# Lecture Notes in Computer Science 8683

Commenced Publication in 1973
Founding and Former Series Editors:
Gerhard Goos, Juris Hartmanis, and Jan van Leeuwen

T0212388

Yuhua Luo (Ed.)

# Cooperative Design, Visualization, and Engineering

11th International Conference, CDVE 2014
Seattle, WA, USA, September 14-17, 2014
Proceedings

 Springer

Volume Editor

Yuhua Luo
University of Balearic Islands
Department of Mathematics and Computer Science
Palma de Mallorca, Spain
E-mail: y.luo@uib.es

ISSN 0302-9743
ISBN 978-3-319-10830-8
DOI 10.1007/978-3-319-10831-5
Springer Cham Heidelberg New York Dordrecht London

e-ISSN 1611-3349
e-ISBN 978-3-319-10831-5

Library of Congress Control Number: 2014946619

LNCS Sublibrary: SL 3 – Information Systems and Application, incl. Internet/Web and HCI

*Typesetting:* Camera-ready by author, data conversion by Scientific Publishing Services, Chennai, India

Printed on acid-free paper

Springer is part of Springer Science+Business Media (www.springer.com)

# Preface

For the first time, the CDVE conference was held in USA after ten times in Europe and Asia. The 11th International conference on Cooperative Design, Visualization, and Engineering, CDVE2014 was held on September 14–17, 2014 in the Pacific Ocean west coast city - Seattle, USA.

After a decade since our first conference, the cooperative design, visualization, engineering, and other cooperative applications are now facing a completely new computing landscape. There are so many important components which have emerged: the cloud computing technology, the ubiquitous broadband internet, and the popularity of mobile devices etc. They provide wide access to social media, e-business, and other online services on a large scale that the human society has never experienced. As a result, the big data become a challenge and an opportunity for the researchers and practitioners.

The papers in this volume convincingly show the answers from our researchers to this great challenge. There is a group of papers a dressing how to use the cloud technology to foster the cooperation. They include the use of cloud for manufacturing, resource selection, service evaluation, and control etc.

To process, perceive, and visualize the big data created by the social media such as Twitter and Facebook, special methods, tools have been presented in the papers in this volume. Activities on social media sites are generating a massive amount of real-time data about human interaction at an unprecedented scale. These papers show their solutions of how to capture the ideas, opinions, feelings, and trends of the people in an efficient and perceivable way. From these papers we can see that the challenge from the new computing landscape is becoming an exciting research opportunity.

To take advantage of the availability of resources in the internet, some papers in this volume made studies on the crowd sourcing such as on location based crowd sourcing. This can be interpreted as a new form of cooperative working in which the information and communication bridge the time and space gaps. In contrast to sourcing help from traditional employees, crowd sourcing looks for contribution and services from a large group of people – the crowd, specially the online crowd.

Facilitating effective teamwork was the center of attention of some papers down to details. Results are presented about how to make annotations for 3D models in collaborative design for communication and coordination.

Cooperative visualization has shown its development strength among the papers of this year. Visualization techniques for engineering open data on the web, for multi-dimensional data etc. are presented. Moreover, the cooperative visualization is no longer for data, but also for sentiment and emotion that are reflected in the big data.

In the field of cooperative engineering, one focus can be seen from this year's papers – using BIM for cooperative design of buildings. Using BIM, the Building Information Model for all the phases of the building life cycle is now becoming popular. Readers can find the papers with the most recent development along this line in the volume.

There are many more topics of cooperative design, visualization, and engineering reported in the papers. New concepts, new methods, new insights are presented in the results and the intermediate results of the research work. Readers are welcome to discover more of them.

I would also like to take this opportunity to thank all of our authors for submitting their papers and presenting their research results to answer the challenges in the new computing landscape. Their research and development achievement will contribute to the society in the long term. I would like to thank all the reviewers for their generous help in reviewing the papers and assuring the quality of this conference. I would like thank all of our Program Committee member Organization Committee members for their continuous support to the conference. My particular thanks go to the Human Centered Design & Engineering Department and the Program Committee members at the University of Washington in Seattle. The success of this year's conference would not have been possible without their enthusiastic help.

September 2014                                                    Yuhua Luo

# Organization

## Conference Chair

Yuhua Luo             University of Balearic Islands, Spain

## International Program Commitee

### Program Chair

Professor Dieter Roller      University of Stuttgart, Germany

### Members

| | |
|---|---|
| Cecilia R. Aragon | Jang Ho Lee |
| Jose Alfredo Costa | Jos P. vanLeeuwen |
| Peter Demian | Ken Lin |
| Carrie Sturts Dossick | Kwan-Liu Ma |
| Susan Finger | Mary Lou Maher |
| Sebastia Galmes | Toan Nguyen |
| Halin Gilles | Moira C. Norrie |
| Matti Hannus | Manuel Ortega |
| Shuangxi Huang | Niko Salonen |
| Jian Huang | Marc Aurel Schnabel |
| Tony Huang | Weiming Shen |
| Claudia-Lavinia Ignat | Ram Sriram |
| Jessie Kennedy | Chengzheng Sun |
| Ursula Kirschner | Thomas Tamisier |
| Harald Klein | Carlos Vila |
| Jean-Christophe Lapayre | Xiangyu Wang |
| Francis Lau | Nobuyoshi Yabuki |
| Pierre Leclercq | |

### Reviewers

| | |
|---|---|
| Cecilia R. Aragon | Susan Finger |
| Marwan Batrouni | Sebastia Galmes |
| Michael Brooks | Halin Gilles |
| Carlos Pampulim Caldeira | Tony Huang |
| Jose Alfredo Costa | Shuangxi Huang |
| Yoann Didry | Claudia-Lavinia Ignat |
| Carrie Sturts Dossick | Ursula Kirschner |

Jean-Christophe Lapayre        Juan Carlos Preciado
Francis Lau                    Guofeng Qin
Pierre Leclercq                Dieter Roler
Jang Ho Lee                    Niko Salonen
Jos P. Leeuwen                 Geetika Sethi
Ken Lin                        Weiming Shen
Jaime Lloret                   Marina Solesvik
Mary Lou Maher                 Ram Sriram
Toan Nguyen                    Chengzheng Sun
Moira C. Norrie                Thomas Tamisier
Manuel Ortega                  Xiangyu Wang
Roberto Pérez                  Nobuyoshi Yabuki
Philippe Pinheiro

# Organization Committee

## Chair

Ying Lin                       Western Washington University, USA

## Members

Tomeu Estrany                  Jaime Lloret
Takayuki Fujimoto              Guofeng Qin
Alex Garcia

# Table of Contents

Collaborative Visual Analysis of Sentiment in Twitter Events . . . . . . . . . .   1
    *Michael Brooks, John J. Robinson, Megan K. Torkildson,*
    *Sungsoo (Ray) Hong, and Cecilia R. Aragon*

Effects of Graph Embellishments on the Perception of System States in
Mobile Monitoring Tasks . . . . . . . . . . . . . . . . . . . . . . . . . . . . . . . . . . . . . . . .   9
    *Frode Eika Sandnes and Kjetil Dyrgrav*

Collaborative Lossless Visualization of n-D Data by Collocated Paired
Coordinates . . . . . . . . . . . . . . . . . . . . . . . . . . . . . . . . . . . . . . . . . . . . . . . . . .  19
    *Boris Kovalerchuk and Vladimir Grishin*

Multidimensional Collaborative Lossless Visualization: Experimental
Study . . . . . . . . . . . . . . . . . . . . . . . . . . . . . . . . . . . . . . . . . . . . . . . . . . . . . . . .  27
    *Vladimir Grishin and Boris Kovalerchuk*

The *Plot-poll* Redesigned: Lessons from the Deployment of a Collective
Mood tracker in an Online Support Group . . . . . . . . . . . . . . . . . . . . . . . . .  36
    *Alex Ivanov and Emma Mileva*

Improving Quality and Performance of Facility Management Using
Building Information Modelling . . . . . . . . . . . . . . . . . . . . . . . . . . . . . . . . . . .  44
    *Heap-Yih Chong, Jun Wang, Wenchi Shou, Xiangyu Wang, and*
    *Jun Guo*

Engineering Open Data Visualizations over the Web . . . . . . . . . . . . . . . . . .  51
    *Rober Morales-Chaparro, Fernando Sánchez-Figueroa, and*
    *Juan Carlos Preciado*

Data Wrangling: A Decisive Step for Compact Regression Trees . . . . . . . .  60
    *Olivier Parisot, Yoanne Didry, and Thomas Tamisier*

Analysis and Visualization of Sentiment and Emotion on Crisis
Tweets . . . . . . . . . . . . . . . . . . . . . . . . . . . . . . . . . . . . . . . . . . . . . . . . . . . . . . .  64
    *Megan K. Torkildson, Kate Starbird, and Cecilia R. Aragon*

A Dynamic Delay Optimization Scheduling Model . . . . . . . . . . . . . . . . . . .  68
    *Chengwei Yang, Ji-Dong Guo, and Jing Chi*

Cloud Computing for Improving Integrity of Data from Biotechnological
Plant . . . . . . . . . . . . . . . . . . . . . . . . . . . . . . . . . . . . . . . . . . . . . . . . . . . . . . . . .  72
    *Dariusz Choiński, Artur Wodołażski, and Piotr Skupin*

Integration of Industrial Control with Analytical Expert Measurements
for Cooperative Operations ........................................    80
  Witold Nocoń, Anna Węgrzyn, Grzegorz Polaków,
  Dariusz Choiński, and Mieczysław Metzger

Fostering Collaboration by Location-Based Crowdsourcing ............    88
  Christine Bauer, Andreas Mladenow, and Christine Strauss

A Web-Based Practice Teaching System in Collaboration with
Enterprise ........................................................    96
  Lin Zhou, Juntang Yuan, Changan Liu, and Aihua Huang

Overdrive Suppression Design Pattern .............................   103
  Marwan Batrouni

RE-Tutor: An Augmented Reality Based Platform for Distributed
Collaborative Learning ...........................................   111
  Weidong Huang, Xiaodi Huang, and Wei Lai

Designing Cooperative Social Applications in Healthcare by Means of
SocialBPM ........................................................   118
  Fernando Sánchez-Figueroa, Juan Carlos Preciado,
  José María Conejero, and Roberto Rodríguez-Echeverría

An Augmented Reality Setup from Fusionated Visualization
Artifacts .........................................................   126
  Maik Mory, Martin Wiesner, Andreas Wünsch, and Sandor Vajna

Messy Work in Virtual Worlds: Exploring Discovery and Synthesis in
Virtual Teams ....................................................   134
  Carrie Sturts Dossick

A Cooperative System of GIS and BIM for Traffic Planning:
A High-Rise Building Case Study ..................................   143
  Jun Wang, Lei Hou, Heap-Yih Chong, Xin Liu, Xiangyu Wang, and
  Jun Guo

An Environment to Foster Scientific Collaborations .................   151
  Tatiana P.V. Alves, Marcos R.S. Borges, and Adriana S. Vivacqua

Supporting Collaborative Decision in Architectural Design
with Synchronous Collocated 4D Simulation and Natural User
Interactions ......................................................   159
  Conrad Boton, Gilles Halin, and Sylvain Kubicki

Collaborative Annotation of Multimedia Resources ..................   163
  Pierrick Bruneau, Mickaël Stefas, Mateusz Budnik,
  Johann Poignant, Hervé Bredin, Thomas Tamisier, and
  Benoît Otjacques

Collaborative Visual Environments for Performing Arts . . . . . . . . . . . . . . .   167
  *Sven Ubik, Jiri Navratil, Jiri Melnikov, Boncheol Goo,*
  *David Cuenca, and Ivani Santana*

Synchronous Mobile Learning System to Cope with Slow Network
Connection . . . . . . . . . . . . . . . . . . . . . . . . . . . . . . . . . . . . . . . . . . . . . . . . . . . . . . .   171
  *Jang Ho Lee*

Data Intellection for Wiser Online Sales the Optosa Approach . . . . . . . . .   175
  *Thomas Tamisier, Gero Vierke, Helmut Rieder, Yoann Didry, and*
  *Olivier Parisot*

Planning for the Microclimate of Urban Spaces: Notes from a
Multi-agent Approach . . . . . . . . . . . . . . . . . . . . . . . . . . . . . . . . . . . . . . . . . . . .   179
  *Dino Borri, Domenico Camarda, and Irene Pluchinotta*

Perception of Space and Time in a Created Environment . . . . . . . . . . . . . .   183
  *Ursula Kirschner*

Studying the Effect of Delay on Group Performance in Collaborative
Editing . . . . . . . . . . . . . . . . . . . . . . . . . . . . . . . . . . . . . . . . . . . . . . . . . . . . . . . . .   191
  *Claudia-Lavinia Ignat, Gérald Oster, Meagan Newman,*
  *Valerie Shalin, and François Charoy*

Collaborative Web Platform for UNIX-Based Big Data Processing . . . . . .   199
  *Omar Castro, Hugo Sereno Ferreira, and Tiago Boldt Sousa*

Efficient Group Discussion with Digital Affinity Diagram System
(DADS) . . . . . . . . . . . . . . . . . . . . . . . . . . . . . . . . . . . . . . . . . . . . . . . . . . . . . . . .   203
  *William Widjaja, Keito Yoshii, and Makoto Takahashi*

Integration of Product Conceptual Design Synthesis into a
Computer-Aided Design System . . . . . . . . . . . . . . . . . . . . . . . . . . . . . . . . . . .   214
  *Alexis Álvarez Cabrales, Enrique E. Zayas, Roberto Pérez,*
  *Rolando E. Simeón, Carles Riba, and Salvador Cardona*

Implementation Challenges of Annotated 3D Models in Collaborative
Design Environments . . . . . . . . . . . . . . . . . . . . . . . . . . . . . . . . . . . . . . . . . . . . .   222
  *Jorge Camba, Manuel Contero, and Gustavo Salvador-Herranz*

Metamorphic Controller for Collaborative Design of an Optimal
Structure of the Control System . . . . . . . . . . . . . . . . . . . . . . . . . . . . . . . . . . .   230
  *Tomasz Klopot, Dariusz Choiński, Piotr Skupin, and Daniel Szczypka*

BIM-Enabled Design Collaboration for Complex Building . . . . . . . . . . . . .   238
  *Jun Wang, Heap-Yih Chong, Wenchi Shou, Xiangyu Wang, and*
  *Jun Guo*

The Impact of Expertise on the Capture of Sketched Intentions:
Perspectives for Remote Cooperative Design . . . . . . . . . . . . . . . . . . . . . . . . .   245
    *Jennifer Sutera, Maria C. Yang, and Catherine Elsen*

Use of Tangible Marks with Optical Frame Interactive Surfaces in
Collaborative Design Scenarios Based on Blended Spaces . . . . . . . . . . . . . .   253
    *Gustavo Salvador-Herranz, Manuel Contero, and Jorge Camba*

A Creative Approach to Conflict Detection in Web-Based 3D
Cooperative Design . . . . . . . . . . . . . . . . . . . . . . . . . . . . . . . . . . . . . . . . . . . . .   261
    *Xiaoming Ma, Hongming Cai, and Lihong Jiang*

Matching Workflow Contexts for Collaborative New Product
Development Task Knowledge Provisioning . . . . . . . . . . . . . . . . . . . . . . . . . .   269
    *Tingyu Liu and Huifen Wang*

A Collaborative Manufacturing Execution System Oriented to Discrete
Manufacturing Enterprises . . . . . . . . . . . . . . . . . . . . . . . . . . . . . . . . . . . . . . .   277
    *Huifen Wang, Linyan Liu, Yizheng Fei, and Tingting Liu*

A Steerable GA Method for Block Erection of Shipbuilding in Virtual
Environment . . . . . . . . . . . . . . . . . . . . . . . . . . . . . . . . . . . . . . . . . . . . . . . . . . .   286
    *Jinsong Bao, Qian Wang, and Aiming Xu*

Service Evaluation-Based Resource Selection in Cloud Manufacturing . . .   294
    *Yan-Wei Zhao and Li-Nan Zhu*

SaaS Approach to the Process Control Teaching and Engineering . . . . . .   303
    *Grzegorz Polaków and Witold Nocoń*

**Author Index** . . . . . . . . . . . . . . . . . . . . . . . . . . . . . . . . . . . . . . . . . . . . . . .   311

# Collaborative Visual Analysis
# of Sentiment in Twitter Events

Michael Brooks, John J. Robinson, Megan K. Torkildson,
Sungsoo (Ray) Hong, and Cecilia R. Aragon

University of Washington, Seattle, WA, USA
{mjbrooks,soco,mtorkild,rayhong,aragon}@uw.edu

**Abstract.** Researchers across many fields are increasingly using data
from social media sites to address questions about individual and group
social behaviors. However, the size and complexity of these data sets
challenge traditional research methods; many new tools and techniques
have been developed to support research in this area. In this paper,
we present our experience designing and evaluating Agave, a collaborative visual analysis system for exploring events and sentiment over time
in large tweet data sets. We offer findings from evaluating Agave with
researchers experienced with social media data, focusing on how users
interpreted sentiment labels shown in the interface and on the value of
collaboration for stimulating exploratory analysis.

**Keywords:** Collaboration, visual analytics, social media, sentiment,
Twitter.

## 1 Introduction

Every day, activity on social media sites like Twitter and Facebook generates
real-time data about human interaction at an unprecedented scale, capturing the
ideas, opinions, and feelings of people from all over the world. These new data
sources present an exciting research opportunity, and researchers across fields
have approached many aspects of social media, e.g. the structure or dynamics of
the social graph, the transmission of information and ideas, or users' emotions,
affect, or sentiment [5,3].

Social media data sets can be quite large, and have complex network structures
that shift and change over time; their main substance is text communication
between users. These characteristics make them challenging to work with, and
even getting a good overall sense of a social data set can be quite difficult.

As in other areas of data-intensive science, data visualization can enable researchers to reach new insights. Numerous examples of visualization systems
for social data such as *Vox Civitas* [4] and twitInfo [13] have demonstrated the
potential for visual analysis to support research on social media. Because these
projects are often interdisciplinary, collaborative visual analysis [11] may be particularly useful. However, so far, there has been little research on collaborative
visual analysis tools for social data.

Y. Luo (Ed.): CDVE 2014, LNCS 8683, pp. 1–8, 2014.

We present Agave, a tool we developed to support collaborative exploration of events in large Twitter data sets, with a particular focus on sentiment. Timeline visualizations of trends and spikes in sentiment help teams of users find relevant events, which can be examined in greater detail through filtered lists of tweets. Annotation and discussion features allow users to collaborate as they explore the data set.

We recruited a group of researchers to evaluate Agave by exploring a data set of almost 8 million tweets from the 2013 Super Bowl, a major sports event. We contribute the findings of our qualitative study, discussing the usefulness of collaboration for exploratory analysis of difficult social media data sets, and implications for the design of sentiment visualizations. Agave and its source code are publicly available[1], to encourage further development and research on collaborative social media analysis tools and sentiment visualization.

## 2  Background and Related Work

We review examples of Twitter research focused on emotion and sentiment to provide context for how Agave might be used. Following this, we discuss related work on visual analysis of Twitter data and collaborative visual analysis.

### 2.1  Emotion in Twitter

Tweets are often explicitly emotional or carry emotional connotations, giving rise to a variety of research on emotion, affect, or sentiment in Twitter.

Dodds et al. demonstrate how Twitter can be used to calculate a metric for social happiness, and analyze temporal fluctuations in happiness on Twitter over days, months, and years [5]. In a similar vein, Quercia et al. calculated a gross community happiness metric based on tweets originating from different census communities in the UK, finding that their metric correlated with socio-economic status at the community level [14]. Mood extracted from Twitter has also been associated with daily changes in the stock market [1].

At a personal scale, a study of individual tweeting behavior has associated sharing emotion in tweets with having larger, sparser follower networks [12]. De Choudhury et al. have used mood patterns in the social media activities of individuals to understand behavior changes related to childbirth [2], and to recognize signs of depression [3]. All of these projects involve analysis of large numbers of tweets. Our goal in this paper is to explore how collaborative visualization can support data exploration in such projects.

### 2.2  Collaborative Visual Social Media Analytics

Visualization and visual analytics are promising tools for tackling complex, dynamic social media data sets, and *collaborative* visual analysis can enable research teams to reach greater insight in interdisciplinary projects.

---

[1] http://depts.washington.edu/sccl/tools

Researchers in the visualization and visual analytics communities have explored visual analysis of Twitter data. The "Visual Backchannel" system developed by Dork et al. presents a stream graph of Twitter topics over time, as well as a display of relevant Twitter usernames, tweets, and photos [6]. The *Vox Civitas* [4] and twitInfo [13] systems use temporal visualizations and sentiment analysis to support journalists exploring tweets about specific events. However, these projects do not address collaborative visual analysis.

Over the past 10 years, there has also been interest in collaborative visual analytics in general. The NameVoyager system was an early example of large-scale public data analysis [15]. Heer et al. followed up on this idea with additional exploration of collaborative features such as graphical annotation, view sharing, and threaded comments [11]. Focusing more on analyst teams, Heer & Agrawala presented a summary of design considerations for collaborative visual analytics systems [10]. However, there is little related work at the intersection of visualization, collaborative data analysis, and social media studies, especially focusing on sentiment.

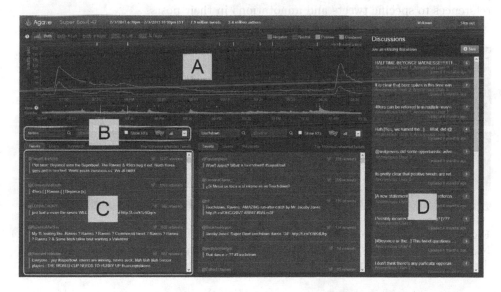

**Fig. 1.** A screenshot of Agave with its four main features: (A) timeline visualizations displaying different representations of the data, (B) data filters to refine searches, (C) data details showing lists of tweets, users, and keywords, and (D) threaded discussions to communicate with other users.

## 3   Design

The interface is illustrated in Figure 1, and a demo is available[2]. A prominent timeline visualization highlights temporal trends. In the default mode (Figure 1,

---

[2] http://depts.washington.edu/sccl/tools

A), the timeline shows the rate of tweets over time as a line graph. Other modes show changes in *sentiment* over time using a streamgraph of positive, negative, and neutral layers representing tweet counts (Figure 2, top) or percents (Figure 2, bottom).

The tabbed panels below the timeline (Figure 1, C) display tweets, users, and "burst keywords" [9] to provide a snapshot of the activity within the selected time range and filters. Zooming and panning on the timeline updates the contents of the detail panels by time range. The tweets displayed can also be filtered by keyword and author, or by sentiment label. Users can define two parallel sets of filters for compare and contrast tasks.

To facilitate shared context between users, we implemented an annotation system for labeling events on the timeline. A bar just above the timeline can be clicked to add an annotation. The user provides a brief description and the annotations are shared between all users. Furthermore, to help users document and share their findings, we also provide threaded discussions (Figure 1, D). New posts are automatically tagged with the current state of the users' view, promoting common ground for discussions. Users may also attach interactive references to specific tweets and annotations in their posts.

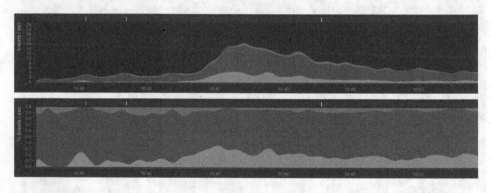

**Fig. 2.** Sentiment streamgraphs for the keyword search "Flacco", the Super Bowl MVP. Negative is red, neutral is gray, and positive is blue. **Top:** overall frequency of tweets, divided by sentiment type. **Bottom:** sentiment as percent of overall volume.

## 4    Evaluation

We evaluated Agave to investigate how collaborative features and sentiment visualizations could support exploratory analysis. Below, we discuss the Twitter data we used in the study, and the study procedure.

### 4.1    Twitter Data Collection

We collected a set of almost 8 million tweets during Super Bowl XLVII, the annual championship football game of the US National Football League. This event was selected based on an expectation of high Twitter volume with emotional content. Data was collected from the Twitter Streaming API, using a tracking list of 142 terms including team and player names, coaches, and entertainers, from Friday, February 1st at 22:30 EST until 20:30 EST on Tuesday, February 5th.

For sentiment analysis, we used the Sentiment140 API [8], which categorizes each individual tweet as positive, negative, or neutral. Based on 500 randomly selected tweets manually labeled by two of the authors, Sentiment140 achieved an overall accuracy of 71%, with a Cohen's kappa of 0.26 (between the two researchers Cohen's kappa was 0.57).

## 4.2 Procedure

Because of the open-ended nature of exploratory data analysis, our evaluation used a qualitative approach. Participants explored real Twitter data in Agave and posted comments and annotations.

We recruited 7 participants experienced with Twitter-based research. Participants' prior grounding and interest supports the validity of their interpretations of the data set and their usage of Agave. After a 5-10 minute tutorial on Agave, participants explored the tool freely for 20-30 minutes, either in our lab or remotely by video conference. We used a think-aloud protocol and observer notes to monitor these open-ended sessions, similar to the lab study used in [11].

We then allowed participants 3-4 days to revisit Agave to continue exploring the data set on their own. After this out-of-lab session, participants completed a questionnaire about discoveries, problems encountered, and attitudes about Agave. Log data were also collected by the system to determine how often each feature was used. Finally, post-study interviews focused on how participants used the visualizations and collaborative features to explore the data.

## 5 Findings and Discussion

Below, we discuss the importance of indirect collaboration for exploring the data, and the interpretation of sentiment visualizations.

## 5.1 Indirect Collaboration

Collaboration we observed in Agave consisted of mostly indirect interactions between people; participants only occasionally addressed other users directly. Because participants did not use the tool at the same time, there was little reason for them to expect a response to a direct interaction. Threads in the study were short (with fewer than 5 posts), and some of these discussions had only one participant. For example, one participant appropriated discussion posts as a way of bookmarking interesting tweets. Of course, these posts were still public, so it was possible for any other user to view and interact with them. As a result, even posts created without any expectation that others would respond were often read by other participants:

> I am looking at a discussion post [in a thread about misclassified senti-
> ment]: "#IRegretNothing is a positive hashtag..." I wonder how many
> people used that. [Searches for the hashtag] Now I'm Looking at RTs for
> #IRegretNothing.                                                    (Peter)

This indirect interaction through the discussion threads was useful for suggesting
and extending lines of analysis. Participants read comments made by other users
and sometimes restored other users' views so that they could easily focus on a
potentially interesting section of the data, often adapting and extending the
filters created by others.

More than discussion posts, annotations created by previous users provided
"jumping off points" for exploration of the data. Allowed to explore the tool
freely, a few participants were initially unsure how to get started with the Twitter
data, and began by opening the discussions or examining the annotations that
had been left by other participants. Many participants seemed to prefer the
annotations:

> The discussions I found harder to look at and understand than just the
> yellow tags [annotations], which were fairly straight forward, and I looked
> at a bunch of those.                                                (Peter)

Participants used existing annotations, which were shown in context as part
of the timeline, as a way of choosing periods of time to focus on (i.e. social
navigation [7]). Just as participants noticed and zoomed in on sharp changes
in the timeline, several participants focused on times surrounding annotations
in order to understand what the annotations were referring to. The following
excerpt shows how Peter used annotations of others to understand how the
49ers fans reacted to their team's defeat:

> Peter focuses the timeline on an interval surrounding the end of the game,
> where another user's annotation has drawn his attention. He then uses
> the sentiment filter to limit the results to negative sentiment. Browsing
> through the details pane, he notices multiple tweets about the 49ers
> losing.

In this case, another participant's annotation at the end of the football game was
useful for highlighting and explaining a shift in sentiment that is visible in the
timeline display. Sometimes, instead of zooming in on annotations, participants
sought out relatively unexplored areas of the data set to focus on, an example
of "anti-social navigation" [10,15]:

> I started by kind of looking in the trough of the blackout period because
> that hadn't had a lot of annotations, so I thought it would be interesting
> to look there. In that dip during the blackout, I saw that [a company]
> was tweeting and got retweeted a bunch of times.                  (Hannah)

Participants expressed appreciation for the annotations feature in particular;
as a low-risk way of indirectly collaborating with other users, annotations were
value for helping people start to explore the data. These observations support
Heer et al. who argued that "doubly-linked" discussions (linked to and from

the relevant data or view) enable users to not only tell what views others were talking about, but to find existing discussions about their current view of the data [11]. Our system did not fully close the "doubly-linked" loop by connecting these annotations to discussions where they were referenced, but our findings suggest that this is a promising idea for future work:

> My goal was very data driven, starting with the data, and there's no real way to end up in the discussion if you start with the data. [...] I think being able to maintain links to the data, narrative centric, vs. marking the data itself (data centric) is really great.                   (Krista)

### 5.2   Exploration of Sentiment

Emotion, affect, and sentiment are important facets of social data sets [4,13,6]. However, the implications of incorporating sentiment in visualizations have not been thoroughly considered. Agave presents information about sentiment in the timeline visualizations and beside tweets in the details panels (Figure 1, C).

Although the visualization of total tweets over time was useful for identifying events of interest, some events were more easily identified using the visualizations of positive, neutral, and negative sentiment (Figure 2). Peter reflected on his use of the sentiment timeline:  *"I think I was most interested in visually seeing where the peaks of positive and negative were and what was clustered around those areas."*

The sentiment timelines successfully facilitated insight about particularly emotional topics or events such as touchdowns or advertisements. However, the sentiment indicators that we attached to individual tweets in the tweet list played a more ambiguous role because they provoked doubt and suspicion in the validity of the sentiment data:

> I saw a few more tweets in there that were in the positive or negative column which were questionably positive or negative and which I felt were more neutral.                   (Allison)

Sentiment classifications were not merely "wrong"; they were ambiguous and subjective. In our study, the presentation of individual sentiment labels was more problematic to participants than the aggregated sentiment timelines. Additional research is needed to understand trust and validity in visual analytics systems that rely on questionable data.

### 5.3   Limitations and Future Work

Future studies should address how people interact with collaborative social media visualization systems in the context of their own projects, e.g. with their own data and with their actual colleagues. The breadth of collaborative interactions we were able to observe in our study was limited by the unfamiliarity of the data set and short-term involvement with the system. More research is needed to understand how the presentation of sentiment in visualization and visual analytics tools affects the way people interpret and interact with sentiment data.

# 6   Conclusion

Agave is a collaborative visual analytics tool supporting exploratory analysis of events in large Twitter data sets, with a focus on sentiment. We conducted a qualitative evaluation to find out how researchers used Agave to develop insights about an 8 million tweet data set. Participants found the timeline visualizations, particularly displays of sentiment changes over time, useful for finding and understanding interesting events. Annotation and discussion were used to share findings, but also served as as jumping off points, enabling indirect collaboration that stimulated broader and deeper exploration of the data.

# References

1. Bollen, J., Mao, H., Zeng, X.: Twitter mood predicts the stock market. Journal of Computational Science 2(1), 1–8 (2011)
2. De Choudhury, M., Counts, S., Horvitz, E.: Major life changes and behavioral markers in social media: case of childbirth. In: Proc. CSCW (2013)
3. De Choudhury, M., Gamon, M., Counts, S., Horvitz, E.: Predicting Depression via Social Media. In: Proc. ICWSM (2013)
4. Diakopoulos, N., Naaman, M., Kivran-Swaine, F.: Diamonds in the rough: Social media visual analytics for journalistic inquiry. In: Proc. VAST (2010)
5. Dodds, P.S., Harris, K.D., Kloumann, I.M., Bliss, C.A., Danforth, C.M.: Temporal patterns of happiness and information in a global social network: hedonometrics and Twitter. PloS one 6(12), e26752 (2011)
6. Dörk, M., Gruen, D., Williamson, C., Carpendale, S.: A visual backchannel for large-scale events. In: Proc. InfoVis (2010)
7. Dourish, P., Chalmers, M.: Running out of space: Models of information navigation. In: Proc. HCI (1994)
8. Go, A., Bhayani, R., Huang, L.: Twitter sentiment classification using distant supervision. Tech. rep., Stanford University (2009)
9. Guzman, J., Poblete, B.: On-line relevant anomaly detection in the Twitter stream: an efficient bursty keyword detection model. In: Proc. KDD Workshop on Outlier Detection and Description (2013)
10. Heer, J., Agrawala, M.: Design considerations for collaborative visual analytics. Information Visualization 7(1), 49–62 (2008)
11. Heer, J., Viégas, F.B., Wattenberg, M.: Voyagers and voyeurs: supporting asynchronous collaborative information visualization. In: Proc. CHI (2007)
12. Kivran-Swaine, F., Naaman, M.: Network properties and social sharing of emotions in social awareness streams. In: Proc. CSCW (2011)
13. Marcus, A., Bernstein, M.S., Badar, O., Karger, D.R., Madden, S., Miller, R.C.: TwitInfo: aggregating and visualizing microblogs for event exploration. In: Proc. CHI (2011)
14. Quercia, D., Ellis, J., Capra, L., Crowcroft, J.: Tracking "gross community happiness" from tweets. In: Proc. CSCW (2012)
15. Wattenberg, M., Kriss, J.: Designing for social data analysis. IEEE TVCG 12(4), 549–557 (2006)

# Effects of Graph Embellishments on the Perception of System States in Mobile Monitoring Tasks

Frode Eika Sandnes and Kjetil Dyrgrav

Institute of Information Technology,
Faculty of Technology, Art and Design,
Oslo and Akershus University College of Applied Sciences, Norway
Frode-Eika.Sandnes@hioa.no

**Abstract.** Monitoring of critical systems such as large server parks require suitable visualization tools that draw the attention to essential aspects of system state to ensure continuous operation. Moreover, administration is increasingly performed using mobile devices giving operators more freedom. Mobile device form factors limit the amount of data that can be displayed. This study explores if visual embellishments in data visualizations improve the perception of system states for mobile administrators. The RRDtool time series data visualizer, which is deployed by the Munin monitoring tool, is used as basis and compared to an experimental monitoring tool that employs visual embellishment enhancements Talk aloud system monitoring sessions were employed with 24 IT-professionals both with and without Munin experience. The results show that the embellishments results in significantly shorter time to interpret the views while they do not significantly help determine the general characteristics of the views. Previous experience with Munin had limited effect on performance. One implications of this work is that embellishments can help focus attention towards important state changes in mobile visualizations.

**Keywords:** system administration, embellishments, mobile monitoring.

## 1 Introduction

Control room visualization has received much attention in certain domains such as nuclear reactor monitoring [1], air control [2], airplane cockpits [3], power grid monitoring [4]. Control room visualization methodology has also reached the mainstream though dashboard design, where control room metaphors are used to communicate business states on websites [5].

Monitoring involves detecting abnormal events causing unfavorable changes to the system states. Time is a crucial factor as system state changes that are detected early may cause less damage if a problem is handled early. Unfortunately, many systems are investigated retrospectively using log files after an anomalous event rather than preventively through active monitoring.

Monitoring is increasingly relying on mobile devices giving the system administrators more freedom while increasing their availability and consequently the

Y. Luo (Ed.): CDVE 2014, LNCS 8683, pp. 9–18, 2014.

quality of service as it is perceived by the users. However, system state visualizations on mobile devices is challenging as there is less real estate available for displaying data compared to large control-room display walls [6]. To compensate for smaller displays mobile visualizations need to rely on alternative means to communicate system states. In this study, visual embellishments are explored as a means for enhancing visualizations and drawing the operators' attention to important data. Graphical representation of timeline data is arguably the most common form of visualization estimated to constitute 75 % of all visualizations [7].

This study focuses on three timeline system state parameters that reflect key recourses in computer system, that is, memory use, disk use and processor use. All of these need to be kept below certain levels in order to maintain a healthy system. These parameters are also interrelated. For example, memory data are cached onto the disk. If the memory runs low more data will be cashed, or paged, to disk, consuming more disk space, and even more importantly, the caching consumes or paging processing power and thus affect the processor load.

There is disagreement among experts regarding the approach to information design. Prominent information designers such as McCandless [8] and Holmes [9] design elaborate visual presentations for newspapers and magazines which contrast the minimalistic, minimum ink principles of Tufte [10] and Few [11].

Icons are believed to have an advantage over text in terms of recognition and recall as the human ability to recall images is superior to that for text. Icons can help make decisions more efficiently. However, the meaning of icons must be learned. The visual context of a pictogram significantly strengthens its ability to be correctly perceived [19]. This is the rationale for putting fire extinguisher pictograms on red doors as it assist visual search [12].

Cartoons are examples of a visual media that use exaggerated imagery to effectively communicate meaning through the use of effects such as speech bubbles, lines to indicate motion, explosions, crashes, etc. Another example is to use Zzz as a metaphor for sleeping as Zzz represents the snoring sound [13].

Fire is a powerful image as humans are instinctively adept at responding to fire. Fire is frequently used metaphorically, for example referring to somebody as "on fire" meaning somebody or something is hot without the presences of actual flames. Fire and flames are associated with danger.

This study set out to explore the effect of embellishments for improving the perception of system states as embellishments have been demonstrated to improve long term memory in certain context [14, 15].

## 1.1   Munin and RRDtool

Current state-of-the-art monitoring tools such as Munin RRDtool have several problems. First, the time series views give misleading information. For example the memory view has an axis which ends at 600 Mb even if the memory device only has a capacity of 512 Mb. The observer may thus be misled to believe that there is more capacity than there really is. Second, the display real estate is ineffectively used. In the previous example, the interval from 512 to 600 constitutes nearly 15% of the view remaining unused. Third, the information provided is inaccurate. The x-axis of many views shows grid lines with 30 hours in total, while the axis date label suggests a 24 hour window. Moreover, the observer has to manually count tick marks to find the time of specific events – a process prone to error and inaccuracies. Four, many views are cluttered. For example, the Munin view shown in Fig. 1a displays 13 parameters, and it is thus hard to identify the individual lines or the overall trend.

## 2    Method

### 2.1    Participants

Evaluating and measuring information visualization are challenging [16] and a methodology involving users are needed. Totally 24 participants volunteered for the study. The participants comprised a) IT professionals with practical system monitoring experience and b) network and system administration master students with system monitoring experience from their studies.

### 2.2    Equipment

A HTC Desire Andriod smartphone was used for the experiment. It contains a 3.7 inch touch-sensitive display that allows zoom and auto-rotation. The resolution was set to 480 x 800 pixels.

Both the Munin tool with the RRDtool visualization extension and a custom made visualization prototype was used for the experiment. The prototype was written in PHP allowing system commands to be issued on the server to obtain system information about disk, memory and processor usage. The graphics was created with GD (Graphics Draw) PHP library using the Portable Network Graphics format.

### 2.3    Materials

The experiment addressed three monitoring categories, namely memory usage, disk usage and processor utilization. For each category the experiment set out to observe the difference between traditional visualizations without embellishments as utilized by the Munin / RRDtool tool, and enhanced visualizations with embellishments as employed by the prototype tool. The experiment thus comprised six stimuli. To achieve a repeatable and consistent experiment the screenshots where fixed such that all participants were exposed to identical stimuli (see Fig. 1).

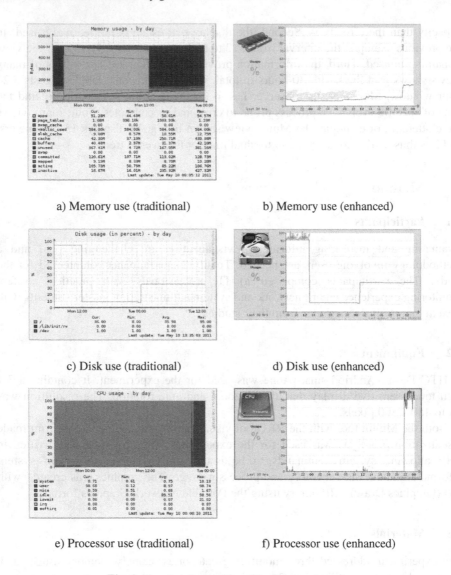

a) Memory use (traditional)      b) Memory use (enhanced)

c) Disk use (traditional)      d) Disk use (enhanced)

e) Processor use (traditional)      f) Processor use (enhanced)

**Fig. 1.** The visual stimuli used in the experiments

The memory scenario starts at low activity during the previous day and lasts for about 16 hours until it increases beyond 10% of full capacity. At 21:30 memory intensive Perl scripts are initiated causing memory use to reach about 30%.

The traditional memory view displays a handful of different memory use categories. During the period of actual low memory use the tool peaks at a very high level due to high cache use (orange). However, cache use does not reflect actual memory use and is somewhat misleading.

The enhanced view is simpler and displays overall memory use in percentage of total capacity. Sleeping cartoon symbols (Zzz) are used to indicate low activity and a red arrow to emphasize the moderate step up from 10% to 30% at 21:30.

The disk scenario starts critically at 8:00 the previous day with approximately 95% of the disk space used. At 13:00 large files are deleted such that only approximately 11% of the disk space is used. Just before midnight new files are created with dd such that disk use increases to 36%.

The traditional view shows disk usage as a simple line graph. The enhanced view employs a red line and cartoon flame embellishments to attract the observers attention to the critical disk levels. No other imagery or embellishments are used in this graph as the step up from 11% to 36% is considered sufficiently noticeable and uncritical.

The processor scenario comprises a timeline where the processor is idle most of the time apart from a few occasional small spikes indicating some system activity. Towards the end of the timeline, that is, at 21:30, the processor usage enters a critical state as it spikes close to 100% due to a processor intensive Perl script.

The traditional view uses different colors for the different classes of processes. It is therefore easy to observe that the first small spike is reflecting system activity (green) and the critical spike towards the end is user activity (blue). Turquoise is used to indicate idle processors. Again the enhanced view shows overall processor use with a red line to indicate the critical state as well as a red line around the entire view.

## 2.4 Procedure

The experiments were conducted individually. Each participant was sitting down in front of a desk. Steps were taken to prevent glare or reflections from the windows and the light fittings. The experiment was balanced to compensate for any learning effects by presenting the six stimuli in different orders to the participants. A digital voice recorder was placed in front of the participants to capture the dialogue. The participants were informed that the recordings were deleted after analysis.

First, the participants provided demographic information. They were also asked if they had prior experience with the Munin system monitoring tool. Next, they were informed of the structure of the experiment. A talk-aloud methodology was employed and participants were thus asked to describe what they observed, their thoughts and impressions during the experiment.

## 2.5 Observations and Measurements

Time measurements and error rates were measured. For each scenario two success criteria were set up and the time to reach these criteria were measured by analyzing the time interval from the beginning of each scenario was shown to the point where the participant uttered the phrases signaling approximately correct graph interpretations. The following success criteria were devised:

Purpose: the participant identifies the domain of the graph, that is, the type of device that is monitored and the type of data that is measured and displayed (percentage or Mb of memory use, percentage disk use).

Timeline: the participants understand the time-span (24 hours), time-scale and time indication on the graph (trend changes at 11:00, 13:00. 20:00 and 21:30).

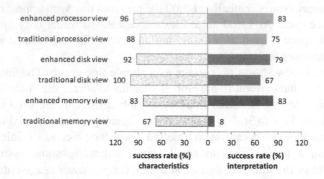

**Fig. 2.** Success rate in identifying the general characteristics (left) and interpreting (right) the view (100% equals 24)

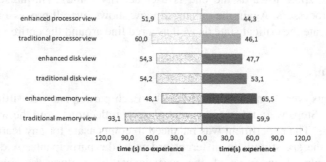

**Fig. 3.** Mean time identifying general characteristics of the traditional and enhanced memory view (red), disk view (green) and processor view (blue), for participants with and without Munin experience

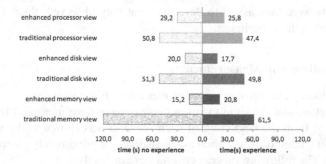

**Fig. 4.** Mean time interpreting the traditional and enhanced memory view (red), disk view (green) and processor view (blue), for participants with and without Munin experience

In particular, to what degree are participants able to comprehend the level of detail down to the 30 minute resolution indicated on the graphs (e.g. 21:30).

Interpretation: the participants are able to interpret the trends in the graph and the implications for system state, that is, low, medium, high and critical values. That is, disk usage is critical at the beginning, then low, followed by a small step up, and memory use is first very low with a few spikes then with a critical high spike. Success rates where thus computed as the rate of criteria identified by the participants.

## 3    Results

The results shows that the associations of the embellishments were reflected in the participants' comments, that is, the most frequent expressions referred to the metaphors sleep (low, idle, calm, quiet), fire (burning, flames) and into-the-roof (high, critical, max, up).

Fig. 2 shows the success rates in identifying the general characteristics of the views (right) and the success rate in interpreting the views (left). Identification of general characteristics of the memory views was associated with the lowest success rates while the disk view was associated with the highest success rate. The general characteristics of the traditional view had the lowest success rate for both the memory test (16 out of 24) and the processor test. All participants identified the general characteristics of the traditional disk view, while two participants did not identify the general characteristics of the enhanced view.

The success rate in interpreting the views (left) is consistently higher for the enhanced views for all scenarios. The traditional memory view has a noticeably low score as only two participants successful interpreted the view.

Fig. 3 shows the mean response time for identifying general characteristics of the three views for participants without (left) and with Munin experience (right). The mean times for the traditional views are consistently longer for all views. The difference is largest for the memory scenario and smallest for the disk scenario. Moreover, the observations are consistent with the success rates shown in Fig. 2 as the memory views are associated with the longest response times and the disk views associated with the shortest response times.

As expected, participants with Munin experience identified the general characteristics of the traditional views faster than the enhanced views, although the differences are marginal. However, the difference between the traditional and enhanced tool is very large for participants with no experience with Munin, as the response time with the traditional view is nearly twice as long as with the enhanced view. Although there is a difference between the traditional and enhanced memory views the difference is not significant ($t = 1.51$; $p > .154$; $df = 13$).

The results for the identifying characteristics of the disk view suggest that there is very little effect of prior experience with Munin, and there is very little effect of enhancements. Consequently, the difference between the traditional and enhanced disk view is not significantly ($t = 1.16$; $p > .258$; $df = 21$).

The results for determining the characteristics of the processor view shows that the experienced participants performed better with both the traditional and enhanced views, and both the experienced and inexperienced participants performed better with the enhanced view compared to the traditional view. However, the differences were not significant (t = 1.78; p > .08 ; df = 20).

Fig. 4 shows the mean response time for interpreting three traditional and enhanced views for participants with and without Munin experience. Note that only two experienced participants completed the task successfully and the mean time thus exceeds the boundaries of the chart. However, the experienced users took nearly three times longer to interpret the traditional memory view than the enhanced view. The response time for interpreting the traditional disk view is more than twice that for the enhanced view and the difference is significant (t = 5.09; p < .0.01; df = 15).

The results for interpreting the processor view show that both groups perform much faster with the enhanced view than the traditional view and this difference is statistically significant (t = 3.3; p < 0.04; df = 15). There experienced participants also perform marginally better than the inexperienced participants.

# 4    Discussion

The experiment revealed that 18 out of 24 participants mentioned the term critical when seeing the flames as opposed to 5 participants identifying the through-the-roof method. Moreover, participants needed a mean time of 19.1 seconds to articulate words related to the flame as opposed to 26.5 seconds for through-the-roof. The data thus confirm that fire imagery is more closely associated with critical states.

The red frame was mentioned by only 5 of 24 participants. Despite occupying a substantial amount of real estate, it may not have received attention due to the other visual elements. Similarly the line color was mentioned by only 8 of 24 participants. One explanation is that it was partially hidden behind the flames, as it was only mentioned by 2 of 24 participants for the disk scenario.

Through-the-roof was a frequent phrase uttered by 14 of 24 participants. The snoring embellishment was not associated with the term snoring. Instead, 19 of 24 participants referred to sleeping suggesting that the participants were familiar with the cartoon sleep metaphor. Furthermore, 20 of 24 participants successfully completed this scenario at the shortest mean time (17.4 seconds) for all scenarios. The snoring embellishment is thus likely to positively impact the perception of low activity states.

The traditional view seemed ineffective in communicating memory state as only two participants managed to recognize the memory usage. This may suggest that either the success criterion was biased against the traditional view, or that interpretation of memory usage in Linux is difficult.

Note that the time recorded participants needed to complete the tasks were longer than due to the talk aloud process. This is also a significant source of error as participants may have different speaking styles, verbosity and speech rates. In fact, some participants commented for well over two minutes, including irrelevant aspects of the displays. Moreover, some participants interpreted the task incorrectly or with a wider scope than intended. The talk-aloud methodology was challenging due to mumbling, hesitations and pauses in the middle of sentences.

The differences in experience did not appear as an important factor. However, this could be linked to the fact that the categorization according to experience was based on the participants self reporting and hence not completely objective.

This study suggests that monitoring visualization could benefit from embellishments. Despite warnings against data-interfering embellishments, critical situations where risk is a considerable factor, the discovery of data state should outweigh the desire to render the data accurately.

# 5 Conclusions

Alternative approaches for enhancing the visual expression of visualized data in system monitoring have been identified though an alternative monitoring tool running in a mobile web browser. It was compared to the commonly used Munin system monitoring visualization tool through three scenarios, namely memory, disk and processor use. Talk aloud sessions were conducted. No significant response time differences were observed in basic graph usage the time difference between the traditional display and the enhanced display, while significant differences were found for monitoring specific usage. The experiment established that use of embellishments significantly improved the perception and interpretation of the state of visualized data.

# References

1. Kim, S.K., Suh, S.M., Jang, G.S., et al.: Empirical research on an ecological interface design for improving situation awareness of operators in an advanced control room. Nuclear Engineering and Design 253, 226–237 (2012)
2. Rozzi, S., Amaldi, P., Wong, W., Field, B.: Operational potential for 3D displays in air traffic control. In: ECCE 2007: Proceedings of the 14th European Conference on Cognitive Ergonomics, pp. 179–183. ACM Press (2007)
3. Pinder, S.D., Davies, T.C.: Interface Design for an Aircraft Thrust and Braking. In: Proceedings of OZCHI 2006, pp. 103–110. ACM Press (2006)
4. Haigh, D., Adams, W.: Why 64 bit computers in the control room. Computing & Control Engineering Journal 7(6), 277–280 (1996)
5. Few, S.: Information Dashboard Design. O'Reilly Media (2006)
6. Chittaro, L.: Visualizing information on mobile devices. Computer 39, 40–45 (2006)
7. Tufte, E.R.: The Visual Display of Quanitative Information. Graphics Press LLC (2009)
8. McCandless, D.: Visual Miscellaneum. Harper Design (2012)
9. Holmes, N.: Designer's Guide to Creating Charts and Diagrams. Watson-Guptill (1991)
10. Tufte, R.R.: Envisioning Information. Graphics Press LLC (1990)
11. Few, S.: Show Me the Numbers - Designing Tables and Graphs to Enlighten. Analytics Press (2004)
12. Abdullah, R., Hubner, R.: Pictograms, Icons and Signs. Thames and Hudson, 2nd edn. (2006)
13. Healey, C.G.: Choosing effective colours for data visualization. In: Proceedings of the Seventh Annual IEEE Visualization 1996, pp. 263–270. IEEE CS Press (1996)

14. Bateman, S., Mandryk, R.L., Gutwin, C., Genest, A., McDine, S., Brooks, C.: Useful junk?: the effects of visual embellishment on comprehension and memorability of charts. In: Proceedings of the 28th International Conference on Human Factors in Computing Systems, CHI 2010, pp. 2573–2582. ACM Press (2010)
15. Borgo, R., Abdul-Rahman, A., Mohamed, F., Grant, P.W., Reppa, I., Floridi, L., Chen, M.: An Empirical Study on Using Visual Embellishments in Visualization. IEEE Transactions on Visualization and Computer Graphics 18(12), 2759–2768 (2012)
16. Plaisant, C.: The challenge of information visualization evaluation. In: Proceedings of the Working Conference on Advanced Visual Interfaces, AVI 2004, pp. 109–116. ACM Press (2004)

# Collaborative Lossless Visualization of n-D Data by Collocated Paired Coordinates

Boris Kovalerchuk[1] and Vladimir Grishin[2]

[1] Dept. of Computer Science, Central Washington University,
400 E. University Way, Ellensburg, WA 98926, USA
borisk@cwu.edu

[2] View Trends International, 15 Wildwood Street, Ste 14, Dracut, MA, 01826-5190, USA

**Abstract.** The collaborative approach is a natural way to enhance visualization and visual analytics methods. This paper continues our long-term efforts on enhancement of visualization and visual analytics methods. The major challenges in visualization of large n-D data in 2-D are not only in providing lossless visualization by using sophisticated computational methods, but also in supporting the most efficient and fast usage of abilities of users (agents) to analyze visualized information and to extract patterns visually. This paper describes a collaborative approach to support n-D data visualization based on new lossless n-D visualization methods that we propose. The second part of this work presented in a separate paper is focused on experimental results of cooperative n-D data visualization described in this paper.

**Keywords:** Collaborative multi-dimensional data visualization, Lossless visualization.

## 1 Introduction

This paper continues our long-term efforts [1-3] on enhancement of visualization performance. While visual shape perception supplies 95-98% of information for pattern recognition, recent visualization techniques do not use it efficiently [4,5]. Another enhancement opportunity is in improving a modern lossy mapping of multidimensional data space onto 2-D plane, by means of:

- dimension reduction such as Principal Component Analysis, multidimensional scaling, projections etc., which represents only a tiny part of initial information from n-D vectors, without a way to restore n-D vectors exactly from it, or
- by splitting n-D data to a set of low dimensional data, that destroys integrity of n-D data, and leads to a shallow understanding complex n-D data. To mitigate this challenge a difficult perceptual task of assembling low-dimensional visualized pieces to the whole n-D vectors must be solved.

Our **collaborative approach** to Enhance Visualization [1] includes:

(1) Shape Perception Priority, i.e., more effective usage of human vision capabilities of shape perception by mapping data vectors into 2-D figures. Its effectiveness is based on the Gestalt laws and psychological experiments.

(2) Lossless Displays, as an alternative way for lossy visualization mentioned above, i.e. primary usage of visual representations in 2-D that fully preserves n-D data, such as lossless methods of Parallel and Radial coordinates, some heat maps, etc. It provides clear interpretation of features of pictures in terms of data properties.

Y. Luo (Ed.): CDVE 2014, LNCS 8683, pp. 19–26, 2014.
© Springer International Publishing Switzerland 2014

(3) Quantitative Modeled Data Structure recognition with different forms of data displays. This includes detecting and describing mathematical structures of given multidimensional data in different visual forms. This is a basis to choose and adjust structures as hyper–tubes, hyper-planes, hyper-spheres, etc.

Current visualization techniques are relatively effective for specific data, but generalizing this success to other data is a significant challenge. Thus, we focus on a formal data structures to enhance generalization of visualization in combination with an interactive collaborative visualization approach. While the modeling of very complex n-D structures is often infeasible the *interactive collaborative piece-wise modeling* is feasible for many data structures.

Gestalt laws motivate advantages of Polar displays (Stars) vs. Parallel Coordinates (PCs) for shape recognition. Our psychological experiments have confirmed these advantages for detection of hyper-tube structures with dimension up to 100. It selects features and classifies objects 2-3 times faster than with PCs [7]. We are interested to link these results with a new and promising visualization methods proposed in [2,5-6,8,9] (see Table 1) and a collaborative approach to enhance visualization.

**Table 1.** Line Coordinates

| Type | Characteristics |
|---|---|
| General Line Coordinates (GLC) | Drawing $n$ coordinate axes in 2D in variety of ways: curved, parallel, unparalleled, collocated, disconnected, etc. |
| Collocated Paired Coordinates (CPC) in 2-D | Splitting an $n$-$D$ *vector* $x$ into pairs of its coordinates $(x_1,x_2),...,(x_{n-1},x_n)$; drawing each pair as 2-D point in the same two axes on the plane; and linking these points to form an oriented graph from these points for each n-D vector. |
| Collocated Paired Coordinates (CPC) in 3-D | Splitting $n$ coordinates into triples and representing each pair as 3-D point in the same three axes; and linking these points to form an oriented graph for each n-D vector. |
| Shifted Paired Coordinates (SPC) | Drawing each next pair in the shifted coordinate system (in contrast with CPC). |

The generated figures allow effective n-D data structure analysis by means of collaborative shape perception. Visualization of large n-D datasets for pattern discovery can be accomplished collaboratively by splitting a dataset between **collaborating agents**, which include both humans and software agents. Each agent analyzes and visualizes a subset of data and exchanges findings with other agents.

There are multiple different *splitting options* to support collaboration based on:

• *Location of data* on n-D space (each agent works of the data from a specific location on n-D space produced by data clustering).
• *Class of data* (each agent works only on the data of a specific class/es),
• *Attributes of data* (each agent works only on the projection of data to the specific subset of attributes.)

Another option is specialization of agents to different visual tasks. Data are not split, but **organized and visualized differently,** e.g., different order of the attributes presented to different agents. Visualization in parallel coordinates and paired coordinates are sensitive to this change. Besides, our experiments [7] had shown that agents recognize the same features with different speed and revealed that the teamwork of agents leads to significant time saving to solve the task.

## 2 Paired Coordinates and Line Coordinates

The algorithm for representing n-D points in 2-D using lossless collocated paired coordinates (CPC) is presented below. We use an example in 6-D with a state vector x=(x, y, x`, y`, x``, y``), where x and y are location of the object, x` and y` are velocities (derivatives), and x`` and y`` are accelerations (second derivatives) of this object. The main steps of the algorithm are: (1) grouping attributes into consecutive pairs (x,y) (x`,y`) (x``,y``), (2) plotting each pair in the same orthogonal normalized Cartesian coordinates X and Y, and (3) plotting a directed graph (x,y) → (x`,y`) → (x``,y``) with directed paths from (x,y) to (x`,y`) and from (x`,y`) to (x``,y``). Fig. 2.1a shows application of this algorithm to a 6-D vector (5,4,0,6,4,10) with the oriented graph drawn as two arrows: from (5,4) to (0,6) and from (0,6) to (4,10).

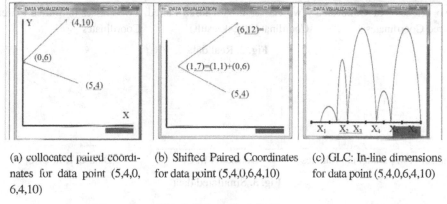

(a) collocated paired coordinates for data point (5,4,0,6,4,10)

(b) Shifted Paired Coordinates for data point (5,4,0,6,4,10)

(c) GLC: In-line dimensions for data point (5,4,0,6,4,10)

**Fig. 1.** Paired Coordinates

The Shifted Paired Coordinates (SPC) show each next pair in the shifted coordinate system. The first pair (5,4) is drawn in the (X,Y) system, pair (0,6) is drawn in the (X+1,Y+1) coordinate system, and pair (4,6) is drawn in the (X+2, Y+2) coordinate system. For vector (5,4,0,6,4,10), the graph consists of the arrows: from (5,4) to (1,1)+(0,6)=(1,7) then from (1,7) to (2,2)+(4,10)=(6,12). See Fig. 2.1b.

The CPC and SPC are in a new class of lossless paired coordinates [2]. It includes also Anchored Paired Coordinates. Another new class is a class of general line coordinates (GLC). It contains well-known parallel and radial (star) coordinates along with new ones that generalize them by locating coordinates in any direction that differ from parallel or radial locations and in any topology (connected or disjoined).

The GLC include In-line Coordinates (IC) shown in Fig.2.1c that are similar to parallel coordinates, except that the axes $X_1, X_2, \ldots X_n$ are horizontal, not vertical. Each pair is represented as a Bezier Curve. The height of the curve is the distance between the two adjacent values, e.g., for (5,4,0,6,4,10), the heights are 1,4,6,2,6.

The *Anchored Paired Coordinates* (APC) represent each next pair starting at the first pair that serves an "anchor". In the example above pairs (x`,y`) and (x``,y``) are represented as vectors that start at anchor point (x,y) with plotting vectors ((x,y), (x+x`,x+y`)) and ((x,y), (x+x``,x+y``)). The advantage of the APC is that the direction has a meaning as actual vectors of velocity and acceleration in this example. In the radial coordinated the directions are arbitrary.

Fig. 2.2 shows these visualizations of real 9-D data (class 1 in blue and class 2 in yellow). The Anchored Paired Coordinates (Fig. 2.2b) did the best in isolating the two classes of technologies: (1) floated processed, (2) non-floated processed. It shows the importance of multiple lossless n-D visualizations to select the best one. Fig. 2.3 shows CPC vs. the Parallel Coordinates for simulated data.

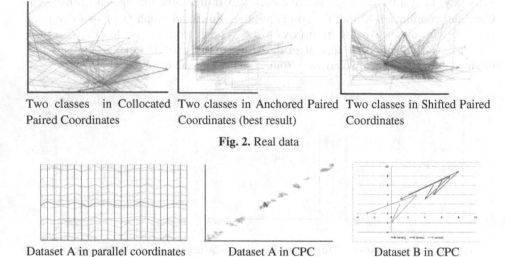

Two classes  in Collocated  Two classes in Anchored Paired  Two classes in Shifted Paired
Paired Coordinates              Coordinates (best result)              Coordinates

**Fig. 2.** Real data

Dataset A in parallel coordinates          Dataset A in CPC          Dataset B in CPC

**Fig. 3.** Simulated data

# 3      Motivation, Tasks and Advantages

The motivation for a new class of coordinates is two-fold: (1) there is a very limited number of available lossless visualization methods of n-D data, and (2) there is no silver bullet visualization that is perfect for all possible datasets. Our experiments [2] had shown the benefits of these new visualizations for World Hunger data, Challenger Disaster, and others. In addition to Fig. 2.2 and 2.3 Fig. 2.4 illustrates advantages of GLC and CPC on modeled data vs. Parallel Coordinates (PCs). Example 1 shows that CPC reveal clearer a structure of specific data than the parallel coordinates. Example 2 shows that CPC represent data structure simpler than the parallel coordinates. In the later each n-D record is just a single point in CPC.

The analytical structure that can be discovered from the dataset 1 within each 8-D vector $x_t = (x_{t1}, x_{t2}, ..., x_{t8})$ is given by the formula: $(x_{t3}=x_{t1})$ & $(x_{t4}= x_{t2}+2)$ & $(x_{t5}=x_{t1}+2)$ & $(x_{t6}=x_{t4})$ & $(x_{t7}=x_{t5})$ & $(x_{t8}=x_{t2})$. The analytical structure that can be discovered from dataset 1 between 8-D vectors $x_t = (x_{t1}, x_{t2}, ..., x_{t8})$ and $x_{t+1} = (x_{t+1,1}, x_{t+1,2}, ..., x_{t+1,8})$ is given by the formulas: $x_{t+1,i}=3x_{ti}$, i=1,3,5, 7 and   $x_{t+1,i} = x_{t,i}$, i=2,4, 6, 8. Here odd attributes grow linearly and even attributes are constants.

At first glance the simple relations above can be easily discovered analytically from the dataset without the need in the collaborative visualization.  In fact, the analytical discovering of relations is done by searching in an assumed class of relations. It is difficult to guess this class. Even when the class is guessed correctly, but the class is very large then, the search of the actual relation is a difficult search of a needle in a haystack. The visual collaborative approach helps to identify and to narrow this class. It even can eliminate the analytical stage, when the goal is only to ensure that a relation that separates two classes exists.

An alternative collaborative way is just looking through a data trying to discover the relation "manually". It is not scalable to the large data tables. Next looking though numbers by each agent in the tables is the sequential process, while the observing that images in the visualization is the parallel process that is much faster.

Below we describe data features that can be visually estimated using CPC and PCs and show their advantages relative to pure computational/analytical ways to describe such features. Let point W be produced by the formula $W=A + tv$, where A is an n-D point, v is an n-D vector, and t is a scalar. A linear segment in n-D is a set of point $\{W: W=A + tv, t\in [a,b]\}$. For $t\in [0,1]$ we have a linear segment in n-D from points A to point $B=A+v$, and a ray from point A to the direction v for $t \in [0,\infty)$.

Statement. An n-D linear segment is represented as a set of shifted graphs in CPC.

Proof: Consider two arbitrary n-D vectors $W_1$ and $W_2$ from this linear segment, where $W_1=A + t_1v$ and $W_2=A + t_2v$ with $v=(v_1,v_2,...,v_n)$. See figure 2.3c as an example. Both $W_1$ and $W_2$ are shifted in the v direction, but with different distances of these shifts in accordance with $t_1$ and $t_2$, respectively. Q.E.D.

Note that for any $W_1$ and $W_2$ their first 2-D points $(w_{11},w_{12})$ and $(w_{21},w_{22})$ are shifted to the directions of $(v_1,v_2)$ on 2-D relative to the first 2-D point of A which is $(a_1,a_2)$. Similarly, the second points are shifted to the direction $(v_3,v_4)$. Thus directions of the linear shifts can differ for different points/nodes of the same graph.

Let we have data of two classes that satisfy two different linear relations: $W = A + tv$ and $U = B + tq$, These data will be represented in CPC as two sets of graphs shifted in v and q directions, respectively. If $W=A + tv + e$, where e is a noise vector, then we have graphs for n-D points W in the "tube" with its width defined by e.

## 4    Supported Visual Features, Pattern Discovery and Data Structures

**Visual Features that CPC Supports.** Analysis of data represented in paired coordinates including figures above show that the following visual features can be estimated visually for each *individual graph*: types of angles (e.g., sharp angle), orientation and direction of lines and angles, length of the lines, color of lines, width of the length (as representation of the number of vectors with such values), width and length of the curves (Bezier curves), number of crossing of edges of a graph, directions of crossed edges, *shape* of an envelope that contains the graph, a "type" of the graph (dominant direction or absence of it: knot, L-shape, horizontal, vertical, Northwest, etc). The analysis of these features is split between different agents in the collaborative visualization process.

There are relations *between graphs* of different n-D data plotted on the same plane that can be *estimated visually by collaborative agents* and split between agents to find these relations: parallel graphs, graphs rotated or generally affine transformed relative to each other, percentage of overlap of graphs, the size and shape of the area of the overlap of envelopes of two graphs, the distance between two graphs.

Fig. 4(b) and 5(b) show that all objects have the same structure in CPC that is less evident in parallel coordinates in Fig. 4(a) and 5(a). These are the same shapes just

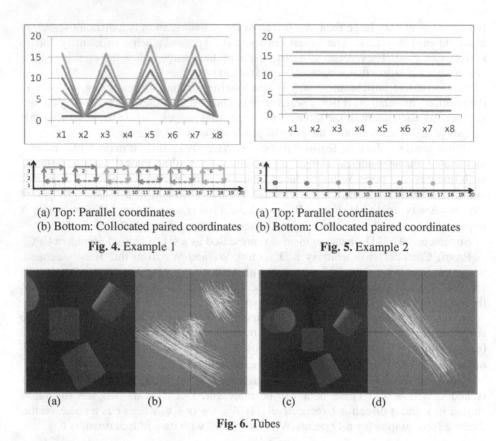

(a) Top: Parallel coordinates
(b) Bottom: Collocated paired coordinates

**Fig. 4.** Example 1

(a) Top: Parallel coordinates
(b) Bottom: Collocated paired coordinates

**Fig. 5.** Example 2

(a)          (b)          (c)          (d)

**Fig. 6.** Tubes

shifted. In the parallel coordinates the shapes are not identical, but similar. It is easier to see identical shapes than similar shapes. Figure 6 shows that all objects within a pipe have practically the same directions, similar lengths and located closely. These similarities help a collaborating agent to distinguish them from data from other pipes. This is critical for the success of collaborative n-D data visual analysis. Figures 6(a) and 6(c) show tubes (cylinders) in 3-D with points in colors. The matched graphs (lines) of CPC representations are shown in the same colors in Fig. 4.3b for the three left tubes and in Fig. 6(d) from the forth (left) tube. This 2-D lossless CPC representation allows easily distinguishing these 4 classes visually. Each agent works on the individual class can extract visual features of each class and then agents combine their features. This speeds up the total visual discovery collaboratively.

The n-D **data structures that fit well to CPC** are pipes and clusters in n-D. For pipes it was shown above, and for clusters in the form of hyper-cubes it is shown below. Consider an n-D *hyper-cube*, that is a set of n-D points {W} that are in the vicinity of an n-D point A within distance $d_i$ from A for each dimension $X_i$ no greater than R, {W: $\forall$ i $d_i(W,A) \leq R$}. We denote this set {W} of n-D points as W(A,R).

Statement. For any n-D point W within the n-D hyper-cube W(A,R) a CPC graphs for W is a graph for A shifted to no more than the distance R in each dimension.

Proof: Let $A=(a_1,a_2,...,a_n)$ then the farthest W of the hyper-cube are $W=(a_1 \pm R, a_2 \pm R_2,...a_n \pm R)$. If these points are shifted relative to A no more than R then all other points are shifted within R too. Therefore we prove the statement for these points. In CPC plane W is shown a an oriented graph that connects pairs $(w_1,w_2)$ $\rightarrow$ $(w_3,w_4)\rightarrow...\rightarrow$ $(w_{n-1},w_n)$. Consider for all i, $w_i=a_i+R$ then $(w_1,w_2)=$ $(a_1+R,a_2+R)$ of W is shifted relative to the first pair $(a_1,a_2)$ of A with the shift (R, R). Similarly the pair $(w_i,w_{i+1})$ of W is shifted relative to the pair $(a_i,a_{i+1})$ of A with the same shift (R,R). Thus to produce the graph for W we need to add shift R in X coordinate and shift R on Y coordinate to the graph for A. Similarly shifts (-R, R) or (R,-R) will happen when some wi will be equal to ai-R keeping the max of distance equal to R. Q.E.D.

Now consider two classes of n-D vectors that are within two different hyper-cubes with property Q: centers A and B of W(A,R) and W(B,R) are with the distance greater than 2R in each dimension i, that is $D_i(A,B) >2R$.

Statement. Graphs of CPC representations of all n-D points from hyper-cubes W(A,R) and W(B,R) with property Q do not overlap.

Proof. Note that $maxD_i(W_k,W_s)=2R$ and max $D_i(W_k,A)=R$ when both $W_k$ and $W_s$ are within W(A,R). The same facts $maxD_i(Wk,Ws)=2R$ and $maxD_i(W_k,B)=R$ are true when both $W_k$ and $W_s$ are within W(B,R). If hyper-cubes W(A,R) and W(B,R) overlap then a dimension $X_i$ must exist such that that $D_i(A,B) \leq 2R$ because it must be less than or equal to the sum of max distances $D_i(A,W)=R$ and $D_i(B,W)=R$ within each hyper-cube that is R+R. This contradicts property Q that requires for all $X_i$ that $D_i(A,B) >2R$. Q.E.D.

The statements for hyper-spheres are similar to statements for hyper-cubes. Another important advantage of CPC is its **lossless**. Our studies had shown that everywhere where parallel and radial coordinates are useful, CPC also useful.

Would it be difficult to separate non-overlapping hyper-cubes and hyper-spheres by using analytical computations without any collaborative visualization in advance? Normally we do not know in advance the centers of the hyper-cubes and hyper-spheres in n-D as well as their lengths. For analytical clustering we need to seed n-D points to start it and the clustering result is sensitive to selection of these points. Not knowing the radiuses of hyper-cubes we need to search thorough many of them. This is difficult especially for clusters with different radiuses. Even when we find a stable clustering we still do not know if this is a local or a global optimum of the clustering objective function. The selection of clustering objective function itself is quite subjective. The collaborative visualization of the clusters found analytically is a way to confirm them and to ensure that they are meaningful. The challenges for analytical methods for discovering more complex data structures such as non-central tubes, piecewise tubes and overlapping structures grow due to complexity of these data.

**CPC Visualization Options**. Fig. 7 illustrates a complete CPC graph visualization. Consider two 4-D records A=(0010) and B=(1000) that are shown in Figure 7 (a) and (b) respectively. In (a) a right (green) node indicates the start point of the graph (0,0), and labels 1 and 2 indicate the sequence of traversing the edges of graph. For record A the sequence is (00) $\rightarrow$ (10) and for record B it is (10) $\rightarrow$ (00).

Often a **simplified CPC visualization** without labels is sufficient. For long graphs produced for higher dimensional data we propose using **animation of the graph** with a point moving on the edges of the graph or jumping from node to node for faster traversing the graph. One of the agents in the collaborative visualization can *drive the* *animation* for other agents. In this case the interactive CPC visualization uses coloring or blinking these graphs. This interactive visualization allows turning off all other graphs showing only such ambiguous graphs, present these graphs in a separate window (CPC plane), and show actual numeric values.

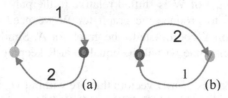

**Fig. 7.** CPC visualizations of the vector

# 5    Conclusion

This paper proposed new lossless n-D data visualizations based on the idea of collocating pairs of the coordinates of n-D vectors and targeted on effective usage of shape perception and interactive collaboration of agents for visual analytics. Advantages of these visualizations are shown with analytical and experimental studies. The experimental results are presented in a separate paper.

**Acknowledgments.** The authors are grateful to CWU students J. Smigai and N. Turnley for coding and producing some visualizations.

# References

1. Grishin, V.: Pictorial Analysis of Experimental Data. pp. 1–237 Nauka Publ. Moscow (1982)
2. Kovalerchuk, B.: Visualization of multidimensional data with collocated paired coordinates and general line coordinates. In: Proc. SPIE 9017, Visualization and Data Analysis, 90170I (2014)
3. Grishin, V., Sula, A., Ulieru, M.: Pictorial analysis: a multi-resolution data visualization approach for monitoring and diagnosis of complex systems. Int. Journal of Information Sciences 152, 1–24 (2003)
4. Kovalerchuk, B., Delizy, F., Riggs, L., Vityaev, E.: Visual discovery in multivariate binary data. In: Proc. SPIE 7530, Visualization and Data Analysis, 75300B, p. 12 (2010)
5. Ward, M., Grinstein, G., Keim, D.: Interactive Data Visualization: foundations, techniques, and applications, pp. 1–496. A K Peters, Ltd., Natick (2010)
6. Bertini, E., Tatu, A., Keim, D.: Quality metrics in high-dimensional data visualization: An overview and systematization. IEEE Tr. on Visualization and Computer Graphics (2011)
7. Grishin, V., Kovalerchuk, B.: Stars advantages vs. Parallel Coordinates (shape perception as visualization reserve. In: Proc. SPIE 9017, Visualization and Data Analysis 2014, 90170I (2014)
8. Kovalerchuk, B., Schwing, J. (eds.): Visual and Spatial Analysis. Springer, Heidelberg (2005)
9. Kovalerchuk, B., Balinsky, A.: Visual Data Mining and Discovery in Multivariate Data Using Monotone n-D Structure. In: Wolff, K.E., Palchunov, D.E., Zagoruiko, N.G., Andelfinger, U. (eds.) KONT 2007 and KPP 2007. LNCS, vol. 6581, pp. 297–313. Springer, Heidelberg (2011)

# Multidimensional Collaborative Lossless Visualization: Experimental Study

Vladimir Grishin[1] and Boris Kovalerchuk[2]

[1] View Trends International, 15 Wildwood Street, Ste 14, Dracut, MA, 01826-5190, USA
[2] Dept. of Computer Science, Central Washington University, 400 E. University Way,
Ellensburg, WA 98926, USA
borisk@cwu.edu

**Abstract.** The major challenges in visualization of large n-D data in 2-D are in supporting the most efficient and fast usage of abilities of users to analyze visualized information and to extract patterns visually. This paper describes experimental results of a collaborative approach to support n-D data visualization based on new lossless n-D visualization methods (collocated paired coordinates and their stars modifications) that we propose. This is a second part of the work. The first part presented in a separate paper is focused on description of the algorithms.

**Keywords:** Collaborative multi-dimensional data visualization, stars visualization, experiment.

## 1    Introduction

This paper is a second part of our work on collaborative visualization of multidimensional data. It is focused on experimental results. The first paper describes a collaborative approach to support n-D data visualization based on new lossless n-D visualization methods that we propose. These new visualizations convert n-D data vectors into multiple shapes in 2-D or 3-D [2,4,7-10]. While all of them are lossless, their perceptual qualities are quite different and this paper explores this issue.

Shape perception plays a key role in human pattern recognition. Visual shape perception supplies over 90% of information for pattern recognition, recent visualization techniques do not use it efficiently [5,6]. Human can detect, compare, describe many figures by hundreds of their local features (concave, convex, angle, wave, etc.) with many attributes (size, orientation, location, etc.) for each feature, and combine them into a multilevel hierarchy (see Fig. 1) [1,3].

A term "holistic picture" denotes an image together with its description that includes image statistics, textures, integral characteristics, shapes, and coloring. Moreover the holistic concept is appearing at multiple levels of image perception. First the image is considered as a set of "spot clusters" and relations between them as an overall structure of the image. Then each spot cluster is considered with the same aspects (statistics, textures, integrals, shapes and coloring) where elements are "spots"

Y. Luo (Ed.): CDVE 2014, LNCS 8683, pp. 27–35, 2014.

and the structure represent relations between these "spots". Next each "spot" is viewed at the holistic level in the same way and at the levels of its elements, denoted in the figure 1 as intermediate and local levels. At these levels the features that are perceptually important are listed in Fig.1. They include symmetry, elongation, orientation, compactness, convexity/concavity, peaks, waves, sharp angle, inside/outside, etc. These general hierarchical image perception principles are applicable to n-D data visualization and we sue them.

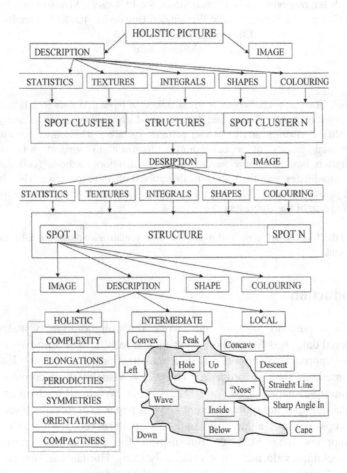

**Fig. 1.** Feature hierarchy of 2-D contour

By mapping data vectors into contours we can recognize and describe very complicated nonlinear structures in data space. Invariance of shape perception under local affine transformations of image radically extends these capabilities. However, modern visualization researches usually refer to just few simplest features on pictures and rarely link it with data structures.

For better understanding and quantitative description of data space structures, which leverage visual capabilities we have to use displays that provide analytically simple connections between data attributes and image features (stars, parallel coordinates, pie- and bar-charts, and other similar displays). Most of the subjects (agents) detect different features of stars that represent the same n-D vector. One subject can detect first feature "a", then "f", then "c", etc. Another subject can detect first feature "d", then "f", etc. Moreover, usually subjects initially detect only the most "impressive" part of current features, e.g., some big angle. Then the subject scans all figures of each class of n-D data to find the details of the shape of the neighbor in the given feature when test goal requires it.

This is an obvious reason for **collaborative visualization** of the same data by a group of users/agents. Comparison of results of visual analysis generated by several users can significantly increase speed and accuracy of recognition of patterns of different data structures. It is especially beneficial for n-D data with $n \geq 30$.

## 2    Stars

**Motivation.** The main goal of this study is getting significant benefits from human shape perception abilities when representing n-D data as 2-D shapes. The 2-D Collocated Paired Coordinates ( CPC) and General Line Coordinates (GLC) displays described in [2, 10] have advantages in representation of:

(1) Attributes of a single standalone n-D vector $x$ for n < 25,
(2) An envelope of an n-D vector $x$ of any dimension n,
(3) Envelopes of hundreds of overlapping n-D vectors {$x$} for n < 25.

Lines in the CPC graph can intersect which can produce a fragmented and complex combination of triangles, squares, etc., that can be difficult to interpret in terms of data space structures. Envelops of CPC graphs allow to mitigate these perceptual difficulties by providing simpler and not fragmented shapes. The envelopes can be compared by using their shape features such as size and symmetries.

These features indicate some relationships between coordinates of the n-D vector $x$, e.g., the orientation of this vector in the data space. The same is true for the envelopes of multiple overlapping n-D vectors in CPC, Parallel and Polar Coordinates. However, these displays are quite cluttered for high-dimensional and overlapped n-D vectors {$x$}. Therefore, only a few statistical properties of data classes such as dominant orientation can be estimating in this way. While this limitation of Parallel and Polar Coordinates is well known such cluttered displays are popular in big database analysis. Thus it is desirable to decrease clutter.

**Stars of Paired Coordinates.** For essentially better use of shape perception for visual analytics with CPC we propose special type of polar displays of CPC (see Fig. 2). These CPC stars are generated as follows: a full $2\pi$ circle is divided on n/2 equal sectors. Each pair of values of coordinates ($x_j$, $x_{j+1}$) of an n-D vector $x$ is displayed in its own sector as a point. This point is located at the distance r from star center, which is a Euclidean length of the projection of vector $x$ on the plane of this two coordinates, $r = \sqrt{x_j^2 + x_{j+1}^2}$ with the angle $\alpha$ of the ray to this point from sector start proportional to the value of $x_j$. In this way we get n/2 points and connect them by straight lines to generate a star. This is a polar representation of *all* 2-D projections of $x_i$ on plane. It is lossless display forming a single connected figure without crossing lines. It satisfies all Gestalt Laws providing an effective application of shape perception capabilities [1,5]. Alternative versions of this polar representation are produced when radius r represents $x_j$ and angle $\alpha$ represents $x_{j+1}$, or vice versa.

These CPC stars provide new visualizations that show 2-D projections directly which could be beneficial for naturally paired data and easily interpretable. In comparison with regular stars such CPC stars: (1) display all information of vector **x** more clear. simultaneously, (2) have twice less break points on the contour of the figure that is significantly decreasing shapes complexity (see Fig. 3). It effectively doubles data dimensions accessible to at least 200 dimensions as Fig. 4 shows obvious advantages of CPC stars vs. regular ones for shape perception.

**Stars Prospects.** Due to limitations described above our next step is studying another representation of CPC and providing a more effective application of shape perception together with extension of possible data dimensions up to 200. It is already shown that a separate polar representation (star) of each individual n-D vector **x** allows distinguishing simple hyper structures in n-D with n ≤ 96 for dozens of vectors for a quite short time required from a user to observe this visualization.

This is for a small number of n-D vectors and relatively small dimensions in comparison with current interests in Big data studies. However, in many practical diagnostics tasks in medicine and engineering dimensions do not exceed 200. Thus, the proposed visualization is beneficial for such tasks.

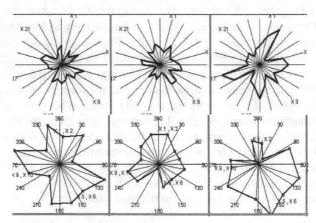

**Fig. 2.** CPC stars (second row) and as regular stars (first row) for the same three 24-D vectors

The expansion of the proposed approach for dimension n up to 1000 is as follows: grouping coordinates $x_i$ of **x** by 100-150 and representing them by separate or collocated colored stars, and/or mapping some $x_i$ into colors. Lossy reduction of n can be applied after visual analysis of these lossless displays which can reveal least informative attributes. Another reduction is based on a priori domain knowledge.

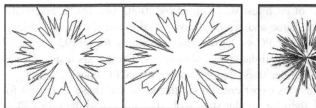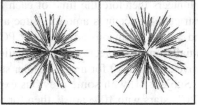

**Fig. 3.** Comparative display of CPC stars and regular stars of the same two 192-D vectors

An important factor of visual analytics is the number of data vectors L. In the mentioned diagnostics tasks it is often no more $10^3$-$10^4$. In other tasks data include millions of records. However, often we have a prior knowledge of data and a specific goal that allow essential data reduction. Our decades of experience have shown that visual comparison of thousands figures in analysis of few classes is feasible *if display allow to effectively apply human shape perception.*

## 3    Experimental Comparison CPC and Standard Stars

Further we quantitatively evaluate advantages of CPC stars vs. regular stars, which figures above clearly show. Comparison of these figures shows that advantages grow with data dimension **n** and therefore we focus our experiments on comparison for maximal **n** yet providing effective shape recognition.

**Recognition of Hyper-Tubes by Shape Features of Their CPC and Common Stars.** Consider five data classes randomly generated as points {**x**} of the n-D Euclidian data space $R^n$, with dimension n=192. Points of each class are laid in a separate hyper-tube around its random rays $r_k$ from its origin (n-D vector $a_k$), where k=1,..,5 is a class label. In each tube 5-15 points are randomly placed within the tube. Then these points have been randomized (by normal multiplicative or additive n-dimensional "noise" with given standard distributions). The distance of each point from tube central line (generatrix) specifies the variation of shapes of stars. Stars are similar in shapes and differ in sizes for narrow hyper-tubes of this type [1]. Many classes of n-D data can be represented as combinations of tubes. For instance, a curved tube can be approximated by a set of linear tubes. A hyper-sphere ("ball") is a "tube" around a single point. Another important aspect is affine invariance of shape perception that allows detecting these shapes that are rotated, shifted and resized. It opens wide possibilities for complex nonlinear structure visual recognition and interpretation.

**Experiment Statement and Results.** Each subject was asked to find a few features separating each of 5 tubes with 6 vectors **x** from others tubes by their randomly placed on one sheet of paper CPC stars (see Fig. 5). The subject solved the same task for regular stars representing the same data sample with the same placement on a paper sheet. The experiment was repeated for different levels of "noise", i.e. tube width (10, 20, 30% of maximum possible value of each coordinate of **x**). All subjects were volunteers therefore the time of each test was limited by 20-30 minutes. It essentially restricted the features amount. Time and errors of task solution are shown in Tables 1 and 2. Due to obvious advantages CPC vs. known stars especially for n=192, we tested initially only 2 subjects to roughly estimate these advantages. These tests results clearly proved that at least for n=192 regular stars cannot compete with CPC ones.

Subject #1, with some previous experience in similar tests, did these tests first for CPC's stars with 10% noise, then for regular stars with 10% noise and then for CPC's stars with noise 20%. During 30 min time limit she detected 4 discriminative features of each of 5 classes for CPCs and 3 such features for regular stars. However, in last test only wide and large features from Fig.5 were detected while comparison of 80-90% of features that consist of the sets of narrow peaks was drastically more difficult. Therefore, subject #1 denied test with 20% and 30% noised stars. For n=192 regular stars do not display data losslessly because they provide visual analytics only of very limited part of adjacent coordinates $x_i$, $x_{i+1}$,... $x_{i+m}$ with large and similar values. Recognition of them with 30% noise is so time consuming that even very experienced Subject #2 could not separate more than two tubes for 30 minutes and only by using large local and integral features. On other hand, CPCs tests showed acceptable time (1-5 min) for all figures and noise up to 30% (see Table 2.)

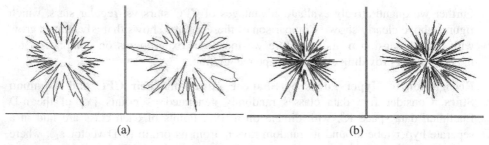

(a)　　　　　　　　　　　　　　(b)

**Fig. 4.** (a): samples of CPCs stars of 2 points of different tubes with n=192 and 20% noise; (b): the same for regular stars

**Table 1.** Subject 1 Time (mean/sd) and errors of one feature detection for 5 tubes (sec)

|  |  | Subject #1 | |
| --- | --- | --- | --- |
| noise |  | Stars | CPC |
| 10% | Time | 124/68 | 92/52 |
|  | Features | 3 | 4 |
|  | Errors | 2 | 2 |
| 20% | Time | n/a | 119/74 |
|  | Features | n/a | 4 |
|  | Errors | n/a | 3 |

**Table 2.** Subject 2 Time (mean/sd) and errors of one feature detection for 5 tubes (sec)

|  |  | Subject #2 | |
| --- | --- | --- | --- |
| noise |  | Stars | CPC |
| 10% | Time | 107/48 | 60/33 |
|  | Features | 3 | 5 |
|  | Errors | 3 | 0 |
| 20% | Time | 159/71 | 84/42 |
|  | Features | 3 | 5 |
|  | Errors | 4 | 1 |
| 30% | Time | n/a | 197/105 |
|  | Features | n/a | 5 |
|  | Errors | n/a | 3 |

Only a half of time difference between results for 10% noise can be explained by subject cognitive training during regular stars analysis that helped with CPCs recognition. Subject #2 with advanced skills performed two times better with CPCs vs. common stars, especially for wide tubes with 20-30% of noise. The success of CPC vs. common stars is due to: (1) two-times less dense placement of the points, and (2) a specific mapping of pairs $x_i$, $x_{i+1}$ into a contour. The magnification can improve performance of the common stars, but with fewer stars in a vision field.

# 4    Collaborative Visualization for Data Exploration

*Collaborative Feature Selection.* A basic part of visual pattern recognition is detection of shape features common for majority of pictures of one class and not typical for others classes of pictures. Therefore, in this experiment figures are compared by selecting sets of local features that are common for certain classes of figures. In the experiment figures of each class include 4-6 identical shape features formed by 5-9 neighboring n-D coordinates. Different random fragments have been placed between these informative features in each figure (see Fig. 6). This can be viewed as "a figurative noise". No additive noise has been added in this experiment

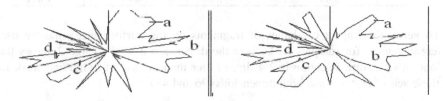

**Fig. 5.** Two stars with identical shape fragments on intervals [a,b] and [d,c]

Consider an n-D data vector is $\mathbf{x}=(x_1, x_2, ..x_i, ..x_n)$ in the data space, where $x_i$ is value of i-th coordinate. The class of vectors illustrated in Fig. 6 can be described by the set of Elementary Conjunctions (EC) of vector coordinates. If all vectors of a given class have the same values of coordinates from $X_i$ to $X_{i+p}$, then all of them have an identical shape fragment E1 with the identical location in all these figures. Appearance of such fragments can be considered as TRUE value of the elementary conjunction, i.e., logical multiplication of logical expression, i.e. "$x_i=a_i$ & $x_{i+1}=a_{i+1}$ &...& $x_{i+p}=a_{i+p}$", where $a_i,a_{i+1},...,$ $a_{i+p}$ are values of indexed coordinates. The length of this fragment is specified by p value.

If a given class has a several common fragments, $E_1$, $E_2...E_n$, then this class is characterized by this set of fragments $E_1$, $E_2...E_n$. Formally all such vectors have a common point as their projection in a subspace of coordinates of these EC's. More generally it is a hyper-ellipse in this subspace if we take into account thresholds of visual perception for shape discrimination. Affine invariance of shape perception extends such hyper-ellipses to complicated nonlinear tubes in these subspaces. Ten data vectors from two classes of figures have been presented to subjects. These classes differ in the shapes of features and their placement on figures (see Fig. 6).

(a)          Features of stars                    (b)          The same features of PC features

**Fig. 6.** Samples of class features in stars and parallel coordinates (PCS)

Subjects knew that the first class of CPV stars is placed in the first two rows and second one in the last two rows. Subjects were instructed to find all first class fragments not existing in the second class and vice versa. Subjects were required to find all coordinates that create each common fragment. Performance time is given in Table 3 for two dimensions. It shows the average time of feature selection (first number) and the standard deviation of this value (second number).

**Table 3.** Separate feature selection time (mean/standard deviation in seconds)

|  | 96 dimensions | 48 dimensions | | |
|---|---|---|---|---|
|  | C | A | D | F |
| Individual | 94/44 | 31/14 | 38/16 | 60/21 |
| Collaborative | 33/12 | 13/11 | 14/13 | 15/12 |

To verify the impact of shapes of fragments on the performance time we used different shapes  for samples A, D, F in the dimension n = 48. Table 3 shows that collaborative feature selection is 2-4 times faster than in case of individual work for all these sets of features and both dimensions (96 and 48).

# 5    Conclusion

This paper demonstrated new lossless n-D data visualizations based on the idea of collocating pairs of the coordinates of n-D vectors. It is targeted on effective collaborative usage of shape perception for visual analytics of real as well as modeled structures of multi-dimensional data. Advantages of these interactive collaborative visualizations are shown with analytical and experimental studies for data dimensions up to 200.

# References

1. Grishin, V.: Pictorial Analysis of Experimental Data. pp. 1–237 Nauka Publ. Moscow (1982)
2. Kovalerchuk, B.: Visualization of multidimensional data with collocated paired coordinates and general line coordinates. In: Proc. SPIE 9017, Visualization and Data Analysis, 90170I (2014)
3. Grishin, V., Sula, A., Ulieru, M.: Pictorial analysis: a multi-resolution data visualization approach for monitoring and diagnosis of complex systems. Int. Journal of Information Sciences 152, 1–24 (2003)

4. Kovalerchuk, B., Delizy, F., Riggs, L., Vityaev, E.: Visual discovery in multivariate binary data. In: Proc. SPIE 7530, Visualization and Data Analysis, 75300B, p. 12 (2010)
5. Ward, M., Grinstein, G., Keim, D.: Interactive Data Visualization: foundations, techniques, and applications, pp. 1–496. A K Peters, Ltd., Natick (2010)
6. Bertini, F., Tatu, A., Keim, D.: Quality metrics in high-dimensional data visualization: An overview and systematization. IEEE Tr. on Visualization and Computer Graphics (2011)
7. Grishin, V., Kovalerchuk, B.: Stars advantages vs. Parallel Coordinates (shape perception as visualization reserve. In: Proc. SPIE 9017, Visualization and Data Analysis 2014, 90170I (2014)
8. Kovalerchuk, B., Schwing, J. (eds.): Visual and Spatial Analysis. Springer, Heidelberg (2005)
9. Kovalerchuk, B., Balinsky, A.: Visual Data Mining and Discovery in Multivariate Data Using Monotone n-D Structure. In: Wolff, K.E., Palchunov, D.E., Zagoruiko, N.G., Andelfinger, U. (eds.) KONT 2007 and KPP 2007. LNCS, vol. 6581, pp. 297–313. Springer, Heidelberg (2011)
10. Kovalerchuk, B., Grishin, V.: Collaborative lossless visualization of n-D data by collocated paired coordinates. In: CDVE 2014 (2014)

# The *Plot-poll* Redesigned: Lessons from the Deployment of a Collective Mood-tracker in an Online Support Group

Alex Ivanov[1] and Emma Mileva[2]

[1] Department of Media and Communication, City University of Hong Kong
[2] Department of Linguistics, Simon Fraser University, British Columbia, Canada
`aivanov@cityu.edu.hk, emileva@sfu.ca`

**Abstract.** The study described in this paper extends our earlier work on improving the user experience in online support groups via embedding social knowledge visualization interfaces. A real online support group was created for the purpose of testing a web-poll mood tracker for 16 weeks. We describe the design and deployment of both 2005 and current plot-polls, and conclude with the mixed results from our qualitative investigation, which yielded useful recommendations for future research.

**Keywords:** data visualization, social visualization, online support group, mood tracker, interface design, ambient displays, collaborative design.

## 1 Introduction

As we write this article, the world continues to search for the lost Malaysian jet. This context brings to mind James Surowiecki's bestseller, *The Wisdom of Crowds* [11]. The book starts out with a case study from the sixties, when a missing submarine was eventually located only after the search team assembled all the 'best guesses' of its whereabouts from hundreds of people with a wide range of knowledge. Of course, the book does postulate several conditions that must be met before we can tap into such collective wisdom and build a composite picture of the 'truth'. Nevertheless, one would think that after all this time, 'social computation' success stories (also refer to [17] would be more common today. Indeed, despite Google's advances in information search and crowdsourcing and data visualization technologies, there still persists a dearth of information on topics that concern millions, even though the knowledge is there somewhere.

Online support groups are one domain that could particularly benefit from capturing and graphically representing knowledge that resides in end-users. In 2005, we started a project with a simple interface for collaborative knowledge visualization – a graphical web-poll for multivariate data that doubled as a collective mood tracker [7]. This interface was embedded within a highly popular forum on the herbal supplement St. John's Wort (sjwinfo.org). Users who were taking this herbal antidepressant were asked to vote for their current mood improvement (if any). As people plotted their data, this web-poll / chart, which we dubbed as a *plot-poll*, began to visualize a certain trend of the product's efficacy across time. For the one week deployment of our

Y. Luo (Ed.): CDVE 2014, LNCS 8683, pp. 36–43, 2014.
© Springer International Publishing Switzerland 2014

plot-poll, new visitors to the forum did not have to ask the one question that arose over and over in the threaded discussions: "how soon can I expect this herb to start working?" In addition to the informative function of the plot-poll, we believed it would also serve an aesthetic purpose, making the web forum more appealing and contribute to its stickiness.

Although a plot-poll is not difficult to create, we have yet to see deployments of such an interface in online forums. Despite the phenomenal advances in interactive information visualization, visitors of support groups like the one mentioned above still spend hours browsing text to find basic data [16]. Most existing web-polls in discussion boards are simply not as useful as they could be; they are typically created as a new thread and get buried quickly. There is also a limitation in that most polls display results in bar or pie charts, which are not suitable for visualizing multivariate data. In sum, online discussion boards can hardly be considered knowledge-building environments [10].

The rest of this paper is structured as follows. In the next section we provide a brief review of social knowledge visualization, plus more details on our 2005 study. In Section 3 we introduce the support group that we created for the purpose of testing our second-generation plot-poll, and describe its design. Section 4 concludes with the lessons from the three-month deployment and gives recommendations for future work.

## 2    Background to the Current Study

Since our first design of the plot-poll in 2005 [7], a number of web forums have provided members with graphical tools for recording personal data. The best-known example is PatientsLikeMe.com, a quantitative personal research platform for patients with life-changing illnesses [16]. Users share their experience with a certain treatment or medication not only via regular posts but also by entering the data into a variety of graphical representations – from bar graphs to Gantt charts. While impressive, these visualizations are different from what we proposed in our original study [7]. Plot-polls not only allow individual users to record their progress data as in a personal journal, they also show the *collective* state of all undergoing the same treatment. Plot-polls are thus more than graphical multivariate web polls; they bear similarities to ambient social displays. Morris 2005 [8], for instance, deployed a social network visualization that induced a positive affective outcome within participants. These were people of age, and the simple star diagram screensaver on their home PCs displayed the activity level of their friends. A similar demographic group was also recruited in a study of a more medical nature by Ferreira et al. [4]. 20 subjects wore various sensors around their bodies for three months, transmitting information about their skin temperature, respiration rate, and other variables. The objective here was to develop a system that captured and transmitted a patient's health condition in real-time, visualizing it for doctors with elegant timeline diagrams instead of the typical flowcharts.

The plot-poll can also be considered a type of social knowledge visualizations, or a mix of data, knowledge, and social visualization. Data and/or information visualization (IV) is defined as the use of computer-supported, interactive and visual representations of abstract data to amplify cognition [2]. IV interfaces such as stock price *heat maps*, for example, enhance the detections of patterns. While these interfaces are typically about presentation of large data sets from databases, knowledge visualization (KV) facilitates the creation of knowledge by giving people graphic means of expressing what they know [12]. Interactive concept maps and affinity diagrams are good examples of KV. The plot-poll can be considered a mix of IV and KV, but we should also mention another type of digital interface that is referred to as social visualization. These are intuitive depictions of interactions in online spaces that aim to recreate a shared sense of context [7]. While the plot-poll does not depict interactions per se, it has the potential to enrich the context of conversation. It is like a digital mural, of sorts, a permanent fixture in the community space that depicts the collective treatment progress.

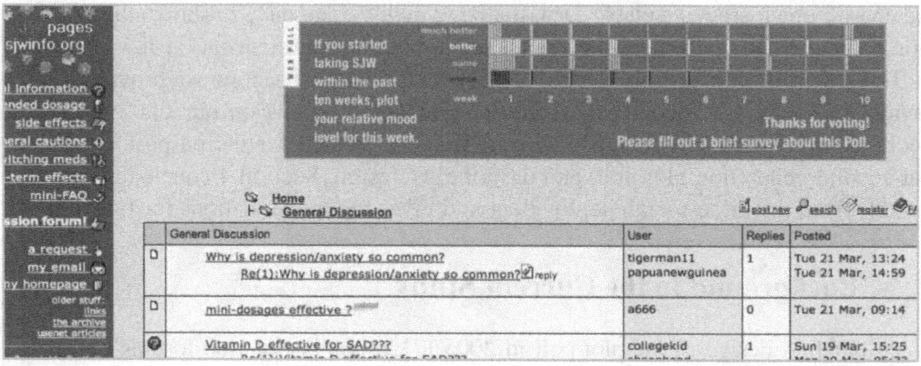

**Fig. 1.** Screenshot of our 2005 plot-poll embedded in the St. John's Wort web forum

This was our intention even with the first plot-poll, which is shown in Fig. 1 as it appeared at the end of the one-week deployment in 2005. The users could click, or 'plot', their mood for others to see in an at-a-glance manner. The experience of mapping or externalizing one's subjective experience into a public space (albeit anonymously) was expected to provide a feeling of contribution, adding to the mutual story (which in this case was the experience of 'hanging in' until the medication 'kicks in'). Three variables were captured and displayed: 1) how long, in terms of weeks, the product has been taken by the user; 2) the degree to which the user's mood has improved (or worsened); and 3) the number of users reporting that particular combination of variables. 76 people voted in the plot-poll to indicate their experience with St. John's Wort. The majority of participation came from 'lurkers', users that were not registered contributing members in the discussions. In other words, people who most likely would have been reluctant to talk now contributed to the site through the plot-poll. In that sense, our 2005 study was a success.

The St. John's Wort plot-poll also had some limitations. First, it was deployed for one week only, and only on certain pages of the forum. (Such was our agreement with the forum's owner.) The second limitation is evident in the skewed nature of the responses: most of them cluster near the beginning of the timeline. This was likely due to the predominance of users in the very first week of treatment. (Note that cookies prevented users from voting twice in the plot-poll.) Although a certain trend of mood improvement could already be detected (note the predominant blue at first, becoming orange later) for a more rigorous test of plot-polling, we needed users reporting their moods progressively, rather than in a one-off snapshot. For technical and other reasons, tracking users across time was not an option with the St. John's Wort forum. Hence, the decision to actually create an online support group from scratch.

We kept our focus on antidepressant medication. A visit to any forum on the topic will reveal a never-ending stream of newbies asking about other people's experiences with the same treatment [6]. Our research also indicated that there was no existing discussion board dedicated to one of the most popular antidepressants on the market. Thus we launched Venlafacts.org, a discussion board exclusively for people starting out treatment with *venlafaxine*.

## 3    The Venlafacts.org Plot-poll

Venlafaxine has proven to be one of the most effective medications for treating depressive and anxiety disorders. Its efficacy, however, varies widely depending on dosage [1], [5]. Some patients do well on a low daily dose of 75 mg, while others feel no improvement until they reach 300 mg or more. Yet, at these higher levels, adverse side effects become common and more serious [5], [13]. The following two posts by actual users taking venlafaxine illustrate the challenges with efficacy, and side effects.

> I was feeling good on 112.5mg, but my doc says time for me to go up to 150mg. I feel okay, but kinda groggy. I was just wondering if anyone feel any differently when you taking dosage higher then necessary?

> My new doc switched me from 20mg Paxil to 150mg Effexor XR daily. There was a two-week ramp-down/ramp-up transition, but now that I'm at full dosage, I feel like my brain is redlining in 6th gear. Has anyone else experienced this?

Accommodating dosage in the design of a plot-poll for venlafaxine was a challenge. The first step in any visualization design is to transform the raw data into a data map, and determine whether a visual structure would improve the textual information display [2]. The data that was to be represented could be summarized as follows:

"I'm in my [W] week of taking
[X] mg venlafaxine daily and at this time and dosage I feel
[Y] in terms of mood relative to week one, just like
[Z] number of users having reported the same W, X, and Y."

We concluded that this information could be presented clearly with a visual structure that enhances pattern recognition. Tufte gives multiple examples of how plots can be extremely effective for illustrating patterns [14]. A key decision is which variable gets spatial coding at the expense of others [2]. In our case, space should arguably be devoted to showing the mood patterns.

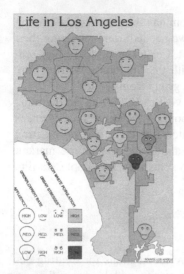

**Fig. 2.** (Left) Eugene Turner's award-winning mood infographic [15] and (right) progresstracking scale for boys with bipolar disorder, by Tracy Anglada (bpchildren.org)

Dozens of formats were mocked-up, as we drew on a range of information design sources (see Fig. 2 for some examples). Emoticons, for instance, may seem like a natural choice, if we had a simpler data structure. A better candidate for extending the small multiples grid format [9] that was central to the plot-poll structure are *Chernoff faces*. This format makes use of facial features to represent multiple variables (e.g. size of mouth for X, width of face for Y, etc.) Yet when it comes to more data visualization, Chernoff faces are not recommended. This is because the human brain likes to minimize the number of perceptual units, and faces are generally processed as single objects other than a collection of individual features [3]. The final version deployed on the site is shown in Fig. 3.

Venlafacts.org was not affiliated with any organization. The site was sponsored by a psychiatrist, who remained anonymous throughout the study yet served as the forum moderator. The forum was supported by the open-source, Vanilla platform. The plot-poll was a Flash application served with a MySQL database.

Promoting and recruiting members for venlafacts.org was achieved via Google Ads. In a week, the site had attracted ten registered members, who were quite active in sharing their experiences. Venlafacts.org also contained several pages worth of relevant information – not only about venlafaxine, but also about the site, and especially, how to use the plot-poll. The site displayed the plot-poll on the top of every page. Depending on the screen size of users, the plot-poll occupied around a third of the browser window. The default view was the collective view, displaying the aggregate of all plotted data. This could be toggled to the personal view, where users reported their progress throughout 16 weeks. Posts could be browsed and read by any visitor, though only registered users could use the plot-poll or write in the discussions.

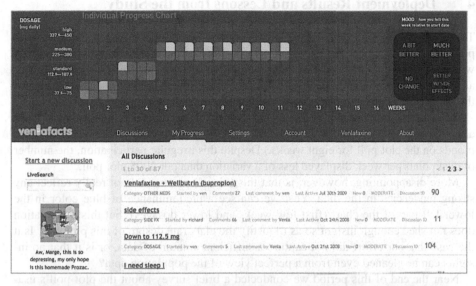

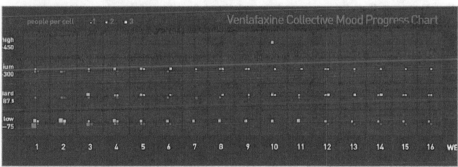

**Fig. 3.** (Top) The *personal* view of the plot-poll, at 11 weeks of one member's treatment progress, and (above) the *collective* view as it appeared after the 16-week deployment.

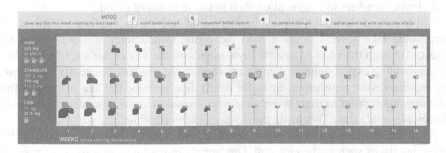

**Fig. 4.** Mock of an alternative visual representation of the data

# 4    Deployment Results and Lessons from the Study

Three months after its launch, Venlafacts.org had accumulated over a thousand user posts. The average post length was 43 words. 80% of posts came from six members, which was 9% of all 65. Some of these committed users posted several times a day, or as much as the moderator. We could not determine how many non-members browsed the discussion board, but 682 unique users visited the site during that 16-week trial.

27 members used the plot-poll to record their treatment progress for at least one week, although only nine used it for the entire 16 weeks. (On average, members recorded their moods on the plot-poll for eight weeks.) Despite this irregular participation, the number of data points per week displayed less of a variation than our 2005 plot-poll.

More disappointing, however, is that this (visual) pattern did not really reflect any strong tendencies in the data. Yes, we can see a predominance of blue color in the lower left part of the chart (first few weeks and lower dosages), but this information does not shed enough insight so as to justify the elaborate design of this plot-poll. Is it the case that our effort did not capture a sufficient amount of data, or is it that no insights can be gleaned even from a perfect view of the population data?

Near the end of this period we conducted a brief survey about the plot-poll's usability. Everyone found the personal (mood diary) function of the plot-poll easy to use, and useful. One third of users, however, admitted to struggling with understanding the collective view.

Another way to gauge the effectiveness of our deployment was the amount and quality of conversation in threads that was about the plot-poll. Remarkably, even though the plot-poll occupied as much as one-third of users' browsers, only two users made comments related to the plot-poll. It was surprising and rather disappointing that among over a thousand user posts there was virtually no interest expressed as to the main feature of our study. One should keep in mind, of course, that users in support groups primarily care about interacting with other people.

Whatever the reasons for the lackluster performance of our second plot-poll, it was clear that it needed to be redesigned. We believed that a 'floral' treatment might appeal better to our predominantly female membership, as the one shown in Fig. 4. Also planned for this visual structure was to organize the discussion board in a way that would invite members to comment on their petals in terms of mood.

As it happened, however, due to the increasing activity on the forum (replying to posts would take several hours a day) the forum's moderator withdrew from the project. Although the site had several loyal members, the moderator's role was essential in providing expert opinion. People returned to the site less frequently, and fewer new members were registering. Still, for nearly five months, the site offered factual and emotional support to users worldwide who wanted to know more details about the efficacy of venlafaxine. This made the deployment worthwhile.

Our first recommendation for future research is to conduct more extensive usability tests of interfaces such as the plot-poll. Our initial pre-deployment tests were positive, but apparently not representative of in-situ conditions. Indeed, more research is needed to evaluate the data structure of the venlafaxine plot-poll, and determine if it is perceptually too complex to be an effective visualization in support group settings.

The second recommendation from this project is about recruiting participants for similar field studies. Relying on the Google Ads program turned out to be an effective method for acquiring site registrations. Although the costs ran in the thousands of (Canadian) dollars, the rich set of user filtering options provides great experimental control. We believe more researchers should take advantage of using Google Ads for conducting field studies with real participants, rather than relying on student subjects.

# References

1. Allgulander, C., Hackett, D., Salinas, E.: Venlafaxine Extended Release in the Treatment of Generalized Anxiety Disorder. British Journal of Psychiatry 179, 15–22 (2001)
2. Card, S., Mackinlay, J., Schneiderman, B.: Readings in Information Visualization: Using Vision to Think. Morgan Kaufman, San Francisco (2008)
3. Chabris, C.F., Kosslyn, S.M.: Representational Correspondence as a Basic Principle of Diagram Design. In: Tergan, S.-O., Keller, T. (eds.) Knowledge and Information Visualization. LNCS, vol. 3426, pp. 36–57. Springer, Heidelberg (2005)
4. Ferreira, H., Sousa, T., Martins, A.: Scalable Integration of Multiple Health Sensor Data for Observing Medical Patterns. In: Proceedings of CDVE Cooperative Design, Visualization and Engineering, pp. 78–84 (2012)
5. Harrison, L., Ferrier, N., Young, A.: Tolerability of High-Dose Venlafaxine in Depressed Patients. Journal of Psychopharmacology 18(2), 200–204 (2004)
6. Hughes, S., Cohen, D.: Can Online Consumers Contribute to Drug Knowledge? A Mixed-Methods Comparison of Consumer-Generated and Professionally Controlled Psychotropic Medication Information on the Internet. Journal of Medical Internet Research 13(3) (2011)
7. Ivanov, A., Erickson, T., Cyr, D.: Plot-polling: Collaborative Knowledge Visualization for Online Discussions. In: Proceedings of the 10th IEEE International Conference on Information Visualization, pp. 205–210. IEEE, London (2006)
8. Morris, E.: Social Networks as Health Feedback Displays. IEEE Internet Computing 9(5), 29–37 (2005)
9. Powsner, M., Tufte, E.: Graphical Summary of Patient Status. The Lancet. 344(8919), 386–389 (1994)
10. Scardamalia, M., Bereiter, C.: Knowledge Building Environments. In: Di Stefano, A., Rudestam, K., Silverman, R. (eds.) Encyclopedia of Distributed Learning. Sage Publications, Thousand Oaks (2003)
11. Surowiecki, J.: The Wisdom of Crowds: Why the Many Are Smarter Than the Few and How Collective Wisdom Shapes Business, Economies, Societies and Nations. Little, Brown (2004)
12. Tergan, S., Keller, T.: Knowledge and Information Visualization – Searching for Synergies. Springer (2005)
13. Thomas, A., Taylor, D.: Evaluating the Relationship of High-Dose Venlafaxine Prescribing to Treatment- Resistant Depression. Psychiatric Bulletin (27), 93–95 (2003)
14. Tufte, E.: Envisioning Information. Graphic Press, Cheshire (1990)
15. Turner, E.: Life in LA. Map reprinted in Harmon, K (author) You Are Here. Princeton Architectural Press, New York (2003)
16. Wicks, P., Massagli, M., Frost, J., Brownstein, C., Okun, S., Vaughan, T., Bradley, R., Heywood, J.: Sharing Health Data for Better Outcomes on "Patients Like Me". Journal of Medical Internet Research 12(2), e19 (2010)
17. New York Times, http://www.nytimes.com/interactive/2011/11/09/us/ows-grid.html

# Improving Quality and Performance of Facility Management Using Building Information Modelling[*]

Heap-Yih Chong[1], Jun Wang[1], Wenchi Shou[1], Xiangyu Wang [1,**], and Jun Guo[2]

[1] Australasian Joint Research Centre for Building Information Modelling,
Curtin University, Australia
[2] CCDI Group, China
{heapyih.chong,jun.wang1,wenshi.shou,xiangyu.wang}@curtin.edu.au,
guo.jun@ccdi.com.cn

**Abstract.** Poor facility management has been attributed to lack of coordination and information during the maintenance process. The need for high quality applies not only to construction works and workmanship, but is also for its subsequent coordination and maintenance of a building. The paper aims to improve quality and performance of maintenance by integrating an advanced technology with a managerial approach, namely, building information modelling (BIM) and facility management. A BIM case study was investigated, which was located in Shanghai, China. Five significant areas were identified to improve the quality and performance of facility management, namely, centralized system, visualization, simplification, modifiable system, and smart emergency escape. The results highlight the benefits in applying the integrated system between BIM and facility management. It draws an insightful inference in enhancing quality services in facility management.

**Keywords:** BIM, Facility Management, Integration, Quality, Benefits, Case Study.

## 1 Introduction

Recent progress in information communication and technology has moved the construction industry forward. It helps in addressing the fragmentation and adversarial issues in construction progress. A well-coordinated work is critical especially dealing with vast of information in building process [1]. It will improve quality performance in whole project lifecycle and dispute avoidance [2,3,4].

Previous studies have shown certain potential benefits in integrating BIM and facility management in building industry [5,6,7,8,9] and even in oil and gas industry [10]. To quality aspect, the earlier studies focused on the construction stage, namely, construction specifications were automated and processed to support the inspection

---

[*] The 11th International Consference on Cooperative Design, Visualization and Engineering, p. 44, 2014.
[**] Corresponding author.

Y. Luo (Ed.): CDVE 2014, LNCS 8683, pp. 44–50, 2014.
© Springer International Publishing Switzerland 2014

and quality control in construction projects [11]; while design information were up-dated to deal with defect in construction [12]. Apart from that, Arayici did a review and forecast about modelling the existing structures for emergency management [6]. There is very rare in previous studies looking at an actual BIM project for facility management, particularly on the quality aspects in post construction stage.

The research reckons better quality facility management through BIM. The research objectives are: (a) to identify the significant areas in improving quality facility management in an actual BIM project, and (b) also to identify benefits derived from the integrated practice in BIM and facility management.  A case study was adopted, where was one of the significant projects located in Shanghai, China.  The integrated BIM model with facility management and related documents were examined. The research would render all the benefits generated from the integrated system. It would render useful references to forecast and schedule the maintenance needs in the building. The system would be able to accommodate the complicated human needs in the physical environments into a simpler and easier platform for overall maintenance for the project.

## 2    BIM and Facility Management

Many philosophies and closely related terminologies have been used to describe facility management. To facility management, many approaches and priorities have been adopted to suit the maintenance requirements and needs. Different countries would have different views and interpretations on its purpose and use [13,14,15,16,17,18]. Some prefer to describe it as an art more than a science for its management philosophy. Nevertheless, the research adopts a popular definition as defined by The International Facility management Association (IFMA), which is "a profession that encompasses multiple disciplines to ensure functionality of the built environment by integrating people, place, process and technology". It is rather a process of integrating the human with the physical environments in a comprehensive manner.  BIM and facility management can be seen from their similar perspectives of encompassing numerous disciplines towards human dimensions. There is a need to incorporate BIM into facility management as to have a better coordination and maintenance of the physical environments.

### 2.1    Quality and Performance of Facility Management

In this research context, a good quality and performance in facility management should be demonstrated from two important perspectives, namely, to address requirements from the technical aspects and to fulfil the high satisfaction level of the client.To technical aspects, the facility management concentrates on the life-span of the client's assets. The maintenance plan and strategy should extend the life of the assets or to reduce the breakdown or downtime of the services in the building. A collaborative virtual environment is one of the best options, where information and communication can be shared and interacted among the stakeholders [19]. On the other hand, human factor is a vital element in the facility management. The services quality should be expressed by client satisfaction indicators [20]. It should minimize the disruption and cost incurred in the maintenance process, which is to provide the best output for the facility management. Yet, different cultural dimensions and diversity issues affect greatly to quality management effectiveness [21]. Therefore, the facility manager should appreciate and take into account of the local culture and practice into the facility management.

# 3    Qualitative Research Approach

The case study approach was adopted. This is qualitative research approach to access the document and BIM model of the project. It is a five-storeys building, namely, Shanghai Disaster Control Centre. The total built-up area is approximately 31180 meter square. The project was completed within a year in 2011. Document analysis and BIM model simulation were the main sources of the primary data. The document analysis is stable and repeatable information, where it can be reviewed many times to fully understand the issues or questions [22]. This method will be able to identify the maintenance needs and potential benefits that can be derived from the BIM model. On the other hand, the informal interviews were also conducted with the related personnel involved in the project. The interview results were to improve the discussion and the primary data that were collected from the document analysis and BIM model.

# 4    Benefits Analysis and Discussion

Five significant areas were identified from the BIM model, document analysis and informal interviews. The data of model and related documents were examined repeatedly. Subsequently, each area has been analysed and elaborated for its quality facility management. The areas are, centralized system, visualization, simplification, modifiable system, and emergency escape.

## 4.1    Centralized System

The conventional facility management always relies on the stand-alone software or systems that are furnished by the service providers, for instance, security system, air-conditioning and so on. It creates many coordination problems and requires different technical personnel to monitor and facilitate each system, especially in handling the maintenance issues caused by several systems together.

  The first significant area of the integrated BIM and facility management were able to provide a centralized system for managing or maintaining all services and components in the building as illustrated in Figure 1. All of them would be monitored and controlled together, where it would save some costs incurred in searching or dealing the issues individually. As a result, this approach has improved the quality facility management as it significantly increases the efficiency in managing and maintaining the building.

**Fig. 1.** Centralized System for FM using BIM technology

## 4.2    Visualization

Another identified area was to have better visualization of the services and components in the building. The services and components were presented in a screen with different colours as illustrated in Figure 2. The details of each component or service can be examined and viewed directly from the screen. This is a very practical solution during the corrective maintenance, where the faulty parts of the services or components can be located easily. It would save a lot of time in searching the parts and this is particularly vital during the emergency breakdown and repairs.

All the minor or major services and components were visualized in a three-dimensional format. It has saved a lot of time in learning and imagining the services or components in the conventional two-dimensional drawings. It also helps in retrieving the related data. As a result, this area has improved the working process on site and also shortens the learning curve for the new employees according to the results of interviews.

**Fig. 2.** Details of each component in different colours

## 4.3    Simplification

Even though the vast of information have been stored and the database might be quite complicated, the most significant feature of the integrated system is to provide a simple interface or platform for direct viewing as illustrated in Figure 3. The personnel will have a very quick learning curve and able to manage and facilitate the building easily via the simplified viewing platform that is directly from the screen. Therefore, the area has benefited the complicated system of the project, especially the flow of piping system can be located easily. Subsequently, the process of maintenance has become more simplified. It will maintain high asset or equipment life through successful planning and coordinating all the maintenance activities.

**Fig. 3.** Simplified system

## 4.4    Modifiable System

As this system is BIM oriented, it will allow modification or improvement in the future. The system is able to upgrade or change the structures, and also to modify the services or components of the building. The changes can be updated easily in the BIM software. Once an item has been changed in the system, the remaining and similar items will be updated accordingly too.

## 4.5    Smart Emergency Escape

As the BIM model can be simulated for obtaining the data from fire and smoke, it will help for designing escape routes during a fire drill. During the fire drill, the system can capture the time and routes for escaping the building. The data were recorded and would be used to develop or to enhance the emergency escape of the building. Regarding the safety and evacuation system, smoke or fire detectors were installed in the building. The data of smoke sensors or fire detectors will be captured in a real time basis. The detectors will send a signal to the system once being activated. Then, the screen will indicate the signal and the facility manager or related personnel will able to make quick and informed decision to guide the occupants escape from the building as illustrated in Figure 4. The fast response is indeed one of the best benefits in integrating BIM into facility management. The system is able to locate a safe route and to guide the occupants to the nearest exit doors. This is contributed by the user-friendly interface of the system. This has improved significantly the decision making based on the interface, instead of referring to personal experience and prediction during the fire.

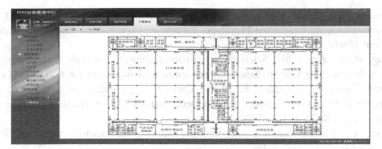

**Fig. 4.** Emergency escape plan

## 5    Discussion and Conclusion

Certain limitations need to consider in the system, the system relies on the accurate data that recorded in the system. The system is unable to check or rectify any possible human errors that might be occurred. Therefore, a comprehensive policy is needed to ensure the quality of the data, One of the possible means is to engage a third party to do the quality check for the system. Next, after having the accurate inputs for the system, it must also need to ensure the data are well exchanged for facility management. Construction Operations Building information exchange (COBie) format is an international standard and should be adopted for exchanging the required asset information. Besides, the data also require proper coordination. It is not solely based on software or know-how of the system, but it requires a comprehensive understanding about the building services, structures and also certain construction knowledge. It is because the poor coordination may worsen a maintenance process if there is any discrepancy information in the maintenance. Although the integrated system is far from perfection, it has served the purpose for having a better facility management. It demonstrates numerous practical areas and benefits through the investigation of the case study.

In summary, five significant areas were identified from Shanghai Disaster Control Centre, namely, centralized system, visualization, simplification, modifiable system, and smart emergency escape. This is an integration between a technology and a managerial approach, which is able to improve the quality and performance of the maintenance. The findings reveal different areas of integration of BIM in facility management, which is able to provide a useful guide and also to accommodate the different human needs in the maintenance. It creates an insight into the effective collaborative platform of facility management in the future.

## References

1. Christensen, L.R.: Practices of Stigmergy in the Building Process. Computer Supported Cooperative Work (CSCW) 23(1), 1–19 (2014)
2. Chong, H.Y., Zin, R.M.: Transforming of Construction Contract Administra-tion: Data Warehouse Modeling. In: 2011 Eighth International Conference on IEEE Information Technology: New Generations, ITNG (2011)

3. Chong, H.Y., Zin, R.M., Chong, S.C.: Employing Data Warehousing for Con-tract Administration: e-Dispute Resolution Prototype. Journal of Construction Engineering and Management 139(6), 611–619 (2012)
4. Chong, H.-Y., Zin, R.M.: Selection of dispute resolution methods: factor analysis approach. Engineering, Construction and Architectural Management 19(4), 428–443 (2012)
5. Becerik-Gerber, B., Jazizadeh, F., Li, N., Calis, G.: Application areas and data requirements for BIM-enabled facilities management. Journal of Construction Engineering and Management 138(3), 431–442 (2011)
6. Arayici, Y.: Towards building information modelling for existing structures. Structural Survey 26(3), 210–222 (2008)
7. Singh, V., Gu, N., Wang, X.: A theoretical framework of a BIM-based multi-disciplinary collaboration platform. Automation in Construction 20(2), 134–144 (2011)
8. Sabol, L.: Building Information Modeling & Facility Management. IFMA World Workplace, Dallas, Tex., USA (2008)
9. Brinda, T.N., Prasanna, E.: Developments of Facility Management Using Building Information Modelling. International Journal of Innovative Research in Science, Engineering and Technology 3(4), 11379–11386 (2014)
10. Hou, L., Wang, Y., Wang, X., Maynard, N., et al.: Combining Photogrammetry and Augmented Reality Towards an Integrated Facility Management System for the Oil Industry. Proceedings of the IEEE 102(2), 204–220 (2014)
11. Boukamp, F., Akinci, B.: Automated processing of construction specifications to support inspection and quality control. Automation in Construction 17(1), 90–106 (2007)
12. Akinci, B., Boukamp, F., Gordon, C., Huber, D., et al.: A formalism for utilization of sensor systems and integrated project models for active construction quality control. Automation in Construction 15(2), 124–138 (2006)
13. Straub, A., van Mossel, H.J.: Contractor selection for performance-based maintenance partnerships. International Journal of Strategic Property Management 11(2), 65–76 (2007)
14. Zavadskas, E.K., Vilutienė, T.: A multiple criteria evaluation of multi-family apartment block's maintenance contractors: I—Model for maintenance contractor evaluation and the determination of its selection criteria. Building and Environment 41(5), 621–632 (2006)
15. Ventovuori, T.: Elements of sourcing strategies in fm services-a multiple case study. International Journal of Strategic Property Management 10(4), 249–267 (2006)
16. Wang, S., Xie, J.: Integrating Building Management System and facilities management on the Internet. Automation in Construction 11(6), 707–715 (2002)
17. Lee, J., Jeong, Y., Oh, Y.-S., Lee, J.-C., et al.: An integrated approach to intelligent urban facilities management for real-time emergency response. Automation in Construction 30, 256–264 (2013)
18. Volk, R., Stengel, J., Schultmann, F.: Building Information Modeling (BIM) for existing buildings—Literature review and future needs. Automation in Construction 38, 109–127 (2014)
19. Gross, T.: Supporting effortless coordination: 25 years of awareness research. Computer Supported Cooperative Work (CSCW) 22(4-6), 425–474 (2013)
20. Atkin, B., Brooks, A.: Total facilities management. John Wiley & Sons (2009)
21. Kull, T.J., Wacker, J.G.: Quality management effectiveness in Asia: The influence of culture. Journal of Operations Management 28(3), 223–239 (2010)
22. Stage, F.K., Manning, K.: Research in the college context: Approaches and methods. Psychology Press (2003)

# Engineering Open Data Visualizations over the Web

Rober Morales-Chaparro, Fernando Sánchez-Figueroa, and Juan Carlos Preciado

Quercus Software Engineering Group,
University of Extremadura, Spain
{robermorales,fernando,jcpreciado}@unex.es

**Abstract.** Data Visualization has been traditionally one of the main pillars for understanding the information coming from Business Intelligence/Analytics based systems. While building visualizations has never been an easy task, moving data visualization for open data over the Web adds extra complexity. The variety of data sources, devices and users, together with the multidimensional nature of data and the continuous evolution of user requirements makes Data Visualization on the Web for open data more complicated as well as challenging. This paper briefly introduces a DSL for engineering open data visualizations over the Web whose aim is twofold. On the one hand, overcoming technological dependencies such as data source, data set, rendering technologies and so on. On the other hand, bringing the possibility of building useful graphics to users with domain expertise but non-technical skills.

**Keywords:** Open Data, Software Engineering, Data Visualization, Domain Specific Language.

## 1 Introduction

Available data on the Internet is growing up more and more every day, with heterogeneous formats and sources. The production of data is being accelerated with the widely use of approaches close related to open data such as linked data, big data, social data and so on. The emergence of new related fields like the Internet of Things and Smart Cities are adding fuel to the fire by providing an immense amount of data that must be processed to be transformed onto useful information and eventually knowledge.

Although the term open data is not new, it is gaining popularity with the launch of open data government initiatives such as data.gov. Currently, many public administrations and enterprises are following open data best practices and publishing their data in RDF format. This format allows users to query the data using a SPARQL endpoint.

The data resulting from these queries need to be explored, analyzed, interpreted or even communicated to/with other people with different profiles. For these actions data visualization is a key concept [1].

However, visualizing open data is not an easy task. It mainly involves issues at two different levels: technical and social. From the technical point of view, the visualization must be rendered in different platforms and devices, connected to different and heterogeneous data sources and it also should make use of the best rendering

Y. Luo (Ed.): CDVE 2014, LNCS 8683, pp. 51–59, 2014.

technologies available at a given moment. Moreover, the visualization must change accordingly to the real-time changes performed on data. From an engineering point of view, it should be desirable for the visualizations to be reusable and defined as much independent as possible from all these technology issues, leading to a self-service data visualization [2]. From the social point of view, the information should be shown in different ways attending to the user changing context (user profile, company interests, colleague interests, market tendencies, social tendencies, etc.). Moreover, some kind of interactions for the user should be desirable in order to change the dimension of the data shown (multidimensional data visualization) or create new graphics in a non-technical way.

Although there is a significant number of methodologies and tools for visualizing data, the real fact is that, for different motives, not all of them are suitable for dealing with open data. This is the reason why we developed Visualligence, a model-driven, data-driven and user-driven approach for visualizing open data [3]. One of the main pillars of Visualligence is a Domain Specific Language (DSL) [4] for defining visual patterns. While an overview of the proposal is provided in [3], the presentation of the main features of the DSL is the main contribution of this paper. This DSL allows both, to capture formally the visualization process and to be used by non-experts users.

The rest of the paper is as follows. Section 2 deals with the limits of existing visualization technologies for coping with open data. Section 3 briefly introduces the main features of the mentioned DSL. Conclusions are omitted for space reasons.

## 2    Limitations of Existing Approaches

From the point of view of open data, this section outlines some of the problems arising in visualization solutions, which have been split in several categories:

- **Spreadsheets.** Microsoft Excel is used to store and visualize data by near to 95% of business around the World. Both Excel and other spreadsheets systems (LibreOffice, Google Drive) lack of full support of data visualization, more if we are referring to open data. They are not extensible, so we cannot make new graphics in an easy way. We are always limited to the initial graphic set. We cannot extract a configured graphic from one document to another, keeping the visualization slave of a dataset. They can connect with external sources, but only for a few technologies, none of them related to Open Data, and with a limited size of the dataset.
- **Statistical tools** such as SPSS and R have been used for years for visualizing scientific results and they can manage very large datasets. However, they usually require importing the dataset to their own format, constraining possibilities of external sources. This is not the ideal solution for managing real time updates. Although they are oriented to general-public, they do not allow for the design of new graphics by non-technical users.
- **Business Intelligence** systems are statistical packages with improved visualization. They have remote data connections but lack of dataset independence of dashboards configured: they lock all the work under the vendor technology. Extensibility options that allow the median user create or share new visualizations are missing.

- **Specific tools,** such as Tableau (www.tableausoftware.com), has gained a foothold in visualization development for bringing the data visualization creation to the non-technical public. It allows certain extensibility, or at least, a great margin for user creativity. However, graphics are locked to the technology and the dataset chosen, and it does not allow for real-time dataset updating.
- Several **programming languages, frameworks, libraries,...** have arisen to help with the web data visualization task. They are very extensible and allows for total control of user experience and interaction. However, developer experience is not the best since high-end technical skills are required, mixed with data visualization and domain experience. Also, final users cannot interchange graphics for a given dataset, limiting the development effort to a specific dataset and technology.
- Many examples of specific **linked data browsers** [5] have been published by Open Data providers. Several cities, international organisms, etc. have developed their own portal to discover, browse, and investigate their own data. This has been inspiring and very useful, but these systems are very related to the dataset and the user experience provided by the vendor. They cannot allow for crossing data with other sources. Also, the effort of developing visualizations is not reused in this case: technological obsolescence make an appearance shortly after release.

Finally, several academic works [6] [7] [8] are being developed aiming easing visualization creation but none of them focuses on reutilization and independence.

## 3      Proposal in a Nutshell

Our proposal follows a Model-Driven, Data-Driven and User-Driven approach. Fig. 1 shows an overview of the system architecture. The entry point is the user(a), who makes a query to the Open Data provider (b) which uses its internal data sources (c) to fulfill the request. The user is offered a default visualization of the results (d) (chosen by the modeler or the system itself based on the user profile). Besides that, the user can change from one pattern to another looking for fulfilling his expectations, since the visualization get the patterns from a server (e) different from the data provider. To render visualizations, the server uses the visualization patterns (f) developed by the modelers (g) with the help of a reasoner system (h) that reads data structure and looks for similar situations in the past. For this purpose a Domain Specific Language (DSL) has been defined. That DSL allows that generator (i) produces final code from the models that connects with the data source, executes transformations over them and outputs the final result.

This work aims to explain the main features of the DSL for building visualization patterns (f) in detail. We split the presentation of the DSL features in two parts. Firstly, those related to design concerns and generic architectural decisions aligned with the problems of visualizing Open Data that we are solving. Secondly, those grammatical details that relate to the usage of the DSL.

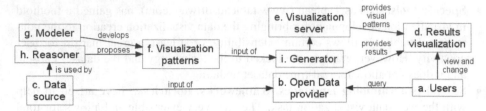

**Fig. 1.** Visualligence architecture

## 3.1    DSL General Concepts

*Independent language*
It is an external DSL. It has no dependencies with others. Its purpose is expressing the behavior of visual patterns until the point in which they can be executed. For this purpose the language provides an underlying computational model.

*Data transformation oriented*
The DSL has 2 essences: **lexical**, for the data values space and **visual**, for the canvas values. The language constructs allow passing from lexical variables to values in the visual domain. This is the way in which the human perception behaves. It is quite natural for a visual shape to be representative of quantitative variables or for a specific color to be representative of qualitative variables. The DSL constructs allow passing from numbers, dates or relationships to sizes, positions, colors and so on. A data-flow paradigm is followed. This means that when data affecting a visualization pattern change then the visualization is recalculated. The DSL provides **operations** for covering data management and to build nested visual objects: with several inputs and outputs. The inputs and outputs of operations are connected among them using typed **flows**. One operation will be executed only when one of its outputs is needed.

*Device independence*
It is not necessary to take care about how to divide the available canvas space. When using the DSL one can assume an unbounded canvas, with generic units. Later on, the graph will adapt to the available space (when rendering it).

*Web enabled*
DSL constructions can be executed in a Web browser. The host technology of the first implementation of the DSL is the Java Virtual Machine, since we have developed the language using Eclipse Modeling Tools such as Xtext. Our Java code generation and large Java runtime package has been tested to be able to run under Google Web Toolkit (GWT). GWT allows Java code to be executed as JavaScript in a browser.

*Supported by standards*
Patterns developed with the DSL will output a node tree when executed. Similarly to semi-structured documents, we will have text nodes and element nodes. Elements can

have attributes, and we need to declare an element before its usage. The system help to the modeler by suggesting elements and attributes they can set. The modeler can import external document schema declarations, such as SVG. With only importing the standard schema, the modeler can use the DSL to build SVG documents. We do not attach the DSL to any particular schema, so we can use the DSL to generate HTML5 nodes, if desired, with only importing the schema.

Several technologies and languages propose their own visual shapes taxonomy, coercing modeler possibilities. The main effort on classifying visual elements and building a dictionary is already done by SVG standard, and our aim is not replicating it.

It does not imply making the DSL more complex, quite the opposite, the modeler can use his SVG knowledge in the DSL. There is no necessity of knowing every SVG element. On the contrary, it is possible to use only known ones to build a graphic.

*Domain experts learnability*

The main public of the DSL are the domain experts. Since we pretend ease the communication with developers, it has two syntax: textual, very simple, and visual. This reduces inconsistencies between modeler desires and what they get. Many experts will refuse to build a pattern from scratch, but they can modify existing ones, if desired, trimming details or extending their functionality, because they understand the semantic. Visual syntax purpose is for improving the communication between tech and non-tech people. However, persistence is always made on textual syntax.

*Reuse of models*

In order to reuse the data processing as well as to package the visual patterns the concept of modules is provided. Modules are interchangeable. For this to be possible they need to have a compatible interface. This is mandatory for compatibility with data flows. Modules can be hierarchically organized to avoid name collisions.

*A typed language*

DSL flows have a type that defines what can be transported through it. Also, it constrains what we can do with the data.

We can use the output of an operation as input of another, only connecting them. Flow type is the output type, and it can only be connected to inputs of compatible types. Types are compatible if the system knows how to convert from one to another, and all the information is available. Native types are proposed, in four categories: lexical, descriptive, auxiliary and visual ones.

*Data sources independence*

The DSL is for visualization purposes and nothing more. Previous issues are already solved in existing tools and they are not the aim of the present work.

We are not developing any mechanism for connecting with data sources. Information systems can and should keep on extracting data and computing results previously to visualization. Anyway, this is relative to implementation and it is source-dependent, so it can be kept transparent to the visual pattern modeler.

*Dataset independence*
The specification of the structure of the data to be received by a visual pattern is defined in a relational schema. This allows the visualization to be independent from specific datasets, making it suitable for all the datasets conforming that schema. Fig. 2 shows equivalent ways of define a data structure, both in a visual syntax and using the canonical, textual one.

data

time when
number mark

```
Box data{
    time when
    number mark
}
```

**Fig. 2.** Data structure defined in a visual and textual ways

## 3.2    DSL Specific Concepts

Once explained why our proposal undertakes the problems that motivate this work, we explain in this section how to use it for getting an input and develop visual constructions.

*Iterating over data*
The data to be represented come as a sequence. However, the construction of visual elements is done individually for each data of the sequence. For this purpose the DSL provides a construction for processing items in a loop, offering one or more outputs depending on the elements and operations used inside the construction. Fig. 3 shows how loops can be defined visually and textually, indicating the input and the outputs.

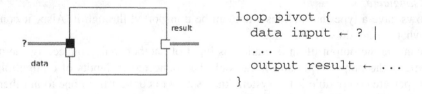

```
loop pivot {
    data input ← ? |
    ...
    output result ← ...
}
```

**Fig. 3.** Loop receiving input (typed as data sequence) and ouputting a result

*Grouping by dominant variables*
The DSL includes the construction *groupby* for choosing the dominant variables of a dataset, inspired by concepts on Data Retrieval [4]. This construction can have one or more keys that are the dominant variables. It is needed to specify in the *groupby* construction the value to be stored in each group list.

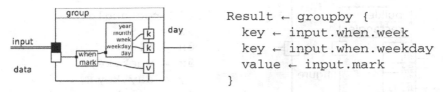

```
Result ← groupby {
    key ← input.when.week
    key ← input.when.weekday
    value ← input.mark
}
```

**Fig. 4.** Two alternatives to specify key (dominant) variables

With this it is possible to create a map (indexed by the keys) that stores a sequence with the grouped valued for each keyset. We can select any computation or output as key, and any desired one as value, as seen in Fig. 4, where data are grouped by week (of the year) and weekday.

*Aggregating secondary variables*

Lists not always are processes in an isolated way. Sometimes it is necessary an additional value. For this purpose the DSL incorporates typical operations of query languages such as *avg, sum, min, max, first*, etc. Given a data sequence (probably, the values from a *groupby*) they returns a single data. The example shown in Fig. 5 is getting the average value of the sequence returned in Fig. 4.

`day.values.avg`

**Fig. 5.** Aggregating sequences into single values

*Ease the creation of scales*

Scales allow doing the mapping between types of values in the lexical space and the visual space. They can be used as axis or for creating whatever type of gradient between two values (angles, colors, etc). Once declared, they transform the input in a value of the indicated range. Scale can automatically infer the input range, as seen in Fig. 6, where there is no indication of it.

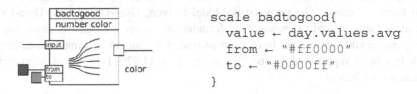

```
scale badtogood{
    value ← day.values.avg
    from ← "#ff0000"
    to ← "#0000ff"
}
```

**Fig. 6.** Mapping between numbers and colors: one example of scales

*Oriented to shape building*

The final purpose of the language is the construction of 2D shapes. The basic attributes must be provided either directly or making references to the output of other artifacts. Fig. 7 shows the building of a rectangle. Some of the inputs are literals, while other ones are obtained from outputs of other operations, most of them described in previous figures.

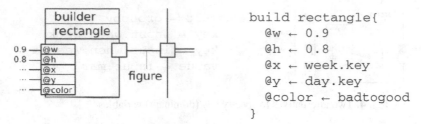

```
build rectangle{
    @w ← 0.9
    @h ← 0.8
    @x ← week.key
    @y ← day.key
    @color ← badtogood
}
```

**Fig. 7.** Build a SVG rectangle, with some values as constants, other ones as input flows

As seen also in Fig. 7, output of the builder is chained as the result of the loop (see Fig.3). Provided this, we know that the loop outputs a sequence of rectangles, that the rectangles have the same size and that they are mapped to 2d-positions using week and weekday. Finally, we can see how their color is mapped in function of the average mark, since the input of color is the output of Fig.6. With some trimming and labeling (building elements <text> of standard SVG) we obtain Fig.8 (a calendar) when executing the pattern over sample data.

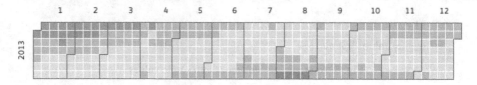

**Fig. 8.** Final result of the execution of the pattern built as an example

## 4    Conclusions

This work discussed the limitations of different alternatives for open data visualization. Then, the main features of a DSL-based proposal that overcomes these problems have been presented. The proposal is Model-Driven, User-Driven and Data-Driven. The main ideas behind its architecture, foundations, language constructions, and both visual and textual grammars have been provided by means of simple samples. The work has been suppported by the Spanish project TIN2011-27340 of Ministerio de Educación y Ciencia.

## References

1. Michael, G.: Brooks. The Business Case for Advanced Data Visualization (2008)
2. Simon, P.: The Visual Organization: Data Visualization, Big Data, and the Quest for better quests. Ed. Wiley (2014)
3. Morales-Chaparro, R., Carlos Preciado, J., Sánchez-Figueroa, F.: Visualizing Search Results: Engineering Visual Patterns Development for the Web. In: Ceri, S., Brambilla, M. (eds.) Search Computing. LNCS, vol. 7538, pp. 127–142. Springer, Heidelberg (2012)

4. Fowler, M.: Domain Specific Languages, vol. 1. Programming the Memory Heirarchy. Addison-Wesley Professional (2010)
5. Approaches to Visualising Linked Data: A Survey; Aba-Sah Dadzie and Matthew Rowe, http://www.semantic-web-journal.net/sites/default/files/swj118_1.pdf
6. Cottam, J.A.: Design and implementation of a stream-based visualization language. PhD thesis (2011)
7. Clarkson, E., Desai, K., Foley, J.: ResultMaps: visualization for search interfaces. IEEE Transactions on Visualization and Computer Graphics 15(6), 1057–1064 (2009)
8. Bozzon, A., Brambilla, M., Catarci, T., Ceri, S., Fraternali, P., Matera, M.: Visualization of Multi-domain Ranked Data. In: Ceri, S., Brambilla, M. (eds.) Search Computing II. LNCS, vol. 6585, pp. 53–69. Springer, Heidelberg (2011)

# Data Wrangling: A Decisive Step for Compact Regression Trees

Olivier Parisot, Yoanne Didry, and Thomas Tamisier

Public Research Centre Gabriel Lippmann, Belvaux, Luxembourg
parisot@lippmann.lu

**Abstract.** Nowadays, modern visualization and decision support platforms provide advanced and interactive tools for data wrangling, in order to facilitate data analysis. Nonetheless, it is a tedious process that
requires a deep experience in data transformation. In this paper, we propose an automated data wrangling method, based on a genetic algorithm,
that helps to obtain simpler regression trees.

**Keywords:** data wrangling, genetic algorithms, decision support.

## 1 Introduction

Traditionaly used as a preliminary step in data visualization and knowledge extraction, data wrangling is a semi-automated process that aims at transforming
data in order to facilitate further usage of them [5]. More precisely, data wrangling consists in iteratively applying different kinds of preprocessing tasks like
*inconsistent data cleaning*, *features selection* or *sampling* [4]. As it induces modifications and information loss, data wrangling has to be carefully applied; in
addition, it is a painful and time-consuming task that requires efficient tools [6].

In decision support and visualization platforms, data wrangling is needed to
build and show comprehensible models [5]. In this field, regression trees are popular because they are easy to visualize [7], more expressive than linear regression
formula [11, section 3.3] and built by well-known algorithms like CART [3].

Unfortunately, regression trees can be difficult to interpret due to their large
sizes [11, section 3.3]. Thus numerous simplication techniques exist and data
manipulation is an indirect but efficient way to solve this issue [7]. In this paper,
we present an original data wrangling method, in a manner that the regression
trees obtained from modified data are smaller and globally accurate.

## 2 Contribution

The presented method aims to wrangle the data before building regression tree,
by applying an ordered sequence of preprocessing operations (like discretization,
merge of features, outliers deletion, duplicates deletion, etc.). To gauge the intensity of the data transformation [10], we use the data completeness ratio [8].
This indicator is obtained by computing the ratio of values that are unchanged

Y. Luo (Ed.): CDVE 2014, LNCS 8683, pp. 60–63, 2014.
© Springer International Publishing Switzerland 2014

during the data wrangling (a value close to 100% indicates a light transformation and a value close to 0% indicates a strong transformation). Moreover, we control the accuracy of the regression trees using a threshold $(T)$. In practice, the error estimation of the produced regression trees should not increase by more than this threshold (i.e. $< T\%$).

Using these metrics, the method aims to find a sequence of operations leading to a modified dataset that can be used to build a simpler regression tree. As a result, we propose a genetic algorithm for this problem [2]. The input is a dataset and the output is a transformed dataset leading to a simpler regression tree (Algorithm 1). The data transformation is controlled with the minimum data completeness ratio and with the accuracy threshold $T$.

The evaluation of a given sequence is a critical step (i.e. the *fitness* of the solution, in the terminology used for genetic algorithms). Firstly, the sequence is applied to the initial dataset and leads to a transformed dataset. Secondly, a regression tree is built on the transformed dataset. Finally, the following metrics are computed: the regression tree size, the regression tree accuracy and the data completeness ratio. Based on this evaluation method, the algorithm aims at finding a sequence leading to a modified dataset whose the data completeness ratio is higher than the minimum data completeness ratio; in addition, the accuracy of the regression tree has to be lesser that the accuracy threshold $T$.

---

**Algorithm 1.** A genetic algorithm for data wrangling

---

**Require:**
 1: a dataset $DS$ & a minimum data completeness ratio & a threshold for accuracy
**Ensure:**
 2: Generate and evaluate a list of sequences $L$
 3: **while** (no stagnation of best sequence) **do**
 4:     Select two *parent* sequences $S_1$ & $S_2$ from $L$
 5:     Cross-over of the two *parent* sequences $S_1$ & $S_2$: build a *child* sequence $S_{new}$
 6:     Mutate the *child* sequence $S_{new}$
 7:     Evaluate the *child* sequence $S_{new}$ and add it into $L$
 8:     Identify and remove the worst sequence from $L$
 9:     Identify the best sequence $S_{best}$ in $L$
10: **end while**
11: Apply the sequence $S_{best}$ on the dataset $DS$ to produce a new dataset $DS'$
12: **return** the dataset $DS'$

---

To find a good sequence, the algorithm follows different steps. First of all, an initial list of $P$ sequences is built, and each sequence is defined with a randomly choosen data wrangling operation (line 2). Then, while the current best solution does not stagnate (regarding $M$, the maximum count of loops with best sequence stagnation) and the list of possible solutions contains different sequences (i.e. leading to trees with the same size) (line 3), the following steps are repeated:

- The *tournament* strategy [2] is used to select two parent sequences (line 4), which are then merged into a new *child* sequence (line 5).

– A data wrangling operation is randomly selected and added into the *child* sequence (line 6); after that, this *child* sequence is evaluated and added into the current list of possible solutions (line 7).
– In order to keep a constant count of sequences (regarding $P$), the algorithm removes the sequence that leads to the biggest regression tree (line 8).
– The current best solution is identified and a stagnation test checks if the best solution remains unchanged over several loops (regarding $M$) (line 9).

# 3   Prototype and Experimental Results

A prototype has been developed as a standalone tool based on WEKA, a widely-used data mining library [11]. More precisely. the induction of regression trees has been done using the REPTree algorithm. The accuracy estimation has been measured using the root mean square error (RMSE) [11, section 5.8], and the error majoration threshold $T$ has been empirically set to 10%.

During the tests, the following data wrangling operations have been considered: discretization, feature selection, constant feature deletion, missing values imputation, outliers deletion, attributes transformation (numerics to nominals, nominals to binaries, etc.). Lastly, the genetic algorithm has been empirically configured as follows: the population count has been set to 500 ($P$), and the stagnation count has been set to 200 ($M$).

**Table 1.** The regression trees' sizes and RMSE before and after data wrangling. The data completeness ratio (DCR) indicates the intensity of the data wrangling.

| Dataset | | | Before wrangling | | After wrangling | | |
|---|---|---|---|---|---|---|---|
| name | #rows | #features | size | RMSE | size | RMSE | DCR |
| wisconsin | 194 | 33 | 9 | 3158.451 | 1 | 3443.455 | 97% |
| cleveland | 303 | 14 | 27 | 78.986 | 3 | 106.883 | 92% |
| housing | 506 | 14 | 41 | 425.407 | 1 | 0 | 92% |
| compressive | 1030 | 9 | 231 | 518.162 | 1 | 0 | 77% |
| winequality-red | 1599 | 12 | 61 | 59.635 | 1 | 0 | 74% |
| crimepredict | 1994 | 127 | 43 | 14.804 | 9 | 15.53 | 96% |
| SkillCraft1 | 3395 | 20 | 17 | 0.020 | 1 | 0.027 | 95% |
| winequality-white | 4898 | 12 | 249 | 65.165 | 57 | 72.71 | 81% |
| bank32nh | 8192 | 33 | 95 | 8.573 | 1 | 0 | 94% |
| ailerons | 13750 | 41 | 139 | 0.018 | 3 | 0.028 | 51% |

Then, we have tested our algorithm on a selection of ten regression datasets with various characteristics [1,9]. According to the results (Table 1), our algorithm allows to produce simpler regression trees with good accuracy. As an example, the *crimepredict* dataset initially leads to a tree of size 43: as is, the tree is not easily interpretable. By applying our genetic algorithm, we found that discretizing the two first numeric attributes modifies the dataset in a way that it is possible to build a regression tree of size 9. As an other example, the *winequality-red* dataset leads to a regression tree of size 61 and the wrangled dataset leads to a tree of size 1. In this case, the data wrangling consists in discretizing the second numeric attribute and then removing the rows containing extreme values. If we consider the *winequality-white* dataset, it is possible to obtain a simpler tree (57 nodes instead of 249): a tree of size 57 is not so easy to interpret, but it is clearly simpler than studying the original one.

Regarding the data completeness ratio, we can see that it is often higher than 75%, which means that in most cases a light data wrangling is sufficient to get simpler regression trees. By contrast, the *ailerons* dataset needs a more intensive transformation to simplify tree (51%).

## Conclusion

In this paper, a data wrangling approach has been proposed to obtain compact regression trees from data. A genetic algorithm has been provided to automatically find an ordered list of data wrangling operations that helps to produce a simplified model. Furthermore, the algorithm is driven by two user-defined parameters that determine the acceptable information loss and regression trees accuracy. A prototype has been developed and tested on several datasets.

In future works, we will try to improve the method in order to handle huge datasets by adapting incremental tree induction methods.

## References

1. Bache, K., Lichman, M.: UCI machine learning repository (2013)
2. Bäck, T., Hoffmeister, F., Schwefel, H.P.: A survey of evolution strategies (1991)
3. Breiman, L., et al.: Classification and Regression Trees. Chapman & Hall (1984)
4. Engels, R., Theusinger, C.: Using a data metric for preprocessing advice for data mining applications. In: ECAI, pp. 430–434 (1998)
5. Kandel, S., Heer, J., Plaisant, C., Kennedy, J., van Ham, F., Riche, N.H., Weaver, C., Lee, B., Brodbeck, D., Buono, P.: Research directions in data wrangling: Visualizations and transformations for usable and credible data. Inf. Vis. 10(4), 271–288 (2011)
6. Kandel, S., Paepcke, A., Hellerstein, J., Heer, J.: Wrangler: Interactive visual specification of data transformation scripts. In: Proceedings of the SIGCHI Conference on H.F.C.S., CHI 2011, NY, USA, pp. 3363–3372 (2011)
7. Kotsiantis, S.B.: Decision trees: a recent overview. Artificial Intelligence Review 39(4), 261–283 (2013)
8. Parisot, O., Bruneau, P., Didry, Y., Tamisier, T.: User-driven data preprocessing for decision support. In: Luo, Y. (ed.) CDVE 2013. LNCS, vol. 8091, pp. 81–84. Springer, Heidelberg (2013)
9. Torgo, L.: http://www.dcc.fc.up.pt/~ltorgo/Regression/DataSets.html
10. Wang, S., Wang, H.: Mining data quality in completeness. In: ICIQ, pp. 295–300 (2007)
11. Witten, I.H., Frank, E., Hall, M.A.: Data Mining: Practical Machine Learning Tools and Techniques. Elsevier (2011)

# Analysis and Visualization of Sentiment and Emotion on Crisis Tweets

Megan K. Torkildson, Kate Starbird, and Cecilia R. Aragon

University of Washington, Seattle, WA, USA
{mtorkild,kstarbi,aragon}@uw.edu

**Abstract.** Understanding how people communicate during disasters is important for creating systems to support this communication. Twitter is commonly used to broadcast information and to organize support during times of need. During the 2010 Gulf Oil Spill, Twitter was utilized for spreading information, sharing firsthand observations, and to voice concern about the situation. Through building a series of classifiers to detect emotion and sentiment, the distribution of emotion during the Gulf Oil Spill can be analyzed and its propagation compared against released information and corresponding events. We contribute a series of emotion classifiers and a prototype collaborative visualization of the results and discuss their implications.

**Keywords:** Sentiment Analysis, Twitter, Machine Learning.

## 1 Introduction and Related Work

Many users turn to Twitter during times of crises to seek and relay information. A tweet transmits not only information, but often emotion. However, research to understand emotion in disaster-related tweets has been relatively unexplored. We seek to better understand how users communicate emotion through analyzing Twitter data collected during the 2010 Gulf Oil Spill.

The Gulf Oil Spill, which began on April 20, 2010, spanned 84 days, during which it evoked an emotional response on many levels, not just as a reaction to the human-induced ecological disaster, but also to negligence of BP and perceived inadequacies of the response efforts. Our dataset contains 693,409 tweets ranging from May 18 – August 22, 2010. All tweets contain "#oilspill," the prevalent hashtag for the event.

Analysis of large tweet corpora is scalable using machine learning. We created a series of classifiers to detect emotion using ALOE (Affect Labeler of Expression), created by Brooks et al. (2013). The tool trains a Support Vector Machine (SVM) classifier on labeled data. SVMs have previously been successful in detecting Twitter emotion in other projects, such as Roberts et al. (2012), who created a series of binary SVM emotion classifiers receiving F-measures, the weighted average of precision and recall, ranging from 0.642 to 0.740.

Analyzing emotion in text-based communication provides insight for understanding how people communicate during disasters. Emotion detection provides context

Y. Luo (Ed.): CDVE 2014, LNCS 8683, pp. 64–67, 2014.

information; for example, identifying tweets labeled as "fear" might support responders in assessing mental health effects among the affected population. Due to the large size of many disaster related datasets, machine learning can help scale analysis. Schulz et al. (2013), use 7-class and 3-class classification to achieve between 56.6% to 55.8% accuracy when trained on random data; however, these classifiers received between 24.4% and 39.5% accuracy when applied to tweets from Hurricane Sandy. This demonstrates the need for a series of emotion classifiers trained on a disaster dataset, due to its unique qualities. Binary classifiers allow for multiple labels, possibly providing better understanding.

## 2      Methods

We created a taxonomy of emotion based on Ekman's six basic emotions: joy, anger, fear, sadness, surprise, disgust (Ekman 1992). Through manual coding, we added "supportive" and "accusation," due to significant occurrences in this corpus. For the sentiment classifiers, we used the scheme: positive, negative, and neutral, intended to be mutually exclusive.

During coding, we disregarded all links because the majority could not be recovered automatically. Article and blog titles in tweets and retweets were used to help label tweets for emotion. Hashtags were also used to determine the emotion content— for example, the hashtag "#ihatebp" exhibits negative sentiment and anger. Emoticons were considered, however they were rarely used in the dataset.

Tweets were randomly sampled. If the author sent an additional tweet within the hour, it was used to help determine the emotional content of the labeled tweet. In total 5054 tweets were coded, 0.7% of the database.

**Table 1.** Example tweets coded for emotion

| Tweet Text | Sentiment and Emotion Label |
| --- | --- |
| #oilspill #bp Oil firms start spill response project – [URL] | Neutral<br>No emotion |
| Note to BP: You do not own the Gulf of Mexico! Public has a right to know what you're doing to it. #oilspill [URL] | Negative<br>Anger |
| BP should be fined for every single bird, fish, sea turtle and human hurt or killed by this disaster. #gulf #oilspill | Negative<br>Disgust |
| What happens when energy resources deplete....? [URL] #oilspill #blacktide | Negative<br>Fear |

## 3      Visualization

To help better understand the coded data, we created a visualization that displays the frequency of emotion labels for events within the dataset. The goal was to support analysis of the emotional impact of events. The stacked area charts allow for easy comparison of values, facilitated by the colored bands. The top 25% of values, the time instances with the highest emotion frequency, have the highest color saturation. The coloring makes these peaks easily distinguishable. From this visualization, there is a large decrease in the number of disgust and accusation tweets after the time of Obama's speech.

Currently, the visualization's collaborative nature stems from its support for analysis. Users can reference the visualization and read example tweets to sensemake about the data. Further collaborative features are planned, such as shared views and annotations, to support the formation of hypotheses between researchers.

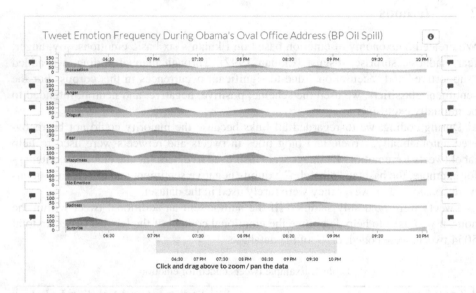

**Fig. 1.** A screenshot of the Oil Spill Visualization. It displays the frequency of emotion detected in Twitter ranging from 2 hours before Obama's Oval Office Address (June 15, 2010 at 8:01 P.M. EDT) to 2 hours after.

## 4     Results and Discussion

Table 2 shows classifier performance. The accuracy is appropriate compared to the small percentage of the coded dataset. The trend of low precision was caused by a high number of false positives. High imbalance within the dataset, such as a significantly low occurrence of positive tweets, also contributed to lower accuracy results. Additional coding of the dataset can improve these problems.

**Table 2.** Classifier performance for all 12 classifiers

| Code | Percent Occurrence (out of 5,054 tweets) | Precision | Recall | Accuracy |
|------|------|------|------|------|
| Positive | 10% | 0.56 | 0.46 | 91% |
| Negative | 41% | 0.71 | 0.69 | 76% |
| Neutral | 49% | 0.71 | 0.71 | 71% |
| Accusation | 5% | 0.03 | 0.53 | 52% |
| Anger | 16% | 0.21 | 0.55 | 64% |
| Disgust | 13% | 0.12 | 0.44 | 55% |
| Fear | 9% | 0.10 | 0.70 | 57% |
| Happiness | 2% | 0.03 | 0.58 | 51% |
| No emotion | 38% | 0.53 | 0.73 | 70% |
| Sadness | 8% | 0.15 | 0.78 | 56% |
| Supportive | 5% | 0.18 | 0.72 | 56% |
| Surprise | 4% | 0.06 | 0.59 | 53% |

## 5 Conclusion and Future Work

Creating emotion classifiers trained on a disaster dataset will improve accuracy for this unique context. If applied to additional datasets, these classifiers may be more accurate than classifiers created for general tweets. The techniques used in this paper can be utilized for creating a taxonomy using ALOE to analyze emotion in additional Twitter datasets. The prototype visualization could also be used with different disaster datasets for sensemaking. In future work, we hope to further improve our accuracy by labeling additional data. We also plan to develop further collaborative features in the visualization and perform usability testing building on our previous experience creating collaborative visualization tools.

## References

1. Brooks, M., Kuksenok, K., Torkildson, M., Perry, D., Robinson, J., Scott, T., Anicello, O., Zukowski, O., Harris, P., Aragon, C.: Statistical Affect Detection in Collaborative Chat. In: Proceedings of CSCW 2013, pp. 317–328 (2013)
2. Ekman, P.: An argument for basic emotions. Cognition & Emotion 6(3-4), 169–200 (1992)
3. Roberts, K., Roach, M., Johnson, J., Guthrie, J., Harabagiu, S.: Empatweet: Annotating and detecting emotions on Twitter. In: Proceedings of the LREC, pp. 3806–3813 (2012)
4. Schulz, A., Thanh, T., Paulheim, H., Schweizer, I.: A Fine-Grained Sentiment Analysis Approach for Detecting Crisis Related Microposts. In: Proceedings of the 10th International ISCRAM Conference, pp. 846–851 (2013)

# A Dynamic Delay Optimization Scheduling Model

Chengwei Yang[1,2], Ji-Dong Guo[1], and Jing Chi[3,*]

[1] Shandong University of Finance and Economic,
College of Management Science and Engineering, Jinan, China
[2] Shandong Provincial Key Laboratory of Software Engineering, Jinan, China
[3] Shandong University of Finance and Economic,
College of Computer and Science, Jinan, China
{yangchengwei2006,gjd730210}@163.com,
peace_world_cj@126.com

**Abstract.** The response time starts to suffer due to the limitation of the Hadoop's FIFO scheduler, and this is unacceptable to execute the large scale instance intensive tasks. To enhance the system resource utilization, we propose a new scheduling solution. To reduce the cost, we use a delay scheduling algorithm to determine the scheduling opportunity. Delay scheduling can ensure that the current service can make full use of the resources, improve resource utilization, and reduce the probability of failure scheduling. The initial experiments demonstrate that the large scale instances intensive workflow tasks will benefit from the Min-Cost delay scheduling algorithm that is proposed in this paper.

**Keywords:** Scheduling, Delay, Cloud.

## 1 Research Background

Cloud computing is a promising solution to provide the resource scalability dynamically[1-2]. The third benefit which Cloud computing provides is the using of virtualized resources for workflow execution. We start review ex-isting solutions for workflow applications and the limitation with respect to scalability and on-demand access. Large scale workflow uses the distributed collection of computation and storage facilities. Therefore, resource scheduling is becoming a critical problem for current workflow system.

However, when we began building the data centers, it found the data consolidation provided by a shared cluster highly beneficial. We found the response times starts to suffer due to Hadoop's FIFO scheduler[13]. This was unacceptable to execute the large scale instance intensive tasks. So as to enhance the system resource utilization, we propose a new scheduling solution. In initial phase, it provides the global users' QoS guarantee ability. Then, at the execution phase, the scheduler can be real-time perception the situation of service resource according the system loading, and determine the best opportunity to perform the scheduling.

---

* Corresponding author.

Y. Luo (Ed.): CDVE 2014, LNCS 8683, pp. 68–71, 2014.
© Springer International Publishing Switzerland 2014

## 2    Dynamic Delay Optimization Scheduling Model

As shown in Figure 2, dynamic delay optimization scheduling model is mainly composed of three core parts, including information service, registration service, retrieval service, analyzer, and scheduler. Analyzer is mainly responsible for the workflow task priority scheduling according to user's QoS constraints, select the best scheduling strategies, and determine the mapping between task allocation and distributed resource. Hence, the design of analyzer guarantees the performance of global optimization scheduling. Scheduler gets the current load of the available resources, and computing the current scheduling cost in the phase of local execution.

So as to reduce the cost, we use delay scheduling algorithm to determine the scheduling opportunity. Delay scheduling can ensure that the current service can make full use of resources, improve resource utilization, and reduce the probability of failure scheduling.

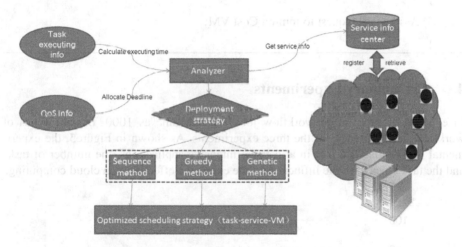

**Fig. 1.** A Dynamic Delay Optimization Scheduling Model

## 3    Min-cost with Delay Scheduling Algorithm

In this section, we consider a new version of delay scheduling which is called Min-Cost with Delay Scheduling. Note that the core of this algorithm is to determine min-cost scheduling under system loading. We have explained the rationale for this design in our analysis of delay scheduling. As a result, when the $\Delta F_{r,M} \geq 0$, the request r is delay scheduled, or if $\Delta F_{r,M} < 0$, the request will be scheduled at once. Pseudo code for this algorithm is shown below:

---

**Algorithm 1.** Mini-Cost with Delay Scheduling

1) For all the ready scheduling instance ti{

2) For all the task requests from ready scheduling instance {

3) For all the ready scheduling machine m{

4) Compute value of $F_M^{start}$, $F_M^{wait}$ and $\Delta F_{r,M}$}

5) If($\Delta F_{r,M}$<0) {

6)  $min_{r,M} = \{r, M\}$;

6)If($F_{r,M}^{penalty} < minCost$){

7)minCost $= F_{r,M}^{penalty}$ ;

}

8) Assign task request to miniumCost VM;

}

---

## 4    Preliminary Experiments

In experiments, the initial workflow jobs are the same as 1000. But the types of workflow are differences in the three experiments. As shown in Figure5, the experimental results illustrate that in a instance intensive applications, the number of tasks and the task types have the influence on the execution effectively in cloud computing.

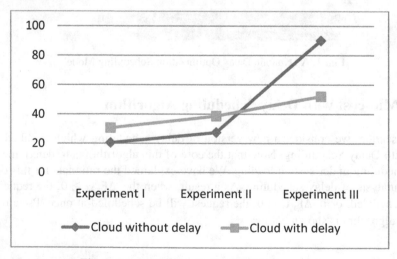

**Fig. 2.** Scheduling Results in Cloud Environment

Less quantity or singleness workflow tasks more adapt to run in cloud workflow environment without delay scheduling. However, the complicated and large scale instances intensive workflow tasks need to be scheduled and will be benefit of the Min-Cost delay scheduling algorithm that proposed in this paper.

## 5    Conclusion

Then, a novel Min-cost with delay scheduling algorithm is presented in this paper. We also focuses on the global scheduling including genetic evolution method and other scheduling methods (sequence and greedy) to evaluate and decrease the execution cost. Finally, three primary experiments divided into two parts. One parts of experiment is carried out demonstrate the global mapping algorithm effectively and the results for execution of a large scale workflow instances with or without delay scheduling.

**Acknowledgement.** This paper is supported in part by Natural Science Foundation of China under Grant 61303088, and part by A Project of Shandong Province Higher Educational Science and Technology Program under Grant J14LN19, and part by the Fundamental Research Funds for Shandong Provincial Key Laboratory of Software Engineering under Grant 2013SE05, The second author is the corresponding author, and his e-mail address is peace_world_cj@126.com.

## References

1. Andrzejak, A., Kondo, D., Anderson, D.P.: Exploiting non-dedicated resources for Cloud computing. In: The 12th IEEE/IFIP (NOMS 2010), Osaka, Japan, April 19-23 (2010)
2. Bowers, S., Ludäscher, B.: Actor-Oriented Design of Scientific Workflows. In: Delcambre, L.M.L., Kop, C., Mayr, H.C., Mylopoulos, J., Pastor, Ó. (eds.) ER 2005. LNCS, vol. 3716, pp. 369–384. Springer, Heidelberg (2005)
3. Bowers, S., Ludäscher, B.: Actor-Oriented Design of Scientific Workflows. In: Delcambre, L.M.L., Kop, C., Mayr, H.C., Mylopoulos, J., Pastor, Ó. (eds.) ER 2005. LNCS, vol. 3716, pp. 369–384. Springer, Heidelberg (2005)
4. Buyya, R., Yeo, C.S., Venugopal, S., Broberg, J., Brandic, I.: Cloud computing and emerging IT platforms: Vision, hype, and reality for delivering computing as the 5th utility. Future Generation Computer Systems 25(6), 599–616 (2009)
5. Zhang, C., De Sterck, H.: CloudWF: A Computational Workflow System for Clouds Based on Hadoop. In: Jaatun, M.G., Zhao, G., Rong, C. (eds.) Cloud Computing. LNCS, vol. 5931, pp. 393–404. Springer, Heidelberg (2009)
6. Yang, C., Wang, L., Yang, C., Liu, S., Meng, X.: The Personalized Service Customization Based on Multimedia Resources in Digital Museum Grid. In: The 3rd International Conference on U-media, Zhejiang Normal University, China, pp. 298–304 (2010)

# Cloud Computing for Improving Integrity of Data from Biotechnological Plant

Dariusz Choiński[1], Artur Wodołażski[2], and Piotr Skupin[1]

[1] Faculty of Automatic Control, Electronics and Computer Science,
Silesian University of Technology,
ul.Akademicka 16, 44-100 Gliwice, Poland
{dariusz.choinski,piotr.skupin}@polsl.pl
[2] Central Mining Institute,
Plac Gwarkow 1, 40-166 Katowice, Poland
awodolazski@gig.katowice.pl

**Abstract.** The extraction of necessary information and its interpretation in the case of biotechnological processes may be a difficult task. This is due to the fact that the large amounts of available data are often a combination of on-line and off-line measurements with a hierarchical structure. Moreover, the measurement data can be geographically dispersed and stored in the different types of databases. To facilitate the extraction of the most significant information on the biological process, the paper presents a model of integration of the hierarchical database with the relational one in the cloud computing environment. The relational database model will allow the less experienced bioprocess designers to find the answers to specific questions. The use of cloud services ensures sufficient data storage space and ease of data management. In turn, data integrity in the cloud environment is realized by means of DataBase Management System with Open DataBase Connectivity drivers.

**Keywords:** cloud computing, relational database, referential integrity, biotechnological process.

## 1 Introduction

A proper conduction of a biological process in bioreactor does not only require the expert knowledge, but also the ability of processing and archiving of large amounts of measurement data. Even in the case of a small laboratory pilot-plant, after twenty-four hours, the amount of collected data is so large that it is a difficult and laborious task to process and interpret the data, but also, to find the answers to specific questions. As it has been presented in [1], [2], the collected data, which is a combination of off-line and on-line measurements [3, 4, 5], have a hierarchical structure making its interpretation dependent on the level of its complexity. In other cases, the required data can be obtained by simulations [6]. Therefore, to extract the desired information, it is often necessary to cooperate with highly skilled experts as shown in our previous studies [7], [8].

Y. Luo (Ed.): CDVE 2014, LNCS 8683, pp. 72–79, 2014.

In another approach, the use of the data (including its processing and interpretation) can be greatly simplified, if it is possible to find relations between stored data items. This can be particularly useful when many users, cooperating with each other and having different levels of knowledge or experience on a biological process, demand the answers to specific questions. In most cases, these questions are similar in form to the inquiries in relational databases. The creation of a relational database provides specific information about the process, but it requires the integration of this database with the hierarchical one collecting the measurements. Moreover, algorithms that allow for creation of relations usually require more space and processing power. At the same time, the use of on-line data requires the extensive database for collection of long-term data.

A recent development and increasing popularity of cloud services offer new tools and possibilities for data storage and access to greater computing power [9], [10]. Hence, the application of cloud computing, including its data storage space and computing resources on demand, allows for further development of cooperation techniques in the cloud. Moreover, the cloud computing ensures sufficient data protection, scalability and elasticity of infrastructure, high efficiency, ease of data management and high reliability at low costs.

Based on the example of biotechnological process, the paper presents a model of integration of the hierarchical database with the relational one in the cloud computing environment. The referential integrity with the hierarchical model allows to ensure the effective data management, data correctness and its transfer. The paper is organized as follows. The next section describes the complexity of data obtained from the biotechnological plant and highlights the problems in extracting the necessary data for the control system design, process set-up and its proper maintenance. In turn, Section 3 describes the integration of data from various sources in the cloud environment. Finally, the last section presents conclusion remarks.

## 2    Extraction of Data from Biological Process

The past decades have witnessed a rapid development of the industrial biotechnology, in which the main role is played by living microorganisms. The yeast *Saccharomyces cerevisiae* is an example of microorganisms that are particularly important in the industrial applications [11] (e.g. in production of biofuels, ethanol or food) and in the genetic engineering (yeast cells are used as host organisms). However, a proper conduction of the biological processes requires preparation of the culture (initial cell pre-cultivation), preparation of the culture medium, and preparation of the equipment for monitoring and control of the process parameters [12]. It is particularly important for ethanol fermentation processes, which may exhibit oscillatory behavior, i.e. the occurrence of self-sustained oscillations of biomass concentration for constant feed and culture conditions [13]. From the industrial point of view, the oscillatory changes are usually undesirable, because they can lead to higher (or lower) average biomass and product concentrations [14], [15]. Moreover, to attenuate the oscillatory changes in the product concentration it is necessary to use a system of surge tanks, which makes the industrial installation more expensive [16]. By a proper choice of the process parameters (e.g. dissolved oxygen concentration, pH, agitation speed or dilution rate D), it is possible to eliminate the oscillatory behavior [17]. Hence, the start-up and maintenance of the biological process requires interdisciplinary knowledge in such fields as: biochemistry, chemical engineering and microbiology.

Based on the example of ethanol fermentation process which uses yeast cells, it is essential to monitor such key parameters as: concentration of the produced carbon dioxide ($CO_2$), dissolved oxygen (DO) levels in the bioreactor medium, respiratory quotient (RQ), biomass concentration (obtained from the measurement of optical density (OD)), residual substrate concentration (S), concentration of the secreted ethanol (P), yield coefficients $Y_{X/S}$ (the mass of dry biomass in grams obtained from one gram of substrate) and $Y_{P/X}$ (the mass of ethanol in grams from one gram of dry biomass), oxygen uptake rate (OUR), dilution rate (D, it is dependent on the input flow rate F to the system), pH and temperature of the bioreactor medium.

These parameters can be obtained from on-line and off-line measurements and are necessary in the determination of the predominant yeast metabolism which has a great impact on the overall process performance. In the considered case, there are three major metabolic pathways and their simplified description is as follows [17]:

$$\text{glucose} + \text{oxygen} + \text{nitrogen} \rightarrow \text{biomass} + CO_2 + H_2O \tag{1}$$

$$\text{glucose} + \text{nitrogen} \rightarrow \text{biomass} + \text{ethanol} + CO_2 + H_2O \tag{2}$$

$$\text{ethanol} + \text{oxygen} + \text{nitrogen} \rightarrow \text{biomass} + CO_2 + H_2O \tag{3}$$

For instance, the first metabolic pathway (1) describes aerobic oxidation of glucose leading to the growth of biomass, production of carbon dioxide ($CO_2$) and water ($H_2O$). This pathway is the most efficient of the three, if the goal of the biological process is production of biomass. In turn, the second metabolic pathway (2) describes the classical ethanol fermentation process, for which utilization of glucose leads to the growth of biomass and secretion of ethanol (P), $CO_2$ and water. Finally, the last pathway (3) describes the growth of biomass, if ethanol is the only available substrate and, from practical point of view, this metabolic pathway is the least preferred. Moreover, it should be emphasized that the self-sustained oscillations can only be observed during aerobic oxidation of glucose (1) or ethanol fermentation (2), which is undesirable behavior.

Monitoring of the process parameters allows us to know, which of these three metabolic pathways is predominant. For example, the first metabolic pathway (1) dominates under strongly aerobic conditions (for high dissolved oxygen levels) and for small dilution rates D [17]. As a result, one can observe small values of the residual substrate concentrations S, about half a gram of the dry biomass per one gram of the substrate (the yield coefficient $Y_{x/s}=0.5[g/g]$) and respiratory quotient $RQ \leq 1$ [13]. In addition to the monitoring and supervision of the process, it is necessary to know how to prepare the culture of living microorganisms (e.g. determination of the composition of culture medium and its optimal conditions, i.e. temperature, pH level, etc.), and how to design and set up the control systems, which are responsible for control and stabilization of the key process parameters.

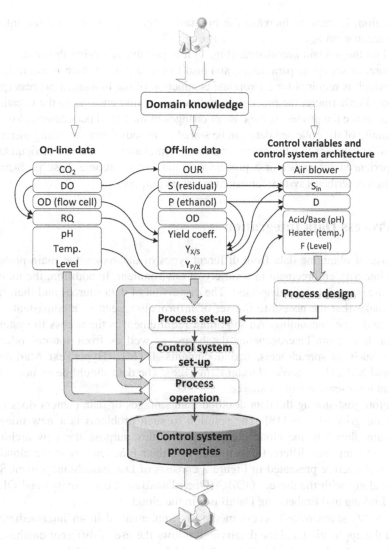

**Fig. 1.** The use of domain knowledge for the process data interpretation, process design and its operation

As shown in Figure 1, the available knowledge, which is the hierarchical domain knowledge, can be divided into three groups describing the on-line and off-line data and the set of control variables. Figure 1 also presents the complexity of interactions between the control and measured variables. In the case of the off-line measured parameters, the arrows indicate some on-line and off-line parameters that are needed to calculate the other parameter values. In turn, in the case of the control variables, the arrows indicate how to interact the process to change the desired parameters. For instance, in order to determine the biomass yield coefficient $Y_{X/S}$, it is necessary to know the residual substrate concentration S and the steady-state value of the biomass concentration. In turn, to increase the biomass yield, one can change the inlet substrate concentration $S_{in}$.

Based on the domain knowledge, (Fig. 1) it is possible to design the control system architecture, to set up its parameters, and also to prepare the culture medium (process set-up), which is required for appropriate conduction of the biological process (process operation). Furthermore, the process data allows us to find answers to the questions on how to influence the process in the case of changes of measured parameters. However, a large quantity of the collected data can be stored in various forms including hierarchical databases. This makes that the processing and interpretation of data is a difficult task for an inexperienced researcher or a process operator. To overcome these problems, the next section describes a system for data integration purposes.

## 3    Process Data Integration

In the case of obtaining data from different types of databases, the main problem is the data integrity enforcement in a variety of environment. In addition, the individual systems are geographically dispersed. The dispersion of data sources and their heterogeneity make that the access to the set of information, seen in a consistent way, is difficult and time consuming. An important requirement is the access to systems information both from heterogeneous databases, as well as from sources other than database, such as spreadsheets, text documents, HTML (HyperText Markup Language) and XML (Extensible Markup Language). The data should be an accurate and consistent representation of its source.

Therefore just storing the data at cloud data storages or data centers does not ensure the integrity of data [18]. The solution to such problems is a new integration architecture placed in the cloud computing. For this purpose the new architecture ensures and integrates different data models and their functionality in the cloud. Integration Architecture presented in Figure 2 consists of Database Management System (DBMS) along with the drivers ODBC (Open DataBase Connectivity) and OLE DB (Object Linking and Embedding DataBase) in the cloud.

The ODBC standardized access method is implemented in an intermediate layer between the application and the database. It allows the use of different database models such as the relational, object-oriented and hierarchical model and ensures data integrity between databases. DBMS based on cloud computing is not only extremely scalable, but also are able to handle large amount of data and processes that cover a typical DBMS. As a result, a greater efficiency and significant reduction of operating costs over the long term can be achieved. In turn OLE DB provides support for data about the functionality of the SQL (Structured Query Language) language and other sources having non-data database. The connection with the use of "generic connectivity" uses ODBC drivers and OLE DB which must be located on the platform that we use to make calls. However, such connections have limited capabilities. All the features of heterogeneous connections are dependent on the possession of ODBC drivers. The other problem is that different databases originate from different producers, where they exert different functionality, data representation and SQL dialects. To solve this problem, the gateway Oracle software is used to transform SQL dialects data types between databases and to provide transactional access to databases. This also allows for synchronous and asynchronous replication of data between databases. This integration architecture ensure a collection and data transfer over different databases. It also maintains the integrity of the interrelated data after hardware or software failures. However, queries to NoSQL database in the cloud provide only access to a non-relational database, whose main disadvantage are the lack of a standard semantics definition, such as DHT (Distributed Hash Table) interface, limited availability of data for multiple services, and also, the lack of "join operation" that significantly impedes writing efficient queries. To deal with the lack of a proper functionality, a programmable software module was put between the DBMS and Database Cloud Storage. The module provides transformation between dialects (including semantics and syntax) and the creation of packages to facilitate programming of databases from different suppliers. It allows data integration and fusion, collaborative management and realization of queries between the different databases models managed by the DBMS in the cloud.

This integration architecture for the biotechnological system ensures a collection and data transfer over different databases. It also maintains the integrity of the interrelated data after hardware or software failures. It uses the potential of cloud computing, accesses to data from various places and provides storage of dynamically allocated resources, virtually through the Internet.

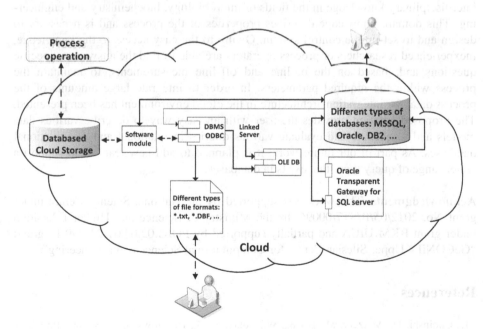

**Fig. 2.** The idea of data integration in the cloud

This study examined the translation of the relational query language to an equivalent program in the cloud that can be processed by a hierarchical database management system and which provides automatic selection of average rates of hierarchical databases. For example, the translation of data from hierarchical to relational model is made by the Entity Relationship (ER) Diagram in the Database Management System [19]. In the presented solution, to represents ER schemas, as a list of entities and their relationships, the Prolog factbase (sequence of predicates) is used. In effect, it is possible to implement structural transformation as a syntactic transformation from data description language to the target data model. This ensures that the data can be easily recoverable, catalogued, and searchable. Furthermore, it also provides tracking, connection and interoperability between them. The basic concept behind cloud computing is that the computing resource is connected to the network environment, so that users can access the resource whenever and wherever it is needed.

The architecture in the cloud introduces a "multi-mercenary" environment with the flexibility to use the allocated resources. It provides access to the indexed hierarchical databases by using the relational query language. This enables the introduction of data integrity on different levels, such as referential, domain and primary keys integrity.

# 4     Concluding Remarks

As has been presented, a proper conduction of the biological processes often requires interdisciplinary knowledge in the fields of microbiology, biochemistry and engineering. This domain knowledge describes properties of the process and is necessary to design and to set-up the control system. Owing to the easy access to the knowledge, inexperienced researchers or process operators are able to find the answers to specific questions and, based on the on-line and off-line measurements, to maintain the process within the required parameters. In order to integrate large amounts of the process data, the integration architecture in the cloud environment has been presented. The proposed solution provides the user with an easy way to describe various data models and to execute and evaluate various queries in relational and non-relational databases. As part of our future work, it is planned to add new features to support a wider range of query types that exists in databases.

**Acknowledgments.** This work was supported by the National Science Centre under grant No. 2012/05/B/ST7/00096, by the Ministry of Science and Higher Education under grant BKM-UiUA and partially supported by POIG.02.03.01-24-099/13 grant: "GeCONiI – Upper Silesian Center for Computational Science and Engineering"

# References

1. Choinski, D., Metzger, M., Nocon, W., Polaków, G., Rozalowska, B., Skupin, P.: Cooperative Access to Hierarchical Data from Biotechnological Pilot-Plant. In: Luo, Y. (ed.) CDVE 2012. LNCS, vol. 7467, pp. 171–178. Springer, Heidelberg (2012)

2. Choinski, D., Metzger, M., Noco, W.: Cooperative Visualization Based on Agent Voting. In: Luo, Y. (ed.) CDVE 2011. LNCS, vol. 6874, pp. 166–169. Springer, Heidelberg (2011)
3. Doan, X., Srinivasan, R., Bapat, P.M., Wangikar, P.P.: Detection of phase shifts in batch fermentation via statistical analysis of the online measurements: a case study with rifamycin B fermentation, J. Biotechnol. 132, 156–166 (2007)
4. Warth, B., Rajkai, G., Mandenius, C.F.: Evaluation of software sensors for on-line estimation of culture conditions in an Escherichia coli cultivation expressing a recombinant protein. J. Biotechnol. 147, 37–45 (2010)
5. Undey, C., Ertunc, S., Mistretta, T., Looze, B.: Applied advanced process analytics in biopharmaceutical manufacturing: Challenges and prospects in real-time monitoring and control. J. Process. Control 20, 1009–1018 (2010)
6. Metzger, M.: Fast-mode real-time simulator for the wastewater treatment process. Water Sci. Technol. 30, 191–197 (1994)
7. Skupin, P., Metzger, M.: Cooperative Operating Control for Induction or Elimination of Self-sustained Oscillations in CSTB. In: Luo, Y. (ed.) CDVE 2011. LNCS, vol. 6874, pp. 66–73. Springer, Heidelberg (2011)
8. Choinski, D., Metzger, M., Nocon, W., Polakow, G.: Cooperative Validation in Distributed Control Systems Design. In: Luo, Y. (ed.) CDVE 2007. LNCS, vol. 4674, pp. 280–289. Springer, Heidelberg (2007)
9. Wang, C., Wang, Q., Ren, K., Lou, W.: Privacy-preserving public auditing for data storage security in cloud computing. In: Proceedings of the 29th Conference on Information Communications, pp. 525–533. IEEE Press, Piscataway (2010)
10. Wu, J., Ping, L., Ge, X., Wang, Y., Fu, J.: Cloud Storage as the Infrastructure of Cloud Computing. In: International Conference Intelligent Computing and Cognitive Informatics, pp. 380–383. IEEE, Kuala Lumpur (2010)
11. Pretorius, I.S., Du Toit, M., Van Rensburg, P.: Designer yeasts for the fermentation industry of the 21st century. Food Technol. Biotechnol. 41, 3–10 (2003)
12. Rani, K., Rao, V.: Control of fermenters – a review. Bioprocess Eng. 21, 77–88 (1999)
13. Parulekar, S.J., Semones, G.B., Rolf, M.J., Lievense, J.C., Lim, H.C.: Induction and elimination of oscillations in continuous cultures of Saccharomyces Cerevisiae. Biotechnol. Bioeng. 28, 700–710 (1986)
14. Balakrishnan, A., Yang, R.Y.K.: Self-forcing of a chemostat with self-sustained oscillations for productivity enhancement. Chem. Eng. Commun. 189, 1569–1585 (2002)
15. Skupin, P.: Simulation approach for detection of the self-sustained oscillations in continuous culture. In: 11th WSEAS International Conference on Mathematics and Computers in Biology and Chemistry, Iasi, pp. 80–85 (2010)
16. Bai, F.W., Chen, L.J., Anderson, W.A., Moo–Young, M.: Parameter oscillation attenuation and mechanism exploration for continuous VHG ethanol fermentation. Biotechnol. Bioeng. 102, 113–121 (2009)
17. Sonnleitner, B., Kappeli, O.: Growth of Saccharomyces cerevisiae is controlled by its limited respiratory capacity: Formulation and verification of a hypothesis. Biotechnol. Bioeng. 28, 927–937 (1986)
18. Buyya, R., Broberg, J., Goscinsky, A.: Cloud Computing: Principles and Paradigms. John Wiley and Sons (2011)
19. Coburn, N., Larson, P.A., Martin, P., Slonim, J.: Cords multidatabase project: Research and prototype overview. In: the Conference of the Centre for Advanced Studies on Collaborative Research, pp. 767–778. IBM, Toronto (1993)

# Integration of Industrial Control with Analytical Expert Measurements for Cooperative Operations

Witold Nocoń[1], Anna Węgrzyn[2], Grzegorz Polaków[1],
Dariusz Choiński[1], and Mieczysław Metzger[1]

[1] Faculty of Automatic Control, Electronics and Computer Science
Silesian University of Technology, ul. Akademicka 16, 44-100 Gliwice, Poland
[2] Faculty of Energy and Environmental Engineering
Silesian University of Technology, ul. Konarskiego 18, 44-101 Gliwice, Poland
{witold.nocon,grzegorz.polakow,dariusz.choinski,
mieczyslaw.metgzer}@polsl.pl, awegrzyn@kbs.ise.polsl.pl

**Abstract.** The paper proposes a framework for incorporating results of the analytical and laboratory measurements directly into the process control system. It is based on an object-oriented framework for cooperative testing of control algorithms implemented for experimental pilot-plants. It enables modification of the control algorithm structure without rewriting the main software component executed on the programmable automation controller (PAC). In this paper the framework is expanded to enable access to web-based services for the purpose of incorporating the results of advanced off-line measurements directly in the process control system.

**Keywords:** process control, control systems engineering, cloud computing, web services, biotechnology.

## 1  Introduction

The modern industry relies heavily on robust control systems being able to counteract the unavoidable disturbances present in all technological systems. In order to ensure the highest quality of the particular product, a strict regime of set point parameters must be maintained throughout the whole production cycle to ensure product quality and the overall process effectiveness. The only practical method of avoiding disturbances is to measure those properties of the process that are the causes of disturbances rather than simply the effects of disturbances already present in the system [1]. However, some measurements are beyond the scope of the available on-line measurements or even of the off-line analyses that can be carried out by the staff operating the particular production process. Therefore, effective off-site analysis of the samples taken from the process is desirable. Moreover, incorporation of the off-site analysis results directly into the control system would greatly enhance the ease of the process operation.

In case of biological systems, early detection of deviations is especially important since changes in the population of living organisms may greatly influence the capabilities of the process. This is the case in the activated sludge process widely used for

Y. Luo (Ed.): CDVE 2014, LNCS 8683, pp. 80–87, 2014.

wastewater treatment [2]. Operation of an activated sludge process requires experts in at least two specialties to cooperate. While control engineers are responsible for implementing and operating the control and visualization system, biological experts are needed to perform analytical and sometimes state-of-the-art investigations. An example of such an analytical method is the fluorescence *in situ* hybridization (FISH) technique. By comparison to standard microbiological methods, FISH enables a relatively fast and reliable identification of microbial species present in the activated sludge. While this technique is well established, it is far from being automated. Thus an expert is necessary to perform the analytical work and microscopic observations. Additionally, some image processing techniques are quite subjective in nature, thus it is advised to use unified and automated protocols for the results to be at least qualitatively representative. Therefore, the existing control system should enable cooperation between experts in biology and the automated control system working with just technician supervision.

This paper presents a framework for incorporating results of the analytical and laboratory measurements directly into the process control system. The main idea is schematically presented in Fig. 1. The existing object-oriented framework for cooperative testing of control algorithms for experimental pilot-plants has been presented in [3]. It is based on the principles stated in the IEC61499 standard [4]. This framework enables modification of the control algorithm structure without rewriting the main software component executed on the programmable automation controller (PAC). Functions realized by particular blocks may be changed dynamically at run-time. The framework is implemented in LabVIEW enabling implementation of algorithms containing advanced analysis functions and complex control algorithms by multiple users, providing an effective practical group support system

## 2    New Trends in Control Systems Architecture

Traditionally, a control system consisted of couple of major components. The lowest level consisted of sensors and actuators connected directly to PLCs (Programmable Logic Controllers), while a supervisory level SCADA system (Supervisory Control and Data Acquisition) provided data logging, visualization of trends, alarms and events and enabled the operator to specify set point values etc. [5].

Nowadays however, an increasing computational power of industrial computers enables more sophisticated architectures. For example, agent technology is gaining popularity as it enables partitioning of the control system code into independent and at-run-time reconfigurable entities thus enhancing the implementation of distributed control systems. Similarly, utilization of an object-oriented structure of components used in the control system's synthesis is now possible enhancing code reuse, code encapsulation and introducing polymorphism [6]. Control systems for biotechnological process especially gain from the growing capabilities of controlling hardware, enabling for example cooperative access to hierarchical data describing the particular process [7], incorporation of simulation procedures directly in the control system thus helping the process operator in the decision-making process [8], [9].

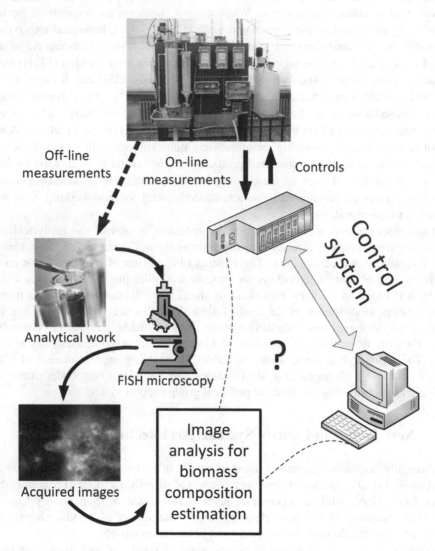

Off-line
measurements

On-line
measurements

Controls

Control system

Analytical work

FISH microscopy

Acquired images

?

Image
analysis for
biomass
composition
estimation

**Fig. 1.** The problem of incorporating analytical measurements into the control system

All those enhancements allow for incorporation of new and advanced features in relatively small installations, even those operating without constant supervision. In this paper we propose an architecture that enables Programmable Automation Controllers (PACs) to access web-based services that would provide additional information about the process being controlled.

## 2.1 Why Clouds in Automation Systems?

A reasonable question one might ask is why cloud technology should be considered for incorporation in automation systems? Generally, control systems are designed to be reliable, fault tolerant and are therefore usually at least relatively closed from the outside world with incoming and/or outgoing internet connections greatly restricted. This is important for preventing malicious software from being able to infect the system. This is a viable concern regarding possible usage of cloud technology in control systems and it requires further investigations and analysis that are beyond the scope of this paper.

On the other hand, new achievements in agent technologies and object-oriented paradigm applied to control algorithms implementation are becoming more and more established and can greatly facilitate the operation of remote and non-supervised control systems [6]. This is especially true in case of small, rural wastewater treatment plants. Therefore, we propose to enable a control system to subscribe to services provided via Web.

## 3 Fluorescent *in situ* Hybridization for Activated Sludge Analysis

Wastewater treatment by activated sludge is one of the most important biotechnological processes. However, the role of microbial consortia in this process is still not completely understood. Previously, the diversity and dynamics of the microbial communities have been analysed by culture-depended methods, but only 15% of the indigenous bacteria in activated sludge could be cultivated [2]. These limitations have lead to techniques using the 16S rRNA approach. Currently, one of the basic tools used in a comparative analysis of bacterial communities without previous cultivation is fluorescent *in situ* hybridization (FISH). FISH uses fluorescently labelled oligonucleotide probes to detect and estimate the abundance of particular bacterial genera or species [10].

The FISH laboratory procedure includes a number of steps: (i) fixation of the samples; (ii) hybridization with the probes for detecting the target sequences; (iii) washing step to remove unbound probes; (iv) visualization and documentation of results [11]. Effective fixation is essential for satisfactory FISH results and should ensure good probe penetration, retention of maximal level of target RNA and maintenance of cell integrity and morphologic detail. Hybridization must be carried out under stringent conditions for appropriate annealing of the probe to the target sequence. For this crucial step of the FISH procedure, hybridization buffer and fluorescently labelled probes complementary to the target RNA are applied to the sample. After the hybridization step, microscopic slides are rinsed with distilled water to remove unbound probe. Finally, the slides are mounted in anti-fading agents to prevent fluorescence 'bleaching', and the results are visualized and documented. Although the laboratory protocol of FISH is well establish, it is far from being automated. Some image processing techniques are quite subjective in nature and results strongly depend on the experience. Therefore it is advised to use unified and automated protocols for the results to be at least qualitatively representative.

In case of wastewater treatment, the elimination of nitrogen compounds is one of the priorities and nitrification is still the most intensively examined and used process. Nitrification involves two stages: nitritation (biological oxidation of ammonia) and nitratation (biological oxidation of nitrite). Respectively, ammonia oxidizing bacteria (AOB) and nitrite oxidizing bacteria (NOB) carry out these steps. Many studies revealed that *Nitrosomonas* sp. and *Nitrobacter* sp. are the most common genera encountered in wastewater systems [12]. The common use of molecular methods proved that nitrifiers' group in activated sludge is much more diverse. Nitrifiers are slower growing, are maintained at much lower populations, and are much more sensitive to operating conditions (temperature, alkalinity, pH, sludge age) than more common floc forming heterotrophic microorganisms [13]. An estimation of nitrifier community variability in activated sludge by FISH allows to ensure that nitrification proceeds without any adverse effects. The preprocessed images obtained in the FISH method could be upload into the proposed framework, while the framework performs an automated image processing. The results of such a processing may for example indicate to changes in nitrifiers composition in activated sludge, thus enabling an automatic modification of the operating conditions (for example sludge age and alkalinity).

## 4    The Proposed System Architecture

The existing object-oriented framework for cooperative testing of control algorithms for experimental pilot-plants has been presented in [3] and it enables the dynamic reconfiguration of the control algorithm structure. Moreover, the control algorithm is fully executed in a PAC (Programmable Automation Controller). To enable access to cloud-based services, a new functional block is needed that implements communication with the particular service. It must be noted, that this block is still executed in the PAC controller, hence it is imperative for this block to guarantee its execution in predefined time. While the PAC controller, running a real-time operating system (RTOS) guarantees timely execution of a properly written code, communication protocols are always prone to timeouts, lost connections etc. Therefore, the proposed functional block is explicitly divided into two treads (Fig. 2).

The main thread implements all the functions of the block than are responsible for communicating with the framework application, responds to events, carries out all necessary computations etc. The communication threat on the other hand, implements the chosen communication protocol, establishes connections, provides for networks exceptions etc. In general, the main thread requests data from the cloud to be retrieved, the communication thread communicates the appropriate service and gets the requested data. However before using this data for control purposes, a 'sanity check' is performed on the data to prevent corrupt data from being used by the control system.

This block, incorporated into the control system's structure, enables direct connection between the controller and the cloud-based service. Fig. 3 presents the general idea of using expert off-line measurements by the control system. In case of FISH, the samples from the biological reactor must be harvested, fixated and hybridized. This is obviously a manual step but because it is relatively routine, it can be performed by the wastewater treatment staff, provided sufficient laboratory equipment is available. Acquisition of microscopic images usually requires a qualified expert because experience is needed and fluorescent microscopes are usually not fully automated. Once good quality images are acquired, a series of such images is uploaded by the microscope technician into the service, where automated procedures are applied to extract information about the condition of the activated sludge. For example, the population of nitrifying bacteria can be estimated, together with the total viable biomass concentration. This information on the other hand is crucial to the proper selection of the set point values for the biomass sludge age.

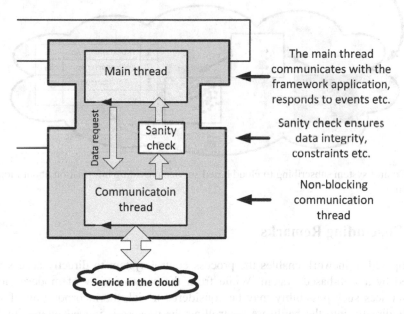

**Fig. 2.** Functional block enabling communication to cloud-based services

The presented use case of the proposed scheme is only an example. Other possibilities exist. The functional block may actually supply images (or other types of data that must be processes by a specialized system) to the cloud-based service. This is indeed possible with National Instruments Compact RIO platform PACs that enable image acquisition by cameras connected directly to the controller. In such cases however, specialized image processing procedures usually exceed the computational power of the controller, hence usage of web-based services is recommended.

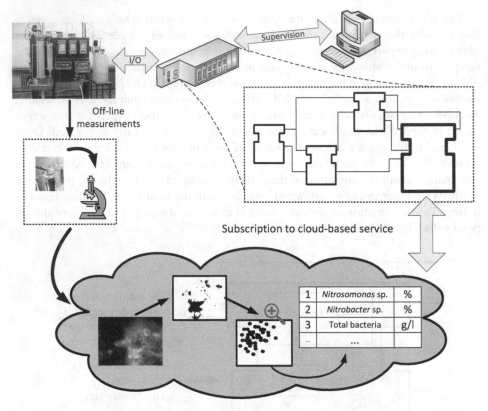

**Fig. 3.** Control system subscribing to cloud based service providing information about biomass composition

## 5    Concluding Remarks

The proposed framework enables the process control system to directly access data provided by a web-based system. While from the point of view of modern cloud-based services such possibility may be considered trivial, the incorporation of such methods directly into the hardware controlling the process is indeed interesting and may prove to be advantageous. In case of biotechnological process, a number of state-of-the-art control strategies, like the utilization of self-sustained oscillations for enhancing the efficiency of the process [14], [15], may be facilitated by allowing access to advanced data processing and simulation services that are beyond the scope of control system hardware at this time.

**Acknowledgments.** This work was supported by the National Science Centre under grant No. 2012/05/B/ST7/00096, by the Ministry of Science and Higher Education under grant BK-UiUA and was partially supported by POIG.02.03.01-24-099/13 grant: "GeCONiI – Upper Silesian Center for Computational Science and Engineering".

# References

1. Sharma, K.L.S.: Overview of Industrial Process Automation. Elsevier (2011)
2. Wagner, M., Loy, A.: Bacterial community composition and function in sewage treatment systems. Current Opinion in Biotechnology 13, 218–227 (2002)
3. Nocoń, W., Polaków, G.: Object-oriented framework for cooperative testing of control algorithms for experimental pilot-plants. In: Luo, Y. (ed.) CDVE 2013. LNCS, vol. 8091, pp. 197–204. Springer, Heidelberg (2013)
4. Vyatkin, V.: IEC 61499 as Enabler of Distributed and Intelligent Automation: State-of-the-Art Review. IEEE T. Ind. Inform. 7, 768–781 (2011)
5. Handbook of Automation. Ed. Nof. Springer Dordrecht Heidelberg London New York (2009)
6. Nocoń, W., Polaków, G.: LabVIEW Based Cooperative Design for Control System Implementation. In: Luo, Y. (ed.) CDVE 2011. LNCS, vol. 6874, pp. 137–140. Springer, Heidelberg (2011)
7. Choinski, D., Metzger, M., Nocon, W., Polaków, G., Rozalowska, B., Skupin, P.: Cooperative Access to Hierarchical Data from Biotechnological Pilot-Plant. In: Luo, Y. (ed.) CDVE 2012. LNCS, vol. 7467, pp. 171–178. Springer, Heidelberg (2012)
8. Metzger, M.: Fast-mode real-time simulator for the wastewater treatment process. Water Science and Technology 30, 191–197 (1994)
9. Metzger, M.: A comparative evaluation of DRE integration algorithms for real-time simulation of biologically activated sludge process. Simulation Practice and Theory 7, 629–643 (2000)
10. Wagner, M., Horn, M., Daimes, H.: Fluorescence in situ hybridization for the identification and characterization of prokaryotes. Current Opinion in Microbiology 6, 302–309 (2003)
11. Motter, A., Göbel, U.B.: Fluorescence in situ hybridization (FISH) for direct visualization of microorganisms. Journal of Microbiological Methods 41, 85–112 (2000)
12. Kelly, J.J., Siripong, S., McCormack, J., Janus, L.R., Urakawa, H., El Fantroussi, S., Noble, P.A., Sappelsa, L., Rittmann, B.E., Stahl, D.A.: DNA microarray detection of nitrifying bacterial 16S rRNA in wastewater treatment plant samples. Water Research 39, 3229–3238 (2005)
13. Zhu, G., Peng, Y., Li, B., Guo, J., Yang, Q., Wang, S.: Biological removal of nitrogen from wastewater. Reviews of Environmental Contamination and Toxicology 192, 159–195 (2008)
14. Skupin, P., Metzger, M.: Cooperative Operating Control for Induction or Elimination of Self-sustained Oscillations in CSTB. In: Luo, Y. (ed.) CDVE 2011. LNCS, vol. 6874, pp. 66–73. Springer, Heidelberg (2011)
15. Skupin, P.: Simulation approach for detection of the self-sustained oscillations in continuous culture. In: Proceedings of the 11th WSEAS International Conference on Mathematics and Computers in Biology and Chemistry, pp. 80–85 (2010)

# Fostering Collaboration by Location-Based Crowdsourcing

Christine Bauer[1], Andreas Mladenow[2,*], and Christine Strauss[2]

[1] Vienna University of Economics and Business,
Department of Information Systems & Operations, Vienna, Austria
chris.bauer@wu.ac.at
[2] University of Vienna, Department of eBusiness, Vienna, Austria
{andreas.mladenow,christine.strauss}@univie.ac.at

**Abstract.** Crowdsourcing is a recently developed method that relies on various alternatives of collaboration to solve problems efficiently. Crowdsourcing is a recent development to solve a variety of problems efficiently, and which implies various alternatives of collaboration. However, as novel technologies are able to exploit location-sensing capabilities of mobile devices, location-based crowdsourcing (LBCS) developed as a new concept. This paper suggests a typology for LBCS as a means for fostering collaboration with the crowd through three types of LBCS: confirmation-based, digital good-based, and physical-based. Each type is underpinned with exemplary applications. Furthermore, opportunities and challenges are analysed; and future trends in LBCS are discussed.

**Keywords:** Location-based Crowdsourcing, LBCS, Collaboration, Collaborative Crowdsourcing, Time-dependency, Location-dependency, Typology, Social Communities, Mobile Crowdsourcing Applications.

## 1    Introduction

Information and communication technologies (ICT) have the capacity to bridge time-space gaps, which in turn forms the basis for collaboration at different times and at different places. In the wide range of ICT-based collaboration alternatives, crowdsourcing represents a novel class of collaboration. In recent years, crowdsourcing concepts flourished: crowdsourcing leverages ICT to interconnect people, and to activate, coordinate, and bundle their collective capabilities to gain synergies [1, 2, 3]. Based on Howe [4], Bayus [1] described the term "crowdsourcing" as an neologism by defining it as the act of taking a task once performed by an employee, and outsourcing it to a large, undefined group of people. However, the basic idea of crowdsourcing is not new: In the 19th century, Charles Babbage, the famous English mathematician and engineer, hired "the crowd" to assist in computing astronomical tables [5]. This indicates that crowdsourcing does not

---

* Corresponding author.

Y. Luo (Ed.): CDVE 2014, LNCS 8683, pp. 88–95, 2014.

necessarily need ICT; ICT is rather to be regarded as an enabler. Still, in recent years, the flourishing phenomenon of crowdsourcing is tightly associated with ICT. Examples given in literature consider the entire value chain including problem statement publication, getting in contact, communicating, carrying out tasks, coordinating activities, reporting on solutions, providing the result to the problem statement, awards, etc. as being carried out online by the crowd and thus using ICT.

One of the key elements in the physical world is "location". For some tasks it is essential that individuals forming the crowd are situated at a certain location to be able to perform a given task. However, such tasks do not seem to correspond with recent conceptions of crowdsourcing, where ICT is regarded as the key enabler supporting all phases of the crowdsourcing value chain. Still, the original crowdsourcing idea did not envisage the use of ICT; accordingly, we argue that even if activities are carried out offline in the physical world, it is still within the scope of the crowdsourcing concept.

This phenomenon of the "collaborating crowd", where tasks are involved that require the crowd to be situated at a certain location, was recently picked up in research and was coined "location-based crowdsourcing" (LBCS) [6, 7]. Still, there is only limited knowledge on the phenomenon itself as well as on its opportunities and challenges.

Against this background, this paper aims to contribute by reducing this research gap. It specifies the concept of LBCS by developing a typology together with its underlying rationale; and selected examples of successful LBCS applications on the market will underpin the typology. Furthermore, we analyse opportunities and challenges associated with LBCS.

This paper is structured as follows: The next section presents related work and provides the theoretical background of LBCS. Built on this, Section 3 discusses the opportunities and challenges for close collaborative LBCS processes, such as saving time and distributing activities among the individuals efficiently. Section 4 introduces a typology of LBCS and presents successful examples of LBCS applications on the market. The paper closes with a conclusion and points to future research opportunities.

## 2    Related Work

Collaboration is an interactive, recursive process [8, 9]. Because it is directed towards an objective, the participants must intend to act or decide [9]. Many collaborative processes in real world involve people interacting with each other [10]. In this regard, the concept of "crowdsourcing," a term coined by Howe [4], describes an interactive form of service delivery on the basis of Web 2.0, where several users are involved in collaborative processes. With crowdsourcing, an organization or individual follows the strategy to outsource tasks by means of an open call (invitation) on a group of unknown actors [3]. Typically, the crowdsourcer and the crowdsourcees benefit from direct economic advantages [3] and form the basic roles in a collaborative setting.

Result-based compensations of crowdsourcing include cash bonuses, small monetary rewards, price incentives, or exclusive information [11]. Furthermore, there are many crowdsourcing projects without direct compensation. In these cases, the participant is typically motivated by the desire to experience something new, to share knowledge with others, or to accomplish common goals [1].

On the Web, crowdsourcing has gained popularity over recent years. There are several websites that serve as platforms to distribute crowdsourcing tasks (e.g., www.mturk.com; www.istockphoto.com; www.innocentive.com; www.cambrianhouse.com; www.threadsless.com) [6]. One common feature among these platforms is that the crowdsourced tasks are location-*in*dependent. With ICT as an enabler, recent research on crowdsourcing tends to assume that all crowdsourcing tasks are carried out online and result in digital products (results). Our work, in contrast, focuses on location-dependent problems and/or tasks. Such work shows how crowdsourcing may generate value and synergies through collaboration, where some tasks are inherently bound to a certain location.

The core concept of the so-called location-based crowdsourcing (LBCS) implies location-dependent collaborative tasks. Individuals, who are currently in close proximity or are promptly issued to the location of the task, may carry out such tasks. In this context, Alt, Shirazi, Schmidt, Kramer and Nawaz [6] describe the concept of LBCS as a crowdsourcing platform that requires tasks to be performed at a specific location; these tasks are then distributed among the voluntary platform participants or the participants select their preferred tasks. As for the types of tasks, LBCS relates to those tasks that can be found in close proximity and that can be carried out fast and easily. Thus, there is a certain degree of context dependency between the situation, which the crowd worker finds him or herself in, and, for instance, the information that he or she has to obtain at a certain location. Thereby the location of the crowdsourcer may be relevant or not; in any case, though, the location of a crowdsourcee is utterly important.

Among the vast attempts to classify crowdsourcing, there are basically two main approaches: One approach is based on the type of task that is crowdsourced, and the other is based on the initiator of crowdsourcing. For instance, Howe [4] differentiates the following three types of crowdsourcing: crowdsourcing idea game, crowdsourced problem solving, and prediction markets. Gassmann, Daiber and Muhdi [12] identify five crowdsourcing initiation approaches: Crowdsourcing initiated and supported by intermediary platforms, user initiated crowdsourcing, company initiated platforms, idea market places, and public crowdsourcing initiatives.

Brabham [13] followed a different approach and introduced a problem-based typology to classify crowdsourcing. He differentiates between knowledge discovery tasks, distributed human intelligence tasks, broadcast searches, and peer-vetted creative productions. For collaborative LBCS, which includes the physical element of location [e.g., 14, 15, 16, 17, 18], these typologies appear to be too narrowly drafted and call for a revised version to integrate the LBCS phenomenon.

# 3    Typology for Collaborative Location-Based Crowdsourcing

Based on Brabham [13], we further differentiate between three LBCS models depending on the nature of the result of the collaborative task: confirmation-based result, digital good-based result, and physical-based result. Based on this novel typology, we analyse successful examples on the market.

## 3.1    Confirmation-Based Result

In the crowdsourcing model with a confirmation-based result, the crowd has to perform a task on site and then confirms online that the task has been accomplished. For instance, the task could be to take some physical good from A to B within a certain town and typically within a defined time-window. The following selected services exemplarily represent successful platforms on the market that support the confirmation-based result type of LBCS.

**WeGoLook.com.** This service works consumer-to-consumer, business-to-business, business-to-consumer, as well as peer-to-peer. One of WeGoLook's services allows crowdsourcers to call crowdsourcees to perform tasks such as inspecting a product, person, or place. This kind of outsourcing is particularly useful, when the task has to be completed in a different part of the world.

**Localmind.com.** This application allows users to direct questions about a specific location to people who have checked-in at this location (e.g., restaurant, club). Users may want to know what is happening at a particular place, or how crowded a club is, or if a restaurant has good seats available. Based on the answers, the crowdsourcer can make better-informed decisions about whether or not to move to a certain location.

**TaskRabbit.com.** This portal supports errands type tasks on a consumer-to-consumer basis. In one part of the services they offer, to find crowdsourcees that act as personal assistants, for instance, cleaning a home or assembling furniture, etc.

## 3.2    Digital Good-Based Result

The crowdsourcing model where a digital good is delivered as a result may be exemplified by asking the crowd to take a picture of a certain object, and submit the digital picture to the crowdsourcer. The following platforms in the field of news reporting represent examples for the digital-good-based result type of LBCS.

**iReport.cnn.com.** The US-based TV channel CNN invites everyone (the crowd) to contribute reports, videos, or photos of breaking news. This is particularly interesting, when the iReporter (i.e., the crowdsourcee) is part of the reported story and could, e.g., eyewitness natural phenomena, disasters or accidents on-site. Such crowdsourced reports have the added value that emotions on-site are passed on unaltered to viewers and readers: amateur reporters typically capture what they are experiencing at the moment, and consequently pass on their own personal story. This added value partly stemming from the immediate and instantaneous reporting combined with the emotional and exciting experiences of iReporters proves to be in demand by news channels.

**Tackable.com.** This application is based on the following idea: An editor or a reporter (i.e., the crowdsourcer) publishes an order within the Tackable application to take a photo from or of a specific location. Users of this application (i.e., the crowdsourcees) may then carry out the indicated task, and share photos on the application's platform. The editor/reporter chooses from the received photos and includes them in online reports or print media. Furthermore, the submitted photos are made accessible on a map (geo-tagging) and users may also share them on various social networks. The great advantage of this concept seems to lie in the fact that it is not based on friendship networks but on the geographical location of the users. This makes it possible to efficiently access actual, relevant photos. In order to motivate users sufficiently, they receive "karma points" for each completed task and top ranked users receive prizes.

### 3.3    Physical-Based Result

The crowdsourcing model, where the crowd shall perform a task on-site, which requires physical distribution, we coined "physical-based result" type. For instance, the crowd has to collect some goods that are only available at the certain location and has to ship them physically to the crowdsourcer. The following two platforms support the physical-based result type of LBCS in their portfolio.

**Table 1.** Overview on LBCS-Typology: Characteristics and Exemplary Applications

| LBCS-Type | Characteristic of Collaborative Task | Exemplary Task | Exemplary Applications |
|---|---|---|---|
| Confirmation-based | online confirmation on the completion of the task | "Take some physical good from A to B under time constraints." | WeGoLook.com Localmind.com TaskRabbit.com |
| Digital good-based | completed task is in form of or contributes to a digital good | "Take a picture of a certain place in town and submit the digital picture to the crowdsourcer." | iReport.cnn.com Tackable.com |
| Physical-based | completion of task requires physical presence at determined location | "Collect some goods that are only available at a certain location and ship it to the crowdsourcer." | WeGoLook.com TaskRabbit.com |

**WeGoLook.com.** Part of the service portfolio allows crowdsourcers to call for customized tasks such as courier and shipping services. For instance, crowdsourcees ensure an item is properly packed and is being shipped. At the destination another crowdsourcee may receive the item at pickup and verify that the item arrived safely.

**TaskRabbit.com.** This portal supports errands type tasks such as delivering groceries or running errands, etc. on a consumer-to-consumer basis. Therefore, many results are physical based.

Against this background, we suggest a revised typology for LBCS, which considers that, while the problem statement is typically published online, a task is involved which has to be carried out offline on-site; thereby the results of going through the crowdsourcing value chain may be of a different nature as depicted in Table 1.

## 4    Opportunities and Challenges for Collaboration in Location-Based Crowdsourcing

To implement the LBCS concept, a system is needed that allows for coordination of the potential crowdsourcing members at the right time at the right place. Thereby, the physical element of LBCS poses some restrictions compared to fully ICT-reliant crowdsourcing in the digital world – still, LBCS also offers great potential. The capabilities of mobile devices are helping people to learn more about their surroundings, solving problems faster and cheaper than traditional methods and support a variety of collaborative tasks on a local basis.

Regarding the challenges for companies to implement a LBCS project, Hammon and Hippner [2] exemplarily outline common problems that may arise in any kind of crowdsourcing ventures; these challenges are likely to be transferrable to LBCS . The major challenges of such an LBCS project may typically arise in an early stage. On the one hand, it is difficult to estimate the costs for the implementation of the project. On the other hand, content (i.e., tasks) and number of users are strong drivers in the project. As a consequence, crowdsourcing concepts may reach their full functionality and, thus, their popularity only with an increasing number of users. Furthermore, the reputation and the success rate of such a concept have mutual influence. Online-traffic generated collaboratively increases with popularity and quality of the LBCS application; and, vice versa, ample online-traffic influences the popularity and quality of the LBCS application positively.

A further challenge is to generate appropriate incentives for the crowd in various situations, so that the result fulfils its intended purpose and creates the expected values for the actors involved [3]. Some issues that might occur are particularly related to LBCS, e.g., reliability issues: if certain information is provided incorrectly or a picture is uploaded by mistake, the crowdsourcer may not be aware of the error. However, it seems even more problematic if a physical product is damaged (e.g., when transporting the product from one place to another). For such cases, critical issues arise, namely damage liabilities and compensation. Other crucial issues refer to security, safety, and privacy aspects.

Furthermore, there is a noticeable difference, whether the crowd is supposed to do a certain task (e.g., many people take pictures of an object) or an individual person carries out some task (e.g., taking an object from A to B, it is likely fulfilled by one person only). If a crowd is taking pictures and one out of a few is good, than then the task is fulfilled. However, if an individual carries out the task, there are high expectations for this individual to deliver a high quality product quickly.

Moreover, quality assurance the different types of LBCS bear different challenges. For instance, if the task is to take a picture of the Eiffel Tower, it could happen that some people of the crowd do not carry out the task correctly (e.g., taking pictures of other construction and uploading these pictures specifying these as ones of the Eiffel Tower). If crowdsoucers are knowledgeable, they will be able to identify the right pictures. Otherwise there are several scenarios: if several people make mistakes by taking pictures of wrong sights, while others fulfil the task correctly, the crowdsourcer will easily be in a position to differentiate between the correct and the wrong pictures. However, if everyone but one is doing a bad job, the crowdsourcer will have difficulty identifying the correct picture.

Further opportunities for novel location-based services may arise by leveraging data collected by LBCS. For instance, the game Ingress, requires the crowd of gamers to tag so-called "portals" (usually special sights at various locations) and provide a picture of the portal. This information that is collected in the game may later be used in another context as a basis for a completely different location-based service.

## 5      Conclusion

Collaboration at any time and any place is enabled by ICT, and crowdsourcing represents one out of numerous alternatives to create value by collaboration. In this paper, we focus on LBCS, and introduced a typology for LBCS to foster collaboration with the crowd. Three basic types are identified, i.e., confirmation-based, digital good-based, and physical-based LBCS. We characterized each type and underpinned them with examples. Furthermore, we discussed opportunities and challenges in the context of LBCS.

Future work may address matching algorithms that identify good crowdsourcee-task combinations. For instance, an LBCS service may use smartphones' GPS signals (or other sensors, which help to derive or to infer a potential crowd worker's location) to match a suitable person for a certain task in order to create a qualitative and/or timely outcome. This idea may be developed further in two possible directions: Either the crowdsourcer would be enabled to identify the "right crowd" immediately, or alternatively, the LBCS portal would suggest to potential and registered crowdsourcees which tasks are available and would be suitable for them in terms of place and time. In addition, building on the concept of ubiquitous computing, the idea of sensors that describe a situation and could tell if someone fits the given task (e.g., suitable in terms of location, skills and equipment as well as in availability of time and resources), might be relevant future trends for LBCS.

# References

1. Bayus, B.L.: Crowdsourcing New Product Ideas over Time: An Analysis of the Dell IdeaStorm Community. Manage. Sci. 59, 226–244 (2013)
2. Hammon, L., Hippner, H.: Crowdsourcing. Bus Inform. Syst. Eng. 4, 163–166 (2012)
3. Mladenow, A., Bauer, C., Strauss, C.: Social Crowd Integration in New Product Development: Crowdsourcing Communities Nourish the Open Innovation Paradigm. Global Journal of Flexible Systems Management 15, 77–86 (2014)
4. Howe, J.: The rise of crowdsourcing. Wired 14, 176–183 (2006)
5. Babbage, C.: On the Economy of Machinery and Manufactures. Knight, London (1831)
6. Alt, F., Shirazi, A.S., Schmidt, A., Kramer, U., Nawaz, Z.: Location-based crowdsourcing: Extending crowdsourcing to the real world. In: NordiCHI 2010, pp. 13–22. ACM, New York (2010)
7. Väätäjä, H., Vainio, T., Sirkkunen, E.: Location-Based Crowdsourcing of Hyperlocal News: Dimensions of Participation Preferences. In: 17th ACM International Conference on Supporting Group Work (GROUP 2012), pp. 85–94. ACM, New York (2012)
8. Marinez-Moyano, I.J.: Exploring the Dynamics of Collaboration in Interorganizational Settings. In: Schuman, S. (ed.) Creating a Culture of Collaboration: The International Association of Facilitators Handbook, pp. 69–86. Jossey-Bass, San Francisco (2006)
9. Wood, D.J., Gray, B.: Towards a comprehensive Theory of Collaboration. J. Appl. Behav. Sci. 27, 139–162 (1991)
10. Kittur, A.: Crowdsourcing, Collaboration, and Creativity. ACM Crossroads 17, 22–26 (2010)
11. Horton, J.J., Chilton, L.B.: The labor economics of paid crowdsourcing. In: 11th ACM Conference on Electronic Commerce (EC 2010), pp. 209–218. ACM, New York (2010)
12. Gassmann, O., Daiber, M., Muhdi, L.: Der Crowdsourcing-Prozess. In: Gassmann, O. (ed.) Crowdsourcing: Innovationsmanagement mit Schwarmintelligenz, pp. 31–55. Hanser, Munich (2010)
13. Brabham, D.C.: Crowdsourcing as a Model for Problem Solving: An Introduction and Cases. Convergence: The International Journal of Research into New Media Technologies 14, 75–90 (2008)
14. Afuah, A., Tucci, C.L.: Crowdsourcing as a Solution to Distant Search. Academy of Management Review 37, 355–375 (2012)
15. Bentley, F., Cramer, H., Müller, J.: Beyond the bar: the places where location-based services are used in the city. Personal Ubiquit Comput. (2014)
16. Celino, I., Cerizza, D., Contessa, S., Corubolo, M.: Urbanopoly: a Social and Location-based Game with a Purpose to Crowdsource your Urban Data. In: 4th IEEE Workshop on Social Media for Human Computation (SocialCom 2012), pp. 910–913. IEEE, New York (2012)
17. Goodchild, M.F., Glennon, J.A.: Crowdsourcing geographic information for disaster response: a research frontier. Int. J. Digit. Earth 3, 231–241 (2010)
18. Pelzer, C., Wenzlav, K., Eisfeld-Reschke, J.: Crowdsourcing Report 2012: Neue digitale Arbeitswelten. epubli GmbH, Berlin (2012)

# A Web-Based Practice Teaching System in Collaboration with Enterprise

Lin Zhou[1], Juntang Yuan[1], Changan Liu[2], and Aihua Huang[3]

[1] School of Mechanical Engineering, Nanjing University of Science and Technology,
zl@njust.edu.cn, mc106@njust.edu.cn
[2] Nanjing Sunnyguys Automatic Machine Co. Ltd.
lchangan@163.com
[3] Office of Academic Affairs, Nanjing University of Science and Technology, China
hah@njust.edu.cn

**Abstract.** It is very important for undergraduate students to learn how to apply the theoretical knowledge to the practical business work. However, the widening gap between the engineering education and the real-world has always been existing. The CDIO(Conceive, Design, Implement and Operate) method is aiming at filling the gap and enables students to take the initiative, practical, integrated way to learn engineering courses based on the complete product lifecycle. The students can study from the initial concept, product development, manufacturing, until the sale and service process. In order to practice the concept of CDIO, a collaboration-based practice teaching mode is presented in this paper. The architecture of web-based practice teaching in collaboration with enterprise and a construction scheme of web-based teaching management system for engineering training are proposed. System architecture and system functions are given. Finally, the implementation and the application examples of this system are described.

**Keywords:** engineering training, collaboration-based mode, web-based management platform.

## 1 Introduction

Engineering training, as the effective way to educate comprehensive and innovative undergraduates, has been one of the required courses at the university, in which undergraduates are taught how to use the theoretical knowledge to actual business work. However, the current education system emphasizes very much on theoretical education. Even in the engineering training course whose main theme is engineering practice, still focuses on theoretical teaching and imitation rather than the guidance of pioneering practical thinking. The widening gap between the engineering education and the real-world has always been existing. Therefore, a Worldwide CDIO Initiative consisted of engineering schools in the USA, Europe, Canada, UK, Africa, Asia, and New Zealand is formed. It is hoped to be a worldwide collaborative educational framework to conceive and develop a new vision of engineering education [1]. CDIO

Y. Luo (Ed.): CDVE 2014, LNCS 8683, pp. 96–102, 2014.

is founded by four universities including the Massachusetts institute of technology and the Swedish royal institute of technology. It provides an effective mode of engineering education. [2,3] CDIO enables students to take the initiative, practical, connected way to learn the engineering courses and the learning process is based on the complete product lifecycle which is from initial concept and product development, manufacturing, and selling and servicing.

According to the principle of CDIO, many scholars studied the reform of practice course. Liu[4] proposes the CDIO-based engineering assignment resources, including design process module, design method module, basic course module, technical data module, modern design analysis software module and academic organization module. Lu[5] proposes a CDIO-based parallel chain teaching system for mechanical engineering talents education, including a basic teaching chain (theoretical teaching - integrated design experiment - course design) and an ability expanding chain (basic training - engineering internship - the training to expand ability). Cao[6] proposes a project-based teaching method, whose teaching process is based on the whole process of a real project so that the students' ability of self-learning, comprehensive information analyzing, creativity, skills and team spirit is effectively developed. Lv[7] proposes that the engineering education should introduce enterprise resources and establish the cooperative relationship with the real enterprise. But most of the studies are just proposed the theory of teaching system and lack of effective implementation and supervision mechanism, and CDIO-based environment and platform.

In this paper, based on the research of CDIO-based engineering education and introducing the concept of enterprise-university-research institute cooperation, a collaboration-based practice teaching mode is presented. In order to implement the workflow under this mode in a scientific and reasonable way, a web-based practice teaching platform is presented to supporting the whole process of engineering education. And finally the system is developed.

## 2    Collaboration-Based Practice Teaching Mode

The purpose of CDIO-based engineering education is to educate engineers with the project elementary knowledge and the ability of solving problem, teamwork and engineering system. The purpose of CDIO is to develop a real engineering talent. There's nothing more effective than simulating the real process of production design and manufacture in a complete engineering education project. What's more, the engineering education is inseparable from the enterprise. But the enterprise and the university are always in different place. Actually, in the real world, the real engineering project is globalism, which means that the members of project are always around the world and they should work together based on the network technology. Therefore, the CDIO-based engineering education mode should consider that the objects are in the different places but should work together.

Based on this, a collaboration-based practice teaching mode is proposed and its model is shown in Fig.1. It supports the cooperation among users who are in the different places with the collaboration platform.

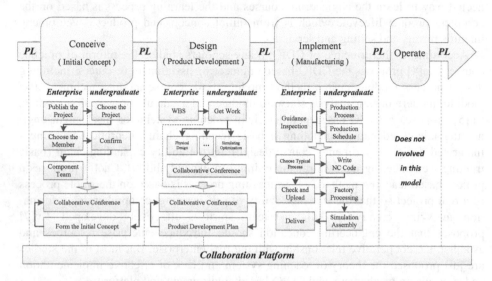

**Fig. 1.** The Model of Collaboration-based Practice Teaching Mode

The collaboration-based practice teaching mode focuses on the authenticity of the manufacturing process and team collaboration. There are two kinds of collaboration, which are (1) the collaboration between enterprise and undergrads, and (2) the collaboration among undergrads in one project.

(1) The collaboration between enterprise and undergrads is mainly reflected in making project team coordination meeting between enterprise and undergrads who are team members to do real-time exchange of views to jointly determine the initial conceptual model, product development programs, production process and production schedule.

(2) The collaboration among undergrads in one project appears in whole project time and is mainly reflected in that every team member has its own task and the task is closely related with others, so that in order to complete the project, everyone must cooperate with each other.

In fact, the practice teaching mode simulates the whole process from production to delivery. The undergrads play designers, technologists, planners, operators and other roles and work together with each other to finish the chosen project issued by the enterprise. The enterprise (or the teacher) should provide guidance and inspection as well as practical conditions (can also be in Engineering Training Center of university if the conditions are met) in the phase of manufacturing. The undergrad educated on this collaboration-based practice teaching mode will be equipped with systematic engineering ability while they have a comprehensive and emotional understanding of enterprise production process.

# 3    Web-Based Practice Teaching System Framework

## 3.1    Requirement Analysis

In order to implement the above model, a complete set of software system supporting the whole process of engineering practice is required. The functions of the system should include process management of project, full control of coordination meetings, quick calling of the local software, version management of sharing files and real-time recording of student performance. Therefore, practice teaching system must meet the following performance requirements:

(1) Distribution: The primary users of the system are undergrads, teachers and the relevant enterprise employees. In most cases, they are in different places especially the relevant enterprise employees. And with the development of MOOC (Massive Open Online Courses), more students will no longer be centralized in one class but be educated through the network in anywhere so that the system must have the distribution characteristics to adapt to the new trend of higher education.

(2) Integration: Systems can be seamlessly integrated with eCWS[8](self-developed software rather than commercial software), ERP, CAD, CAPP, CAM and DNC systems. It means that the user can call each local software application through this system to deal with the current file even the sharing file.

(3) Flexibility: As the software applications interacted with the system are varied and often updated, the system must be flexibility enough to adapt the unforeseeable change of the software applications.

(4) Instructional: The positioning of this system is a teaching software, so that the system should have the basic elements of teaching system, such as syllabus, teaching content, error correction, scoring and so on.

## 3.2    System Framework

According to the functions and performance requirements of practice teaching system, a web-based practice teaching system is proposed and its system framework is shown in Fig.2. System architecture is B/S (Browser/Server) [9]. The user operates the system through the browser. A very few business logic is implemented in the front (which means the web-browser) and the main are on the server side [10]. The framework includes three layers: client layer, server layer and data layer. The function of each layer is as follows:

(1) Client layer, which provides access for users to do conversation with system based on Web Server. The user can access and manage system file and other resource, call and access relevant local software application system, and initiate or participate in collaborative meeting. It's a HCI (Human - computer interaction) window.

(2) Server layer, which provides service packaging and integration. The basis of each function can be abstracted to four logical calculations, including adding data, deleting data, editing data and querying data to communicate with the database. The function modules are packaged into collaborative server, project management, process management, data management and system management. These five kinds of servers

obtain the relevant data through logical interface instead of directly interacting with the database. Three core services are detailed as follows.

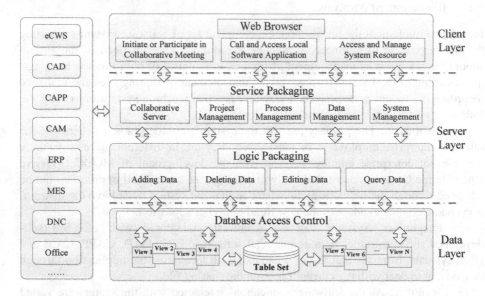

**Fig. 2.** The Framework of the Web-based Practice Teaching System

Collaborative server: It provides the function of initiating and participating in a collaborative meeting. The enterprise or undergraduate who has the right can initiate a collaborative meeting through collaborative server while the other relevant enterprise or undergraduate can see the meeting invitation and accept it. Then collaborative server calls the eCWS to hold the meeting.

Project management: It provides the function of managing the practice teaching project. The enterprise can start a project and manage it, including publishing a project, choosing the member, composing and managing the team and so on. The undergraduate can scan the published project and choose one interested project.

Process management: It provides the function of managing the workflow of practice teaching process. The enterprise can set the workflow and manage it. The workflow usually should include scoring each team member in each process node. The undergraduate learn engineering knowledge step by step following the workflow.

(3) Data layer, which provides system database environment including the database tables and database view sets, and in which the management works such as data storage, data query, data update and data deletion are implemented. The interaction with the server layer only occurs through logical interface so that the security of data is increased.

# 4    Implementation

According to the above design, a web-based practice teaching system is developed using ASP.NET (one kind of Web programming techniques) and SQL Server (one kind of database techniques) under the development environment of Visual Studio C#.NET on the Windows platform. The system has been commissioning operation in the laboratory and the operating interfaces of the system are shown in Fig.3.

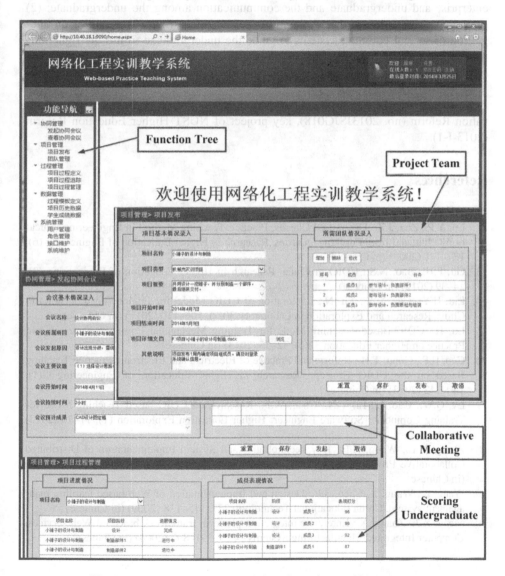

**Fig. 3.** The running sample of web-based practice teaching system

## 5    Conclusions

Based on the concept of CDIO, a collaboration-based practice teaching mode is presented. Combined with the networked collaborative technology, a web-based practice teaching system is proposed and finally developed to support the collaboration with enterprise for engineering education. The main contribution of this system is as follows: (1) providing an interactive platform to support the communication between enterprise and undergraduate and the communication among the undergraduate; (2) providing a simulation of the whole process of manufacturing; (3) providing an integration of several common systems to guide the undergraduate to use the right software application at the right phase. All in all, this system provides an engineering education environment and collaboration platform to practice the concept of CDIO.

**Acknowledgements.** The project is supported by key project of Jiangsu Higher Education Reform (no. 2013JSJG018), key project of NUST Higher Education Reform (2013-I-1).

## References

1. The Worldwide CDIO Initiative, http://www.cdio.org
2. Lu, Y.P., Zha, J.Z.: Diversified Classes: Practice Teaching Method in Engineering Education Originated from Foreign Countries. Research in Higher Education of Engineering (6), 137–141 (2009) (in Chinese)
3. Gu, P.H., Bao, N.S.: CDIO in China. Research in Higher Education of Engineering (3), 24–39 (2012) (in Chinese)
4. Liu, H.Y., Gai, Y.X., Xu, N.: Exploration of CDIO Model for Engineering Education in China. Research and Exploration in Laboratory 30(7), 106–110 (2011) (in Chinese)
5. Lu, H.: CDIO-Based Teaching Mode for Training Mechanical Engineer. Research and Practice on Higher Education 32(3), 32–35 (2013) (in Chinese)
6. Cao, H.P., Guan, T.H.: Reform and Practice of Electrical and Electronic Practice Teaching Based on the CDIO Concept. Research in Higher Education of Engineering 32(1), 140–142 (2013) (in Chinese)
7. Lv, Q.W., Cao, L., Li, Y.N., Chen, W.F.: Research on CDIO-based Teaching Mode for Training Composite Software Engineer. Higher Education Exploration (1), 71–76 (2013) (in Chinese)
8. Zhang, Y.L., Wang, H.F.: Key Technologies and System Implementation of Distributed Collaborative Product Design & Manufacturing. Engineering Design 9(2), 53–59 (2002) (in Chinese)
9. Wang, P., Wang, J., Chen, S.P.: Design and Implementation of Web-based learning management system. China Educational Technology 277, 115–118 (2009) (in Chinese)
10. Meng, X.J., Zhang, X.: Enterprise integration platform framework based on Web services. Computer Integrated Manufacturing Systems 14(5), 891–897 (2008) (in Chinese)

# Overdrive Suppression Design Pattern

Marwan Batrouni

Vertafore Corp,
11724 NE 195th St, Bothell, WA, USA
mbatrouni@vertafore.com

**Abstract.** Design patterns are architectural artifacts that are the results of solutions that have been applied successfully and repeatedly to a set of problems. In computer science design patterns play a crucial role in maximizing code reuse and architectural best practices.

The overdrive suppression design pattern outlined in this paper targets mainly the computing, although it can be applied to any field where simple robustness through managed redundancy is paramount.

**Keywords:** Design patterns, robustness, redundant, cloud computing, resilient, heart, ODS (overdrive Suppression).

## 1 Introduction

In a highly distributed and collaborative environment, such as cloud computing, many components may fail, continuing normal operations and processing during these failures is vital. The problem is how to implement a simple recovery mechanism that is fully automatic without complicated logic and heavy processing.

The keyword here is simplicity; being able to deploy a system with built in resiliency, not only assuming that a failure can happen but that it will happen and frequently.

A few years ago as part of a team working on a cardiology software, one heart mechanism in particular attracted my attention. Overtime it became apparent that it could be translated into an applicable design pattern.

The over drive suppression design pattern described in this paper can be relevant in many domains especially distributed computing in cloud space, where fault tolerance and redundant events handling are crucial, this pattern can help simplify the fault recovery process permitting a robust and efficient cloud software eco system.

Transforming and adapting the overdrive suppression principle into a design pattern would require some adjustments.

These adjustments are based on the targeted field; we can separate these fields into two main categories: analogue and digital.

The analogue realm is out of scope for this paper which will focus exclusively on the digital/computing aspect.

Y. Luo (Ed.): CDVE 2014, LNCS 8683, pp. 103–110, 2014.

## 2    Terms and Definitions

**Instance.** A process running in a cloud[1] hosted virtual machine.

**Overdrive Suppression.** The term comes from cardiology[2] and it lies at the core of how the electrophysiology of the heart works, it is a simple mechanism that allows the heart to function flawlessly for decades, pumping the equivalent of an oil tanker in volume during the average life span of a human being.

## 3    Pattern

**Definition.** Over drive suppression is the mechanism by which a group of software instances produce a set of synchronized events for the purpose of providing a simple and automatic recovery process.

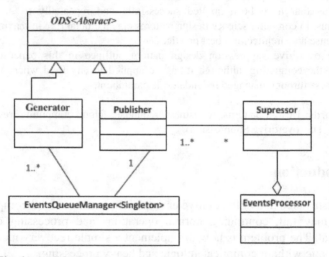

**Fig. 1.** possible class structure implementation (expressed in UML)

---

[1] Cloud computing is a Technology built around abstracting sets of heavily networked and virtualized servers, a virtual machine or server is a piece of software that emulate a physical hardware, allowing a full-fledged operating system and applications to run seamlessly within its context.

A physical server can run multiple virtual machines (or VM); in this case the physical hardware will be called the host.

The cloud allow users and organizations to execute computing operations with scalability on demand, a cloud can be public, private or hybrid of the two.

[2] In a nutshell, several special groups of cells in the heart are natural pacemakers (called nodes) they're role is to send an electric signal to the heart muscles to contract, ALL these nodes continuously fire their signals with different frequencies and signal strength, the Sino atrial node (or SA node) is the main operator (i.e. loudest), the heart muscles hears only the loudest, but let's say the SA node fails for whatever reason then the heart muscle will hear the second loudest, namely the AV node, which up until now was drowned by the SA loudness. If the AV node fails as well then the third loudest node will automatically become the loudest and so forth until the last line of defense (in the heart it is the Purkinje fiber) .
http://www.cvphysiology.com/Arrhythmias/A018.htm
http://en.wikipedia.org/wiki/Sinoatrial_node

**Participants.** The classes participating in this pattern are:

- **ODS.** An abstract base class defining a set of common methods related to events frequency configuration.
- **Generator.** Source of the events generated by the instance, it may also be a collector or consolidator of events
  Produced by other software components (classes, objects or other services)
- **Publisher.** Responsible for throttling and sending the software events to a recipient based on a preset frequency.
- **EventsQueueManager.** A singleton class responsible for queuing events produced by the generator classes.
- **Suppressor.** An events listener class responsible for receiving the events and suppressing redundant ones.
- **EventsProcessor.** Defines the methods responsible for consuming the events received by the suppressor.

**Mechanism.** Given the following variables:

- **P** :  A set of publishing instances
- **E** : A set of  events produced by **P**
- **$R_e$**: A set of  redundant events produced by **P**
- **$f$** : The send frequency of  events in **E**
- **$t$** : The starting time for each event sent
- **$c$** : A small time constant offset for events in **E**
- **L** : An event listener recipient and container

  The ODS pattern behave following these rules:
- Events sending frequencies decreases for each new instance

$$f_i < f_{i-1} \qquad\qquad (1)$$

- Start time for sending events is offset by a constant for each new instance.

$$t_i = t_{i-1} + c \qquad\qquad (2)$$

- Assuming $R_e \subset E$ then all events sent by P to L are idempotent[3]:

$$P \rightarrow R_e \cup L \equiv L \qquad\qquad (3)$$

---

[3] An operation is called Idempotent if it can be applied multiple times without changing the result beyond the initial application.
http://en.wikipedia.org/wiki/Idempotence

**Description.** In a computing context an overdrive suppression mechanism is laid out as a system with two major components; the first component is a set of client instances sending events, the second component is a one or more listener service(s) responsible for processing the received events. Each client instance sends events following a different frequency relative to the rest of its peers.

Events sent by the client instances are generated similarly by each instance, meaning each event generated by an instance is identical to all the events generated by the other instances for a given time sequence.

All identical events shares the same id (such as a prefix+ timestamp for example), the receiving service will process the event and keep the event id in a list of processed events, once the listener service receives a new event then it will look up its ID in the historic list of received events, if the event has been already processed then it will just ignore it.

If the most frequent (loudest) instance fails for whatever reason then the instance second in rank (less frequent that is) will become automatically the primary, if the secondary fails then the tertiary will become primary automatically and so forth.

**Components Layout.** Following is a detailed description of the publishing and listening instances in the diagram below (Fig. 2.).

**Publishing Instance Configuration.** In Fig 2 each instance contain two main threads, one that produce and process the event, the other thread is responsible for sending the event to the listener service following a preset frequency.

The event sending operation has the following properties:

*Start time.* Actual moment in time when the instance starts sending events.

Suppose instance1 with frequency $f_1$ starts at $T_0$ then:

- Instance2 with frequency $f_2$ starts at $T_1=T_0+c$   where $c$ is a small time constant delay
- Instance3 with frequency $f_3$ starts at $T_2=T_1+c$.

The small constant delay $c$ helps minimize the receipt by the listener instance of multiple events at once, reducing load in the process.

*Frequency.* Number of events sent per period of time; this frequency value can be a multiple of the primary instance frequency value.

*Example.* Suppose we have three instances:

- Instance1 (primary), Instance2 and Instance3
- Instance1 start time is 10:0:0 UTC with a frequency $f_1$ equal to 5 minutes.
- Instance2 is half as frequent as instance1 (multiple =2)
- Instance3 is one third as frequent as instance1 (multiple=3)
- $c=1$ minute

Then:

- Instance2 start time = 10:0:0 UTC+1 minute or 10:1:0 UTC.
- Instance2 frequency $f_2$ =10 minutes.
- Instance3 start time= 10:1:0 UTC+1 minute or 10:2:0 UTC.
- Instance3 frequency $f_3$ =15 minutes.

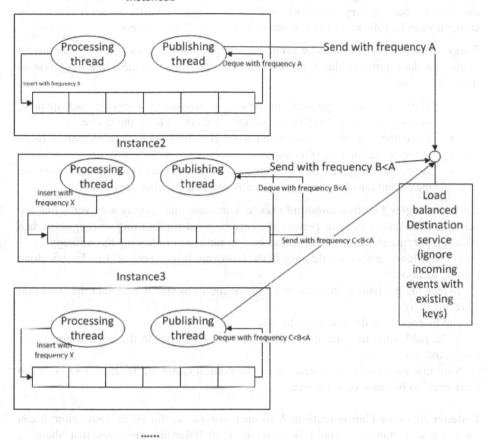

**Fig. 2.** Cloud instances publishing and sending events with different frequencies

**Table 1.** Events timeline of different instances

| Time\Instance | Instance1 –Primary- (start time 10:0:0) | Instance2 (start time 10:1:0) | Instance3 (Start time 10:2:0) |
|---|---|---|---|
| 10:0:0 | $E_1$* | | |
| 10:1:0 | | $E_1$ | |
| 10:2:0 | | | $E_1$ |
| 10:5:0 | $E_2$ | | |
| 10:11:0 | | $E_2$ | |
| 10:17:0 | | | $E_2$ |
| 10:10:0 | $E_3$ | | |
| 10:21:0 | | $E_3$ | |
| 10:32:0 | | | $E_3$ |
| … | … | … | … |

*$E$ symbolizes an event to send.

**Queue Purges Strategies.** The difference in frequencies between queuing and de-queuing in non-primary instances will cause a queue build up over time, few strategies can be followed to help control the growth of these queues:

*Purge strategies for time-bound events.* A time bound event is an event that has an expiration date, purging this type of events can be accomplished following one of these strategies:

- Mark the event type with an expiration timestamp, then for each queuing operation check for expiry events and purge them from the queue.
- Limit the size of the queue and when the limit is reached execute a batch purge operation on expiry events.
- A third strategy can be a combination of the two, by limiting the size of the queue and checking for expiry events on each queuing operation.

*Purge strategies for time-unbound events.* Time-unbound events are events that are timeless from an application perspective (maybe used for auditing or long term data mining), purging this type of events can be accomplished following this strategy:

1-The listener service would publish the last event it has received to a known cloud storage location.

2-Once the publishing instance reach the queue limit size it will read the last event Id received by

The listener from the common storage.

3-The publishing instance then will purge all events prior to the last event received by the listener.

Note that the read/write operation on the common storage location can be set to dirty-read[4] to increase performance.

**Listener Instance Configuration.** A listener instance is the event destination; it can be a single instance or could be a set of load balanced instances that shares a dictionary as in Fig. 3.

The listener events dictionary is the repository that keeps track of received events helping in the process suppressing redundant ones.

*Listener event- dictionary purge.* At some point the event dictionary would reach a size limit, one strategy to purge the listener events dictionary can be as follow:

1-Create time based partitions for events (this is very easy to do in cloud storage such as Microsoft Azure© for instance)

2-Use a rule to drop partitions that are old enough.

3-Store the last dropped partition Id in a shared storage location.

4-If an old staggered event reach a listener then it will read  the Id of the last dropped partition (from the storage) to see if the dictionary did contain it at some point but it cleaned it up, if so it will just ignore the event.

---

[4] Dirty read is a mechanism by which a read request to a database can be executed regardless of other ongoing Write access to the same database record.
http://en.wikipedia.org/wiki/Isolation_(database_systems)

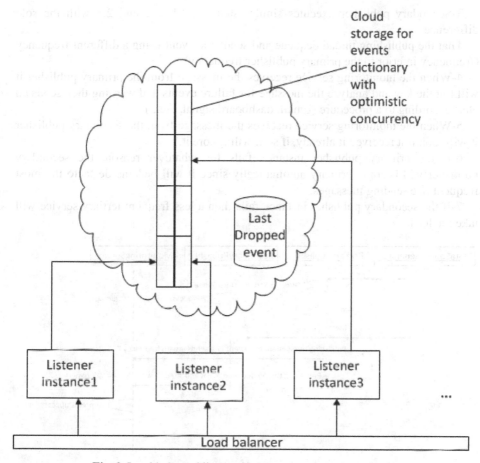

**Fig. 3.** Load-balanced listener instance memory management

# 4    Real World Example

Consider a system where its health monitoring is done using dedicated services, these dedicated monitoring services collect health metrics data then they process/aggregate the data and publish the result to a central dashboard service,

Following is the sequence for the operation:

1-Primary publisher receives health metric events.

2-Primary publisher accomplishes the following steps:

2.1-Aggregation thread sorts events by priority, aggregate stats, watch for certain performance thresholds and compose the event message with a unique key.

2.2-Aggregation thread inserts the message into a queue.

2.3-Publishing thread picks up the message from the queue and sends it to the monitoring service using a configured frequency.

3-Secondary publisher executes similar steps to 2.1, 2.2 and 2.3 with the sole difference

That the publishing thread dequeue and sends the event using a different frequency (frequency inferior to the primary publisher frequency).

4-When the monitoring service receives the message from the primary publisher it will log the key and analyze the message for failure events and warning then sends an alert according to a procedure (Email, dashboard signal, etc...)

5-When the monitoring service receives the message from the secondary publisher it will look if it received it already, if so it will ignore it.

6-If the primary publisher instance fails for whatever reason, the secondary publisher will become primary automatically since it will become de facto the most frequent one sending messages.

7-If the secondary publisher instance fails then a less frequent tertiary service will take the lead.

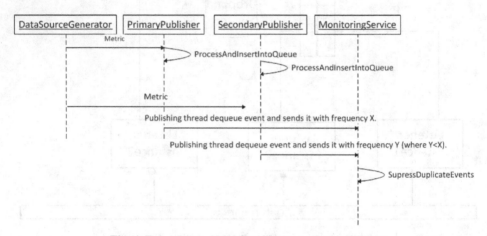

**Fig. 4.** Example sequence diagram (expressed in UML)

## 5     Conclusion

The over drive suppression design pattern extends Mother Nature's design to the digital realm, helping build a more resilient software and allowing for a simple recovery mechanism. The cloud software eco system is a natural use case for this pattern; however it can also be applied in other fields covering digital and analogue systems.

## References

1. http://msdn.microsoft.com/en-us/library/dd129913.aspx
2. http://msdn.microsoft.com/en-us/library/aa480027.aspx
3. http://www.omg.org/soa/Uploaded%20Docs/EDA/bda2-2-06cc.pdf
4. https://enterprisearchitecture.nih.gov/Pages/EventDrivenArch
   itecturePattern.aspx
5. http://www.oracle.com/technetwork/middleware/complex-event-
   processing/overview/ocephawhitepaperbenchmark-193519.pdf

# RE-Tutor: An Augmented Reality Based Platform for Distributed Collaborative Learning

Weidong Huang[1], Xiaodi Huang[2], and Wei Lai[3]

[1] University of Tasmania, Australia
[2] Charles Sturt University, Australia
[3] Swinburne University of Technology, Australia
tony.huang@utas.edu.au, xhuang@csu.edu.au, wlai@swin.edu.au

**Abstract.** Many ICT technologies have been used to develop systems to support collaborative learning. These systems are mainly developed to support interaction between users when they collaborate with each other to learn knowledge and solve a problem. However, there are many situations for collaborative learning in which geographically distributed participants play distinct roles and work together to produce or manipulate physical objects. For example, a teacher in a major city teaches a disabled child at a remote area; a remote tutor provides a tutoring service to a local student at home to finish an art or handcraft assignment; or more often, a teacher guides a class of students online through a series of activities in which physical objects are involved such as drawing a picture using different pens. In these scenarios, traditional learning systems may be limited since students not only need to see and hear their teacher, but also need to interact with their teacher to use or manipulate physical objects. In this paper, we introduce a novel system platform called RE-Tutor that is proposed to support this category of collaborative learning scenarios. In this system, while physically distributed, a teacher is enabled to talk to his students, see what the students are working on, and provide guidance information using hand gestures or annotations which are often needed for physical tasks.

**Keywords:** remote guidance; collaborative learning; augmented reality, hand gestures.

## 1    Introduction

It is generally accepted that an easy access to education resources is one of the key factors that affect the quality of people's everyday life. It is also commonly agreed that sustainable participation or engagement in education is important for them to be successful in their career and to live a quality life in this now increasingly competitive society [1]. However, people around the world do not have the equal chance to be educated due to various reasons. Among them, a limited access to education resources is one of the major circumstances that face both adult students and young people who live in remote areas. Schools and teachers are mostly located in more populated areas

Y. Luo (Ed.): CDVE 2014, LNCS 8683, pp. 111–117, 2014.

such as cities. It is often costly for them to leave their homes and come to the major cities to get educated, not only emotionally but also financially. This is particularly true in Australia: a report revealed that in 2008, there were around 80,000 students living in remote areas and a further 876,000 students in provincial areas [2].

Although much effort has been made to help students get into classrooms or teachers go to students' home [3, 4], tools that support remote interaction between teachers and students will be beneficial; these tools would allow two sides to stay where they are and at same time perform their tasks properly, therefore making the education resources more readily available and saving time and money for both students and education providers. In this paper, we introduce a technology called Re-Tutor that can be used for a teacher or a tutor to help a student remotely with home assignments or hand-craft activities. Re-Tutor was inspired by HandsOnVideo, a wearable technology developed for mobile tele-assistance to be used for remote repair or maintenance in the mining industry [6].

In Section 2, we briefly discuss the current trends of developing computer supported collaborative learning (CSCL) systems. We will show that the current focus for CSCL is mainly on supporting interaction between participants (students and/or teachers). The less attention has been paid to collaboration in which physically distributed participants work together to use or build physical objects. Then in Section 3, the HandsOnVideo system is described and a model of RE-Tutor, an augmented reality based platform for distributed collaborative learning, is proposed. Section 4 describes two versions of the RE-Tutor system. Finally the paper concludes in Section 5 with a short summary and future work.

## 2     Related Work

CSCL is a term used to describe a form of teaching and learning activities that are supported by ICT technologies and conducted by a group of participants who interact with each other and with the technologies for the purpose of better learning performance [9, 10]. In this section, we give two examples of CSCL with one for co-located learners and the other for distributed learners. We also briefly review some research on remote guidance in the field of Computer Supported Collaborative Work (CSCW) which is related to CSCL.

### 2.1     CSCL for Co-located Users

Echeverria et al. [11] designed two technological platforms for teaching electrostatics through co-located collaborative games in classrooms. One platform is based on multiple mice technology that makes it possible for users to provide multiple inputs. The other is based on augmented reality technology that enables users to explore and interact with a virtual classroom. Using a tablet, users can interact with the virtual objects and perform different tasks. The authors also conducted a user study comparing the impact of them on students' understanding of electrostatics concepts. The results suggested that when designing games for co-located collaborative learning, the technology used to support the game is also an important factor to consider.

## 2.2    CSCL for Distributed Users

Kumar et al. [12, 13] introduced two projects that aimed to develop systems to facilitate collaborative learning in distributed organizations. These two systems, PHelpS and PAD, were developed in the context of just-in-time workplace training and program analysis and debugging respectively. The rationale behind these systems is that geographically distributed organizations are increasingly involved in activities that are coordinated and integrated with the use of a range of ICT methods. With PHelpS, a worker can select the best one from a list of helpers provided by the system who are ready and available to help when he is running into a problem. The worker can also interact with the selected helper through the system. In this sense, the system acts as a moderator to stimulate collaborative learning between the helper and worker. With PAD, networked users can use a set of tools to help with each other with a series of domain-specific tasks related to software development and testing. These tasks include analyze/debug and advocate programming styles and conventions, analyze and assess internal documentation of a program, walk-through the versions of a developed program, perform time-based analysis of the programming process, and so on.

## 2.3    Systems that Support Remote Guidance

A number of systems have been developed to support a helper to guide a remote worker on physical tasks (e.g., [8]). For example, the DOVE system of Ou et al. [5] connects two networked computers with additional input and control devices such as tablets, video cameras and digital pens. The collaborators can work together by sharing their workspaces through video connections. The helper can draw on the video feed of the workspace of the worker to provide gesture information while communicating with his partner verbally.

## 3    HandsOnVideo and the Model of RE-Tutor

HandsOnVideo [6] has two units, one for the helper and the other for the worker, which are connected through a wireless network. As shown in Figure 1, there are a video camera and a display on each side. The camera on the helper side is to capture the hand over the big display, while the camera on the worker side is mounted on a helmet and is to capture the scene of the workspace. The system augments the hand image along with the object of the workspace and shows it on the display on the worker side as a common ground for communication (see Figure 2). This is also the main feature of this system.

User studies have shown this setup is effective for remote guidance. Although this system is developed to be used in the mining environment, it also can be tailored to be used for teaching and learning scenarios. More specifically, we propose RE-Tutor, a CSCL platform for distributed users, as shown in Figure 3.

**Fig. 1.** HandsOnVideo setup

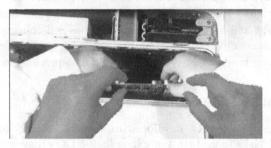

**Fig. 2.** A shared visual space with the worker's workspace augmented with the helper's hands (grey)

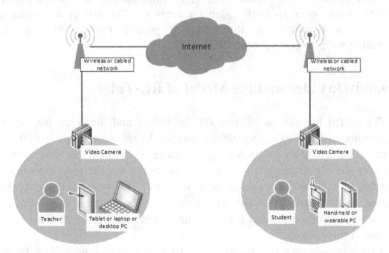

**Fig. 3.** RE-Tutor model

In this model, the big display of the helper unit is replaced by a monitor of traditional devices. The original big display is specifically designed for the commercial world with professional standards and also for making it possible for the helper to gesture with natural hands. But this is expensive and requires a relatively large office space, which is not suitable for the education setting. Therefore, the proposed RE-Tutor uses traditional fixed desktop or mobile laptop or tablet settings. Accordingly, the original implementation of the unmediated hand gestures based on a big display no longer applies. Instead, two approaches to the conveying of the gesture information are employed, which we discuss in the next two sub-sections.

## 3.1 RE-Tutor 1

In this setup, the two units use the same hardware that includes a light-weight see-through device such as a Google glass connected to a headset and a wearable PC. But each unit runs a different piece of software. On the teacher side, the system is responsible for displaying the scene of the student's workspace and captures the hand image of the teacher when he talks to the student and performs some hand gestures. The captured hands are augmented with the student scene and the resulting video feed is displayed on the see-through device on both sides.

On the student side, the student can hear the teacher and talk to the teacher with the headset attached to the system. He can also see both the visual aid and the physical workspace through the see-through device. This setup uses the same concept of HandsInAir [7] as shown in Figure 4, but the display mechanism of visual aids is implemented through see-through devices, rather than near-eye displays which were originally considered mainly for safety considerations in industrial workplaces.

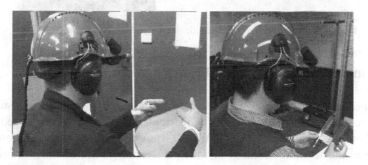

**Fig. 4.** Illustration of a teacher guiding a student in assembling toy blocks

## 3.2 RE-Tutor 2

In this setup, the teacher uses a tablet, a laptop or a desktop PC to display the shared visual workspace. The student can use any mobile device that has a camera attached. In the case shown in Figure 5, the student uses a smart phone and the teacher uses a laptop. When the student needs help on fixing a device, he can call the teacher and face the camera of the phone to the device that he is working on. The video of the device is sent to the teacher and shown on the teacher's laptop. The teacher sees the picture, talks to the student and makes some digital annotations or sketches such as a circle on a specific part of the object. While the student is listening to the helper, he can also see the annotations the teacher made on his phone.

Therefore, in this setup, the teacher's gesture information is conveyed to the student through the digital representation of the gesture. This gesture can be any free sketches that the teacher thinks are meaningful to the student. In addition, for the teacher to be able to make sketches, a digital pen needs to be installed and integrated to the system.

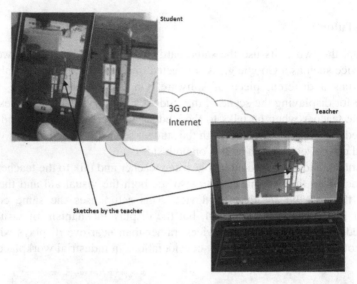

**Fig. 5.** A teacher is introducing a device to a student using annotations

## 4    Concluding Remarks and Future Work

In this paper, we briefly reviewed two most common formats of CSCL systems: one is for co-located users and the other is for distributed users. We also reviewed systems that are from the community of CSCW. We showed that not enough attention has been paid to the learning scenario in which a teacher guides a student remotely on physical objects. But this category of the scenarios has been well researched in CSCW. We therefore proposed two formats of RE-Tutor based on a wearable tele-assistance system. In the future work, we will further improve the design of the system and conduct user studies to test its usability.

## References

1. Purdie, N., Buckley, S.: School attendance and retention of Indigenous Australian students. AIHW Publication (September 2010)
2. Beavis, A.: Addressing educational disadvantage. Research Developments 26, Art. 4 (2011)

3. McIntosh, G., Phillips, J.: Disability Support and Services in Australia. E-Brief: Online Only issued March 2001,
   http://www.aph.gov.au/About_Parliament/Parliamentary_Departm
   ents/Parliamentary_Library/Publications_Archive/archive/disa
   bility (updated October 16, 2002)
4. Action Plan for Rural and Remote Education for 2011-2015: Department of Education, Training and Employment,
   http://education.qld.gov.au/ruralandremote/index.html
5. Ou, J., Fussell, S.R., Chen, X., Setlock, L.D., Yang, J.: Gestural communication over video stream: supporting multimodal interaction for remote collaborative physical tasks. In: Proceedings of the 5th Conference on Multimodal Interfaces, pp. 242–249 (2003)
6. Alem, L., Tecchia, F., Huang, W.: HandsOnVideo: Towards a Gesture based Mobile AR System for Remote Collaboration. In: Recent Trends of Mobile Collaborative Augmented Reality Systems, pp. 35–148. Springer, NY (2011)
7. Huang, W., Alem, L.: HandsInAir: A Wearable System for Remote Collaboration on Physical Tasks. In: The 16th ACM Conference on Computer Supported Cooperative Work and Social Computing (CSCW 2013), San Antonio, Texas, USA, February 23-27 (2013)
8. Tecchia, F., Alem, L., Huang, W.: 3D Helping Hands: a gesture based MR system for remote collaboration. In: The 11th International Conference on Virtual Reality Continuum and Its Applications in Industry (VRCAI 2012), Singapore, December 2-4 (2012)
9. Lipponen, L.: Exploring foundations for computer-supported collaborative learning. In: CSCL 2002 (2002), http://newmedia.colorado.edu/cscl/31.html
10. Ludvigsen, S., Mørch, A.I.: Computer-supported collaborative learning: Basic concepts, multiple perspectives, and emerging trends. In: International Encyclopedia of Education. Elsevier, Amsterdam (2010), doi:10.1016/B978-0-08-044894-7.00493-0
11. Echeverría, A., Améstica, M., Gil, F., Nussbaum, M., Barrios, E., Leclerc, S.: Exploring different technological platforms for supporting co-located collaborative games in the classroom. Comput. Hum. Behav. 28(4), 1170–1177 (2012)
12. Kumar, V.S.: CSCL environments for distributed peer collaboration,
    http://www.gerrystahl.net/cscl/cscl97/consort/
    Kumar.html (accessed on April 27, 2014)
13. Greer, J.E., McCalla, G.I., Kumar, V.S., Collins, J.A., Meagher, P.: Facilitating Collaborative Learning in Distributed Organizations. In: International Conference on Computer Support for Collaborative Learning (CSCL 1997), Toronto, Canada, December 10-14 (1997)
14. Al-Qaraghuli, A., Zaman, H.B., Olivier, P., Kharrufa, A., Ahmad, A.: Analysing tabletop based computer supported collaborative learning data through visualization. In: Badioze Zaman, H., Robinson, P., Petrou, M., Olivier, P., Shih, T.K., Velastin, S., Nyström, I. (eds.) IVIC 2011, Part I. LNCS, vol. 7066, pp. 329–340. Springer, Heidelberg (2011)

# Designing Cooperative Social Applications in Healthcare by Means of SocialBPM[*]

Fernando Sánchez-Figueroa[**], Juan Carlos Preciado, José María Conejero, and Roberto Rodríguez-Echeverría

Quercus Software Engineering Group,
University of Extremadura. Avda. de la Universidad, s/n, 10003, Spain
{fernando,jcpreciado,chemacm,rre}@unex.es

**Abstract.** The appearance of the so-called first-generation of social tools such as blogs, wikis or CMS made possible for the Web to be used as an interaction arena for healthcare purposes. Currently, this interaction has been improved by means of different social networks such as PatientsLikeMe, HealthVault or Inspire, just to cite a few. The business world, not to be left behind, is rapidly catching up with this change in interpersonal communications, allowing third parties (clients, patients, colleagues, providers, etc) to participate in the process execution by performing social operations such as voting, commenting, ranking, sharing, following, inviting, etc. However, this integration is being done in an ad-hoc manner, not existing understandable notations to include social interactions in Business Process Modelling (BPM). Moreover, the user has to face several social applications to perform simple social tasks, i.e., scheduling a meeting and sharing a diagnostic must be done through different applications. While the former problem affects the design phase, the latter affects the execution phase. In this paper we present a case study in order to illustrate how the use of SocialBPM solves these problems, where SocialBPM denotes to the combination of social technologies and BPM. SocialBPM eases both, the cooperative design of social processes, and their cooperative execution.

**Keywords:** Web 2.0, Social technologies, BPMN, Social BPM, Health social networks.

## 1 Introduction

Social technologies are being rapidly adopted inside the organizations and enterprises improving the way business is done. Today, the business processes are being enriched from a more social than technical point of view of the end-users involved. The non technical staff, such as employees, partners and customers, conforms the end-users group and they are every day more and more in touch with each other simultaneously,

---

[*] Partially supported by MEC project TIN2011-27340 and EU project FP7-SME-2011-285929.
[**] Corresponding author.

Y. Luo (Ed.): CDVE 2014, LNCS 8683, pp. 118–125, 2014.

offering support, answering questions, voting on the quality of a service, commenting, following the progress of a service request, networking with other colleagues to share experiences and so on, improving collaboratively their daily tasks. The appearance of techniques such as Cloud Computing that simplifies data storage, processing and security, is accelerating its broad adoption.

The health-related information domain is a representative example of this social technology adoption [1], fed by physicians blogs, posts, or portals for sharing diagnostics, offering services, sharing patients or professionals experiences, etc. As stated in [2], knowledge intensive processes, such as those defined at the healthcare field, may take advantage of using social software techniques.

There exists a good number of social networks for healthcare purposes attending to different criteria. Some of them are business oriented such as Medical Mingle[1], MedXCentral[2] or MyMedPort[3]. Sermo[4] is a network for physicians that allows them share clinical information and do case studies. Sharing information is also the aim of cureTogether[5], rareShare[6], Inspire[7], PatientOpinion[8] or PatientsLikeMe[9]. Other social networks with an API to interact with are Microsoft HealthVault[10] and, prior to be closed, Google Health[11].

However, all these tools (being health oriented or not) share a common weakness: they don't provide any way for structuring the interactions, dependencies or constraints between the different tasks. Moreover, the orchestration between all of them has to be done in an ad-hoc manner, forcing the user to lose the context quite often. Consider, for example, a doctor using LinkedIn for inviting colleagues to help him to take a decision on a pathology, using Doodle for setting up a meeting with these colleagues and using PatientsLikeMe [3] to see similar pathologies to serve as a reference before taking the final decision. Currently, there are tools that allow integrating different social networks using a simple syntax, such as ifttt[12] or zapier[13]. However, this syntax is not integrated with the notation used for the rest of the business processes. To solve these problems SocialBPM comes to the scene.

BPM can be seen as a systematic approach to make an organization's workflow more effective, more efficient and more capable of adapting to an ever-changing environment. Business can be seen here as whatever organization: a company, a public administration, a hospital or a set of colleagues, just to cite a few. Process

---

[1] http://www.medicalmingle.com/
[2] http://healthcare.medxcentral.com/
[3] http://www.mymedport.com/
[4] http://www.sermo.com/
[5] http://curetogether.com/
[6] http://www.rareshare.org/
[7] http://www.inspire.com
[8] https://www.patientopinion.org.uk/
[9] https://www.patientslikeme.com
[10] http://www.microsoft.com/en-gb/healthvault/
[11] http://www.google.com/intl/en_us/health/about/index.html
[12] www.ifttt.com
[13] www.zapier.com

orientation is one of the essential elements of quality management systems, including those in use in healthcare. A business process can be defined as an activity or set of activities that will accomplish a specific organizational goal, i.e., a medical clinical pathway. BPMN (Business Process Modeling Notation) is a graphical language for expressing the concepts involved in the BPM using flowcharting techniques. Its notation is easily readable and comprehensible for end-users and all other technical people involved in the BPM project definition. Processes can be visually described by users and implemented by technicians, breaking the existing gap between both profiles. In this sense, BPMN is a point of connection within an organization between the non-technical staff and the IT department. This fact has brought about its quick adoption by users of different fields and domains, such as e-Goverment, Agriculture, Travel Booking or Health [4][5][6].

SocialBPM [7] can be seen as the combination of both, social technology and BPM. While SocialBPM has been gaining maturity during the last years on the academic and industrial setting, the possibilities for end users have been ignored. Our position is that it is time for SocialBPM to exploit new scenarios for the end users inside business processes. And the healthcare field is a fertile ground for it.

The aim of this paper is twofold. On the one hand, showing some of the problems arising for healthcare professionals when using social technologies in a non-structured way. For this purpose a simple case study is presented. On the other hand, showing how these professionals can take advantage of SocialBPM by solving the case study using an extension of BPMN to include social interactions. This extension, developed under the BPM4PEOPLE project, allows a general practitioner or a hospital manager to easily design a process, but now incorporating social extensions with the typical operations of this kind of applications: tagging, voting, commenting, following, networking, etc. The aim of BPM4PEOPLE is not only allowing a non-technical person designing a process that includes a social behaviour, but also generating automatically a prototype of the application that implements that process. This last step is of capital importance when you do not want the IT professionals to intervene until they are really needed.

The rest of the paper is as follows. Sections 2 and 3 are devoted to the case study. While Section 3 introduces the problem, Section 4 solves it. Finally, Section 5 presents conclusions and future work.

## 2    Case Study: Highlighting the Problem

Let us suppose a rural region with small villages more than one hundred kilometres far from a little hospital. These villages share a primary care physician who can solve common pathologies. However, when the patient presents a difficult diagnostic and the general practitioner has doubts, then the health expedient of such patient is remitted to a hospital through an intranet system in order to be analysed by a specialist. If the specialist can diagnose it, then the treatment is prescribed. On the contrary, if the pathology is complicated enough or the specialist has also doubts, then the opinion of other colleagues must be considered. Figure 1 shows the BPMN diagram for our case study. It does not deserve further explanations.

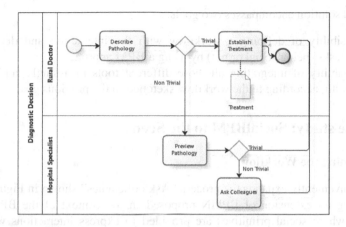

**Fig. 1.** BPMN diagram for the workflow described for our case study

The process of "asking colleagues" can involve typical social operations such as sharing similar pathologies, commenting the original pathology, voting on a proposed treatment, etc., so it is a potential process to be performed through social networks. A possible workflow for this process could be:

1. Finding similar clinical cases by using PatientsLikeMe.
2. Finding the appropriate colleagues for building a team to treat the pathology. This can be done using the Hospital's contacts in LinkedIn.
3. Setting up a meeting for discussing the pathology. This can be done using Doodle, a social application for scheduling events.
4. Documenting and sharing the conclusions through HealthVault, once the treatment is prescribed.

From the healthcare professional point of view there exist problems at two different levels:

1. On the one hand, the interactions and dependencies between different tasks are not formally established. Different tools are used by the professional just based on his own previous experience without defining a systematic workflow. This problem affects the design phase of the process.
5. On the other hand, the number of different social tools to be used can be high and heterogeneous, and it is always increasing. Then the healthcare professionals must continuously learn how to use several evolving systems with different characteristics distracting them from their main duties. Moreover, those tools are not integrated in a single system making the user to lose his context quite often, that is, the login operation must be done sometimes in different platforms with different user interfaces and different modus operandi. This problem affects the execution phase of the process.

The ideal solution encompasses two goals:

1. The possibility of defining a workflow with the interaction and dependencies between tasks (being social or not) by using a BPM approach.
2. The possibility of integrating all those different tools in a single application to interact with, according to the workflow sketched in the previous goal.

# 3    Case study: SocialBPM to the Scene

## 3.1    Defining the Workflow

Figure 2 conveniently expands the process "Ask colleagues" shown in Figure 1. Now we are using an extension of BPMN proposed in the context of the BPM4People project [7] where social primitives are provided to express interactions with social networks [8]. The case study only uses a simple subset of the proposed extensions. However, it is enough for our purposes. This subset is shown in Table 1. A detailed description of the extensions can be seen in [8].

**Table 1.** Subset of social icons used in the case study

| Icon | Meaning | Icon | Meaning | Icon | Meaning |
|---|---|---|---|---|---|
| | Login using a social profile | | Data flow to a community pool | | Voting on an activity |
| | Comment the activity | | Dynamic enrolment to a task in the process case | | Event raised by the community |

In Figure 2, the medical specialist logs in into the application by using one of his own social network credentials (e.g., LinkedIn credentials). Then, he can retrieve information of similar pathologies from PatientsLikeMe and make them available for future collaborators in a repository. He also establishes one or more candidate treatments. Then, he can search for those professionals closer to the pathology among his contacts (hospital collaborators). Observe that the search activity can be supported by the social platform he is connected to (LinkedIn in our case), without losing of context. The connection with PatientsLikeMe can be done using the user credentials previously stored in his application profile. Then, the colleagues can comment on the pathology and vote on the candidate treatments. The doctor can collect the comments and votes after a period of time and decide if he has enough information for prescribing a treatment. If this is the case then the process ends by sending the pathology and the treatment to a social network to be "commented" by patients (patient pool) with the same pathology. If there is no agreement between colleagues, then the doctor creates a poll (using a connection to Doodle) and the collaborators are invited to mark their preferences among a predefined list of dates (by sending a message to the collaborators using their inbox at LinkedIn). Finally the doctor chooses the final date for the meeting and publishes it. After the meeting, a treatment will be established and, again, the relevant information will be broadcasted to a social network to contribute to enhance the knowledge in the field.

## 3.2    Obtaining the Application

To validate the viability and usability of BPM4People in the biomedical field, we have implemented the case study using Webratio and RUXTool [9], two Model-Driven Web application development (MDD) tools allowing one to edit BPMN models and automatically transform them into running Java applications with a Web interface. Webratio is used for data and business logic modelling and RUXTool for presentation modelling.

MDD is mainly characterised by: (i) the use of models as primary entities in the software development process and (ii) model transformations that perform several refinement operations until (semi)-automatically generating the final code of the systems from these models.

From the Social BPMN model one obtains automatically two different models, data and business logic models. They are expressed in WebML, the web modelling language used in Webratio. These generated models, among other functionalities, provide the logic needed to interact with the most used social networks and perform typical operations, such as voting, commenting, ranking, following, sharing, and so on.

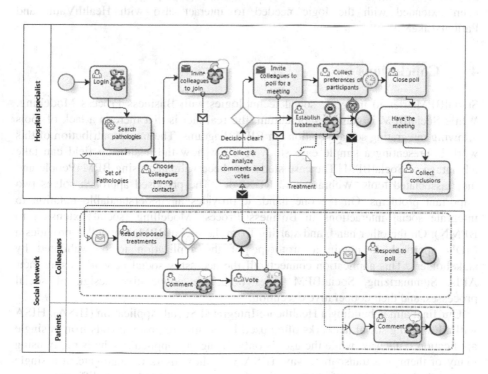

**Fig. 2.** Extended BPMN for the case study

Application developers can fine-tune the Web application for enacting the process, by enriching the skeleton application model produced automatically from the BPMN process diagram. Additionally, they can use RUXTool to improve the appearance of the interface. Finally, a second transformation is performed, automatically obtaining a prototype of the application that can be validated by stakeholders.

Note that providing a public API becomes a key feature for the social networks used in our work. This issue may be considered an important thread of validity for the work, since most of the health networks analysed do not provide such an API. However, this is also one of the main contributions of the approach, since those networks that include the API have been easily integrated and connected by BPM4People (e.g. PatientsLikeMe and HealthVault). In particular, Doodle and LinkedIn provide APIs that allow developing external applications that access to these networks based on web services (using REST). Regarding the health networks, PatientsLikeMe uses the clinicaltrials.gov API, which is a registry and results database of publicly and privately supported clinical studies of human participants conducted around the world. HealthVault provides an API through .NET, a Microsoft technology.

Currently, BPM4People provides connections with Facebook, LinkedIn, Twitter, WordPress, Xmpp, Google Docs, Doodle, WordPress, Xmpp, Google Calendar, Google Maps, Yammer, Cloud Storage (Dropbox, SugarSync, Box.net, and Microsoft SkyDrive). Additionally, and for the sake of adapting the project to this work, it has been extended with the logic needed to interact also with HealthVault and PatientsLikeMe.

## 4    Conclusions

SocialBPM tries to integrate social technologies with Business Process Modelling. While SocialBPM is gaining momentum, the real fact is that there is a lack of tools allowing integrating social notations in BPM diagrams. The main contribution of this work is presenting a simple case study to show how the healthcare field can take advantage of SocialBPM. The case study has been validated using BPM4People and their associated tools, Webratio and RUXTool. The proposed approach solves two important problems. On the one hand, it provides an understandable notation to integrate social interactions in Business Process Modelling (social extension to BPMN). On the other hand, and starting from the social BPMN model, it provides a MDD approach to obtain a prototype of the application to be validated by stakeholders. This application connects all the necessary social networks using their APIs. Summarizing, SocialBPM eases both, the cooperative design of social processes, and their cooperative execution.

Our final aim is building a Healthcare Integrated Social Application (HISA). HISA will allow using social networks often used by healthcare professionals from a single application. This way, while the user is only facing one application, he is really using many of them in a transparent way. HISA will allow users to aggregate in a single place all the relevant information for them that is spread over different social networks. Moreover, the possible interactions with these networks will be also available, easing their work and increasing their productivity. However, for this purpose we need healthcare social networks to provide an API for external interactions. We are convinced that this fact will be occurring soon as it has been the case of PatientsLikeMe and HealthVault.

# References

1. Lupiáñez, F., Mayer, M.A., Torrent, J.: Opportunities and challenges of web 2.0 within the health care systems: an empirical exploration. Informatics for Health & Social Care 34, 117–126 (2009)
2. Erol, S., Granitzer, M., Happ, S., Jantunen, S., Jennings, B., Johannesson, P., Koschmider, A., Nurcan, S., Rossi, D., Schmidt, R.: Combining BPM and social software: contradiction or chance? Journal of Software Maintenance and Evolution: Research and Practice 22, 449–476 (2010)
3. Wicks, P., Massagli, M., Frost, J., Brownstein, C., Okun, S., Vaughan, T., Bradley, R., Heywood, J.: Sharing health data for better outcomes on PatientsLikeMe. Journal of Medical Internet Research 12 (2010)
4. Altman, R.L., Altman, K.W.: Dynamic Clinical Pathways-Adaptive Case Management for medical professionals. In: Fisher, L. (ed.) Social BPM: Work, Planning, and Collaboration Under the Impact of Social Technology. BPM and Workflow Handbook Series (2011)
5. Rojo, M.G., Rolón, E., Calahorra, L., García, F., Sánchez, R.P., Ruiz, F., Ballester, N., Armenteros, M., Rodríguez, T., Espartero, R.M.: Implementation of the Business Process Modelling Notation (BPMN) in the modelling of anatomic pathology processes. In: Proceedings of 9th European Congress on Telepathology and 3rd International Congress on Virtual Microscopy, Toledo, Spain (2008)
6. Rolón, E., García, F., Ruiz, F., Piattini, M., Calahorra, L.: Healthcare Process Development with BPMN. In: Cruz-Cunha, M., Tavares, A., Simoes, R. (eds.) Handbook of Research on Developments in E-Health and Telemedicine: Technological and Social Perspectives, pp. 1024–1047. Medical Information Science Reference, Hershey (2010)
7. Brambilla, M., Fraternali, P., Vaca, C., Butti, S.: Combining Social Web and BPM for Improving Enterprise Performances: the BPM4People Approach to Social BPM. In: Proceedings of the 21st International Conference Companion on World Wide Web, European-projects track, New York, USA (2012)
8. Brambilla, M., Fraternali, P., Vaca, C.: A Notation for Supporting Social Business Process Modeling. In: Dijkman, R., Hofstetter, J., Koehler, J. (eds.) BPMN 2011. LNBIP, vol. 95, pp. 88–102. Springer, Heidelberg (2011)
9. Linaje, M., Preciado, J.C., Morales-Chaparro, R., Rodríguez-Echeverría, R., Sánchez-Figueroa, F.: Automatic Generation of RIAs Using RUX-Tool and Webratio. In: Gaedke, M., Grossniklaus, M., Díaz, O. (eds.) ICWE 2009. LNCS, vol. 5648, pp. 501–504. Springer, Heidelberg (2009)

# An Augmented Reality Setup
# from Fusionated Visualization Artifacts

Maik Mory, Martin Wiesner, Andreas Wünsch, and Sandor Vajna

Otto-von-Guericke-Universität Magdeburg, Germany
firstname.lastname@ovgu.de

**Abstract.** Merging three-dimensional visualization artifacts interactively from arbitrary sources is a promising approach to support interoperability in engineers' software landscape. Based on previous work, which yielded a framework for asynchronous processing of OpenGL, we present a component, which combines three-dimensional visualizations from OpenGL-streams into one three-dimensional visualization space in real-time. In our current setup, CAX software is integrated with pointcloud rendering from an RGBD-camera to resemble an orthoscopic virtual mirror, which combines a user's reality in front of the mirror with the CAX software's virtual reality inside the mirror. We present results, how the tested augmented reality setup fosters cooperative decisions in product development and engineering.

**Keywords:** cooperative decision, mixed reality, three-dimensional visualization, distributed system, interoperability.

## 1 Introduction

Simulations commonly are used to support decisions and for staff training. Together with the advent of cheap graphics hardware, computer-based visualization has become part of virtually every computer-based modelling or simulation software. Even more, users recognize visualization as a simulation's natural element today. To pick a random example, Teizer et. al. [3] put it "a variety of technologies ... to produce visualizations" when they talk about software, which actually processes sensor data.

Given the popularity of simulations and their visualizations respectively in science and engineering, it is temptating to research lightweight interoperability concepts based on three-dimensional visualizations in engineering. Thus, technologies that capture, stream and process 3D content from arbitrary software live have become available. This paper has a special focus on a technology, where two, basically independent, proprietary software applications are merged into one three-dimensional visualization.

The field of simulation is broad and the number of potential pairings is too huge and heterogeneous to be discussed in general from the perspective of cooperative decision making. Therefore, this paper discusses one application scenario, which is concrete enough to clarify some effects, but still is general from the engineering domain where it may be applied.

The first component to be fusionated resembles augmented reality applications. An rgbd-sensor system (top of Figure 1) scans a reality (right in Figure 1). An associated

Y. Luo (Ed.): CDVE 2014, LNCS 8683, pp. 126–133, 2014.

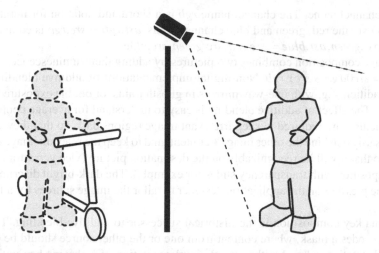

**Fig. 1.** The setup's basic idea: A virtual mirror fusionates virtual content from an arbitrary simulation into the mirror image. The resulting impression should be as plausible as possible and must not require modification of the fusionated simulation/visualization software.

3D-graphics system renders the sensor system's data, so that the reality appears to be mirrored (left in Figure 1) on a screen (middle of Figure 1).

The second component to be fusionated resembles virtual reality applications. Please note, that we use the term "virtual reality application" in a broad sense of an established taxonomy called the Virtuality Continuum [8]. Therefore, you may consider most known desktop, tablet, or smartphone applications that show three-dimensional content as a virtual reality application.

This paper discusses, whether and how it is possible to create a plausible experience for participants in a product development process in the given application scenario.

## 2    Background

### 2.1    Image Combining Examples

This section presents common applications of image combining by example. We focus on the relation between the algorithms and their application scenarios in science and engineering. For a deeper discussion on the graphics algorithms' properties, see Section 2 from Heirich and Moll [5] for example. Of course, the set of examples presented here can not be complete.

Image combining is a technique, where an operator is applied pixel-wise on pictures or series of pictures, which fusionates multiple sources into one destination. Throughout this paper we assume two input picture streams as sources. The first input image is $src0$. The second input is $src1$. The image that the output is written to is the destination $dst$. In the running example, our images have red, green and blue channels. Where declared, the images have an alpha or depth channel. We will access the channels following the notation from OpenGL's traditional pixel shader with a dot operator and the channel name. The channel name *rgb* is a shorthand notation for iterative application over the red, green and blue channel. Thus, $dst.rgb = src.rgb$ is equivalent to $dst.red, dst.green, dst.blue = src.red, src.green, src.blue$.

Additive composition combines two pictures by adding their luminescences. This is $dst.rgb = src0.rgb + src1.rgb$. Non-digital implementations of additive blending have a long tradition, e.g. with one-way mirrors in ghosth trains, or double exposure in photography. The effect of additive blending is easy to understand for average people. The source pictures are required to keep irrelevant image regions dark, so that they will not unnecessarily outshine the other image's content; and to keep the relevant image content bright, so that it will be recognizable on the destination picture (vice versa for subtractive composition with transparency slides for example). The dark-bright discrimination puts some pressure on the application designer to tailor the image sources for a feasible result.

Chroma key composition is the historical successor to additive blending. The first picture encodes a mask, where content from one or the other source should be placed, using a distinctive color. A rather simple implementation of a chroma key with green backdrop might be $dst.rgb = $ if $src0.green > .5$ and $src0.red < .5$ and $src0.blue < .5$ then $src1.rgb$ else $src0.rgb$. The mask in chroma keying wastes much less information space than the dark-bright discrimination in additive blending. The remaining requirement is, that the relevant content from the first source must not use the key color. Thus, the requirements how to tailor the inputs are looser than with additive blending, but there is still potential conflict to adhere. On the other hand, the algebraic properties of chroma keying are more restrictive than the properties of additive blending.

Alpha composition adds a (not directly visible) alpha channel to the images. The alpha channel determines the mask how to blend the sources and thus does not waste bandwidth of the visible rgb-channels. A rather simple alpha blender might be $dst.rgb = src0.alpha * src0.rgb + src1.alpha * src1.rgb$. In contrast to additive blending and chroma keying, the mask does not depend on visible content. But there is the new requirement to provide the alpha channel. Thus, alpha blending primarily is used on static content like corner logos and virtual HUDs.

Depth composition requires a depth channel besides the rgb-channels. From the sources, the pixels with the shorter distance to the viewpoint are drawn – the nearer content occludes the more far content. Simplified this is $dst.rgbd = $ if $src0.depth < src1.depth$ then $src0.rgbd$ else $src1.rgbd$. The mathematical properties are not too different from alpha-based composition. The main difference is, that an alpha channel is more or less artificial, while depth channels are increasingly available. The majority of scientific visualizations uses or resembles OpenGL's immediate mode, where the depth channel is part of the rendering pipeline (cf. [11]). Cameras that provide a depth channel have become generally available some years ago and evolve rapidly on the market.

## 2.2 A Depth-Based Composition for Independent Visualizations

Using the vanadium framework [10], we assume two nodes (A and B) in the network that publish the OpenGL client-server dialogues (say OpenGL-streams) from two distinct software applications. Now it's trivial to create a third node (C) that subscribes to the two original OpenGL-streams. For the sake of comprehensibility, we initially assume that node C would create two OpenGL windows. In the first window, node C replays the OpenGL-stream from node A. In the second window, node C replays node B's OpenGL-stream. In effect, node C's display shows node A's and node B's visualization side by side at interactive framerates.

Once the data is there, we now describe the merging algorithm in particular. We discard the hypothetical two side-by-side windows and use one target window at node C. We slice the two source streams into frames at invocations of the SwapBuffers function [7]. Node C replays the two streams' frames alternating in its target window. If one frame finishes rendering and on the alternate stream is no new frame available completely, then the alternate stream's last completely received frame is replayed. The choreography avoids congestion issues and determines the display window's frame rate at the faster one of node A's and node B's OpenGL-streams. Each frame from either stream contains a sequence of invocations that clears the window and draws the visualization. Thus, the alternating streams in one window overdraw each other on the screen.

As final step in the algorithm, we remove all invocations that cause the effect of overdrawing. From the alternating sequence of frames, we drop the SwapBuffers invocation at the end of each frame from node A. At the start of frames from node B, we remove invocations that clear the screen or draw background graphics. Thus, node A's frames clear the screen and draw their contents; then node B's frames draw their respective contents and swap buffers to make the new drawing appear on the display. Since OpenGL's drawing is done with three-dimensional geometry data, the two streams' contents appear to be present in one three-dimensional space.

## 3 Results

The mirror component that should be merged with the engineering tool provided many constraints, how the fusion had to be configured in detail. Basically, the mirror component scans the reality in front of the mirror with a Microsoft Kinect 360 and renders the gathered point cloud to a screen. Among others, an 1.5 m × 2 m monoscopic display and a 65" stereoscopic display were tested.

The mirror software is run-time configurable for two modi: a preferred crowd mode and an available single-user mode. In crowd mode, the data is projected orthogonally, so that the display mimics an orthoscopic mirror, as if orthogonal (virtual light) rays would reflect in the display's surface. This metaphor yields evenly plausible impressions for multiple viewers. In single-user mode, one selected user is tracked by the Kinect. The user's head position relative to the screen is derived to a rotation of the mirror content, so that the user has a basic impression of motion parallax. Perception quality for other viewers is decreased in single-user mode.

We used Siemens NX – an off-the-shelf CAX suite – as the engineering tool that should be merged into the mirror. NX embeds a window-on-the-world as presence metaphor [8] into a menu landscape. In its central view, NX uses an orthoscopic projection by default. Straight fusion with the mirror's visualization without other supporting configurations rendered all three rotation axes and translation along the screen plane useful. NX provides a metaphor that gives the user the impression that the model would translate along the screen normal.

At the second glance, NX adapts the orthogonal projection symmetrically, so that the virtual content looks to be scaled when rendered in relation to the mirror content. A translation along the screen normal that is plausible in the mirror was implemented by a node, that modifies NX' near and far plane during setup of the projection matrix. In summary, one should consider seven degrees of freedom – rotation, translation and scaling – for plausible alignment of orthogonal projections.

(a) The virtual mirror on a stock TV set ...                    (b) ... and on a powerwall.

**Fig. 2.** The setup's objective layout: The RGBD-camera scans the area in front of the screen and publishes the OpenGL-stream of a real-time pointcloud rendering. On a desk to the side of the public screen, a Siemens NX is modified to deliver its content as OpenGL-stream. The mixed stream appears to integrate the pointcloud and the CAD model in one three-dimensional space. The geometries are setup to mimic an orthoscopic mirror – the persons are life-size on the screen. Another node adds stereoscopic rendering to NX' and Kinect's contents.

The mirror's rotation in single-user mode could be identified in the stream as a matrix operation. One node extracts the rotation from the mirror's stream and another node injects the rotation into NX' stream. The two contents kept their consistent alignment throughout all our tests with the head tracking.

### 3.1 Related Work

OpenGL's strict client-server architecture suggests itself for research about distributed rendering. The oldest documented research that we know of, is Bourke's discussion of load distribution in a cluster of OpenGL servers [1] and Silicon Graphic's specification of an OpenGL Stream Codec [4].

In 2005, Miyachi et al. showed that OpenGL Command Fusion [9] from arbitrary sources is feasible. Besides minor technical differences between their and our work, we see two major differences in the results. First, their presentation may suggest that visualization fusion directly enables multi-physics. Forsooth, when many of our experiment

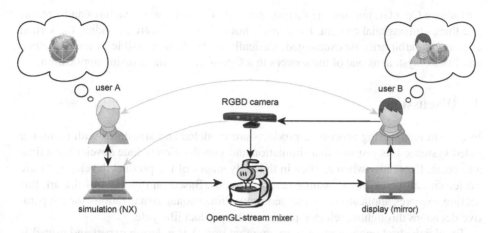

**Fig. 3.** The setup's conceptual layout: User A uses NX as simulation. An RGBD-camera scans User B. The OpenGL-stream processing framework splices the two OpenGL-streams. The stereoscopic display mimics an "orthoscopic mirror", which presents the user together with NX' virtual content. Optionally, scanned user data is used as input to NX. Optionally, User A and B interact in reality too, or even are the same person.

participants experienced the plausible mirror image with virtual content, they intuitively expected something to 'happen'. But there is no direct interaction in the image domain. Combining the 'physics' from two simulations has to be done either in mind or on model level (or on "equations level" as they put it). Ignoring model-based integration of simulations, which is a well-studied field of research, we were able to shift the cooperative aspect into focus, when domain specific knowledge should be transferred from mind to mind.

French company TechViz claims to have implemented an OpenGL Fusion. As far as we know, documentation on their approach does not exceed advertisement material [2].

Although Heirich and Moll [5] research distributed rendering for load balancing, their proposal of a "pixel-by-pixel merge" might be an alternative approach for the fusion technique. Each distributed node renders into a local pixel buffer. The collected buffers are fused with a pixel-based operation into one buffer, which shows the fused scene. Future work may discuss, whether this approach might be more robust than the 'pure' command fusion used in this work. A more robust fusion would increase flexibility on the sources that can be fusionated.

The mirror component that we used in our experiments has some similarities with a telepresence system presented by Maimone and Fuchs [6]. It shares the approach to use an rgbd sensor's features to provide a user with a "non-disruptive" telepresence and head tracking. Still, Maimone and Fuchs' work is much more complete than ours with respect to their use of multiple sensors and a better presentation of the data. Our approach is different with respect to incorporation of virtual objects (Figure 1E and last paragraph of Future Work in [6]). Since we use the vanadium framework [10] for the insertion, the source of the (dynamic) virtual object is potentially arbitrary. As long as there is a software that visualizes the wanted virtual content, there is neither a special

API above OpenGL nor any file format required. The framework captures and streams live three-dimensional content. Even more, not only the software providing the virtual content can arbitrarily be exchanged. Basically it should be possible to use Maimone and Fuchs' system as one of the sources in a OpenGL command fusion application.

## 4   Discussion

In current engineering processes, products are modeled and simulated with computer aided systems. It is justified that simulation and visualization reduce development time and costs. Especially when applied in the early stages of the product development life cycle, virtual prototypes substitute real prototypes. Based on this state-of-the-art, this section explores applications of merged three-dimensional visualizations for cooperative decisions throughout selected phases of the product lifecycle.

To take the first opportunity, we assume that user A is a design expert and user B is expert in another domain. During a session, the design expert (A) uses a desk workplace with his common hard- and software for minimal ergonomic barrier. The other expert (B) uses the virtual mirror. As an experience from our experiments, there are three primary effects that foster cooperative decisions about the model.

1. The life-size appearance in the mirror and the interactive three-dimensional inter-section with the model appeal to baser human instincts. User B experiences immersion into the virtual reality. All senses are available at full capacity to comprehend the model and user A's statements, if present.
2. Due to the immersion, user B feels natural to act gestures, simulate interactions with the model, and build mockups in front of the mirror. Thus, he is enabled to highlight aspects of his statements towards user A.
3. In comparison to an interview or to a shared session at a desk, the non-frontal situation between the users gives a diverse setting for higher social interaction.

At the second glance, there is another effect: User A may immediately edit his model/simulation according to cooperative decisions that are made in front of the mirror. Because OpenGL-streaming is real-time, user B promptly experiences the then new simulation from user A. In the tight loop, we expect faster development of more accurate simulations from virtual products to digital mockups. Nevertheless, the tight-loop-benefit applies for decisions on the virtual product's static structure, too.

The expert in front of the mirror is especially useful, when it comes to decisions that require some kind of 'test drive'. Moreover, due to the natural experience of the virtual product, experts with commonly lower degree of formal education can be involved into the development process, when they try assembly, maintenance or recycling procedures with their own tools in the virtual mirror. 'Test drives' can be used for tests on feasibility, for authoring of product documentation, and for ergonomic optimizations. Likewise, it is easy to use the virtual mirror for virtual training when training objects are scarce.

Due to the fact, that the presented technology is based on OpenGL only, it is easy to combine arbitrary simulation software to new applications. This explicitly includes CAx-software, FEM-solvers, fringe plots, flow analyses and other simulations that present their results in three-dimensional visualizations.

# 5   Summary

In this paper, we showed that OpenGL command fusion is a useful technology to setup augmented reality applications from existing software. We used a running example of a virtual mirror that embeds virtual content from a CAD software live. We discussed the application context with respect to cooperative decisions.

# References

1. Bourke, P.: Distributed OpenGL Rendering (1996),
   http://paulbourke.net/miscellaneous/distropengl/
2. Boutin-Boila, E.: TechViz Fusion (March 2011),
   http://www.techviz.net/wp-content/uploads/TechViz_Fusion_2011.pdf
3. Costin, A., Pradhananga, N., Teizer, J., Marks, E.: Real-Time Resource Location Tracking in Building Information Models (BIM). In: Luo, Y. (ed.) CDVE 2012. LNCS, vol. 7467, pp. 41–48. Springer, Heidelberg (2012)
4. Dunwoody, C.: The OpenGL Stream Codec – A Specification. Silicon Graphics (1996),
   http://www.opengl.org/documentation/specs/gls/glsspec.txt
5. Heirich, A., Moll, L.: Scalable Distributed Visualization Using Off-the-shelf Components. In: Proceedings of the 1999 IEEE Symposium on Parallel Visualization and Graphics, PVGS 1999, pp. 55–59. IEEE Computer Society, Washington, DC (1999),
   http://dx.doi.org/10.1145/328712.319337
6. Maimone, A., Fuchs, H.: Encumbrance-free telepresence system with real-time 3d capture and display using commodity depth cameras. In: ISMAR, pp. 137–146. IEEE (2011)
7. Microsoft Developer Network (MSDN): SwapBuffers function (2013),
   http://msdn.microsoft.com/en-us/library/windows/desktop/dd369060.aspx
8. Milgram, P., Kishino, F.: A Taxonomy of Mixed Reality Visual Displays. IEICE Transactions on Information and Systems 77(12), 1321–1329 (1994),
   http://etclab.mie.utoronto.ca/people/paul_dir/IEICE94/ieice.html
9. Miyachi, H., Oshima, M., Ohyoshi, Y., Matsuo, T., Tanimae, T., Oshima, N.: Visualization PSE for Multi-Physics Analysis by using OpenGL API Fusion Technique. In: First International Conference on e-Science and Grid Computing, pp. 530–535 (July 2005)
10. Mory, M., Masik, S., Müller, R., Köppen, V.: Exposing Proprietary Virtual Reality Software to Nontraditional Displays. In: Proceedings of the 20th International Conference in Central Europe on Computer Graphics, Visualization and Computer Vision. WSCG Communication Proceedings, Union Agency, pp. 35–43 (2012),
   http://wscg.zcu.cz/wscg2012/short/B03-full.pdf
11. Silicon Graphics, Inc. and The Khronos Group: glDepthFunc function (2013),
   https://www.opengl.org/sdk/docs/man/docbook4/xhtml/glDepthFunc.xml

# Messy Work in Virtual Worlds: Exploring Discovery and Synthesis in Virtual Teams

Carrie Sturts Dossick

Department of Construction Management, University of Washington, Seattle, WA, USA
cdossick@uw.edu

**Abstract.** The challenges of engineering team collaboration—establishing trust, fostering productive informal communication, cultivating knowledge exchange—are often exacerbated in virtual teams by geographical separation as well as team members' cultural and linguistic differences. Researchers have observed that powerful collaboration in collocated teams is supported by shared visualizations with which the team engages in informal, flexible and active ways. In studying virtual team interactions in a virtual world known as the CyberGRID, we see that just as with AEC collocated teams, shared visualizations were instrumental for the teams as they define, understand, and generate knowledge when working on interrelated tasks. Emerging from this analysis is an empirically supported theory that while avatar-model interaction supports mutual discovery, more messy interactions of brainstorming, knowledge exchange and synthesis requires flexible, active, and informal shared visualizations.

**Keywords:** Global Virtual Teams, Collaboration, Communication, Visualization, Information Technology, Building Information Modeling, Virtual Worlds.

## 1 Introduction: Shared Visualizations in AEC Teams

As communication technology enable globally distributed teams, the architecture, engineering and construction (AEC) scholars have had an increasing interest in how AEC teams collaborate across distances. There is extensive research literature on virtual teams that spans from engineering management, organizational science and human-computer interaction. For example, previous studies have explored cultural and linguistic differences [1,2,3], conflict [4], and trust development [5] in distributed virtual teams. Architectural and engineering design as well as construction planning present particular challenges for work in virtual teams [6]: namely, multidisciplinary problem solving and using complex shared visualizations for collaboration. As the use of virtual teams to support design and construction activities increases [7,8,9], the need for solving these challenges will as well. Consequently, in this paper, we seek to understand the collaboration needs of AEC teams and then explore how the affordances of virtual worlds support or hinder this collaboration.

Y. Luo (Ed.): CDVE 2014, LNCS 8683, pp. 134–142, 2014.
© Springer International Publishing Switzerland 2014

## 1.1     Collaboration in Architecture, Engineering and Construction Teams

For collocated teams—teams who are physically present together—much work has been done around how shared visualizations, such as emergent 3D modeling technology known as Building Information Modeling (BIM), support knowledge exchange through interaction, collaboration and communication in AEC teams [10,11,12]. For the practitioner who creates them, visualizations and models both serve as a way to communicate knowledge and as a means of knowing [12]. Those who receive a drawing or a model reinterpret it through their own domain lens, their role on the project, and their disciplinary expertise [13]. Consequently, for AEC teams, models and documents are sites for conversation where meaning is made through talk when practitioners exchange perspectives, knowledge and interpretations [14]. In 2011, Dossick and Neff introduced the concept of messy talk—"unplanned, unforeseen and unanticipated" dialog that supports brainstorming and mutual discovery [15, p. 85]—as a way to typify AEC design solution-generative interactions. In subsequent research we used Ingram and Hathorn's method of analyzing collaboration: participation, interaction, and synthesis (creation of new knowledge) [16]. We add a fourth element: discovery, which is a key element for AEC interaction. As Suwa, et al. noted, shared visualization helps lead to "unexpected discoveries" through designers' rapid-fire process of sketching, analysis, and synthesis [17, p. 240]. Combining Ingram and Hathorn with Suwa's notion of discovery, we formalized an operational definition for Messy Talk [18] to identify when teams mutually discovered (MD) issues in their models, critically engaged (CE) each other by asking questions and proposing solutions, exchanged knowledge (KE) about their own analysis, systems or technical knowhow, and then finally resolved (R) the issue together, at time creating a solution that was a synthesis of their collective know-how.

If the work of AEC teams is intensely visual, informal and dynamic, how then do geographically distributed teams, who are mediated by technology, accomplish this messy interaction? What affordances do the team members need? Which affordances inspire "unexpected discoveries" and solution generating dialog? In this paper, the focus is on the affordances of virtual worlds and compare and contrast team discussions in two virtual world environments, 1) avatars walking through a 3D model and 2) avatars using shared screen displays and discussing a 3D model upon the shared screen.

## 1.2     Virtual Worlds

Virtual teams of geographically distributed members who collaborate to accomplish planning and design tasks are more prevalent in global engineering projects [9], [19], [20]. Virtual teams require increased management emphasis, social and cultural understanding, and emphasis on common goals as well as technical elements such as compatibility of systems, security, and the selection of appropriate technologies [7], [21].

The research reported here is part of a larger research effort wherein researchers from Virginia Tech lead the development of the CyberGRID, (Cyber-enabled Global Research Infrastructure for Design), an avatar-based virtual world built on Unity. This work evolved from earlier efforts to support collaboration in SecondLife. Iorio et al. identified a number of factors that "impact tool usage patterns and adoption, including the simplicity of the tool, whether the tool promotes group cohesion, the emergent need for the tools, and local factors specific to the experiences of the domestic teams." [22, pg 209]. In their study of AEC teams in SecondLife, they found that users sought out tools that helped them work together. The CyberGRID was developed specifically to support distributed collaborative work in AEC settings and to study how virtual world tools can support AEC teams in their rich collaborative tasks with shared 3D models. In the CyberGRID, 3D human avatars represent participants and they share a 3D virtual world with a meeting space and a 3D model of their building project (see Figs 1 and 2). They communicate via VoIP (Voice over Internet Protocol), text chat, and file exchange. In the virtual meeting room, a "team wall" enables members to share their computer desktop in real-time. Team members provided non-verbal cues within the system akin to hand-raising or nodding with head bubble gestures or avatar position reinforcing the sense of copresence, i.e. the sense of being there together [23] (Figure 2). Thought bubbles used for backchannel communication such as the green bubble for "I agree," are located at the top center of image and the team wall shared desktop tool (showing Revit, a BIM tool, in this image).

In light of the messy interactions required of AEC teams, in this paper we focus on one aspect of the virtual world and ask: What affordances do avatar-3D model spaces provide for these teams, particularly when they are separated by geographic distances?

## 2    Setting and Methods: Students in CyberGRID

We analyzed ethnographic observations and team meeting transcriptions of a 10-week long experiment to examine the dialog of distributed virtual AEC project team members. In the winter/spring of 2013, thirty-six graduate students from the University of Washington (UW), Virginia Tech (VT), University of Twente (UT) and Indian Institute of Technology-Madras (IIT) met in six teams. Three of the teams were assigned to work once per week in an online environment called the CyberGRID (Cyber-enabled Global Research Infrastructure for Design), a virtual collaborative space [22]. To study the relationship of CyberGRID affordances with team interaction, the researchers designed a set of interrelated tasks. In the 2013 CyberGRID experiment the students designed a three room addition to an existing building in Revit (IIT), created a construction schedule (VT), created a 4D model (3D + schedule, UW) and developed a cost estimate of the project (UT). Teams then optimized their models. It was in the design and optimization processes that we expected the teams needed shared visualizations for joint decision making and brainstorming that typifies this work in the industry [15].

All interactions that took place in the virtual collaboration space were audio- and video-recorded. Researchers also took detailed ethnographic notes and completed ethnographic observation sheets to document the use of tools, teamwork, and communication. Analysis of meeting interactions are underway, and in this paper we present preliminary analysis of team interactions from week 3 for all six teams. Examples are shown from Team 1. We used the operational definition of Messy Talk [18] to identify the types of interactions the team members had throughout the process. We coded the student dialog as Mutual Discovery (MD), Critical Engagement (CE), Knowledge Exchange (KE), Resolution (R) or none (N). We mapped the dialog codes against how the participants used the technological affordances (see Tables 1 and 2). This allowed us to study if and how team interactions differed when using different virtual world features.

# 3      Findings: Mutual Discovery and Messy Talk

The focus of this analysis was on week 3 interactions, when the students reviewed the 3D model with new three-room addition. Team interactions took place in two settings. First, teams used their avatars to "tour" their models and discuss their designs (Avatar-Model interactions, Fig. 1). Second, the teams also used their virtual meeting rooms to share desktop content (Avatar-screen interactions, Fig. 2). From this analysis emerged a proposition that suggests that while the avatar-model space proved to be very productive for discovery, when virtual world users were able to "mess up" the shared visualization we saw higher levels of collaboration (e.g., brainstorming, joint decision making).

## 3.1      Avatar-Model Interaction

Once per week the 3D models were imported into the 3D space and the team members walked through these models with their avatars. The interactions during these walk throughs were characterized by discovery. Note, the IIT students were not copresent in the virtual world due to bandwidth limitations. UT, VT and UW created a word document list of 3D model issues to share with their IIT teammates. Table 1 illustrates team exchanges in the virtual model and the messy talk coding process: Mutual Discovery (MD), Critical Engagement (CE), Knowledge Exchange (KE) and Resolution (R), [18].

**Table 1.** Avatar-Model Interaction Example (excerpt)

| Transcription | Code | Virtual and Local Affordances |
|---|---|---|
| UT: I'm in the model now, it looks real funny. It's just a mistake in the model [referring to an earlier issue with a wall on the third level] | MD | As they navigate the virtual model, UT opens the Revit |
| UW: Pretty funky up here. | MD | model locally |
| VT: Yeah, it's like they added the features but they didn't remove the existing items. | MD | because he cannot see the details of |
| UW: did they just copy on of the other additions and paste it up here? | MD | the wall from the virtual world |
| UT: yeah, that's one and they failed to implement phasing. So now it is as if it is all built in the same phase. So they should implement phasing in the model so we can see what is new. ... | MD, KE | model view. |
| VT 2: we're we going to keep the roof or did we want them to change that too? | CE | VT2's question goes unanswered |
| UW: so, this stairwell doorway should connect to our room, (ugh, I just fell down), without going outside. ... | CE, MD | UT continues to review the Revit |
| UT: I am just checking the model and they seem to be on top. Yeah, they are aligned. | MD | model locally throughout the |
| UW: ok, then the façade just needs to be over. | MD, R | virtual tour. |

**Fig. 1.** View of Model-Avatar interaction: Team 1 tours the model together

**Fig. 2.** Avatar-Screen interaction showing the Revit Model on the Team Wall with the use of multicolored pens to sketch ideas

## 3.2    Avatar-Screen Interaction

In Team 1, after 25 minutes in the model, UW asks "Could we run through the list ". Since the model was on a shared screen, everyone quickly agreed to go back to the meeting room. Once there, they opened the Revit model on a second shared screen (the word document showing on the first screen) and began to discuss the design (see Fig. 2). In these exchanges, the teams brainstormed new design ideas.

**Table 2.** Avatar-Screen Interactions, Team 1 Week 3 (excerpt)

| Transcription | Code | Virtual and Local Affordances |
|---|---|---|
| UW: I agree. I, ah, just looking at it, it's just weird lookin'. I just think that it should all be the same height and it should definitely be connected on the interior. It's just strange. | CE | UT moves the view in Revit so everyone can see in the model. He tries to change the wall |
| UT: So, I think you can basically do two things, you can extend this wall to here and make a new wall. Hum, I'm trying to model but it is too hard. I'll just use the drawing function on the board. You make a new wall here, and here, and extend the old one. … | CE | real time, but cannot easily. He changes to using the team wall pens. (Fig. 2). The team uses pens from this point forward to illustrate |
| UW: Then you can also blow out that whole doorway for the new room and just have it be the entire width of that hallway… | CE | different ideas. |

# 4    Discussion

From this analysis emerges a clear difference in interaction styles between the two settings, 1) Avatar-model and 2) Avatar-screen. The Avatar-model interactions are dominated by mutual discovery while the avatar-screen interactions are characterized by critical engagement, and knowledge exchange as the team reviews options. In the avatar-model setting, they are able to use deictic references such as "this window", because their avatar location provides location cues as to which level, room, door and window they are refereeing to. In the Avatar-model setting, there were some moments of critical engagement where a team member suggested a different configuration between the stair and the room, but these questions went unanswered as the avatars continued to look around. There seemed to be limitations to this view of the model.

As the teams moved to the shared screen space to review their list of items, they quickly changed their interaction style. Their comments become longer as they critically engage the design, exchange their disciplinary knowledge and made design proposals. Whereas the design suggestions went unanswered in the Avatar-model space, here the teams focused on creating and discussing design alternatives. Students were able to pull and push the model, shown on the shared screen, in real time to explore an idea. Or, when the Revit software did not support an idea, the students used the shared screen pens to sketch on top of the view.

# 5    Conclusion

This paper summarizes preliminary findings from a 2013 experiment of student teams collaborating on a complex set of AEC planning and design tasks in a virtual world. This is analysis of 6 student teams, three of which were in the 3D virtual world. These student teams were made up of graduate students from four universities with a variety of professional backgrounds (0-10 years of experience). Most of these students are in the early stages of there careers. Each team had some members with industry experience. They were all learning the tasks a fresh during the experiment as part of a class, e.g. UW students were learning to do 4D models, while IIT students were learning to use Revit. Only a few of the students had virtual world experience and the first day of the team meetings were dedicated to user training for the CyberGRID. For this experiment, we provided the same experience (training, meeting duration, assignment scope) to each team. These findings are preliminary, but hold valuable cues as to the potential of virtual world tools for supporting "messy" AEC distributed team work.

In this analysis, we propose that it was the mutability of the shared screen that enabled and engendered the messy interactions of brainstorming and joint-problem-solving. Shared visualizations in the Avatar-model space alone lead to Mutual Discovery. In the generative messy talk exchange in the avatar-screen space however, the shared mutable visualizations on the team wall provided contextual cues for the distributed teams to understand each other's ideas and dynamically joint-problem solve while the task—the creation and optimization of a 3 room addition—was being conducted. Just as with AEC collocated teams [10], [12], [15], shared visualizations were instrumental for the teams to define, understand, and generate when working on interrelated tasks. We conclude then that when virtual team members make their knowledge work more explicit through modifying shared visualizations in real time, thereby visualizing the dynamic knowledge creation process, they can overcome the barriers to geographic distances and share opportunities for the co-production of knowledge through first mutual discovery in avatar-model space then second messy talk in avatar-shared screen space. This makes the collaboration more dynamic and lends itself to opportunities for knowledge synthesis in the case of messy talk and more straightforward interaction in the case of mutual discovery.

**Acknowledgements.** This material is based in part upon work supported by the National Science Foundation under Grant No. IIS-0943069 and Grant No. SES-0823338. Any opinions, findings, and conclusions or recommendations expressed in this material are those of the authors and do not necessarily reflect the views of the National Science Foundation.

# References

1. Steel, J., Murray, M.: Constructing the Team - A Multi-Cultural Experience. In: Proc., The Chartered Institution of Building Services Engineers Dublin Conference, Dublin, Ireland (2000)
2. Comu, S., Unsal, H.I., Taylor, J.E.: Dual Impact of Cultural and Linguistic Diversity on Project Network Performance. Journal of Management in Engineering 27(3), 179–187 (2011)
3. Di Marco, M.K., Taylor, J.E., Alin, P.: Emergence and Role of Cultural Boundary Spanners in Global Engineering Project Networks. Journal of Management in Engineering 26(3), 123–132 (2010)

4. Hinds, P.J., Mortensen, M.: Understanding conflict in geographically distributed teams: The moderating effects of shared identity, shared context, and spontaneous communication. Organization Science 16(3), 290–307 (2008)
5. Jarvenpaa, S.L., Leidner, D.E.: Communication and Trust in Global Virtual Teams. Journal of Computer-Mediated Communication 3(4) (1998)
6. Carrillo, P., Chinowsky, P.: Exploiting Knowledge Management: The Construction and Engineering Perspective. Journal of Management in Engineering 22(1), 2–10 (2006)
7. Chinowsky, P., Rojas, E.: Introducing Virtual Teams in Construction and Engineering. Journal of Management in Engineering 19(3), 98–106 (2003)
8. Messner, J.: Offshoring of engineering services in the construction industry. In: The Offshoring of Engineering: Facts, Unknowns, and Potential Implications, pp. 137–148. National Academies Press (2008)
9. Nayak, N.V., Taylor, J.E.: Offshore Outsourcing in Global Design Networks. Journal of Management in Engineering 25(4), 177–184 (2009)
10. Liston, K., Fischer, M., Kunz, J., Ning, D.: Observations of Two MEP iRoom Coordination Meetings: An Investigation of Artifact Use in AEC Project Meetings. In: CIFE Working Paper, Stanford University (2007)
11. Taylor, J.E.: Antecedents of Successful Three-Dimensional Computer-Aided Design Implementation in Design and Construction Networks. Journal of Construction Engineering and Management 133(12), 993–1002 (2007)
12. Whyte, J., Ewenstein, B., Hales, M., Tidd, J.: Visualizing Knowledge in Project-Based Work. Long Range Planning 41, 74–92 (2008)
13. Dossick, C.S., Neff, G.: Organizational Divisions in BIM-Enabled Commercial Construction. Journal of Construction Engineering and Management Special Issue on Governance and Leadership Challenges of Global Construction 136(4), 459–467 (2010)
14. Neff, G., Fiore-Silfvast, B., Dossick, C.S.: A Case Study of the Failure of Digital Media to Cross Knowledge Boundaries in Virtual Construction. Information, Communication & Society 13(4), 556–573 (2010)
15. Dossick, C.S., Neff, G.: Messy Talk and Clean Technology: Communication, problem solving, and collaboration using Building Information Modeling. Engineering Project Organizations Journal 1(2), 83–93 (2011)
16. Ingram, A.L., Hathorn, L.G.: Chapter X. Methods for Analyzing Collaboration in Online Communications. In: Roberts, T.S. (ed.) Online Collaborative Learning: Theory and Practice. Information Science Publishing (2004)
17. Suwa, M., Gero, J., Purcell, T.: Unexpected Discoveries and S-invention of Design Requirements: important vehicles for a design process. Design Studies 21(6), 539–567 (2000)
18. Dossick, C.S., Anderson, A., Azari, R., Iorio, J., Neff, G., Taylor, J.E.: Messy Talk in Virtual Teams: Achieving Knowledge Synthesis through Shared Visualizations. Journal of Management in Engineering (accepted for publication, 2014)
19. Gibson, C.B., Gibbs, J.L.: Unpacking the Concept of Virtuality: The Effects of Geographic Dispersion, Electronic Dependence, Dynamic Structure, and National Diversity on Team Innovation. Administrative Science Quarterly 51(3), 451–495 (2006)
20. Kirkman, B.L., Rosen, B., Gibson, C.B., Tesluk, P.E., McPherson, S.O.: Five Challenges to Virtual Team Success: Lessons from Sabre, Inc. The Academy of Management Executive (1993-2005) 16(3), 67–79 (2002)
21. Ramalingam, S., Mahalingam, A.: Enabling conditions for the emergence and effective performance of technical and cultural boundary spanners in global virtual teams. Engineering Project Organization Journal 1(2), 121–141 (2011)

22. Iorio, J., Peschiera, G., Taylor, J.E., Korpela, L.: Factors impacting usage patterns of collaborative tools designed to support global virtual design project networks. ITcon, Special Issue Use of virtual world technology in architecture, engineering and construction 16, 209–230 (2011), http://www.itcon.org/2011/14

23. Anderson, A., Dossick, C.S., Iorio, J., Taylor, J.E., Neff, G.: Avatars, text, and miscommunication: The impact of communication richness on global virtual team collaboration. In: Proceedings of Annual Conference - Canadian Society for Civil Engineering, vol. 4, pp. 2767–2775 (2011)

# A Cooperative System of GIS and BIM for Traffic Planning: A High-Rise Building Case Study[*]

Jun Wang[1], Lei Hou[1,**], Heap-Yih Chong[1], Xin Liu[1], Xiangyu Wang[1], and Jun Guo[2]

[1] Australasian Joint Research Centre for Building Information Modelling,
Curtin University, Australia
[2] CCDI Group, China
{jun.wang1,lei.hou,heapyih.chong,
xin.liu,xiangyu.wang}@curtin.edu.au,
guo.jun@ccdi.com.cn

**Abstract.** Design of localized traffic is a decision-making process for producing the viable solutions of where the parking lots, roads, entrances, exits, and the associated facilities should be built. In a traditional design case, a planner may take into account numerous factors, such as economy, constructability, geological impacts, layout constraints, connection of localized and external traffic, etc., and the process is mainly relied on a master plan and two-dimensional design drawings. Such pattern has certain limitations as these important factors can hardly be overall considered at the same time. It is promising to cope with the issues using a cooperative system where Geographic Information System (GIS) incorporates with Building Information Modelling (BIM). The research aims to optimize and evaluate the site layout for effective traffic planning based on the integrative approach of BIM and GIS. From the case study, the paper also demonstrates: 1) the approach of analyzing the statistical data to represent the existing traffic condition around the building via GIS and 2) the approach of making use of the advanced vehicle simulation models to optimizing the localized traffic facilities design, considering the possible impact of the localized traffic to the ambient traffic. Referring to the cooperative system, the bottlenecks of the initial design of parking facilities are identified, and the corresponding improvements are suggested.

**Keywords:** Traffic Planning, BIM, GIS.

# 1 Introduction

Nowadays road congestion in urban areas has been a serious problem confronting both communities and individuals. Among numerous factors that incur the issue, it is believed a lack of proper traffic planning along with the rapid development and

---

[*] The 11th International Consference on Cooperative Design, Visualization and Engineering, p. 143, 2014.
[**] Corresponding author.

Y. Luo (Ed.): CDVE 2014, LNCS 8683, pp. 143–150, 2014.

construction projects can be a critical factor. An effective planning is required to ensure efficient traffic flow and coordinate ambient traffic movements related to arrival and departure at all time, as well as ensure the users obtain the desired quality service in terms of addressing traffic demands and congestion control [1,2,3,4]. It is therefore imperative to assess the traffic conditions of a region where the building is situated, and design the ambient traffic facilities of the building, such as roads, entrances, exits and parking spaces building.

## 2    Literature Review

The traffic planning is of significant influence to the operation of modern urban transportation system. The topic regarding traffic planning has drawn a growing attention to the urban dwellers that heavily rely on automobiles for travel. Nowadays, how to address the ever-increasing traffic congestion issues has been the main research focus of numerous researchers [5]. Unfortunately, an overview of previous literatures identifies very limited approaches been produced for streamlining the traffic planning in architectural engineering, particularly in the design stage. Talking about the design of building peripheral traffic facilities, such as parking bays, roads, entrances and exits, a planner normally conducts a traditional manner, for instance, based on experience and socioeconomic data [6]. Unfortunately this may not be able to produce very effective designs along with the building settings [6]. Motivated by this fact, there is a sufficient need to pay attention to produce more promising approaches and apply these approaches as a series of effective planning support tools that can optimize the sequencing and scheduling of traffic around the architecture and minimize the congestions of vehicle between the inner and outer region.

To address the issues, it is envisaged that Building Information Modeling (BIM) is one of the promising technologies [7, 8, 9]. With BIM platform, the accurate as-planned building models and the building surroundings can be precisely digitalized and attached with all sorts of properties [10, 11, 12, 13, 14, 15,16]. The traffic planners or engineers can easily simulate the traffic conditions and flexibly play with the planning scenarios under different circumstances [17, 18, 19]. Compared with BIM, Geographic Information System (GIS) has also been tentatively researched to streamline the traffic network design and conduct spatial statistics, considering its advanced capability in spatial pattern analysis under multi-criteria [20, 21][]. GIS refers to a concept which integrates computer-based visualization and storage, aiming at better mastering the spatial information in traffic accessibility research [22]. Notwithstanding, there are more research works starting to think about how the integration of BIM and GIS can be applied to achieve the similar goal, very few research outcomes indicate effective solutions. Taking this as a starting point, the case illustration stated below innovatively presents a cooperative GIS and BIM system framework, under which the statistical data regarding the existing traffic condition can be acquired and the effective traffic planning can be conducted by comprehensively considering the possible impact of the localized traffic flow to the ambient traffic.

# 3      Case Illustration

## 3.1      Case Description

The case study aims at simulating and optimizing the site layout for effective traffic planning based on the approach of BIM and GIS. The data regarding the architecture periphery traffic were collected from Beijing City Planning Technology Centre and were used for simulation under the BIM simulation. The results of planning indicate this approach can produce effective design in addressing the current design issues. The scenario simulated is a high-rise building located in the CBD of Beijing. The architecture design for the parking facilities includes the parking paths, entries/exits of the underground parking lot, pick-up zones, and entries/exits connecting to the arteries. The layout of the design can be seen as Fig. 1. Two entries/exits of the underground parking lot are located on the parking paths of east and west sides (shown in green color). Entries/exits connecting to the arteries are designed for the north, east, and west arteries (shown in green color). And three pick-up zones are located aside the building at the north, west, and east sides (shown in blue color).

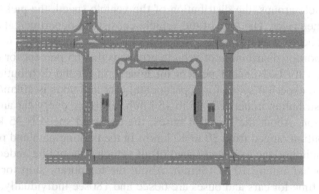

**Fig. 1.** The design of surrounding parking facilities

## 3.2      Simulation Model I/O and Parameters

One of the parameters required by the simulation model is the traffic flow, which can be analyzed and represented on the GIS platform. In this study, the average hourly traffic flow was calculated the long-term real-time monitor about the traffic conditions and the annual statistics. As of the attributes for the road network in the format of shapefile (.shp), the hourly traffic flow was symbolized on the ArcGIS [23]. The information of traffic flow from ArcGIS is able to be directly integrated with the simulation model as of the input parameters. Furthermore, to better visualize the traffic situation and make a reasonable decision to evaluate the parking facilities design, spatial analysis was applied to identify the high density of the busy traffic.

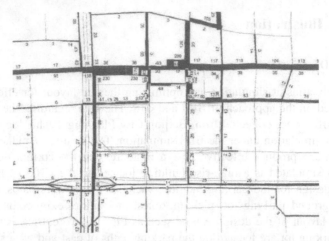

**Fig. 2.** The spatial-statistical analysis about the hourly traffic flow around the office building

For better simulating traffic flow of the office building, besides the traffic flow, other parameters considered in VISSIM system include the type of the vehicle, the consist of vehicle groups, the distribution of the vehicle speed, the pick-up time, and behaviors of the driver. The type of the vehicle consists of departmental car, bus, and taxi. They can be set with different driving patterns, paths, speeds, and temporary stop time. The proportion distribution of vehicle groups is that 65 percent for departmental cars, 34 percent for taxis, and 1 percent for buses. As for the distribution of the vehicle speed, the expected speed for departmental cars and taxis is 40km/h. And there is a normal distribution in between 35 to 45 km/h regarding every car and taxi shown in the simulation. About the speed of buses, the expected speed is 35 km/h and the normal distribution ranged from 30 to 40 km/h. In the parking path and pick-up zones of the office building, the expected speed of all vehicles should be under 15km/h and normal distributed among 10 to 18km/h. About the temporary stop for pick-up, the expected stop time for cars and buses are 60sec and 180sec individually, with normal distributed among 40 to 80sec and 120 to 240sec.

The vehicles in the simulation are generated at eight positions, 6 from the entry point of arteries, and 2 from the entry/exit of building parking facilities. Thus, the traffic flow of each entry/exit connecting arteries can be seen as follows:

- East entry: 102 PCU/h exit: 98 PCU/h
- North entry: 242 PCU/h, exit: 153 PCU/h
- West entry: 275 PCU/h, exit: 158 PCU/h

# 4    Data Analysis

As shown in Fig. 3, there is no significant bottleneck existed during the simulation. Sometimes queuing and waiting situations can happen while vehicles are going to exit the artery and enter the entry path of the building, and vice versa. But the simulation shows no seriously jam in general. With the appropriate paths, entry, and exit gates design of the building, traffic flow can be control under low vehicle speed condition, giving the circumstances that designed the paths surrounding the building are complex, and highly chances of vehicles passing over.

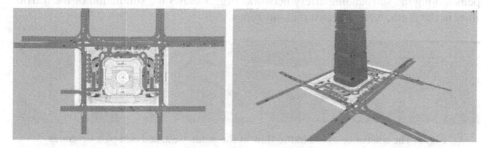

**Fig. 3.** The traffic flow simulation of the case: in (a) 2D and (b) 3D environment

According to the simulation results, there are sometimes one or two vehicles are in the queue waiting for passages at both north and west entry gates. As for the east entry gate, no waiting situation happens because of three lanes of the road and the pick-up zones are at the both side of the road. As shown in Fig. 4, waiting for driving into the arteries can happen but the queue size never bigger than three, which cannot influence to the entire traffic flow among each path and artery surrounding the building. This proved that it is useful to set up multiple entry and exit paths.

**Fig. 4.** The waiting queue of vehicles entering artery

The parking paths surrounding the building are designed in both one-way and two-way. One-way path can apparently avoid the potential conflicts when vehicles are passing over. Two-way path can guarantee the convenience of connecting parking facilitate and surrounding arteries. From the results of simulation, the rate of serviceability of every parking path is high in average. It will sometimes decrease at the intersections of the paths and arteries, because the speed of vehicles is decreased and queue existed.

Due to the features of an office building, 50 percent of vehicles which enter the parking paths and pick-up zones are going to leave in a short duration once they finish their pick-up missions. The potential bottlenecks may exist when there is not enough space for pick-up zones. So the simulation also target on evaluating the utilization rate of the pick-up zones. The results show that there is approximately 60 percent of utilization on the pick-up zones in despite of queues may sometimes exist in the north and west pick-up zones. It provides highly serviceability for this case. And no jam happens among the surrounding artery network. Fig. 5 shows the simulation of the traffic flow in the north, west, and east pick-up zones.

**Fig. 5.** The simulation of the traffic flow in the north, west, and east pick-up zones

The simulation results show that the serviceability rate of the intersections on the north main artery is slight lower than that of the intersections on the south. The traffic flow of the artery and serviceability are two factors significantly influencing how smooth the vehicles arrive and leave the office building. In general, the traffic conditions on the intersections during simulations are all acceptable considering the influences of the office building and its connecting paths. Fig. 6 shows the traffic conditions of the north-east and north-west intersections of the office building.

**Fig. 5.** The traffic conditions of the artery intersections surrounding the office building

## 5     Conclusion

The simulation results of the office building and its parking paths and pick-up zones design indicate that the parking paths and pick-up zones design fulfilled the design requirements. The traffic conditions surrounding the office building are smooth in general. The serviceability rates of every functional facilitate are all within an acceptable range, including that of pick-up zones, interactions between parking paths and arteries, and intersections between arteries. These results show that the design requirements have been achieved based on the cooperative system of BIM and GIS. The design requirement of the building will significantly influence the traffic conditions of the surrounding area. In the simulation, there are queues existed sometimes in the entry/exit points of parking paths and arteries, so does the pick-up zones in the north and east of the building. This prediction is made considering high utilization rate of the bus, which means the traffic conditions could be worst once the rate has decreased. Potential jam can still happen between parking facilities and surrounding arteries of the building. The traffic flow of the north main artery needs further examinations. As a key traffic and main evacuation way of the building, the precise information about the traffic flow of the north main artery is necessary, to guarantee the accuracy of the simulation. Once the traffic condition has changed for the artery, bottlenecks could existed and weaken how smooth the traffic flow between parking paths and surrounding arteries.

**Acknowledgement.** Acknowledgement goes to CITIC Real Estate and CCDI Group, which provided the BIM models, project information presented in this paper, and the contributed time of their experts to the research and developmental work that have been described and presented in this paper.

# References

1. Managing Urban Traffic Congestion, http://www.transportstrategygroup.com
2. Jain, R.: Congestion Control and Traffic Management in ATM Networks: Recent Advances and a Survey. Computer Networks and ISDN Systems 28(13), 1723–1738 (1996)
3. Cheng, M.Y., Yang, S.C.: GIS-based Cost Estimates Integrating with Material Layout Planning. Journal of Construction Engineering and Management 127, 291–299 (2001)
4. Ma, Z., Shen, Q., Zhang, J.: Application of 4D for Dynamic Site Layout and Management of Construction Projects. Automation in Construction 14(3), 369–381 (2005)
5. Chiu, Y.C., Zhou, X., Hernandez, J.: Evaluating Urban Downtown One-way to Two-way Street Conversion using Multiple Resolution Simulation and Assignment Approach. Journal of Urban Planning and Development 133(4), 222–232 (2007)
6. Bustillos, B.I., Shelton, J., Chiu, Y.C.: Urban University Campus Transportation and Parking Planning through a Dynamic Traffic Simulation and Assignment Approach. Transportation Planning and Technology 34(2), 177–197 (2011)
7. Wang, Y., Wang, X., Wang, J., Yung, P., Jun, G.: Engagement of Facilities Management in Design Stage through BIM: Framework and a Case Study. Advances in Civil Engineering (2013)
8. Park, C.S., Lee, D.Y., Kwon, O.S., Wang, X.: A Framework for Proactive Construction Defect Management using BIM, Augmented Reality and Ontology-based Data Collection Template. Automation in Construction 33, 61–71 (2013)

9. Wang, X., Love, P.: BIM+ AR: Onsite Information Sharing and Communication via Advanced Visualization. Paper presented at the 2012 IEEE 16th International Conference on Computer Supported Cooperative Work in Design (2012)
10. Wang, X., Truijens, M., Hou, L., Wang, Y., Zhou, Y.: Integrating Augmented Reality with Building Information Modeling: Onsite construction process controlling for liquefied natural gas industry. Automation in Construction 40, 96–105 (2013)
11. Wang, X., Love, P.E., Kim, M.J., Park, C.-S., Sing, C.P., Hou, L.: A Conceptual Framework for Integrating Building Information Modeling with Augmented Reality. Automation in Construction 34, 37–44 (2013)
12. Kovacic, I., Oberwinter, L., Müller, C., Achammer, C.: The BIM-sustain Experiment–simulation of BIM-supported Multi-disciplinary Design. Visualization in Engineering 1(1), 1–11 (2013)
13. Zhu, Z., Donia, S.: Spatial and Visual Data Fusion for Capturing, Retrieval, and Modeling of As-built Building Geometry and Features. Visualization in Engineering 1(1), 1–10 (2013)
14. Shin, D.H., Dunston, P.S., Wang, X.: View Changes in Mixed Reality-based Collaborative Virtual Environments. ACM Transactions on Applied Perception, Association for Computing Machinery (ACM) 2(1), 1–14 (2005)
15. Wang, X.: Using Augmented Reality to Plan Virtual Construction Worksite. International Journal of Advanced Robotic Systems 4(4), 501–512 (2007)
16. Wang, X., Schnabel, M.A.: Mixed Reality in Architecture, Design, and Construction. Springer (2009) ISBN: 978-1-4020-9087-5
17. Zhang, C., Zhao, K., Li, J.Q.: BIM Application Analysis in Transportation Project. Advanced Materials Research 671, 2986–2989 (2013)
18. Cho, A.: Document Building Information Modeling Boosters are Crossing That Bridge. ENR (Engineering News-Record) 263(5), 28–29 (2009)
19. Hammond, R.: BIM Transportation Sector: LiDAR and Mobile Mapping
20. Berglund, S.: GIS in transport modelling. Royal Institute of Technology, Department of Infrastructure. Report, 2001 (2013)
21. Keshkamat, S., Looijen, J., Zuidgeest, M.: The Formulation and Evaluation of Transport Route Planning Alternatives: a Spatial Decision Support System for the Via Baltica Project, Poland. Journal of Transport Geography 17(1), 54–64 (2009)
22. Maguire, D.J., Goodchiled, M., Rhinds, D.: An Overview and Definition of GIS. In: Geographical Information Systems: Principals and Applications, pp. 9–20 (1991)
23. ESRI Inc. ArcGIS. Redlands (2013)

# An Environment to Foster Scientific Collaborations

Tatiana P.V. Alves, Marcos R.S. Borges, and Adriana S. Vivacqua

Graduate Program in Informatics (PPGI),
Federal University of Rio de Janeiro (UFRJ),
Rio de Janeiro, RJ, Brazil
`tatiana.pimentel@ufrj.br`,
`{mborges,avivacqua}@dcc.ufrj.br`

**Abstract.** Collaboration is an integral part of modern scientific research. It is hard to imagine any modern scientific endeavor that does not involve a group of people. However, collaboration is frequently constrained to close partners or proximal groups. Finding new potential partners with whom to exchange ideas is an important step in establishing new working groups. We propose to use automated system to recommend potential collaborators, and present a system for this purpose. One of the problems involved is establishing criteria to select these potential partners. We address this issue by (1) automatically constructing users profiles from publicly available data to establish areas of expertise and (2) employing an analysis of users' networks to select partners with the potential for fruitful relationships.

**Keywords:** collaboration, social network analysis, group recommendation.

## 1 Introduction

Cooperation among researchers is in high demand by institutions and funding agencies. Nowadays, scientific production requires associations, negotiation, strategies and a varied skill set to come to fruition. Multidisciplinary research requires the interconnection of different knowledge, which usually involves work by individuals from different domains to generate new knowledge [1]. Knowledge generation is driven by common goals between researchers, who join forces, share information and apply their skills [2]. Additionally, joint work reduces time and resources [3].

Collaboration happens usually among researchers who already have some degree of social proximity, such as working in the same university or having common contacts, for instance. Establishing connections between geographically distant researchers (especially those located in different countries) is still hard. Researchers are frequently unaware of others' work even though they might work in the same research area. This may lead to the duplication of efforts, instead of cooperation converging towards one result. Even worse are the cases of lack of awareness of others within the same research group.

There is a need to bring researchers closer, especially those who work in the same research group. This means making introductions, looking to create new relations,

Y. Luo (Ed.): CDVE 2014, LNCS 8683, pp. 151–158, 2014.

independent of their physical locations. Given a virtual proximity, researchers should be able to discover new affinities, exchange ideas and start actual collaborative work.

Scientific collaboration happens in many ways [4]. They may be indirect interactions between scientists, informal meetings, discussions at conferences or exchange of ideas over a meal, for instance. Thus, scientific interaction does not present itself solely as co-authorship of research papers. These casual interactions are more free form and may generate valuable ideas for innovative research and exchange of information. In this paper, we present an environment for social combination and interaction, which helps users find peers and engage in informal interaction. Through the analysis of prior work and the application of specific rules, we suggest potential partners. The environment supports informal interaction, in order to jump start collaboration.

This paper is organized as follows: in the next section, we present background research on which this work is based. In section 3, we present the CollPesq environment, followed by a case study. We finalize with a discussion in Section 5.

## 2      Background

Studies about Scientific Collaboration are plentiful. However, due to the large variety of domains and work styles, there is no consensus regarding the ideal way to engage in cooperative work. Cooperative arrangements might be made between scientists, universities or countries, and each one entails a different style, as a function not only of the parties involved, but also of the knowledge domains in which it happens. Scientific collaboration can be defined as joint work conducted by researchers with a common goal of producing new scientific knowledge [4].

Besides producing scientific knowledge, interaction among researchers is also sought after to facilitate the execution of tasks [5], as parties involved may divide activities according to their specialties or affinity with the subject at hand. This usually leads to a reduction in time needed to obtain results. Scientific collaboration is an intrinsically personal process, tied to human communication forma to enact communication and share competencies and resources. When individuals collaborate, there is a natural exchange of resources, be they knowledge, material or financial. Given these definitions, we note that scientific collaboration is a social interaction process, which brings researchers with common interests closer to each other, with a common goal of producing new knowledge and making contributions to science [6].

In [4], Katz e Martin studied how close researchers have to work to become collaborators. Researchers may be physically close but not interact for a lack of common interests. In reverse, researchers from different countries may be strong collaborators. Modern network and communications technologies have made this easier than ever. These studies indicate that a common research interest, within a domain of expertise is a strong motivator for collaboration.

Connections between researchers' ideas are established through informal social interaction [7], and studies are being conducted to better understand what motivates researchers to collaborate with one person as opposed to another. A worldwide research network, COLLNET (*Collaboration in Science and Technology*) [8], has been established to study the different aspects of scientific collaboration and how it presents itself in the distinct knowledge areas.

## 2.1    Recommender and Social Combination Systems

Recommender systems are systems which seek to provide to a user information he or she may need, according to some strategy. They are similar to personal recommendations, where individuals take into account the opinions of others who have some knowledge on a given domain [9]. Many recommendation systems use social relations to help a user find/select among a set of options. One of the challenges in the construction of recommendation systems is creating the recommendation strategy that will lead to the correspondence between what the user wants and what is suggested to him or her. Most systems identify the user, construct a profile, saving their choices and preferences and recommend items based on these [10].

Social matching systems are a particular type of recommender system, one that brings people together based on individuals' personal characteristics such as competencies, skills or interests [11]. These systems seek to establish relationships between people, and have four phases:

1. Modeling: construction of preference databases and user models.
2. Combination: matching of users according to (1) explicit user requisitions or (2) implicit opportunities identified by the system.
3. Introduction: bringing users together, according to matches made in the previous step. This only happens when one of the users considers the suggested matches to be interesting.
4. Interaction: this phase will only happen when there is a mutual interest (both users find the match interesting). Users will then interact according to their interests and available media.

Our proposed environment follows this process to create social recommendations of individuals with given expertise. In the next section, we present the CollPesQ environment and how it supports each of these four phases.

## 3    An Environment for Scientific Social Matcing

Our research fits into social matching for *Information Needs*, where users need some information and search for experts in the topic at hand [11]. In these situations, users wish not only to find someone with a given expertise, but also someone trustworthy, with whom they might collaborate. Finding individuals to recommend is not a simple task.

The CollPesQ environment builds on the principle that individuals who participate in a research group will have common interests and possibly work in cooperation. Individuals have a tendency to collaborate with others who are close and have similar research areas. Prior research has shown that physical proximity plays a part in the establishment of collaboration [12]. We corroborated these findings through a preliminary study conducted with potential system users. Following this research, the environment offers mechanisms to help users identify and approach potential collaborators. It takes into account academic characteristics of each individual, based on information about publications, research projects, courses taught and student committees, among others. The environment has three main functionalities:

1. *User profile construction*: this involves load user data from standard databases and integrating information from different sources about each user's activities.
2. *Collaborator discovery*: in this phase, the system attempts to match individuals following available data and information needs. It takes as input a querying user and an information need and searches for matches, providing an explanation as to why they are being suggested.
3. *User interaction*: the system provides functionality to jump start interaction, which is the first step towards establishing a collaborative relationship.

In the following sections, we delve deeper into the proposed solution and how it works.

## 3.1     Construction of Researcher Profiles

The CollPesQ environment works with data about users academic life, originating from official resumes and consolidated organizational systems data. It currently uses two official governmental sources:

- DataCAPES [13], an annual report each graduate program must provide to Brazilian governmental funding agencies; and
- LATTES [14], the country's official research curriculum vitae system, where researchers report all of their work.

Bootstrapping is a major problem in recommender systems, so we chose to preload the system with these data. It should be noted that other sources could be used, such as DBLP [15] and other publication databases or manual input. Data is extracted from these sources and added to the system database, where it is used to create each user's research profile and network. This information provides not only information about a user's current expertise and work domains, but also about his or her collaborators and acquaintances.

Expertise areas are extracted from these data through the use of text mining techniques. Titles and keywords for papers and thesis, syllabi for courses taught and titles and project descriptions, for instance, are solid indicators of research themes, as they comprise the body of work for a researcher. Besides these data, the system also maps the relations between researchers.

Additional data analysis is conducted over these data to construct each researcher's academic network. These are established through the identification of joint authorship, co-participation in thesis committees, co-participation in projects, participation in courses and the like. These will help establish the network of research acquaintances for each user. Five criteria help establish these relationships and build each user's research network (Fig. 1):

- *Supervision-based relationship (student/supervisor)*
- *Project-based relationships (may be two participants in the same project or coordination/participant)*
- *Publication-based relationships (co-authorship)*
- *Committee-based relationships (co-participation in qualifying or thesis examinations committees)*
- *Course based-relationships (either two students taking the same course or teacher/student relationship)*

Potential partners are pulled from the pool of researchers in a users' extended network. When looking for new partners, the system will search for those with whom a user has not yet published papers.

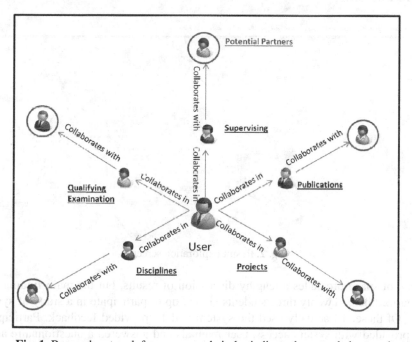

**Fig. 1.** Research network for a user - red circles indicate the extended network

## 3.2     Searching for Collaborators with the CollPesQ System

Some heuristics were created for the search for matches. First, co-authorship is a strong signifier that two individuals already collaborate: a research publication is the result of their collaboration. Therefore, co-authors are never recommended as potential collaborators, as the system attempts to pair up individuals who might otherwise be unaware of each other. Similarly, a supervision relationship already denotes joint work, even if no papers have been published yet.. The types of collaboration mentioned before are color coded in the results, to help with the navigation of the network and identification of potential collaborators. This way, the user can know why a

certain individual is being suggested as a potential collaborator, which should help
with the decision of whether or not to contact them.

The CollPesQ system's main goal is to help users find others with whom they may
want to start to collaborate. Thus, users may start this process by providing keywords
to guide the search. To reduce the number of results, only individuals one hop away
from the user (one degree of separation distant) who are not current collaborators (no
co-authors or supervisors) and whose expertise matches the desired keywords are
potential partners. Results are color coded to indicate the origin of the link, which
helps users evaluate whether or not to contact each person. Fig. 2 shows a screenshot
of the result exploration screen.

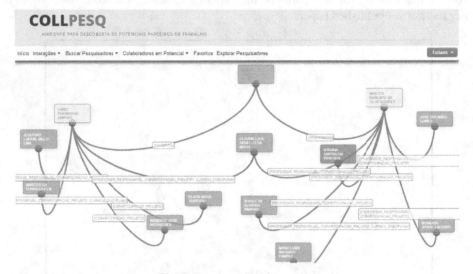

**Fig. 2.** Result exploration screen

Lack of space precludes a lengthy discussion of results, but the main findings are
summarized here. Twenty three students signed up to participate in a study of system
usage. Of these, 18 actually used the system and 12 provided feedback. Participants
were provided with system access, user manuals and answered a questionnaire at the
end of a few day usage of the system.

The majority of users found the system useful, and was satisfied with the recommendations received. The ones who weren't were those whose information was not in
the database, which reduced the utility of recommendations. They saw the system as a
way to increase interaction between researchers, and especially liked one of the system's features, a "favorites" tag, which allows a user to bookmark his or her preferred
potential collaborators for later reference. This action is later used by the system to
perfect profiles and matching. In addition, the environment features a messaging system to allow initial contact between researchers after matches have been suggested.
These interactions are also taken into account to perfect the profiles and matching
system.

# 4    Discussion

Scientific knowledge is in constant evolution, with new developments happening frequently. Researchers must be able to follow these changes and deal with increasingly complex problems. Research is now more interdisciplinary and involves several individuals working together. Thus, individuals must seek collaborators, and finding the right people is sometimes a difficult task.

We present an environment for scientific social matching, based on analyses researchers curricula and interests. The search strategy uses the researcher's work network, using current collaborators as bridges to find new ones. Using this network has an advantage in that there is a social contract already in place. Theoretically, individuals will not want to create a negative impression with their new collaborators, as it might affect their existing relations (with the bridge individual). This social accountability could potentially lead to better collaboration, as both parties strive to maintain their existing relations. This point deserves further investigation, which is possible now that the system is in place.

In addition, Social Network theory provides concepts that may be applied in this case. In particular, the definition of strong and weak ties may prove useful. First defined by Granovetter in 1973, the strength of ties depends on the level of interaction between participants [16]. While these concepts were first introduced prior to the internet, they can be adapted to this situation. In our case, we consider that strong ties are those that involve frequent interaction and joint work. Thus, both supervision and co-authorship characterize the existence of strong ties between parties. Courses and committees by themselves are not enough to characterize strong ties, we therefore consider them to be an indication of a weak tie. Project relationships are harder to determine, so we consider them a mid-level tie, in between strong and weak. in addition, ties between participants can have an implied hierarchy: courses, supervision and projects are indicative of a hierarchical distinction between parties (project coordinator vs participant; course instructor vs student, supervisor vs student.) These elements are under study for incorporation for the next iteration of this research. A combination of these properties could be used to drive the search for collaborators. Weights could be assigned for the links between individuals, providing scores to rank the suggestions. This is currently under implementation And studies will be conducted to ascertain the combination or elements that will yield the best results.

With the CollPesQ project we have taken a first step towards an environment for social matching in academia. Initial feedback has been good and we expect to make it more widely available soon. One shortcoming is that it currently only works with the Brazilian standardized curricula formats. We are implementing links to other sources (e.g., DBLP) to enrich the dataset. This will also open up possibilities for the design of new algorithms and matching strategies, which should yield even better results.

**Acknowledgements.** Marcos R.S. Borges and Adriana S. Vivacqua are supported by grants from CNPq and FAPERJ. Tatiana Pimentel was supported by a CAPES scholarship.

# References

1. Silva, E.L.: Rede científica e a construção do conhecimento. Informação e Sociedade: Estudos 12(1), 120–148 (2002)
2. Balancieri, R.: The analysis of scientific collaboration networks under new information and communication technologies: a study of the Lattes Platform. Ciência da Informação 34(1), 64–77 (2005) (in Portuguese)
3. Maia, M.F.S., Caregnato, S.E.: Co-authorship as an indicator of scientific collaboration networks. Perspectivas em Ciência da Informação 13(2), 18–31 (2008) (in Portuguese)
4. Katz, J.S., Martin, B.R.: What is research collaboration? Research Policy 26, 1–18 (1997)
5. Sonnenwald, D.H.: Scientific Collaboration. Annual Review of Information Science and Technology 42(1), 643–681 (2008)
6. Vanz, S.A.S., Stumpf, I.R.C.: Scientific Collaboration: conceptual and theoretical review. Perspectivas em Ciência da Informação 15(2), 42–55 (2010) (in Portuguese)
7. Ziman, J.M.: Public Knowledge, p. 164. Itatiaia, Ed. da USP, Belo Horizonte, São Paulo (1979) (in Portuguese)
8. COLLNET - Collaboration Network, http://www.collnet.de/ (last accessed February 2014)
9. Cazella, S.C., Nunes, M.A.S.N., Reategui, E.B.: Science of Opinion: state of the art of recommender systems. In: XXX Congresso da SBC Jornada de Atualização da Informática, Porto Alegre, Brasil, vol. 52, p. 146 (2010) (in Portuguese)
10. Motta, C.L.R., Garcia, A.C.B., Vivacqua, A.S., Santoro, F.M., Sampaio, J.O.: Reccomendation Systems. In: Pimentel, M., Fuks, H. (eds.) Sistemas Colaborativos, p. 416. Elsevier, Rio de Janeiro (2011) (in Portuguese)
11. Terveen, L., McDonald, D.W.: Social Matching: A Framework and Research Agenda. ACM Transactions on Computer Human Interaction 12(3), 401–434 (2005)
12. Olson, G.M., Olson, J.S.: Distance Matters. Journal of Human Computer Interaction 15(2) (September 2000)
13. Coleta de dados CAPES, http://www.capes.gov.br/avaliacao/coleta-de-dados/ (last accessed February 2014)
14. Plataforma LATTES, http://lattes.cnpq.br (last acessed November 2011)
15. DBLP - Digital Bibliography and Library Project, http://www.informatik.unitrier.de/~ley/db/index.html (last accessed May 2014)
16. Granovetter, M.S.: The Strength of Weak Ties. The American Journal of Sociology 78(6), 1360–1380 (1973)

# Supporting Collaborative Decision in Architectural Design with Synchronous Collocated 4D Simulation and Natural User Interactions

Conrad Boton[1,2], Gilles Halin[2], and Sylvain Kubicki[1,2]

[1] Public Research Centre Henri Tudor, 29, avenue JF Kennedy,
L-1855, Luxembourg-Kirchberg
[2] CRAI - Research Centre in Architecture and Engineering,
2, rue Bastien Lepage, 54001 Nancy, France
gilles.halin@crai.archi.fr,
{conrad.boton,sylvain.kubicki}@tudor.lu

**Abstract.** The work presented in this paper is part of a more comprehensive one which aims to propose appropriate natural user interactions to support collaborative decision making in synchronous 4D simulation. It presents the issue and previous works on natural user interfaces in 4D simulation. It also introduces a first prototype and a 4D case study from a real construction site.

**Keywords:** CSCW, 4D simulation, Human-Computer Interfaces, Natural User Interaction, Decision support, Architecture, Engineering and Construction, Collaborative 4D.

## 1 Introduction

According to Kvan, "in discussions about computer systems for collaborative design, their behaviours, specifications and implementation, the most fundamental arguments appear to be encountered on the issues of interaction" [9]. This is about both the interaction between participants and the interaction with the systems, and the issue have been well discussed in related literature [9, 10, 12]. But during the last decade, new devices (smartphones, tablets, digital tabletops, etc.) are appearing with new interaction capabilities. Construction practitioners are increasingly using such devices including, in addition to common mobile devices, the VCE [13], the TATIN [1], the ValueLab [7], and the iRoom [6]. Because of the diversity of innovative devices, it is important to take into account the novel interaction mechanisms they provide users with.

## 2 Previous Works on Natural User Interfaces in 4D Simulation

In the line of Building Information Modeling (BIM) approaches, collaborative 4D simulation is being increasingly used to visually simulate the construction process in

Y. Luo (Ed.): CDVE 2014, LNCS 8683, pp. 159–162, 2014.

order to detect constructability inconsistencies in the planning or in the design [3]. 4D simulation consists in linking a 3D model to the construction activities planning (time) to simulate the construction process over time [11]. In synchronous 4D simulation, all collaborative work participants are working on the 4D model at the same place at the same time [3]. If the interaction with 3D models has been extensively discussed in the literature, the interaction principles with the fourth dimension are much less studied [4, 8].

After Command Line Interfaces and Graphical User Interfaces, the last evolution in the Human-Computer Interaction paradigm lies in Natural User Interfaces (NUI). NUI reuse the human capabilities, behaviors and gestures to interact with IT systems [2]. NUI are not really new in 4D simulation. In 2002, Waly and Thabet proposed a virtual construction environment (VCE) for pre-construction planning [13]. They introduced an Interactive Virtual Interface (IVI) where users can graphically "drag and drop" elements from the 3D model and rebuild the building by putting side by side the components in the order received for the actual construction. The IVI offers intuitive and interesting interaction mechanisms such as 'click to take' or 'release to place' or 'navigate to the walk through' [13].

## 3    A NUI me-fi Prototype to Support Collaborative 4D Decision

In Human-Computer Interfaces design, "prototype fidelity expresses the similarity between the final user interface and the prototyped UI" [5]. Medium-fidelity (me-fi) tools "support designing UI mock-ups giving more importance to the contents than the style with which these contents are presented" [5]. The proposed prototype is composed of:

-    A digital tabletop (Fig. 1c), used to display the 3D model, allowing all participants to visualize the model and providing the designer with appropriate natural interaction to make changes on the model (using a CAD software);
-    4 digital tablets (Fig 1a), used to display the planning, allowing each practitioner to make changes on his part of the planning. The validations performed by Zaidi [14] on lo-fi prototypes showed that interactions with the 3D model on tablets are not useful and actors prefer to interact with 3D on the tabletop;
-    A whiteboard (Fig. 1b), used as viewer, displaying the 4D model resulting from the 3D model and the planning sequences.

The prototype business scenario is based on a case study from a real construction site in Luxembourg. The studied detail is about the construction sequence of wooden wall which is built through many steps with various subcontractors (woodwork, insulation, and cladding). Moreover windows have to be installed during and after the assembly of the wall itself. A smooth coordination among actors is then necessary to drill accurate reservations within walls and to ensure that the openings on the wall fit the windows dimensions. A 4D simulation for this case study showed that it is possible to involve at the early construction stage the sub-contractors in the

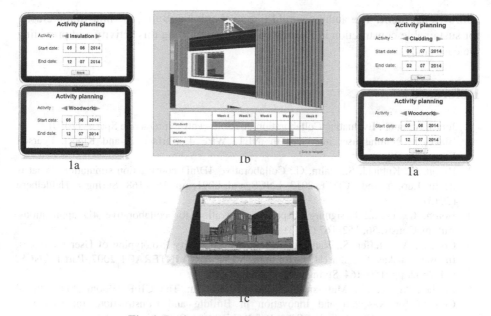

**Fig. 1.** Devices composing the Me-Fi prototype

construction process planning, and to provide them with a visual support in order to interact with the model and to find out the optimal construction sequences.

On the technical level, a built-in screen is integrated to the tabletop. This screen is multitouch and at least 12 points. A 4D software is implemented on the tabletop in order to manipulate the 3D/4D model with multitouch gestures. The digital tablets are connected to the tabletop and the via Wi-Fi connection.

The research project is still at its beginning and experimentations are planned to be conducted in architecture and engineering agencies. Such experimentations will be studied by some psychologists and specialists in ergonomics in order evaluate the usefulness and the usability of the proposed prototype for collective decision making supported by 4D models in a synchronous and collocated environment.

# 4    Conclusion and Future Works

In this paper, we presented the very first steps of an ongoing comprehensive work which aims at supporting collaborative decision making in architectural design with synchronous collocated 4D simulation and Natural User Interfaces. A first prototype and a 4D case study from a real construction site are introduced. These elements provide a good basis to understand the research project approach. Future works will validate the proposed prototype in the line of the business case. It will then be possible to propose a real NUI-based collocated and synchronous 4D system, according to the prototype.

**Aknowledgement.** The authors would like to thank NeoBuild, the innovation cluster for sustainable construction in Luxembourg, for supporting this activity and providing the case study.

# References

1. Jones, A., et al.: Evaluating Collaboration in Table-centric Interactive Spaces (2010)
2. Blake, J.: Natural user interfaces in .NET. WPF 4, Surface 2, and Kinect. Pearson Education (2012)
3. Boton, C., Kubicki, S., Halin, G.: Collaborative 4D/nD construction simulation: What is it? In: Luo, Y. (ed.) CDVE 2013. LNCS, vol. 8091, pp. 161–168. Springer, Heidelberg (2013)
4. Boton, C., et al.: Designing adapted visualization for collaborative 4D applications. Autom. Constr. 36, 152–167 (2013)
5. Coyette, A., Kieffer, S., Vanderdonckt, J.: Multi-fidelity Prototyping of User Interfaces. In: Baranauskas, C., Abascal, J., Barbosa, S.D.J. (eds.) INTERACT 2007, Part I. LNCS, vol. 4662, pp. 150–164. Springer, Heidelberg (2007)
6. Fischer, M., et al.: Multi-stakeholder collaboration: The CIFE iRoom. International Council for Research and Innovation in Buildig and Construction. In: CIB w78 Conference, pp. 12–14. Aarhus School of Architecture (2002)
7. Halatsch, J., et al.: Value Lab: a Collaborative Environment for the Planning of Future Cities. In: eCAADe 2008, pp. 507–514 (2008)
8. Halin, G., Kubicki, S., Boton, C., Zignale, D.: From collaborative business practices to user's adapted visualization services: Towards a usage-centered method dedicated to the AEC sector. In: Luo, Y. (ed.) CDVE 2011. LNCS, vol. 6874, pp. 145–153. Springer, Heidelberg (2011)
9. Kvan, T.: Collaborative design: what is it? Autom. Constr. 9(4), 409–415 (2000)
10. Lahti, H., et al.: Collaboration patterns in computer supported collaborative designing. Des. Stud. 25(4), 351–371 (2004)
11. McKinney, K., et al.: Interactive 4D-CAD. In: Proceedings of the third Congress on Computing in Civil Engineering, Anaheim, CA, USA, pp. 383–389 (1996)
12. Plume, J., Mitchell, J.: Collaborative design using a shared IFC building model—Learning from experience. Autom. Constr. 16(1), 28–36 (2007)
13. Waly, A.F., Thabet, W.Y.: A Virtual Construction Environment for preconstruction planning. Autom. Constr. 12, 139–154 (2002)
14. Zaidi, F.: Identification des usages et interactions de la 4D collaborative synchrone exploitant une interface utilisateur naturelle. Mémoire de master, Nancy (2013)

# Collaborative Annotation
# of Multimedia Resources

Pierrick Bruneau[1], Mickaël Stefas[1], Mateusz Budnik[2], Johann Poignant[2],
Hervé Bredin[3], Thomas Tamisier[1], and Benoît Otjacques[1]

[1] Public Research Centre - Gabriel Lippmann, 41 rue du Brill, L-4422 Belvaux,
Luxembourg
[2] LIG CNRS UMR 5217, BP 53, F-38041 Grenoble Cedex 9, France
[3] LIMSI-CNRS, BP 133, F-91403 Orsay, France

**Abstract.** Reference multimedia corpora for use in automated indexing
algorithms require lots of manual work. The Camomile project advocates
the joint progress of automated annotation methods and tools for improving the benchmark resources. This paper shows some work in progress in
interactive visualization of annotations, and perspectives in harnessing
the collaboration between manual annotators, algorithm designers, and
benchmark administrators.

**Keywords:** multimedia annotation, interactive visualization, collaborative annotation

## 1 Introduction

Wide amounts of multimedia data are accessible over the Internet, but for efficient search and retrieval, those have to be properly annotated. Such annotations
can also be useful for improving the user experience in the context of multimedia content consumption. However, the growing pace of these data are largely
exceeding the abilities of manual annotators: automated means are thus needed.

The Camomile project fosters the development of tools for the Multi-modal
and Multi-language processing of Multimedia content (often gathered under
the acronym MMM in this domain). This naturally includes contributing to
the state-of-the-art of content-based multimedia indexing algorithms. But the
project also considers tools for facilitating the constitution of realistic and reliable benchmark resources, thus favoring a general improvement of the contributed literature.

This paper presents on-going work, with a focus on perspectives for the latter
aspect. Section 2 shortly introduces the data framework designed for the project,
and overviews first results on the use of interactive visualization to support
the error analysis of indexing algorithms. Then in Section 3, we consider the
perspective of extending this fine-grained task to the context of multiple manual
annotators and algorithm designers, that collaborate in the dual objective of
improving the quality of both algorithms and the benchmark resources they are
evaluated on.

Y. Luo (Ed.): CDVE 2014, LNCS 8683, pp. 163–166, 2014.
© Springer International Publishing Switzerland 2014

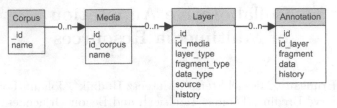

(a) Entity-relation diagram of the annotation data.

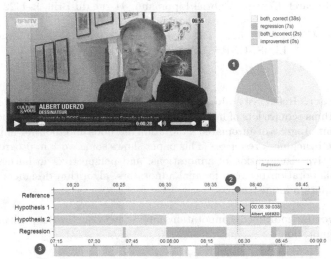

(b) Overview of the visual tools for algorithmic results analysis. *1)* Summary statistics displayed in a pie-chart view. *2)*
Synchronization of the video playback with an interactive annotation timeline. A tooltip shows the annotation data underlying glyph colors. *3)* A context line shows the summary of all
loaded layers, and supports brushing interactions. The time
scales are updated interactively.

**Fig. 1.** Data framework and visual tool in the Camomile project

## 2    Visual Analysis of Algorithmic Results

Annotations can be summarized as any kind of metadata affecting a fragment
(with respect to space or time) in a given medium. For the discussion in this
paper, we restrict to speaker (i.e., who speaks) and face (i.e., who is seen) annotations in video media, materialized by temporal fragments.

With a view to scale up the processing of benchmark corpora and associated
algorithmic results, a general data framework (see Figure 1(a)) was implemented
using NoSQL storage technologies. This design facilitates its further use and
extension for a variety of clients, including mere web browsers. It logically stores
annotations in a nested structure, gathering annotations in layers, and ultimately
referring to *corpora*, i.e. benchmark databases.

Speech and video recognition practitioners are primarily concerned by the design of effective automatic indexing algorithms [2]. They classically assess the quality of their algorithms by aggregated quality metrics w.r.t. a benchmark database.

Taking advantage of the data framework evoked in Figure 1(a), and inspiration from tools such as Advene [1], we recently proposed to use visual and interactive tools to allow a finer analysis of algorithmic results [3] (see Figure 1(b)). With the joint use of timeline and pie-chart views, practitioners can perform the differential analysis of their algorithmic results w.r.t. the benchmark.

In the machine learning literature, algorithms are generally compared to what is often called a *ground truth*, the veracity of which not being questioned. As for automatic annotation, benchmark databases are the result of the intensive manual work of many annotators, and errors are likely to occur in the reference layers used by algorithm designers. Actually, in annotation challenges such as REPERE [5], the *adjudication* step is specially dedicated to debunk potential mistakes highlighted by users of the benchmark [4].

The next section discusses the current perspectives in the project, where multiple manual annotators and algorithms can be considered, with referees filtering the notifications issued by algorithm designers (further known as *adjudicators*).

## 3   Perspectives in Collaborative Support

In a first stage, the tools presented in the previous section could be extended for the notification of errors in reference annotation layers. Algorithms may occasionally recover the actual ground truth, that was not correctly annotated in the benchmark reference. This capability could be exploited, through the definition of a specialized kind of layer, allowing algorithm designers to highlight the suspected error in the reference. Its visual restitution could emphasize this information, facilitating the decision process by the adjudicator.

We could also add full editing functionalities to the current tool. But taken independently, this feature retains the usual, long, and error-prone annotation sessions, just solving for a more efficient way of distributing the workload. In itself this can be seen as a notable improvement w.r.t. the current, completely manual, procedure, but we decided to aim at a more ambitious target, and harness such distributed editing functionalities towards a greater integration of learning, visualization, and interaction with the data.

Classical automated indexing algorithms proceed in a *supervised* fashion: a predictor is trained to minimize its errors on media where the annotations are known *a priori*. This way of proceeding is demanding in manual annotation effort. Alternatively, *active learning* [6] starts from a completely unlabeled setting, and selects elements to be annotated iteratively, so as to reduce the uncertainty of the model at the current step. We propose to combine this approach with the data framework and visual tools respectively evoked by Figures 1(a) and 1(b). An active learning algorithm could feed a waiting queue of video segments to be annotated in a server. Manual annotators could then process this workload in a distributed fashion. From the interactive point of view, the required research pertains to providing an adequate context for annotators, so that they make informed decisions, and appropriate controls to reduce the noise of annotations (e.g. dynamic dictionary of named entities in the case of speaker annotations).

Another important direction of research regards findings relevant visualization and interaction metaphors at the corpus scale. Adjudicators could for example inspect and filter the corpus for relevant statistics, navigate in the history of actions taken by all annotators and algorithms, or estimate the annotation coverage currently achieved. Possibilities of integrating the active learning paradigm in the shape of a visual data mining tool, where the algorithm designer and the annotator use a visual abstraction of the currently learned model, both for picking new elements to annotate, and understanding the ongoing learning process, could also be sought.

## 4    Conclusion

This paper summarized work in progress in the context of the Camomile project. Shortly recalled here, a low-granularity visual tool has already been proposed to support the analysis of errors made by annotation algorithms. We then drew perspectives on scaling up the analysis, and harnessing machine learning and collaborative interactions between involved actors using visual tools.

**Acknowledgments.** This work was done in the context of the CHIST-ERA CAMOMILE project funded by the ANR (Agence Nationale de la Recherche, France) and the FNR (Fonds National de la Recherche, Luxembourg).

## References

1. Aubert, O., Prié, Y.: Advene: active reading through hypervideo. In: ACM Conference on Hypertext and Hypermedia, pp. 235–244 (2005)
2. Bredin, H., et al.: Fusion of speech, faces and text for person identification in TV broadcast. In: Fusiello, A., Murino, V., Cucchiara, R. (eds.) ECCV 2012 Ws/Demos, Part III. LNCS, vol. 7585, pp. 385–394. Springer, Heidelberg (2012)
3. Bruneau, P., Stefas, M., Bredin, H., Ta, A.-P., Tamisier, T., Barras, C.: A web-based tool for the visual analysis of media annotations. In: International Conference on Information Visualisation (2014)
4. Giraudel, A., Carré, M., Mapelli, V., Kahn, J., Galibert, O., Quintard, L.: The REPERE Corpus: a Multimodal Corpus for Person Recognition. In: LREC (2012)
5. Kahn, J., Galibert, O., Quintard, L., Carre, M., Giraudel, A., Joly, P.: A Presentation of the REPERE Challenge. In: International Workshop on Content-Based Multimedia Indexing, pp. 1–6 (2012)
6. Krogh, A., Vedelsby, J.: Neural network ensembles, cross validation, and active learning. In: Advances in Neural Information Processing Systems 7, pp. 231–238 (1994)

# Collaborative Visual Environments
# for Performing Arts

Sven Ubik, Jiri Navratil, Jiri Melnikov, Boncheol Goo,
David Cuenca, and Ivani Santana

CESNET, KAIST, i2CAT, Universidade Federal da Bahia

**Abstract.** Our objective was to verify whether modern computer network and audio-visual technologies can enable collaborative work of performing artists over large distances. Such collaborative environments
would bring new opportunities for artists, audience and engineers. We
describe our experience obtained during a three-continent cyber performance done during the 36th APAN meeting.

**Keywords:** cyber performance performing arts, remote collaboration,
cultural exchange, e-learning.

## 1 Introduction

Low-latency sharing of visualizations can enable real-time collaboration in multiple fields. We wanted to explore whether real-time collaboration is possible
among performing artists in music and dance across large distances. If possible,
the technology can enable creative collaboration during learning, training and
performances among people of different cultures in different parts of the world.

## 2 Related Work

Probably the lowest latency is required for playing music together. Experiments
have shown that the maximum acceptable latency is approx. 30 ms [2].

LoLa software [3] developed by GARR is now used in musical institutions
around the world for remote collaboration and lectures. Lola uses an analog
camera and a grabber card for minimal visual latency and added sound latency
approx. 6 ms.

Using networks to interconnect artists is a subject studied at NPAW (Network
Performing Arts Workshop) organized once a year. A two-point demo transmis-
sion between two dancers have been done during the last workshop in Vienna in
March 2013[1].

Low-latency sharing of high-definition visualizations has been used for remote
collaboration experiments in several fields, for example, architecture design and
remote access to 3D models of cultural artifacts [4], often making use of large
visualization devices, such as CAVE [1] and SAGE [2].

---

[1] http://www.terena.org/activities/network-arts/vienna
[2] http://www.sagecommons.org

Y. Luo (Ed.): CDVE 2014, LNCS 8683, pp. 167–170, 2014.
© Springer International Publishing Switzerland 2014

## 3    Experimental Work

The APAN (Asia-Pacific Advanced Network) eCulture working group organized a networked music and dance performance, as a joint effort of artists and engineers located across the world, working together in real time. The performance was named "Dancing beyond TIME" and involved approx. 100 people in three continents. The final event took place at the 36th APAN Meeting held in Daejeon, Korea on 21 Aug 2013. The event began at 08:55 UTC/GMT simultaneously in Salvador, Brazil (BR), Prague, Czech Republic (CZ), Barcelona, Spain (ES) and Daejeon, Korea (KR). The team included network engineers and researchers, audio-visual technicians, programmers, musicians, dancers, scene designers and choreographers, with some people spanning multiple areas.

*Performance organization.* The overall inter-connection is illustrated in Fig. 1. There was a live chamber music in CZ, dancers in KR, ES and BR and the main audience in KR.

To mitigate the latency issue, computer generated skeleton data using Kinect sensors generated by a MaxMSP program were used between sites. The delay was shorter when compared to video transmissions.

1. Music was played in a concert hall in CZ. The video in ultra-high-resolution (4K) along with audio were transmitted to KR.
2. In KR, a dance was performed to the music from CZ in front of a kinect sensor. The skeleton data of a dancer and sound of the chamber music from CZ were sent to ES and BR simultaneously.
3. In ES and BR, an avatar created by the skeleton data from KR was shown on the screen. Both dancers each interacted with the avatar to the music from CZ via KR in front of the kinect sensor.
4. Each skeleton data of dancers in ES and BR were exchanged and sent to KR at the same time. All dancers could see avatars of each other.
5. Each video from ES and BR was also sent to KR. Then the all avatars and videos were shown on one screen in KR.

There are several ways for signal propagation among multiple performers.

– All performers in a sequence. Each performer can react to all preceeding performers who are seen in sync. However, the audience sees the total picture as a set of non-synchronized contributions.
– One to all other performers. Each performer can react to only one remote performer. The audience sees all performers with smaller time differences.
– Full mesh. Some performers are seen delayed after own movements.

We used the last option. We wanted to verify if a performer can react to other performers even though some remote views come after a short delay. The audience was approx. 100 people in Daejeon and additional participants in other locations. The venue in KR is shown in the illustration in Fig. 2.

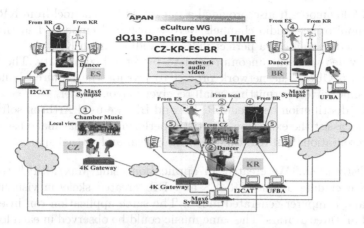

Fig. 1. Network inter-connection

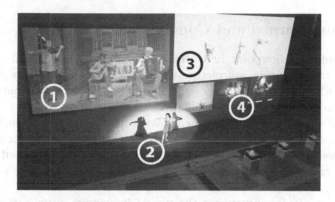

**Fig. 2.** The stage in APAN venue. 1 - live 4K video and music from CZ, 2 - a dancer in KR reacting to the music in front of Kinect, 3 - avatars from KR, ES and BR, 4 - video from ES and BR.

*Network.* The network traversed a wide range of links of the GLIF (Global Lambda Interchange Facility)[3] infrastructure, and in the public Internet. The connected networks and inter-connection centers included KRLight and KRE-ONET (Korea), GLORIAD (Korea to US), StarLight (Chicago), C-wave and NLR (US), RNP (Brasil), NLLight (the Netherlands), i2Cat (Spain) and CES-NET (Czech Rep.). The average delay between end points was Prague - Daejeon 140 ms, Daejeon - Barcelona 165 ms, Daejeon - Salvador 155 ms and Barcelona - Salvador 170 ms.

*Video streaming.* The music performance was captured by a 4K camera and delivered from HAMU to KAIST by a pair of FPGA-based 4K Gateway devices[4], adding approx. 2 ms latency in an uncompressed mode and a subframe latency

---

[3] http://www.glif.is

[4] http://www.4kgateway.com

in a JPEG 2000 mode. It also provided a backward HD channel from KR to CZ for stage monitoring. Audio channels were transferred embedded in the video channel, which guaranteed a perfect video to audio sync in KR.

The 4K video was sent uncompressed to preserve high quality. The bitrate was approx. 5 Gb/s. The network proved to provide the required bandwidth with very small jitter, permitting small receiver playout buffer.

For video distribution between KR, ES and BR, we used Arthron software [5], developed to assist the execution of artistic performances that make use of multimedia presentations and real time sharing of real and virtual spaces.

*Skeleton distribution.* We created an application using Max/MSP [6] that distributed Kinect data among KR, ES and BR, created skeleton visualizations (avatars) and computer-generated music. The same application ran in each location and all three avatars. The same music could be observed in each location. Eight joints were obtained from the Kinect.

## 4    Lessons Learned and Conclusions

From the audience viewpoint in Korea, the performance smoothly combined high-quality remote music and picture with dancers collaboratively reacting to the music and to each other, although all performers were distributed in four countries, across three continents and three time zones.

There had been previous experiments with multipoint dance performances. We advanced this area by adding distribution of computer-generated skeletons that decreased observable delay between participants. We also used full-mesh distribution and found that it was possible for dancers to react to each others performing.

In future we plan to investigate the use of immersive visualizations for collaboration in performing arts, such as the CAVE devices, involving other kinds of artistic expressions, such as fine arts and paintings and installation of more permament infrastructures fo the use in university lectures.

## References

1. Cruz-Neira, C., Sandin, D.J., DeFanti, T.A., Kenyon, R.V., Hart, J.C.: The CAVE: Audio Visual Experience Automatic Virtual Environment. CACM 35(6), 64 (1992), doi:10.1145/129888.129892
2. Urban, O., Pinkas, M., Travnicek, Z., Ubik, S.: Notes from experimental work in HAMU (June 2012), http://perfmon.cesnet.cz/public/video/hamu_harp_flute
3. Drioli, C., Allocchio, C., Buso, N.: Networked Performances and Natural Interaction via LOLA: Low Latency High Quality A/V Streaming System. In: Nesi, P., Santucci, R. (eds.) ECLAP 2013. LNCS, vol. 7990, pp. 240–250. Springer, Heidelberg (2013)
4. Ubik, S., Travnicek, Z., Zejdl, P., Halak, J.: Remote Access to 3D Models for Research, Engineering, and Art. IEEE Multimedia (October-December 2012)

---

[5] http://www.lavid.ufpb.br
[6] http://cycling74.com/products/max

# Synchronous Mobile Learning System to Cope with Slow Network Connection

Jang Ho Lee

Dept. of Computer Engineering, Hongik University, Seoul, Korea
janghol@cs.hongik.ac.kr

**Abstract.** The network connection of a mobile device can get slow temporarily due to its high mobility. This could make synchronous mobile learning system unable to receive the video and audio from the server, thereby making students find difficulty understanding the real-time lecture on their mobile devices. Thus, we propose a synchronous mobile learning system that enables students to follow the ongoing lecture in such temporary slow network connection. The system allows students to watch an instructor and slide with annotation in real time. The students can send questions to an instructor and discuss together in text. To make students not to miss the lecture while the video and audio can't be delivered due to low-speed network connection, live speech text is supported by converting the instructor's speech to text in real time.

**Keywords:** mobile learning, distance learning, synchronous collaboration, slow connection, live speech text.

## 1 Introduction

As mobile devices have rapidly spread and their performance become more powerful, the researchers became interested in distance learning system running on those mobile devices [1]. MLVLS [2] is a Symbian smartphone-based synchronous learning system that provides real-time video and slide. However, one of the drawbacks of the smart-phone-based learning system is that the display of the most smartphones is too small for students to easily recognize small letters on the slide. Classroom Presenter [3] is a tablet-based synchronous learning system that provides sharing of slides and annotation among a teacher and students collocated in the same room. It doesn't support mobile device or real-time video. Thus, previously we developed a tablet-based synchronous learning system that allows students to watch an instructor and slide with annotation on their tablets [4]. It also allows students to send questions in real time.

However, there are still problems with these mobile synchronous learning systems. One of them is that they are prone to temporary slow network connection because of its high mobility. While a student's mobile client is experiencing slow connection, it can no longer receive live data at a normal rate so that the student misses a part of the live learning session. This could make the student have difficulty understanding the later part of the learning session even after the network connection gets back to normal. As a result, this could lead to the student's poor learning experience.

Y. Luo (Ed.): CDVE 2014, LNCS 8683, pp. 171–174, 2014.

Thus, we propose a synchronous mobile learning system to deal with such tempo-rary slow network connection. When the network is normal, the students can watch an instructor and slide with annotation in real time. They can ask questions to the instruc-tor and discuss together in text. The instructor's speech is also converted to text in real time and sent to the students. When the network connection becomes slow and the video and audio are not smooth, it allows a student to choose the speech text only mode that disables the video and audio while leaving the speech text on. Since the video and audio consumes the network the most, disconnecting video and audio chan-nels gives room for other less network consuming channels such as speech text, slide, annotation, and text chat. In this speech text only mode, the student can still follow the ongoing lecture by reading the live speech text with slide and annotation.

## 2     Synchronous Mobile Learning System to Support Slow Network Connection

Fig. 1 shows the system consisting of a broadcasting server and mobile clients. An instructor client encodes the video in H.263, audio in G.723.1, and slide in JPEG along with annotation from an instructor and sends the encoded data to the server.

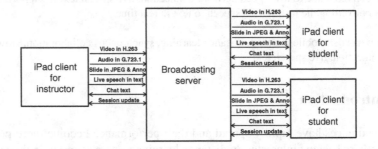

**Fig. 1.** Run-time architecture of the proposed system

The instructor's speech is also converted to live speech text and sent to the server. There are third-party iOS frameworks for speech recognition. OpenEars [5] provides local or offline speech recognition for English. DaumSpeechRecognizer [6] provides server-based or online speech recognition for Korean. Local speech recognition pro-vides faster response since it doesn't use network but uses smaller vocabularies. We use DaumSpeechRecognizer because it supports Korean. The connection between the instructor client and the speech recognition server is omitted in Fig. 1.

The chat text is also sent to the broadcasting server. The broadcasting server rece-ives those data from the instructor client and sends them to all the student clients. A student client decodes data (video, audio, slide, annotation) from the server and presents them to a student with speech text and chat text. It also sends student's chat text. The client also sends session update to the server which updates its own copy and broadcasts it to clients.

In Fig. 2, the UI of the instructor client consists of video, slide with slide controls (arrows and pen), text chat, live speech text, and participants. In Fig. 3, the UI of the student client consists of video, service-level selection ("Video + Audio + Speech Text" and "Speech Text Only"), slide, text chat, live speech text, and participants.

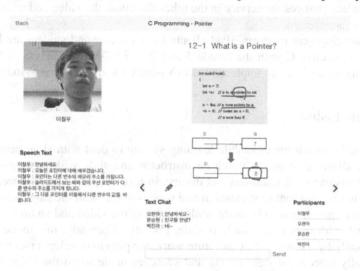

**Fig. 2.** User interface of the instructor's iPad client

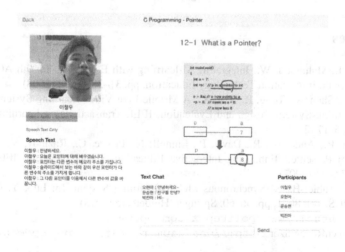

**Fig. 3.** User interface of the student's iPad client

In Fig. 3, a student can choose between two levels of service depending on the network situation. When the network connection is fast enough to support video and audio, a student can choose the "Video + Audio + Speech Text" service that provides video, audio, live speech text, slide with annotation, and text chat. Currently, the "Video + Audio + Speech Text" service is selected in Fig. 3. When the network connection is not fast enough for video and audio, a student can choose the "Speech Text Only" service that provides live speech text, slide with annotation, and text chat. When a student changes the service from "Video + Audio + Speech Text" to "Speech Text Only", the video channel and audio channel to the server are disconnected. When a student changes the service in the other direction, the video and audio channel to the server are created.

About development platform, iPad clients for instructor and student are being developed in Objective-C with the Xcode 5 and iOS 7 SDK on Mac OS X 10.9. The broadcasting server is being implemented in Visual C++ and MFC on Windows 7.

## 3      Conclusion

We proposed a synchronous mobile learning system to deal with slow network connection. It allows students to watch an instructor and slide with annotation in real time. Students can send questions and discuss in text. The instructor's speech is also converted to text and sent to students in real time. To deal with the slow connection, it provides live speech text-only mode while disabling the video and audio that requires higher bandwidth than others such as slide, text, etc. Currently, this mode switch is done manually by a student. But, as future work, we plan to develop a mechanism that automatically detects the right timing and switches mode when the video and audio need to be disabled. When our current implementation of the proposed system is completed, we will develop various usage scenarios and conduct usability testing.

## References

1. Wains, S.I., Mahmood, W.: Integrating M-learning with E-learning. In: 9th ACM SIGITE Conference on Information Technology Education, pp. 31–38. ACM (2008)
2. Ulrich, C., Shen, R., Tong, R., Tan, X.: A Mobile Live Video Learning System for Large-Scale Learning-System Design and Evaluation. IEEE Transactions on Learning Technologies 3(1), 6–17 (2010)
3. Anderson, R., Anderson, R., Davis, P., Linnell, N., Prince, C., Razmov, V., Videon, F.: Classroom Presenter: Enhancing Interactive Education with Digital Ink. IEEE Computer 40(9), 56–61 (2007)
4. Lee, J.H.: Tablet-Based Synchronous Mobile Learning System. In: Luo, Y. (ed.) CDVE 2013. LNCS, vol. 8091, pp. 56–60. Springer, Heidelberg (2013)
5. OpenEars, http://www.politepix.com/openears
6. DaumSpeechRecognizer, http://dna.daum.net/affiliate/speech/ios

# Data Intellection for Wiser Online Sales
# the Optosa Approach

Thomas Tamisier[1], Gero Vierke[2], Helmut Rieder[2],
Yoann Didry[1], and Olivier Parisot[1]

[1] Centre de Recherche Public - Gabriel Lippmann,
41, rue du Brill, L-4422 Belvaux, Luxembourg
[2] InfinAlt Solutions SA, 2a, Ennert dem Bierg L-5244 Sandweiler

**Abstract.** This article presents the basic concepts of Optosa, a visual analytics solution for the optimization of online sales, designed to support manufactures in all phases of the online sales process from the product specification to the price fixing and more. Optosa combines a data processing module that builds and constantly updates operational knowledge related to sales positioning with a decision assistant that uses relevant aspects of the knowledge for helping the tasks of the different teams along the integrated chain of the sales. After reviewing the challenges of the approach, we discuss the first significant experiments with Optosa on some formalized use-cases.

**Keywords:** Visual Data Mining, Knowledge-based Support, Integrated chain.

## 1    Introduction

Everybody realize that the future of selling lies on the Internet. Therefore, most manufacturers and uncountable merchants devote themselves in a hard and continuous competition over the online marketplaces. However, many of them do not develop any structured approach to increase their market shares. Others use rather naive procedures, commonly based on lowering prices and thus reducing sales margins. An intelligent approach, based on timely usage of dynamic information directly available from the Internet will give us unique and decisive advantage.

Generally speaking, one of the greatest challenges for the manufactures is that in online sales the distributors in the online market do not fulfill the same function as in the stationary market. In particular, in the stationary market the distributor, especially the procurement manager, supports the manufacturer with his know how on the consumer needs, namely the optimal specification and presentation of products. In contrast, in the online distribution, the manufacturer is given full freedom to manage all aspects of the sale process.

There is therefore a strong need to provide the sales business with an alternate solution that could make up for the human competence that is not at hand any more. This is the purpose of the Optosa system, developed in a partnership with researchers and practitioners, and specified after a thorough operational state of the art driven by three progressive investigation steps:

Y. Luo (Ed.): CDVE 2014, LNCS 8683, pp. 175–178, 2014.

1. in what way it would be possible to rely on data nowadays at disposal with a view to maximizing turnover and margin
2. based on this knowledge from the data, which processes in online sales could be automated
3. last, which decisions within the other processes could be supported by a knowledge based assistant.

With regard to the data, there has been a lot of research done and some tools are available in the domain of Search Engine Optimization (SEO), in particular [1,2], or tools from the search engines themselves like Google Analytics.   However, those tools focus on search engines like Google and not on online market platforms. The ranking mechanism of search engines and market places are similar but not identical, the essential difference being that search engines aim to deliver most relevant content while market places aim to deliver products that are most likely to be bought. The goal of Optosa goes beyond this current state of the art, in order to figure out those differences and to develop algorithms that for instance analyze the meta-content of successful products and to extract the most relevant key-words and to compute the optimal structure for our meta-content.

Complementarily, a lot of data sources like [3] propose business information that could be formalized to automatic handle or optimize several tasks in the sale process. Made of static knowledge about common best practices, this information can be outdated when applied to the fast evolving domain of online sales. In contrast, the Optosa system is based on the monitoring of live data in view of delivering to the sales collaborators an accurate business handling and a pro-active decision support.

## 2     Data Challenges and Functional Overview

Within the preliminary state of the art, we identified two main challenges towards a system that could cure the lack of expert knowledge.

The first one is to extract business information from the available data. A lot of sales data are available from online marketplaces, either directly to the general public or to registered users. As such, the raw data cannot be straightforwardly used to solve any concrete problem such as optimizing the sales through a given platform. We need to understand the data in their specific context of use, and then to mine them according to the knowledge we intend to build: remove outliers, find correlations... Moreover, user control and interaction should be possible during the processing of so diversified bunches of data: we follow here the *visual analytics* paradigm, a way of addressing such complexity through an efficient combining of the respective powers of the computer and the human brain [4].

The second challenge is to process this business information within concrete use cases by means of a collaborative expert system and a transparent data model. The Optosa system primarily intends to generate recommendations for operating on an online platform, dedicated to the sales collaborators.  The recommendations must be in any case supported by a clear and suitable justification. The justification exhibits both the trace of the reasoning and available references to knowledge extracted from the data. The traceability brings constraints on the architecture and the technology used to implement the system. In particular, Optosa will use a referencing mechanism associates rules with documentary sources. Also, when updating the knowledge base, the references allow identifying the impact of a given knowledge source on the rules model, in order to replace them.

Sales processes are modeled through different procedures and algorithms. We structured the functionalities of the Optosa system according to separate optimization needs that could be refined independently:

1. Direct optimization of the sale of a product.
2. Optimization in relation to sales and delivery channels: How to deal with competitors?
3. Reporting and analysis: How to improve the offer through the consolidation of the sale channels?

As mentioned above some of the functionalities can be fully automated, given the values of parameters asked by the system. An example is the dynamic price adjustment: for each product to be sold, the user can specify a minimal and maximal price. Optosa will autonomously monitor the market situations, especially the prices of the competitors, and finally adapt the product price in such a way that turnover and margin is optimized. Other functionalities can be only partially automated and serve as decision support for the user. For instance, when description text or search tags are to be defined, Optosa will scan other, comparable product descriptions on the sales platforms, and evaluate which key words correspond to sales success. From this it computes suggestions that are presented to the user. In any case, the input data processed by the rules is information extracted through data mining from recorded characteristics of past sales. The business knowledge to process the data is specified and tested in partnership with intended users of the system.

## 3    Experimental Tests

For our first technical trials, we processed datasets relevant to different business use cases. The knowledge is formalized on the shape of decision trees [5], a user readable formalism, the trees being directly extracted from real life data.

Data considered as input are: the list of products and information about each product (features description, prices, sales ranks, etc.) The information can be structured in the shape of clusters of products, and for each cluster the products profile is defined (core features, prices ranges, sales rank ranges, etc.). The use cases are groups of tasks defining some concrete sales activity, such as the following examples. Some use cases are principally handled by data mining (on relevant data) such as "Price fixing" based on similar products. Other ones contain more domain related knowledge (from vendor or buyer point of view) such as "Calculation of a similarity index between products".

The following figures illustrate the "Price positioning" use case for a laptop. First, from a dataset, a decision tree is computed to determine the price range according to the features of the laptop. The decision model is then applied to evaluate and justify the price of a given product. Second, the knowledge is used for the computation of a clustering of the laptops recorded on a dataset, according to their main features. A planar projection (using multi-dimensional scaling [6]) of the laptops shows the correspondence between the features (horizontal axis) and the price (vertical).

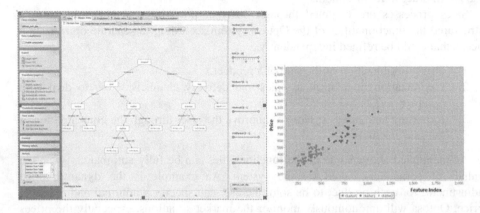

**Fig. 1.** Visual Analytics for Price Positioning

The processing of the use cases shows the possibility to extract knowledge, track evolutions and build decision models. From the debriefing on the data mining results, it was also clear that a lot of business information must be taken into account to reinterpret the results, in order to be able to formalize rules that could automate the handling of marketing activities.

## 4     Conclusion

The first experiments with Optosa show the feasibility of a computerized expert assistant that on the one hand builds knowledge with respect to the dynamic of sale contexts and on the other hand uses the knowledge for helping in operational sales activities. Such customized information and assistance is hardly available otherwise in the domain, neither directly nor through computing artifacts.

**Acknowledgments.** The project Optosa is supported by a grant from the Ministry of Economy and External Trade, Grand-Duchy of Luxembourg, under the Law RDI.

## References

1. Sistrix, http://www.sistrix.com
2. Wiseseosuite, http://www.wiseseo.de
3. Channel Advisor, http://www.channeladvisor.com
4. Heer, J., Agrawala, M.: Design considerations for collaborative visual analytics. Information Visualization 7(1) (2008)
5. Kotsiantis, S.B.: Decision trees: a recent overview. A. I. Review 39(4) (2013)
6. Kruskal, J.B., Wish, M.: Multidimensional Scaling. Sage Publications (1978)

# Planning for the Microclimate of Urban Spaces: Notes from a Multi-agent Approach

Dino Borri, Domenico Camarda, and Irene Pluchinotta

Technical University of Bari, Italy
irene.pluchinotta@gmail.com

**Abstract.** Agents, agent-oriented modelling and multi-agent systems (MAS) introduce new and unconventional concepts in computer science. These elements are able to sparkle new modelling perspectives in behavioural knowledge and in environmental domain, where interactions between humans and natural/artificial agents are not standardized. MAS are considered as "societies of agents" interacting to coordinate their behaviour and often cooperate to achieve some collective goal. In order to show the involved agents and their roles in a quasi-hierarchical scale of interaction behaviours, we propose the setting up of schemes aimed at simplifying the behaviors and the interactions between human and non-human agents in indoor spaces for urban microclimate management.

**Keywords:** Urban microclimate planning, Multiple agents, Behavioural knowledge, Cooperative models, Multi agent System, Interactions.

## 1   Introduction

Agents inhabiting a shared environment are expected to coordinate their activities and share common resources. Important works have been done in Artificial Intelligence towards modelling social intelligence, behaviors and the Multi-Agent Systems (MAS) offer a modelling method based on the principles of distribution and interaction [1][2][3][4]. Indeed, MASs allow to model complex phenomena and different interacting entities with specific behavior patterns, belief systems and cultural norms structures. Since models started to be conceived for reasoning and acting in open unpredictable worlds, characterized by limited and uncertain knowledge, bounded (both cognitive and material) resources, hybrid architectures, interfering either cooperatively or competitively with other systems [5], a new key concept is interaction [6] with evolving environment and with distributed and heterogeneous human-artificial systems in a network. Thus, this study shows interesting insights and suggestions particularly from methodological and modelling, rather than substantial, point of view, in connection with its inherent agent-based perspective. In this context, the use of a multiple-agent approach shows new potentials to support the complex scenarios embedded with the multifaceted problem of managing urban heat islands (UHIs). After this introduction, a second chapter shows results coming from field surveys, carried out with a multiple-agent-based approach on urban microclimate in managing indoor spaces. The paper ends up with remarks on results and follow-ups.

Y. Luo (Ed.): CDVE 2014, LNCS 8683, pp. 179–182, 2014.

## 2     A Multi-agent Approach in Urban Microclimate Management

Our research started with surveys, that have contributed to the definition of action frameworks of urban (single or multiple) agents and their skills and knowledge in thermal behaviours. Agents have been broadly considered as either natural (namely human) and/or artificial (e.g., equipment, building elements, town features etc.), toward the consideration of a hybrid and intrinsically interacting system. In relation to our case study, we identified a number of agents involved in the management of the housing unit: non-human agents (equipment) and human agents and their relations. According to Ferber [1], an interaction occurs when two or more agents are brought into a dynamic relationship through a set of reciprocal actions. Thus, interactions develop out of a series of relations and actions whose consequences in turn have an influence on the future behavior of agents. Moreover, considering the possible relationships between agents, several researchers converge on basically four types of MAS environments: (i) cooperative MASs, agents cooperate in their work and every agent helps another agent if help is required and possible; (ii) competitive MASs, agents compete between themselves and winner agents are allowed to perform their actions and to influence the behavior of a system; (iii) semi-competitive MASs, agents can be selfish, but they are willing to work together because their gain will be greater if they cooperate than it would be without cooperation: a known example is iterated prisoner dilemma; (iv) a single agent, i.e., an agent that does not belong to any MAS and therefore does not communicate with other agents.

The typologies of mutual relations were also investigated through surveys, singling out relations of power, usefulness, as well as functional, causal and sensorial relations. This allowed fine-tuning agents' characters and roles in a quasi-hierarchical scale of interaction behaviors. Furthermore, the micro level analysis of our surveys is based on social psychology models, which have been widely applied to environmental management issues, such as, the *theory of planned behavior* [7]. Such theories hypothesize that attitudinal (both cognitive and emotional) factors are predictors of behavioral intentions which, in turn, influence behaviors themselves. For this reason, the final survey, formalized through focus groups and used in our case-study, allows the building up of a model with a taxonomy of agents. It aimed at analyzing user profiles, studying preferences, attitudes and beliefs, investigating also the relations of agents with their environment, looking into aptitudes, behavior intentions, constraints.

To say it formally, let $A_{a-b}$ be a set of abiotic agents inside the building b (equipment, structure), let $A_{u-b}$ be a set of human agents inside the building b, let $A_{u-h}$ be a set of human agents who live in a housing unit h inside the building b. We consider a housing unit h, in order to divide the set of human agents in three subsets disjoint:

$$A_u = (A_{u-h}) \text{ OR } (A_{u-b} \text{ AND NOT } A_{u-h}) \text{ OR } (\text{NOT } A_{u-b})$$

In our model, the actions performed by a human agent who is in a certain state are also determined by the relationships with other human agents. To formalize their behavior we consider two human agents $A_{u1}$ and $A_{u2}$ and a relation $R(A_{u1}, A_{u2})$ which describes the various levels of interaction (*dominant-dominated, collaboration, partially dominated, totally dominated*) (see, e.g. [8][9][10][11]). $A_u$ can be in a state of "well-being" or "malaise" and $A_u$ can perform a number of steps: $A_u$ will not make any action (NOP) or $A_u$ will interact with other $A_u$ (INT), (e.g. request an opinion); $A_u$ can make two different kinds of interaction, such as INT{WEAK}, i.e. operation that does not involve interaction with other agents (e.g. changing clothes) or INT{STRONG}, i.e. operation that has an effect on other $A_u$ involving interaction with some (at least one) abiotic agents $A_{a-b}$ (e.g. system on/off for heating or cooling, opening or closing windows). This set of operations has a greater environmental impact. The action/operation chosen by $A_{u1}$ depends on the relationship $R$ with other human agents $A_{ui}$:

— If $A_{u1}$ is *dominant* over the other $A_{ui}$, then $A_{u1}$ decides autonomously whether to perform an operation of INT{WEAK or STRONG} type, without interacting with other $A_{ui}$ agents and regardless of the presence of them;
— If $A_{u1}$ is *totally dominated*, then $A_{u1}$ can only perform operations like INT{WEAK} or NOP, even in the absence of other $A_{ui}$ (for example children);
— If $A_{u1}$ is related to *collaboration* (i.e., is *twin agent*), then $A_{u1}$ can perform an operation of INT type, interacting with another $A_u$, and after the outcome of this interaction s/he will decide whether to perform an operation like NOP, INT{WEAK or STRONG}. In case of absence of other $A_u$, then $A_{u1}$ decides autonomously;
— If $A_{u1}$ is *partially dominated*, $A_{u1}$ can perform INT{WEAK} operations in the presence of other $A_u$;
— If $A_{u1}$ is an agent that does not belong to a housing unit (Agent Collaborative Not Hierarchical), then $A_{u1}$ can interact with other $A_u$; and in case of housing unit with only one $A_u$, s/he can be modeled as a dominant single agent;

# 3    Conclusion

This study has tried to work out if and how agents with different roles and behaviors could affect urban microclimates while performing their single and/or collective (particularly mutually interacting) activities. When focusing on our case study more in detail, a certain number of agents was identified and formally characterized, following their different degrees of involvement in the MA framework. This allowed the setting up of schemes aimed at simplifying the behaviors of and the interactions between human agents and non-human agents (such as equipment and structures). As to human agents, they were considered as either belonging to the family, or outside the family but inside the condo (neighboring agents), or even external agents (i.e., acting in public spaces). Together with the identification of agents, the typologies of mutual relations were also investigated, so singling out relations of power, usefulness, as well as functional, causal and sensorial relations. This allowed the fine-tuning of agents' characters and roles in a quasi-hierarchical scale of interaction behaviors. However, beyond the indoor outcomes reached, only few attempts were carried out to extend the agent-based investigation to external outdoor spaces, mainly due to the time constraints of the project agenda. As far as the indoor investigation is concerned, the characterization of agents' roles, behaviors and mutual interactions toward microclimate management was not free from biases and misconceptions. It was partly dependent on families' scarce responsiveness or friendliness with survey processes, but also on the difficulties of drawing formal results out of quail-quantitative questionnaires. Yet, when moving toward the subsequent phase of sketching out a multi-agent model structure, oriented to the formalization of a system architecture to support UHI-managing decisions. In particular, the data drawn out from our case study were connected by and structured on a system of IF-THEN causal rules. As a matter of facts, one of the priority perspectives of the research was supposed to be the completion of a "condition-action" domain of rules, useful for the next UHI management system architecture. At present, this set of rules is still in an embryonic phase, just allowing an exemplary working module aimed at understanding the potentials of a more complex MAS. Research efforts will be oriented toward such modelling direction, for the future development of the management of the UHI problem in confined areas, with an agent-based approach.

# References

1. Ferber, J.: Multi-Agent Systems: An Introduction to Distributed Artificial Intelligence. Addison-Wesley, London (1999)
2. Sandholm, T.W., Lesser, V.R.: Coalition formation among bounded rational agents. In: International Joint Conference on Artificial Intelligence (IJCAI 1995), pp. 662–671. American Association for Artificial Intelligence, Montreal (1995)
3. O'Hare, G.M.P., Jennings, N. (eds.): Foundations of Distributed Artificial Intelligence. Wiley, London (1996)
4. Bond, A.H., Gasser, L.G. (eds.): Readings in Distributed Artificial Intelligence. Morgan Kaufmann, San Mateo (1988)
5. Castelfranchi, C.: Modelling social action for AI agents. Artificial Intelligence 103, 157–182 (1998)
6. Bobrow, D.G.: Dimensions of interaction. AI Magazine 12, 64–80 (1991)
7. Ajzen, I.: The theory of planned behavior. Organizational Behavior and Human Decision Processes 50, 179–211 (1991)
8. Camarda, D.: Cooperative scenario building in environmental planning: Agents, roles, architectures. In: Luo, Y. (ed.) CDVE 2008. LNCS, vol. 5220, pp. 74–83. Springer, Heidelberg (2008)
9. Borri, D., Camarda, D., Pluchinotta, I.: Planning urban microclimate through multiagent modelling: A cognitive mapping approach. In: Luo, Y. (ed.) CDVE 2013. LNCS, vol. 8091, pp. 169–176. Springer, Heidelberg (2013)
10. Parsons, S.D., Gymtrasiewicz, P.J., Wooldridge, M.J.: Game Theory and Decision Theory in Agent-Based Systems. Kluwer Academic Publishers, Dordrecht (2002)
11. Li, J., Sheng, Z., Liu, H.: Multi-agent simulation for the dominant players' behavior in supply chains. Simulation Modelling Practice and Theory 18, 850–859 (2010)

# Perception of Space and Time in a Created Environment

Ursula Kirschner

Leuphana University Lüneburg, Faculty of Humanities and Social Sciences,
Institute of Urban and Cultural Area Research, Scharnhorststr. 1, 21335 Lüneburg, Germany
kirschner@uni.leuphana.de

**Abstract.** A built environment is ambiguous, because space can be understood in a Euclidean way, symbolically, socially as well as architecturally, image-scientifically or psychologically. This conference paper is dedicated to learning about the correlations of these perceptions in a wider sense with means to disclose time-dependent and functional layers related dynamically to the space.

We have chosen our campus for the case study, which was a garrison beginning in the 1930s and served different armies before it was converted to a university in the 1990s. Our intention is to offer social, informative benefits and knowledge about the campus, which in turn contributes to participatory development of the campus and hence to identification with the place as well as with collective memory, for everyone on site.

We are developing an app that facilitates innovative space perception. The digital tools in the app consist of geocaching, an interactive map, communication tools and various multimedia information components. This so-called "geo knowledge-caching" shall be used to expand a university campus to a complex knowledge construct with buildings in which knowledge is imparted and a library that houses knowledge and a place for discussion, encounters and leisure activities.

**Keywords:** Perception of space, app, geocaching, multimedia exhibition.

## 1 Introduction

Students expressed many spontaneous thoughts on the term of "open space":
"Open up open space"; "Open space has no fences"; "Open space means that you behave yourself anyway"; "Open spaces are flying thoughts"; "Rarely any open space between the beer and the foam"; "Open spaces are dreams"; "Open space is a scarce commodity in big cities"; "Open space is not good for me"; "Create open space"; "Rent out open space"; "Open spaces usually fill up quickly".

Although colloquial use of the word "space" is generally straightforward, scientific applications have led to differentiations that make it difficult to find a common context. In physics "space" is related to fields, while in mathematics "spaces" are understood to be sets of points. Philosophy contains spatial theories that pertain to: ontology, examining what the space is when not related to the experience and what it constitutes; epistomology, focusing on space as a condition for the experience; and

Y. Luo (Ed.): CDVE 2014, LNCS 8683, pp. 183–190, 2014.

phenomenology, which analyzes the ways in which space is experienced. [1] "Their potential in terms of architecture is to be used to develop space concepts that have their starting point in sensory experience, actions, motion and the subsequent correlations. Space is not static. It emerges from the vivid, corporal orientation of humans and the world." [2]

Our behavior in all areas depends on and is closely linked to the acceptable social system of standards and values and to the derived behavioral expectations of the social environment. [3]

This study examines the constructed space - in this case the historical garrison now used as a university - in regard to the interaction between erected structures and action. So there is no distinction between the consideration of the territorial, material space on the one hand and the social interaction space on the other; instead there is correlated interaction between these two components of space. This is based on the assumption that the space is experienced subjectively and serves as a source of information perceived differently in terms of the cultural socialization of a person.

Human perception is influenced by complex structures and correlations, so it varies greatly. Thus the structure of the methodology and the approach of the substantive work is of a deconstructivist nature. The next step is to ascertain how this information can be made available for the specific location while enabling interaction and how the information will impact the space perception.

## 2     How a Location Deals with Its History

A distinct characteristic of the selected campus of the Leuphana University Lüneburg along Scharnhorststrasse is the rows of red brick buildings, symmetrically arranged, that used to be a military barracks. Conversion of the former garrison to a university was significant for the city of Lüneburg - instead of the 10,000 soldiers who lived here during worldwar II, there are now 7000 students living on campus and around the city. [4]

But simply converting the military edifices to classrooms and offices was not enough to create a properly functioning university. The campus needed a library, a cafeteria and lecture halls. The new structures demonstrate the attempt to rid the site of the previously predominant military character.

When entering the campus, one first becomes aware of the combination of red brick buildings and the many grassy areas created on the barracks site. The new building complexes, characterized by their open and transparent style, are a stark contrast to the severe garrison architecture. But the streams of people offer the first hint that the heart of the university is the glass center: the lecture halls, the library and the cafeteria. The buildings were designed by the architectural firm MWP v. Mansberg, Wiskott + Partner and were built between 1994 and 1998. In one popular city guide of Lüneburg published in the late 1990s, a regional author described the barracks compound reborn as a university as "[o]ld brick buildings and modern architecture [that] harmonize well with each other on the partially park-like grounds." [5]

To meet the university's need for additional space resulting from merging the various locations in one place, the previously unused attics were converted to offices and classrooms beginning in 2007 and continuing on at present. The architects were Robert Ketterer, Ulrich Tränkmann and KBNK Architekten.

The third step in using construction to demonstrate the new purpose of the buildings occurred with the hiring of the architect Daniel Libeskind to design a new central building. As the core of campus development, the new central structure is intended to once and for all break up the prevailing grid structure. Libeskind was appalled at the sight of the garrison architecture on the campus - but at the same time he was particularly inspired by the idea of adding something to the decisively military environment that could embody the sentiment of the 21st century. In an interview, he told students, "I recreate the whole image of the campus." [6] Despite everything that has already been done, Libeskind is convinced that fundamental reinvention is essential. For Libeskind, the challenge of the original idea is to create a democratic style of buildings and make the structures accessible to everyone.

Art and the sustainability concept are ubiquitous themes in consistently envisioning this process in day-to-day campus life. Art in various forms of presentation around campus provides food for thought, including graffiti, in galleries and as artistic productions such as environments, etc. The quest for the spirit of a new university in old

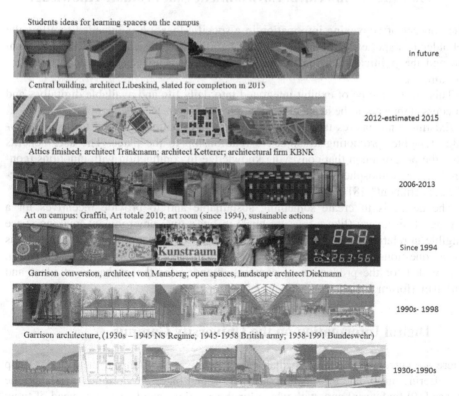

Students ideas for learning spaces on the campus

in future

Central building, architect Libeskind, slated for completion in 2015

2012-estimated 2015

Attics finished; architect Tränkmann; architect Ketterer; architectural firm KBNK

2006-2013

Art on campus: Graffiti, Art totale 2010; art room (since 1994), sustainable actions

Since 1994

Garrison conversion, architect von Mansberg; open spaces, landscape architect Diekmann

1990s- 1998

Garrison architecture, (1930s – 1945 NS Regime; 1945-1958 British army; 1958-1991 Bundeswehr)

1930s-1990s

**Fig. 1.** Impressions from the campus as a multi-layer model from different eras. (Illustration by the author).

buildings, with the aid of the artist Christian Philipp Müller and a group of Culture Studies students, should be accentuated. 110 silkscreens depicting the theme "The campus as a work of art" (1996 - 1999) were produced. Müller and the students researched the blueprints of 100 campuses around the world, superimposing them onto a map of the Lüneburg campus, whereby the libraries were always placed one over the other as the heart of a university.[7]

All of the students are familiar with sustainability issues. They are reminded of the topic by $CO_2$ meters in classrooms, by an electronic display indicating energy consumption, by the rental bike stations and by other rules on campus.

At the same time, the students' visions should be revealed in real places.  The students are convinced that there are many areas on campus that could be converted to ideal places to study, such as the rooftop of the library, a learning tower or a glass sphere over a biotop.

To teach the students about the various eras of campus development, we developed text modules, photos and audiovisual segments by the respective architects for the various geographic topics.

## 3    How the Architectural Environment Can Promote Knowledge

The concept of conveying information in a specific location is intended to allow the beholder to experience the history of the buildings in the context of the historical use and the political situation. People are made aware of spaces without signs or monuments.

This creates a type of exhibit integrated into daily life and available digitally - and it occurs at the site of the happening (past, present, future).

Existing atmospheres that aid in conveying information are used to make knowledge tangible: promoting a subjective relationship to the place. The user benefits from the phenomenon that conveying knowledge in conjunction with emotions (conjured e.g. by atmospheres) tends to reinforce perception. Bear talks about an "affective concernment". [8]

The desire is to create something sustainable and to provide incentives for a voyage of discovery (like a treasure hunt) in one's own environment, making space tangible in relation to time. In this context, supplying answers is just as important as posing questions, e.g. on the use of open spaces inside as well as outside. A platform is provided for the production of contents intended for the exchange of ideas and criticism. (forum concept)

## 4    Digital Information on the University Campus

There are currently four apps available on the university campus: the StadtRad app [9], offering up-to-date information on where rental bikes are currently available; the Mensa [10] (cafeteria) app, with which lunch selections can be chosen ahead of time; the mystudy app [11], which provides an interactive course catalog with communication and material storage features; and the Bib app, an app currently being developed to enable books to be more easily located in the open access library. In addition, there are eight public screens, installed at the students' request, providing information on campus development and current events at the university. To find out which presentation platform the students prefer to use to find day-to-day university information, the student body was surveyed[1] via the public screens and asked about the daily use of apps. This research revealed that the screens are rarely acknowledged and not highly valued, but that the apps are used regularly throughout the day. This confirms that an app better suits the zeitgeist of today's university students.

## 5    Technical Basis for "Geo-Knowledge-Caching"

In this context the name "geo-knowledge-caching" is applied to this app, to make clear that knowledge can be found in a playful manner.

To make the moving history of the selected university campus - beginning with the conversion from a military barracks - comprehensible, new ways of conveying information will contribute to the explanation. In conjunction with stationary knowledge transfer and storage, a digital architecture guide is to convey the idea and background of the constructed environment. Visions for the future and for planning are integrated into the process of finding individual spaces or special places.

Applying the principle of geocaching, spaces are intended to be playfully discovered, and with an open content principle users are to be involved in suggestions through interaction with the map data. An assessment and evaluation platform will continue to improve the app for the community.

The functional basis is geocaching [12] with a GPS tracking system, combined with an interactive map[2] and a digital exhibition concept[3]. Beyond the physical existence of the university campus, this app offers its users special insight: historical photos, video tours complete with commentary as well as in-depth background information from the architects themselves. Interviews have been prepared by students with the architects who are still living. This enables three differing perspectives on the campus to be gained: that of the architect, that of the curator and that of the students. The program, e.g. ArcGis ©[4], [13] is used to create the map, to implement the pop-ups with documentation material and to navigate on campus. The basis for the map is a 3D model of the campus which was imported from Google Earth, Fig. 2. In addition, geographic data can be imported via openstreetmat, e.g. from Geofabrik. [14]

---

[1] The survey was conducted as part of a seminar. 105 persons on campus were questioned and more than half stated that they do not pay attention to the contents on the screens around campus.

[2] A reference to a digital map can be found at nexthamburg.de. Members of the community can upload photos or text modules for specific coordinates.

[3] Sauerbruch created a digital exhibition concept for the exhibition Kultur:Stadt in Berlin in 2013. The exhibition consisted exclusively of models, and visitors were given an I-map with different information blogs (films, maps, photos, etc.)

[4] © Copyright 2013 Esri

Various so-called "spotlights" for the app menu items should be implemented to generate and convey information: The following contents have been created for the three spotlights:

- Space-Spotlight: self-guided tour using a digital architecture guide without changing the actual place, based on an architecture guide for the campus with historical image, sound and video documents, interviews with architects and contemporary witnesses; places of remembrance, participation by introducing reminders (e.g. old, digitalized souvenir photos and maps, videos, audio recordings, music, radio reports on historical events, text) and specifying "places of remembrance" by GPS coordinates on the website or in the app; also visualization of the energy concept and the art on campus, Fig. 2.
- Action-Spotlight: organizational scheduling tool (e.g. use of sports facilities, putting together teams); develop new interim use; publicize events and appointments.
- Future-Spotlight: campus planning; planners can share their concepts (pool of ideas), users can upload their suggestions for campus improvements as images or text.

Information about the campus is imparted digitally, without signs or extra exhibition pieces. Information can be called up with the GPS coordinates. All of the spotlights are allocated a communication tool to link the members of the university communities.

A CampusApp [15] - which 20 universities throughout Germany and their respective Student Affairs have joined - is currently available. Potentially integrating geo-knowledge-caching is being investigated.

**Fig. 2.** Campus model in Google Earth with pop-up signs: brown - garrison architecture; green - new buildings after the conversation in the 1990s; yellow - roof extensions; light yellow - art on the campus; light brown - central building; blue - future ideas from students. (Illustration by the author)

# 6    Conclusion

With this suggested app the user will receive a single tool to interact with the environment. In the context of urban development, the app should be considered an intervention. According to Krüger, an intervention is (usually) an artistic, temporary action in a public urban space intended to make a sociopolitical statement.[16] The aspired to statements are sociopolitical in regard to conversion of the barracks (military use vs. civil institution of education); sociological in regard to the differentiated communication spaces; artistic in regard to the various styles of architecture; ecological in regard to the visualization of the energy concept; and social in regard to the accessibility and the communication platform. The last aspect could be meaningfully expanded by adding recommendations for wheelchair-accessible routes on campus.

The fundamental objective is to create a specific communication level that encourages people to reflect on certain topics of the architectural history and to potentially change their perception of space. We aim to measure the effect on the user regarding his perception of the space by applying an existing tool to determine a semiotic differential.

A digital model of the campus could increase use of the app and would allow the students to creatively experiment. Additionally providing the students with this virtual model and tools to perceive and modify according to their associations should train their cognitive understanding.

We aim to measure the effect on the user regarding his perception of the space by applying an existing tool to determine a semiotic differential.

**Acknowledgments.** This research work would not have been impossible without the great efforts of all students in the seminar "Project: Architectural guide for the Leuphana Campus, Lüneburg" and the members of the group responsible for campus development of Leuphana.

# References

1. Janich, P., Mittelstraß, J.: Raum. In: von Hermann Krings, Baumgartner, H.M., Wild, C. (eds.) Handbuch Philosophischer Grundbegriffe, München, pp. 1154–1168 (1973)
2. Hauser, S.: Körper, Leib und Raum. Zur Einführung. In: von Susanne Hauser, Kamleithner, C., Meyer, R. (eds.) Architekturwissen Grundlagentexte aus den Kulturwissenschaften, Bd. 1: Zur Ästhetik des sozialen Raumes, Bielefeld, pp. 192–201 (2011)
3. Tessin, W.: Freiraum und Verhalten. Soziologische Aspekte der Nutzung und Planung städtischer Freiräume. Eine Einführung, p. 27, Wiesbaden 2011
4. Holst, U., Sefrin, M.: Die Lüneburger Heide, Clenze (2008); Wuggenig, U., Kastelan, C.: Saltcity, Soldiers City, University City; Fogarsi, A., Sander, K. (eds.), Moirés, Lüneburg, Urtica (2011)
5. Trägerverein Wasserturm Lüneburg e.V. (edt.): Lüneburg...auf neuen Wegen, Lüneburg, p. 109 (2001); Wuggenig, U., Kastelan, C.: Saltcity, Soldiers City, University City; Fogarsi, A., Sander, K. (eds.), Moirés, Lüneburg, Urtica (2011)
6. Interview with Daniel Libeskind based on questions from the students in context of a seminar (January 2014)

7. http://kunstraum.leuphana.de/projekte/prototypen/projekte/leereseite.htm (access on April 2014)
8. Bear, M.F.: Neurowissenschaften. In: Ein grundlegendes Lehrbuch für Biologie, Medizin und Psychologie, Heidelberg, pp. 632–655 (2008)
9. http://stadtrad.hamburg.de/kundenbuchung/ (access on April 2014)
10. http://mensaapp.de/ (access on April 2014)
11. https://mystudy.leuphana.de/portal/android (access on April 2014)
12. http://www.geocaching.de/ (access on April 2014)
13. http://www.esri.com/software/arcgis (access on April 2014)
14. http://download.geofabrik.de/europe/germany/niedersachsen.html
15. http://www.campus-app.de/ (access on April 2014)
16. Krüger, T.: Künstlerische Interventionen im Stadtraum. Grußwort des Präsidenten der Bundeszentrale für politische Bildung (2003), http://www.bpb.de/presse/kuenstlerische-interventionen-im-stadtraum (access on April 2014)

# Studying the Effect of Delay on Group Performance in Collaborative Editing

Claudia-Lavinia Ignat[1], Gérald Oster[1], Meagan Newman[2],
Valerie Shalin[2], and François Charoy[1]

[1] Inria, Universit de Lorraine, CNRS, France
[2] Department of Psychology, Wright State University, France
claudia.ignat@inria.fr

**Abstract.** Real-time collaborative editing systems such as Google Drive are increasingly common. However, no prior work questioned the maximum acceptable delay for real-time collaboration or the efficacy of compensatory strategies. In this study we examine the performance consequences of simulated network delay on an artificial collaborative document editing task with a time constant and metrics for process and outcome suitable for experimental study. Results suggest that strategy influences task outcome at least as much as delay in the distribution of work in progress. However, a paradoxical interaction between delay and strategy emerged, in which the more generally effective, but highly coupled strategy was also more sensitive to delay.

**Keywords:** Collaborative editing, groupware, delay, usability measurement.

## 1 Introduction

Real time collaborative editing [3] allows a group of people to modify a shared document simultaneously. One user's changes appear to other users almost immediately, with very small time intervals of inconsistent document status. Real-time collaborative editing has gained in popularity due to the wide availability of free services such as Google Drive. With several tools to support collaborative editing, the practice is increasingly common, e.g., group note taking during meetings and conferences, and brainstorming activities.

While collaborative editing tools meet technical goals, the requirements for group performance are unclear. One system property of general interest is network delay. Despite several years of continuous increase in network bandwidth, network delay has not decreased. In fact, network delay is presently considered as the constraining factor. This delay is due to the physical communication technology, be it copper wire, optical fiber or radio transmission. Additional delay in real-time collaborative editing can result from underlying architecture or merging algorithms associated with collaborative editing tools.

As in all collaborative work, in collaborative editing, users must "divide, allocate, coordinate, schedule, mesh, and interrelate their contributions" [6]. Unanticipated interactions between subtasks can emerge [8]. Both the avoidance and

Y. Luo (Ed.): CDVE 2014, LNCS 8683, pp. 191–198, 2014.

resolution of such interactions requires communication among the team members [4]. However, not all tasks are sensitive to delay [2] and users might pursue strategies that are not sensitive to delay, or they might adjust their strategies if they are aware of delay [5].

To our knowledge no prior work questioned the maximum acceptable delay for real-time collaboration or the efficacy of compensatory strategies. In this paper we study the effect of delay on group performance on an artificial collaborative editing task where a group of four participants i) located the release dates for an alphabetized list of movies and ii) re-sorted the list in chronological order. The task is not unlike job shop scheduling [9]. We examine how strategy interacts with delay to affect task outcome and process in this task.

We start by describing the methods we used for designing our experiment. We then continue by presenting our results organised by measures. We next discuss our results and we end the paper by some concluding remarks.

## 2   Methods

*Participants.* Eighty students affiliated with a European university participated in this experiment, in mixed gender groups of 4. The participants ranged in age from 21 – 27. All participants used French in their daily activities, although they had sufficient working knowledge of English to comprehend the movie titles in the task stimuli. An electronic announcement solicited participation. All participants received a 10 Euro gift certificate for their participation.

*Apparatus.* The experiment was conducted using four desktop computers in a classroom setting. Participants were separated by partitions and could not directly observe other team members while they worked, although typing activity was audible. The server running the Etherpad application was hosted on an Amazon EC2 instance located in the US East (Northern Virginia) Region. Each desktop ran the Mozilla Firefox web browser executing the Etherpad web client application. Etherpad hosted the task stimuli and a Chat dialogue facility. User operations appeared color-coded in both the text and chat. Etherpad relies on a client-server architecture where each client/user edits a copy of the shared document. When a user performed a modification it was immediately displayed on the local copy of the document and then sent to the server. The server merged the change received from the user with other user changes and then transmitted the updates to the other users. When a user edited a sequence of characters, the first change on the character was immediately sent to the server, while the other changes were sent at once only upon reception of an acknowledgement from the server. With each change sent to the server, it created a new version of the document. Gstreamer software enabled the video recording of user activity. We also instrumented Etherpad to register all user keyboard inputs on the client side and to introduce delays on the server-side. The editor window displayed 50 lines of text. Users editing above the field of view of a collaborator could cause the lines within the collaborators' view to "jump" inexplicably. Such a property is consistent with the inability to view an entire document as it undergoes modification from multiple team members.

*Task and Stimuli.* Participants conducted a 10 minute search and sorting task, starting with an alphabetized list of movies. They used the internet to locate the release year for each movie and sorted the list in chronological order. The list contained 74 movies, extending beyond the window size of the editor.

*Procedure.* The entire procedure was approved by a US University IRB. Participants began the session with informed consent. The present sorting task was second in a three-task series. Scripted instructions (translated into English) for the sorting task follow: *"We will provide you with the list of movies. Your task is to search for the release dates of the movies and assemble a single list of movies sorted and labeled with their release dates. You can use the browser for finding the year of release of a movie. The year of release of a movie should be placed before the movie title and the movies should be sorted in an ascending order, starting from the oldest to the newest movie. You will have 10 minutes for finishing the task. Please work as accurately as you can while still being efficient. You are free to coordinate your efforts with your teammates throughout the task using the chat interface at the bottom right side of the screen".*

*Design.* The sorting task was conducted with four teams of 4 participants for each level of the continuous independent variable Delay, tested at 0, 4, 6, 8 and 10 seconds in addition to the 100 msec delay inherent to client-server communication. While participants viewed their own document changes in real-time, they viewed other participants' changes according to delay condition. Chat was implemented in real time for all conditions. Delay conditions were tested in random order, and all groups experienced a single level of delay across the three-task session.

*Dependant Measures.* We examined sorting accuracy as an outcome measure. We also examined a set of process measures such as average time per entry and chat behavior, as well as strategies.

- *Sorting Accuracy* is measured by an insertion sort metric which is the most likely strategy for human sorting [7]. Insertion sort iterates over an input list of elements and generates an output sorted list. At each iteration, an element in the input list is removed and inserted in the proper location within the sorted list, terminating when no more input elements remain. The insertion sort metric quantifies the distance between the input list and the output sorted list. Here the group provides the input list and the output list is the target list of movies, ordered according to their release dates. The distance between an element in the input list and the corresponding element in the sorted list is measured in terms of the number of swaps between adjacent elements required to place the input element properly in the sorted list.

We normalized this distance with the distance in the worst case scenario, i.e. when the input list is sorted in reverse order. We additionally had to accommodate duplicated or missing movies, or movies with incorrect release dates. Therefore we eliminated the duplicated movies and the movies with an incorrect release date from the final list of movies generated by each group. We also eliminated from the output list the missing movies in the input list. The distance computed by the insertion sort metric was adjusted to be proportional to the number of movies that are not duplicated and for which users assigned the correct release dates. The formula that we used for each group score is : $\left(1 - \frac{\#Swaps}{\#SwapsWorstCase}\right) \times \#Movies$

$\#Swaps$ represents the total number of swaps between adjacent movies required using an insert sort method on the group's final list of movies. $\#SwapsWorstCase$ represents the total number of swaps between adjacent movies required by an insert method in the worst case, i.e. when the list of movies contains the movies in a descendant order according to the release dates. $\#Movies$ represents the number of movies in the final list of movies after a removal of duplicated movies or those with an incorrect release date. Two co-authors independently coded the insertion sort metric in different programming languages with identical results.

– *Average Time Per Entry* was computed as the period of activity in question divided by the number of characters input. Because the task characteristics potentially changed over the 10 minutes, with the first half corresponding to the identification of movie dates and the second potentially corresponding to the sorting, we also calculated separate average response times for the first and second halves of the session.

– *Chat behavior* was quantified as the number of turns, the number of words, agreement words (yes and OK), group oriented pronouns (You, your, one, us, who, each one, someone, no one, others) and ego oriented pronouns (I, my, me, mine). We examined agreement words, group-oriented pronouns and ego-oriented pronouns as a function of the number of words.

– *Strategies* emerged through detailed analysis and are described below.

## 3   Results

We provide results in three subsections, organized by measures. First we examine task strategies. Next we examine task outcome, followed by several measures of task process. For both outcome and process measures, we conduct regression modeling, using Delay condition and Strategy as predictors, and follow up with simple effect analyses by Strategy. We examine additional facets of process in the indicators of coordination as apparent in Chat.

### 3.1   Strategies

As we had no a priori hypotheses about how users would divide up the work, we developed a coding scheme based on a review of the videos, supplemented by the chat discussion. Two strategies emerged:

- Sort at the end (Strategy 0) where sorting starts after all years have been added for all movies. This strategy enables loose coupling among participants at the beginning of the task, but leaves a highly coupled sorting task for end, with no pre-established assignments.
- Continuous sorting sorting (Strategy 1) is done immediately after adding a year for a movie. This strategy begins with a highly coupled distribution of work among participants.

## 3.2  Outcome Measure

An insertion sort metric served as the outcome measure. Figure 1 displays the relationship between Delay, Strategy and insertion sort.

Strategy alone accounts for insertion sort score, $r(18) = .68$, adjusted $R^2 = .34$, $F(1, 18) = 10.89$, $p = .004$, $b_0 = 44.17$ $t(18) = 14.54$, $p < .001$, $b_1 = 4.53$, $t(18) = 3.30$, $p = .004$.

We examined the 9 groups who pursued Strategy 1 separately from the 11 groups who pursued Strategy 0. Among the 11 Strategy 0 groups, Delay does not predict insertion sort ($r(9) = .11$, adjusted $R^2 = -.10$, $F(1, 9) = .12$, $p = .742$). Among the 9 Strategy 1 groups, a linear model for Delay predicts insertion sort score ($r(7) = .69$, adjusted $R^2 = .39$, $F(1, 7) = 6.21$, $p = .042$). The intercept for the linear model is 66.46, $t(7) = 17.69$, $p = .000$ and the unstandardized slope is $-1.38$, $t(7) = -2.49$, $p = .042$. That is, each increment in Delay decrements the outcome measure by 1.38 Insertion Sort score units. A quadratic model does provide a better account for Strategy 1 groups ($r(7) = .75$, adjusted $R^2 = .50$, $F(1, 7) = 8.98$, $p = .020$). The intercept for the quadratic model is 65.99, $t(7) = 21.15$, $p = .000$ and the unstandardized Delay slope is $-.15$, $t(7) = -3.00$, $p = .020$. This model raises the possibility that Delay condition 10 results in qualitatively different behavior than the other conditions.

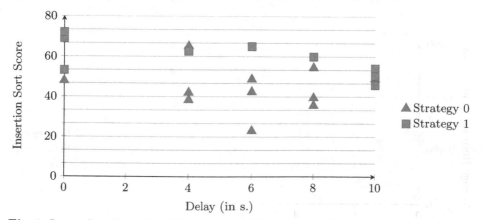

**Fig. 1.** Insert Sort Score by Delay, separated by strategy. Strategy 0 groups pursued sorting after finding movie years. Strategy 1 groups pursued continuous sorting.

### 3.3   Process Measures

We examined the average time between task inputs based on client recordings. Software error caused the loss of data for 4 groups. At the group level we used regression analysis to describe our results, treating Delay condition as a continuously valued independent variable. At the participant level, we used a nested ANOVA, using Delay condition as a categorical variable. The nested analysis allowed us to determine whether significant group effects precluded analysis of the Delay main effect. We examined Delay condition and Strategy as independent variables, with tests based on Type III Sums of Squares to account for the unbalanced design and an $\alpha = .10$ due to the small number of groups [1].

Significant group effects precluded statistical analysis of response time data across the entire experimental session. We proceeded with response time data from the session's first 5 minutes, where group effects were absent.

Group response time over the first 5 minutes accounts for insertion sort score, $(r(14) = .49$, adjusted $R^2 = .19$, $F(1, 14) = 4.48$, $p = .053$, $b_0 = 70.37$ ($t(14) = 7.20$, $b_1 = -.01$, $t(14) = -2.12$, $p = .053$). Slowing down decreases outcome.

Delay alone accounts for response time, $r(14) = .45$, adjusted $R^2 = .15$, $F(1, 14) = 3.56$, $p = .080$, $b_0 = 2504.77$ msec $t(14) = 4.81$, $p < .001$, $b_1 = 141.84$, $t(14) = 1.89$, $p = .080$.

As suggested in Figure 2, separate Strategy models suggest quadratic effects of Delay on response times. For Strategy 0 the best model missed overall significance $r(6) = .75$, adjusted $R^2 = .38$, $F(2, 5) = 3.12$, $p = .132$, $b_0 = -6331.84$ msec $t(5) = -1.54$, $p = .183$, Delay $b_1^* = 5.05$, $t(5) = 2.42$, $p = .060$, Delay$^2$ $b_2^* = -4.81$, $t(5) = -2.30$, $p = .070$. For Strategy 1, the best model had an $r(6) = .71$, adjusted $R^2 = .42$, $F(1, 6) = 6.12$, $p = .048$, $b_0 = 2281.23$, $t(6) = 7.02$, $p < .001$, Delay$^2$ $b_1^* = .71$, $t(6) = 2.47$, $p = .048$.

*Chat.* We examined chat metrics as predictors of insertion sort score. Proportion of accord words predicted insertion sort score ($r(18) = .54$, adjusted $R^2 = .25$,

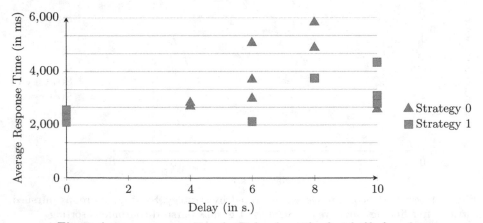

**Fig. 2.** Average response time by Delay from the first half of session

$F(1, 18) = 7.24$, $p = .015$, $b_0 = -40.00$, $t(18) = 8.49$, $b_1 = 3.83$, $p = .000$, $t(18) = 2.69$, $p = .015$). We also examined Strategy and Delay as predictors of chat metrics. Of these analyses, only total words was sensitive to the independent variables. For Strategy 0, Delay predicts total words ($r(9) = .64$, adjusted $R^2 = .34$, $F(1, 9) = 6.22$, $p = .034$, $b_0 = 29.08$, $t(9) = .79$, $p = .448$, $b_1 = 14.32$, $t(9) = 2.49$, $p = .034$). For Strategy 1, Delay does not predict total words ($r(7) = .34$, adjusted $R^2 = -.01$, $F(1, 7) = .92$, $p = .368$, $b_0 = 123.36$, $t(7) = .5.39$, $p = .001$, $b_1 = -3.23$, $p = .034$, $t(7) = -.96$, $p = .368$).

## 4   Discussion

An artificial document editing task captures the upper limit of dependency and interactivity in collaborative editing, and permits the measurement of task outcome. Here we return to our original question regarding the relationship between delay and strategy on process and outcome.

The effect of delay depends on strategy. Such an interaction between strategy and experimental manipulation on outcome is consistent with prior studies in game-like motor control environments. However, somewhat counterintuitively, and unlike previous research, the overall superior strategy does not overcome the effect of delay. In fact, the insertion sort score declined with delay for continuous sort, but did not for sort-at-the-end. We suspect that continuous sort entails more coupling, because years must be in place prior to positioning, and because text position is changing frequently throughout the entire task as sorting proceeds. To manage the coupling in continuous sort, we see participants slow down with delay. However, the negative slope on the insertion sort metric for continuous sort relative to the flat slope for sort-at-the-end suggests that the continuous sort strategy is only adaptive within a range of delay. Untested levels of delay could actually result in worse performance for continuous sorting than a sort-at-the-end strategy.

The sort-at-the-end strategy did not encounter coupling until the later phases of task completion. However, the chat metric suggests that sort-at-the-end requires more local coordination as delay increases. Thus the coordination established by formal agreement at the outset in continuous-sort appears to favor efficient communication over the ability to respond to local perturbations. On the other hand, sort-at-the-end appears to favor the ability to respond to local perturbations at the expense of efficient communication.

Performance on a family of related tasks will help to address the relationship between delay and task properties. We have data for the effect of delay on two other artificial editing tasks that vary both the task time constant and the degree of subtask coupling. The analyses presented here suggest the need to add Delay levels, with 2 and 12 second delays and beyond. This will help determine whether the models that relate performance to delay are appropriately linear, or quadratic, with more rapid declines in task performance with delay.

## 5    Conclusions

The general effect of delay on an artificial document editing task is to slow the individual participant, which for the present task, decrements the outcome metric. However, similar to game-like tasks (e.g., [5]), the effect of delay on document editing, as measured by outcome, depends on strategy. A tightly coupled subtask decomposition that enhances outcome in the presence of minimal delay becomes detrimental at higher levels of delay, potentially less effective than a more loosely coupled task decomposition at the beginning of the task. Nevertheless, a loosely coupled strategy at the beginning of the task leaves a poorly coordinated, tightly coupled sorting task to the end of the task, increasing the need for communication and hampering overall performance. Given the time constant of the present task, strategy is at least as important as delay in the distribution of participant inputs to the team.

**Acknowledgments.** The authors are grateful for financial support of the US-Coast Inria associated team and of the research program ANR-10-SEGI-010 and for sabbatical support from the Department of Psychology, Wright State University. Many thanks to Olivia Fox for her help on statistical analyses.

## References

[1] Cooke, N.J., Gorman, J.C., Duran, J.L., Taylor, A.R.: Team cognition in experienced command-and-control teams. Journal of Experimental Psychology: Applied 13(3), 146–157 (2007)

[2] Dourish, P., Bly, S.: Portholes: supporting awareness in a distributed work group. In: Proceedings of the SIGCHI Conference on Human Factors in Computing Systems, Monterey, California, USA, pp. 541–547 (1992)

[3] Ellis, C.A., Gibbs, S.J., Rein, G.: Groupware: Some Issues and Experiences. Communications of ACM 34(1), 39–58 (1991)

[4] Erkens, G., Jaspers, J., Prangsma, M., Kanselaar, G.: Coordination processes in computer supported collaborative writing. Computers in Human Behavior 21(3), 463–486 (2005)

[5] Gutwin, C., Benford, S., Dyck, J., Fraser, M., Vaghi, I., Greenhalgh, C.: Revealing delay in collaborative environments. In: Proceedings of the SIGCHI Conference on Human Factors in Computing Systems, Vienna, Austria, pp. 503–510 (2004)

[6] Schmidt, K., Bannon, L.J.: Taking cscw seriously. Computer Supported Cooperative Work 1(1-2), 7–40 (1992)

[7] Sedgewick, R.: Algorithms. Addison-Wesley (1983)

[8] Simon, H.A.: The architecture of complexity. In: Proceedings of the American Philosophical Society, pp. 467–482 (1962)

[9] Tan, D.S., Gergle, D., Mandryk, R., Inkpen, K., Kellar, M., Hawkey, K.: MaryCzerwinski: Using job-shop scheduling tasks for evaluating collocated collaboration. Personal and Ubiquitous Computing 12(3), 255–267 (2008)

# Collaborative Web Platform for UNIX-Based Big Data Processing

Omar Castro[1], Hugo Sereno Ferreira[1,2], and Tiago Boldt Sousa[1,2]

[1] Department of Informatics Engineering, Faculty of Engineering,
University of Porto, Portugal
{omar.castro,hugo.sereno,tiago.boldt}@fe.up.pt
[2] INESC Technology and Science (formerly INESC Porto), Portugal

**Abstract.** UNIX-based operative systems were always empowered by scriptable shell interfaces, with a core set of powerful tools to perform manipulation over files and data streams. However those tools can be difficult to manage at the hands of a non-expert programmer.

This paper proposes the creation of a Collaborative Web Platform to easily create workflows using common UNIX command line tools for processing Big Data through a collaborative web GUI.

**Keywords:** Big Data, UNIX Shell, End-User Programming, Cooperative Programming.

## 1 The Expansion of Data

The volume of data being generated globally has been growing exponentially [1] which is increasing the complexity of managing it using traditional tools. Five dimensions can be identified while evaluating how data is growing [2]: *Volume*, managing terabytes to petabytes and up; *Variety* of different types of data (musics, videos, images, text); *Velocity* of flowing data in all directions, *Variability* inconsistent data flow speeds with periodic peaks; and *Complexity* , correlating and sharing data across entities. Considering the specific needs while dealing with Big Data, new paradigms are being adopted to simplify how information can be processed optimally, both for achieving results faster, as well as to simplify the process of creating new computing pipelines.

## 2 UNIX Shell: A Studied Solution

The UNIX shell adopted concurrency paradigms that are being applied today by modern programming languages [3] since they were introduced [4], e.g. the *stream processing*[5], which is a similar paradigm to the *Pipes and Filters* architecture applied in the UNIX Shell [6].

New tools were created in the UNIX environment that allow the execution of workflows in more conventional ways, like executing commands in a remote computer using the Secure Shell (SSH) tool, parallel execution of UNIX shell code in one or multiple computer by using the *parallel* command.

Y. Luo (Ed.): CDVE 2014, LNCS 8683, pp. 199–202, 2014.

However the UNIX shell also has shortcomings, it is difficult to design complex big-data workflows, because not only the user have to study the functionality of each command, which can differ greatly, Furthermore, commands documentation ("man pages") might be complex to read by non expert users.

Due to their native concurrency and distribution and large amount of stream processing commands, UNIX Shells are a relevant platform to consider for Big Data processing.

## 3    A Block-Based Collaborative Solution

The authors propose a collaborative web based framework for creating dataflow-based processing using common UNIX shell commands[1], abstracted as connected block components. The metaphor of a component with inputs and outputs is a common representation in software engineering. Black box testing, per example, uses this metaphor. A user creates components with a set of inputs that transform incoming data, making the result available in an output. These outputs can be connected with inputs of other components, creating a model that is similar to a data-flow diagram. Our approach was implemented as a collaborative web application, with a drag and drop editor to create and connect components. A parsing engine then converts this representation into its textual version, compatible with common UNIX Shells. Figure 1 shows an example of the execution of a workflow and its resulting command line at the bottom.

Being a realtime collaborative framework, the system allows for users to co-operate while building their dataflows. The processing workflow is formed by making typed connections, avoiding possible errors such as infinite loops by creating cycles in the dataflow. The workflow can be created or managed using the dataflow GUI, or using text code that should be compatible with UNIX Shell. All block management, connection, abstraction and information propagation on blocks would be controlled by our framework using a data-flow [7] approach.

### 3.1    Prototype Implementation

The authors identified a potential in the usage of UNIX tools to execute big data related tasks, while it provides command line interpreters for the users to interact those tools, adding a collaborative aspect of managing it. It was decided to develop a framework for the browser, starting by using technologies that would help developing the application efficiently.

The implementation started in the creation of a parser, to translate text commands to a data representation of a data-flow graph that will be used to generate a graph visually. Since most commands in the UNIX shell code are executables, and many of them are not related to data processing of files, we would need to restrict the number of allowed commands. The transformation of text code to visual information has been done for a number of commands the authors believed it was sufficient to advance to the implementation of the GUI, the authors

---

[1] The source code is in the link `https://github.com/OmarCastro/ShellHive`

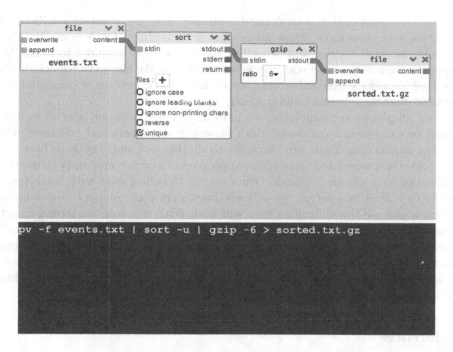

**Fig. 1.** An example of a command line and it's visual representation

also explored the automatic generation of graphs from a text command, which an expert user can create a workflow by using text commands, since creating workflows with a keyboard can be faster than creating manually with a GUI.

The parse and execution of the workflow in the server has been done initially in a local machine to find security problems. The dataflow would be executed in an isolated container in the server, allowing a safe execution of the workflow. The isolation environment of the commands will be done using the LXC tool [8] to execute the commands without compromising performance and security for those who do the execution. When a user runs a dataflow, every connected peer receives a notification about the execution, and also information about the execution of the application, such as percentage done and time remaining to finish the execution with the help of the *pv*(pipe viewer) command line utility. Every workspace allows uploads and downloads of files, and any generated files after executing the workflow will be added in the workspace so that the user can download them later.

## 4   Future Work

While the presented prototype can already be used to experiment with the concept, a final product would require further development to increase the products maturity. Another plan is the usage of Docker  [9] as the container engine to execute the commands in a sandboxed container. The engine uses the LXC tool to create said containers. Then we are going to begin to implement the user management in the server and as well as the technologies required to make the application a collaborative realtime web application. We also plan to include an interface to manage external servers, which allow the execution of commands in multiple machines, or in a remote server.

After all phases are completed, we plan to test both our end-user as well as expert programmers frameworks. Both expert programmers and end-users will test the application. There are two ways to do this test, one way is to host the application in a server and ask interested people in the web community to use the application and ask for feedback, Other way is to collect data with interviews, locally or hosted in a server, we will ask for expert programmers to develop a workflow and see the difficulties they will find. With this test, we intend to get answers for: Do we provide sufficient debug options? Is our application intuitive? Then we will ask them to compare their experiences with the usage only text commands. After those tests, we will analyze the data, fix some bugs and test again. Final goal will be to open-source our work and freely distribute it within the community, allowing private deployments of the system.

# References

1. Big data and the creative destruction of today's business models, strategic it article, a.t. Kearney
2. Big Data Meets Big Data Analytics, SAS White Paper (2011)
3. Robbins, K.A., Robbins, S.: Practical UNIX Programming: A Guide to Concurrency, Communication, and Multithreading. Prentice-Hall, Inc., Upper Saddle River (1995)
4. Bourne, S.R.: An introduction to the UNIX shell. Bell Laboratories (1978)
5. Bartenstein, T.W., Liu, Y.D.: Green streams for data-intensive software. In: 2013 35th International Conference on Software Engineering (ICSE), pp. 532–541. IEEE Press (2013)
6. Scheibler, T., Leymann, F., Roller, D.: Executing pipes-and-filters with workflows. In: 2010 Fifth International Conference on Internet and Web Applications and Services (ICIW), pp. 143–148 (May 2010)
7. Johnston, W.M., Hanna, J.R.P., Millar, R.J.: Advances in dataflow programming languages. ACM Comput. Surv. 36, 1–34 (2004)
8. LXC - Linux Containers, https://linuxcontainers.org (accessed April 18, 2014)
9. Homepage - Docker: the Linux container engine, https://www.docker.io (accessed April 19, 2014)

# Efficient Group Discussion with Digital Affinity Diagram System (DADS)

William Widjaja*, Keito Yoshii, and Makoto Takahashi

Department of Management of Science and Technology,
Graduate School of Engineering, Tohoku University, 6-6-10 Aramaki Aza Aoba,
Sendai, 980-8579, Japan

**Abstract.** Collaborative discussion is an integral part of exchanging ideas and solving important problems. However, traditional approaches to group discussion have used analog tools that create problems for collaborative contributions. Many researchers have tried to use technology to overcome these limitations, but current digital collaboration systems isolate users from each other and do not promote efficient idea creation or allow users space to support ideas with evidence. The Digital Affinity Diagram System (DADS) presents a solution that encourages better group discussion by implementing three features: 1) Separation of private and common areas during initial phase to allow ideas to mature without initial critique 2) Intuitive input and navigational design to help users create, edit, view and manipulate generated ideas, and 3) Multi-platform synchronization technology to create real-time visual feedback on the discussion accessible to all users. DADS' dual-monitor setup uses real-time network socket infrastructure so that multiple users can interact with each other under one discussion environment. We capitalize on multi-touch hardware to create a natural, deep and structured collaborative environment.

**Keywords:** Human Factors, Design, Measurement, CSCW, Brainstorming, Affinity-Diagram, Idea-generation, Collaboration.

## 1 Introduction

Collaborative development is a mainstay of most industries and is central to technology, education, and design. Many groups struggle to enhance creativity and maintain an efficient collaborative process[1]. Most collaborative work is initiated by face-to-face group meetings [2]. Research has shown mixed results for collaborative idea generation: some find that the number of ideas generated by groups is significantly higher and broader than mere individuals[3], while others have pointed out that collaborative idea generation does not necessarily produce more or better ideas than individual idea generation[4]. Digital brainstorming

---

* Mr. William Widjaja is the principal designer and developer of the DADS with the support of the Mr. Keito Yoshii for experiment design and advise from Dr. Makoto Takahashi

Y. Luo (Ed.): CDVE 2014, LNCS 8683, pp. 203–213, 2014.
© Springer International Publishing Switzerland 2014

tools have not solved these problems by improving the efficiency of collaboration, but have instead tried to accurately replicate collaboration using digital paper or large-scale digital "idea boards." Digital collaboration tools that do increase efficiency may isolate collaborators from each other. Our challenge was to design a system that takes advantage of technology to overcome these problems without constraining group interactions or continuing the inefficiency of analog collaborations.

## 1.1    Issues with Collaboration in Analog Methods

Teams often use collaborative methods like brainstorming and affinity diagrams[5] to gather and organize new ideas at the beginning of a project. However, most of these teams are working on digital products in a digital environment. Transitioning from analog meetings to digital collaboration creates a bottleneck in the project's timeline. There are three major problems with analog collaboration: 1) Social factors such as anxiety, production blocking, and negative evaluation, 2) Articulating and supporting ideas, and 3) Record-keeping and transferring between mediums. Anxiety and fear of negative evaluation can reduce the volume and creativity of ideas that people share during collaboration[6]. Production blocking during collaboration can close off innovative ideas; contributors with very different ideas can feel "blocked" from producing them because they are so dissimilar to the more popular ideas[7]. And lastly, initial idea generation meetings are difficult to record in the digital space, although many tools have been developed that attempt to capture the analog output of this complex process. Given the severity of these problems, many researchers have tried to use technology to solve them.

## 1.2    Digital Tools for Collaboration

One reason people in technologically sophisticated organizations end up collaborating and generating ideas using analog techniques is the lack of efficient, easy-to-use digital solutions. Teams hold meetings that rely on analog tools largely because that is the best solution so far. However, many teams are recognizing that analog collaboration is inefficient, especially when transitioning back and forth to digital creation and development mediums. Digital collaboration tools have generally taken one of two forms: "big screen" shared group displays that encourage face-to-face interaction, but still have most of the drawbacks of analog idea generation, and "small screen" methods that are able to coordinate large remote teams, but which don't lend themselves well to idea generation and face-to-face meetings.

"Big screen" digital collaborative environments have focused on exactly replicating the physical constraints of analog techniques in a digital format, as in Geyer and colleagues' Affinity Table[8]. Their device allows users to create virtual sticky notes with digital ink and organize them over a multi-touch surface.However, these systems still force participants to negotiate physical space with others when generating ideas and collaborating on a grouping and sorting task. Haller's Nice [9] discussion solution uses this specialized digital Anoto pen to detect two different users. This allows users to digitally collaborate with each other using different colored pens, just as they would in the analog method. More traditional "small screen" methods for collaboration range from email to version-control processes and project management applications, all of which are adapted to serve distributed teams. Some systems allow users to create an input using a distributed interface such as PDA, mobile phone, or tablet [10]. Ballendat and colleagues' Proxemic Brainstorm system[11] separates public and private space by giving users hand-held devices to synchronously contribute to brainstorming activity without interrupting larger group discussions. This system could be considered a hybrid big screen/small screen tool. Greenberg's SharedNotes system [12] used PDAs to create a private space for users to develop ideas before sharing them with other users. Many of these distributed systems are still focused on a monolithic shared group display (SGD) and specialized technology, such as an overhead projector and camera, or digital pen and microdot paper. We think it is important to give users a familiar setup to express their thoughts. Access to a familiar system with a keyboard, mouse, and browser will allow users to efficiently research, build and nurture ideas.

Collaborative web-browsing tools take a different approach to these problems. Paul and Morris' CoSense tool enables group web-based investigation by making better sense of how individuals reach solutions and look for information to support them.[13] In our experiences with collaborative idea generation, we often found that a sticky note was much too small for some of the ideas that users wanted to contribute, especially if the process required people to express persuasive opinions. Our tool gives users the ability to attach source material using familiar digital mechanics.

### 1.3 Proposed Solution

Our goal in developing DADS is to create an efficient tool for collaboration that uses **Dual-Screen Terminal** design which separates private input space from common interactive space for idea generation and discussions. DADS is a multi-user real time digital sticky note discussion system that gives users a personal space to create their ideas while allowing users to also have control of their ideas in common interactive spaces during discussion. To make digital collaboration more accessible, DADS uses a multi-touch gesture-based monitor and stable Microsoft database server technology. The two goals of the system include 1) private space is to create an intuitive user input system that quickly converts users' thoughts into text with minimal steps, and 2) a natural collaborative environment where users can easily cluster and link similar ideas to provide structure to their collaboration.

## 2 System Architecture Design

DADS was designed and developed at Tohoku University . The basics of the system can be seen in our previous work, the Discusys system[14]. The current

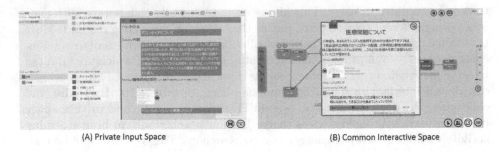

(A) Private Input Space                    (B) Common Interactive Space

**Fig. 1.** (A) Private Input space for data input and (B) Common interactive space for collaboration

system presents significant technical and design improvements and is more robust than its predecessor. We have extended the system so that it accommodates 3 users instead of only 2, we have incorporated a system for attaching sources that support discussion points, and we have added two creative features to help users express their points: a Vector Free Draw feature and a digital pointer that can highlight text or images when activated.

**Private Input Interface.** The private input interface maximizes visibility and navigation capabilities for users viewing and creating discussion points. Figure 1(A) shows the private interface's 3 column dashboard: in the top right hand users can select different topics and switch from one topic to another; the middle column lists all the ideas written by each participant; the bottom right corner is where users select and view different participants' points; the lower center column lists the titles of other participants' points. Finally, the full screen right-hand column is where users construct their own points. Three distinct areas allow users to give each idea a title, description, and source documents that support each idea.

Users can switch freely between the input dashboard and a browser window when they are searching for supporting material. DADS' source attachment function gives users the ability to attach articles or sources from the Internet to their ideas. Two new features allow users to enhance their ideas with evidence: Internal Browser and Media Attachment. The system's internal browser makes it easier for participants to search for evidence to support their ideas, and for other participants to view this evidence by clicking a URL. Media Attachment allows users to right-click images from a browser search to copy and paste the image url to our media text box in the system's private input form.

**Common Interactive Space.** In the common space interface, points written in the private input space are displayed as cards with the author's identity color, the point's title and the author's name. These cards can be rearranged by touching and dragging them to a new location on the multi-touch screen. We believe that successful collaboration requires the common space to be synchronized smoothly across different users. To achieve this goal, our system was optimized for low latency between common interface monitors so that participants' collaboration was seamless.

Four key features of the common space allow users to assemble an affinity diagram more easily than they can with the traditional sticky-notes-and-pen "analog" method.

- **In-depth Card Details** - Cards on the common interactive board display only the title of the user's idea. Users expand the card details by double-clicking on the card. The expanded window displays all of the in-depth information including the description, attached links, and media sources.
- **Commenting System** - This function replicates the commenting phase of the analog Affinity Diagram process by allowing users to comment on each other's ideas, ask questions, and write comments via the system. Users can expand any card and write comments on another person's ideas. In addition, users are notified of new comments via the system, which allows users to have real-time exchanges with each other.
- **Grouping and Linking** - Grouping and linking cards can be accomplished using certain motions on the multi-touch monitor. If a user presses the 'Group' button and touches cards on the common board with a circular motion between several cards, a border around these cards is created, and these grouped cards can be moved as a unit. Groups of cards can be reorganized by moving any card within the group, and any ungrouped card can be inserted into that group. Users can link cards or groups to each other by pressing the 'Link' button and clicking two cards in sequence.
- **Vector Free Drawing** Previous digital collaboration systems have allowed users to draw in collaboration, but these drawings quickly become confused and overlapping. DADS' drawing system creates vectored image components from each free-form drawing on the common board. Because users' drawings are converted to vector images that can be moved and resized, users have more flexibility to create and re-shape their own objects on the board.

(A) Individual Terminal Setup          (B) Group Terminal Setup

**Fig. 2.** (A) Single individual setup with dual extended multi-touch monitor at the left side (B) 3 person group setup with a larger public monitor at the center

## 2.1   Hardware Setup

The system described above requires a hardware setup that can provide reliable low latency performance and real-time updating. It also needs to allow discussion and conversation to flow easily. We designed a three-person seating arrangement(Fig 2(B)) with synchronous access for this experiment. Each user's laptop displays the private input interface, and users access the common interactive board via the auxiliary multi-touch monitor(Fig 2.(A)). A large central monitor displays the common interactive space and acts as a central focus during discussion. The Windows Server 2008 infrastructure prefers low latency in order to allow the high-frequency refresh of simultaneous workspaces; it acts as both a database system and input-output traffic center.

## 2.2   Software Architecture

The system's software was developed using C#, using Microsoft libraries to increase compatibility across critical server, database, and client infrastructure. In addition, we also took advantage of the touch framework library that is currently maturing in Microsoft's framework to develop the system's interactions with the extended 22" multi-touch monitor. The laptop and multi-touch monitor give users access to the private and common interactive spaces, respectively.

**Multi-user Real-Time Synchronization Technology.** We believe that successful collaboration requires the common interactive space to be synchronized smoothly across different users. To achieve this goal, we used an optimized network socket method, core technology from a multi-player on-line game engine, and adapted this technology to suit our system. Participants are given a unique identity and color for their idea cards. They can also manipulate idea cards and enlarge the details of other participants' ideas. These manipulation input commands are constantly sent to the server, and updates are broadcast to other clients at up to 10 commands per second. Low latency determines the smoothness of the common board's control and manipulation responses.

## 3   User Study Experiment

In this direct comparison study, we hypothesize that the system's attachment and comment features can enhance users' ability to show and explain their ideas. Increasing users' powers of expression using technology may improve their satisfaction with the result of group discussion. We expect that higher usability and flexibility can result in more movements executed by users in the digital condition.

### 3.1   Analog Condition and Digital Condition

We tested the usability of our Digital system against the Analog method commonly used for collaborative affinity diagrams. The analog method uses traditional tools: a whiteboard, colored sticky notes, and colored markers. Users in the Analog condition could search the Internet and print out any sources they wished to use, and magnets were provided to connect these materials to the idea notes. In the Digital environment, users interacted with our system to conduct the experimental tasks. Before the experiment, participants were given a 60-minute tutorial on the digital system and a 30-minute tutorial in the analog conditions. The longer tutorial time for digital ensured that users were reasonably comfortable with the system. Afterward, participants completed a survey comparing the systems' features in terms of usability.

## 3.2 Participants

A total of 15 participants (8 men, 7 women) performed this experiment. They were recruited by word of mouth, and were all undergraduate students, mainly from the faculties of engineering and science, between the ages of 18 and 24. Experiments were conducted with groups of 3 individuals, and all groups went through both Analog and Digital conditions. The subjects were all right handed, and 11 of 15 had experience with a dual-screen monitor system in the past.

## 3.3 Experiment Procedure

This experiment compares the analog method of affinity diagramming to our digital approach. The affinity diagram process was originally developed to overcome some of the problems inherent in brainstorming and exchanging ideas[5]. During the creation of a collaborative affinity diagram, users perform 4 tasks from the modified Nominal Groups technique developed by Delbecq and colleagues[15]:

- Task 1:Create Ideas Points and Attach Source (**30 mins**)
- Task 2:Sharing and Explaining points (**15 mins**)
- Task 3:Exchanging opinions and Comments (**20 mins**)
- Task 4:Collaborative affinity diagram (**15 mins**)

## 3.4 Observations

We measure our system's usability in two ways: a usability survey administered to participants and counts of behavioral performance metrics. Our analyses determine user preference and whether DADS supports better collaboration. Table 1 shows the result of user responses to all 15 survey questions. In this paper, we focus on reporting three distinct relationships: 1) participants' use of attachments and how this influenced their ability to clearly explain their ideas; 2) participants' use and feelings about making and reading comments and comment functions; and 3) the relationship between flexibility in the digital system and users' tendency to move and re-group ideas, leading to increased feelings of usefulness. We also report the number of card moves, attachments, and comments in both analog and digital conditions. Paired t-tests were used to determine the relative strengths and weaknesses of the two methods (Analog and Digital), as perceived by participants.

**Table 1.** Full Experiment Self reporting Usability Survey result

|  | N | Mean | Std. Dev | Std. Err | 95%LCI | 95%UCI | t.test | P-Value |
|---|---|---|---|---|---|---|---|---|
| Create Ideas AN | 15 | 3.87 | 0.92 | 0.24 | 3.36 | 4.37 | 2.32 | 0.04 |
| Create Ideas DI | 15 | 4.53 | 0.92 | 0.24 | 4.03 | 5.04 | | |
| Edit Ideas AN | 15 | 3.27 | 1.10 | 0.28 | 2.66 | 3.88 | 5.00 | 0.00 |
| Edit Ideas DI | 15 | 4.80 | 0.41 | 0.11 | 4.57 | 5.03 | | |
| Attach Source AN | 15 | 2.13 | 1.06 | 0.27 | 1.55 | 2.72 | 6.62 | 0.00 |
| Attach Source DI | 15 | 4.53 | 0.64 | 0.17 | 4.18 | 4.89 | | |
| Show Ideas/Source AN | 15 | 2.87 | 1.25 | 0.32 | 2.18 | 3.56 | 3.68 | 0.00 |
| Show Ideas/Source DI | 15 | 4.47 | 0.83 | 0.22 | 4.00 | 4.93 | | |
| Explain Ideas AN | 15 | 3.13 | 0.92 | 0.24 | 2.63 | 3.64 | 2.75 | 0.02 |
| Explain Ideas DI | 15 | 3.87 | 0.83 | 0.22 | 3.40 | 4.33 | | |
| Navigate AN | 15 | 2.93 | 1.03 | 0.27 | 2.36 | 3.51 | 4.07 | 0.00 |
| Navigate DI | 15 | 4.47 | 0.83 | 0.22 | 4.00 | 4.93 | | |
| Understand AN | 15 | 3.27 | 0.80 | 0.21 | 2.82 | 3.71 | 3.29 | 0.01 |
| Understand DI | 15 | 4.07 | 0.80 | 0.21 | 3.62 | 4.51 | | |
| Read Comments AN | 15 | 3.40 | 1.18 | 0.31 | 2.74 | 4.06 | 2.30 | 0.04 |
| Read Comments DI | 15 | 4.27 | 0.88 | 0.23 | 3.78 | 4.76 | | |
| Write Comments AN | 15 | 2.93 | 0.96 | 0.25 | 2.40 | 3.47 | 5.77 | 0.00 |
| Write Comments DI | 15 | 4.67 | 0.62 | 0.16 | 4.32 | 5.01 | | |
| Reply Comments AN | 15 | 3.13 | 0.99 | 0.26 | 2.58 | 3.68 | 3.67 | 0.00 |
| Reply Comments DI | 15 | 4.33 | 0.90 | 0.23 | 3.84 | 4.83 | | |
| Affinity Diagram AN | 15 | 3.00 | 1.07 | 0.28 | 2.41 | 3.59 | 2.75 | 0.02 |
| Affinity Diagram DI | 15 | 4.13 | 0.83 | 0.22 | 3.67 | 4.60 | | |
| Teamwork AN | 15 | 3.53 | 1.06 | 0.27 | 2.95 | 4.12 | 1.05 | 0.31 |
| Teamwork DI | 15 | 3.87 | 0.83 | 0.22 | 3.40 | 4.33 | | |
| Comfort AN | 15 | 3.60 | 0.91 | 0.24 | 3.10 | 4.10 | 2.65 | 0.02 |
| Comfort DI | 15 | 4.27 | 0.70 | 0.18 | 3.88 | 4.66 | | |
| Usefulness AN | 15 | 3.27 | 0.96 | 0.25 | 2.73 | 3.80 | 5.10 | 0.00 |
| Usefulness DI | 15 | 4.53 | 0.64 | 0.17 | 4.18 | 4.89 | | |
| Satisfaction AN | 15 | 3.47 | 1.06 | 0.27 | 2.88 | 4.05 | 3.56 | 0.00 |
| Satisfaction DI | 15 | 4.20 | 0.68 | 0.17 | 3.83 | 4.57 | | |

Users found it easier to attach sources and support to their ideas in the digital than in the analog condition. This difference is echoed by the reported ease of explaining points, since users are mainly attaching points in order to enrich their ideas and make them easier to explain to the rest of the group. Users also found it slightly easier in the digital condition to both read comments on their own work, and write comments on others' work. The digital environment was reported to be more flexible/easier to use as well as a more useful system than the analog environment. However, there was no significant difference between systems in how well they promoted teamwork.

We used a video analysis of each session to count how many times users attached source documents, commented on another person's ideas, and moved the idea cards on the common interaction board. We also measured how long it took groups to complete the Affinity Diagram phase of the task and the number of card movements per person over time.

**Table 2.** Performance Metrics Results

|  | Analog (SD) | Digital(SD) | p-value |
|---|---|---|---|
| Number of source | 2.07(1.01) | 5.87(2.77) | <0.01 |
| Number of comments/person | 6.47(1.77) | 12.87(6.16) | <0.01 |
| Number of card movement/person | 7.00(3.85) | 17.0(10.82) | <0.01 |
| Total time to complete AD (minutes) | 6.31(1.63) | 9.94(3.31) | <0.01 |
| Frequency of moves/user (minutes) | 3.19(0.69) | 5.42(2.30) | <0.05 |

Users moved cards more often in the Digital environment compared to Analog. Digital collaboration also took longer than analog. To illustrate this, users also perform faster in digital, resulting in higher rates of card moves per minute in digital than in analog. Users may spend more time on discussion using the digital system, but they perform manipulations faster compared to analog.

### 3.5   Discussion

The above results present four interesting patterns that link behavior to user experiences. First, the attachment system's ease and usefulness is also related to how easily users were able to show and explain their points to others. Showing and explaining points are an essential part of discussion, thus the results show that digital system was perceived as easier and more useful. Second, all questions about the comment system are interrelated, and the performance metrics validate users' self-reports about their experience of the system: those who thought the commenting system was easier left more comments. Third, the synchronous features of our system enabled more movements of the idea cards, higher reported usefulness and easier diagram creation. Again, this demonstrates the relationship between what people actually do in the system (move idea cards around during the affinity diagram phase) and how they feel about it (easier in digital). Lastly, teams did not think the digital system - which they slightly preferred over the analog system- produced better perceptive teamwork.

During the experiment, we discovered that the individual dual-monitor setup encourages flexibility and efficient participation. However, having this level of individual control may have reduced perceptions of teamwork and coordinated action. Because our system spared users the awkwardness of having to negotiate physical space in front of a single affinity diagram, they may have felt a lower level of interaction with their teammates. Users who felt they had not had enough practice with the system may have been too involved in coordinating with the system to pay attention to how much they were coordinating with other people. It may be harder to experience teamwork as we know it in a digital medium compared to the familiar analog medium. However, we believe this can be learned, and is worth further exploration. We also observed that analog users who had trouble navigating the large common board would sometimes ask other users to pass sticky notes to an unreachable part of the board. Actions like this may be interpreted as "teamwork" by users, but are eliminated by the more efficient digital system. Gaining control and independence through technology reduces our dependence on other people, which can be perceived as lower levels of teamwork.

### 3.6    Conclusion and Future Research Directions

Based on the the experiment results, DADS proves to be more usable than traditional methods, and newly incorporated functions result in greater efficiency and improved usability. Despite the many benefits of the digital system, the digital tool's environment may make it harder for people to experience teamwork, even if usability results are superior. It would be worth testing a system that varied the perceived distance between users to explore subjective perceptions of teamwork and how this feeling predicts (or fails to predict) performance. Other possible analyses include linear regression or correlation, and a content analysis of user output could reveal interesting findings. The system's inherent learnability is also an area that can be further evaluated.

### References

1. Osborn, A.: Applied imagination (1953)
2. Sutton, R., Hargadon, A.: Brainstorming groups in context: Effectiveness in a product design firm. In: Administrative Science Quarterly, pp. 685–718 (1996)
3. Diehl, M., Stroebe, W.: Productivity loss in brainstorming groups: Toward the solution of a riddle. Journal of Personality and Social Psychology; Journal of Personality and Social Psychology 53(3), 497 (1987)
4. Isaksen, S.G., Gaulin, J.P.: A reexamination of brainstorming research: Implications for research and practice. Gifted Child Quarterly 49(4), 315–329 (2005)
5. Kawakita, J.: The original kj method. Kawakita Research Institute, Tokyo (1991)
6. Mullen, B., Johnson, C., Salas, E.: Productivity loss in brainstorming groups: A meta-analytic integration. Basic and Applied Social Psychology 12(1), 3–23 (1991)
7. Herrmann, T., Nolte, A.: The Integration of Collaborative Process Modeling and Electronic Brainstorming in Co-located Meetings. In: Kolfschoten, G., Herrmann, T., Lukosch, S. (eds.) CRIWG 2010. LNCS, vol. 6257, pp. 145–160. Springer, Heidelberg (2010)
8. Geyer, F., Pfeil, U., Budzinski, J., Höchtl, A., Reiterer, H.: Affinitytable-a hybrid surface for supporting affinity diagramming. Springer, Heidelberg (2011)
9. Haller, M., Leitner, J., Seifried, T., Wallace, J.R., Scott, S.D., Richter, C., Brandl, P., Gokcezade, A., Hunter, S.: The nice discussion room: Integrating paper and digital media to support co-located group meetings. In: Proceedings of the SIGCHI Conference on Human Factors in Computing Systems, pp. 609–618. ACM (2010)
10. Burtner, E.R., May, R.A., Scarberry, R.E., LaMothe, R.R., Endert, A.: Affinity+: Semi-structured brainstorming on large displays. tech. rep., Pacific Northwest National Laboratory (PNNL), Richland, WA, US (2013)
11. Ballendat, T., Marquardt, N., Greenberg, S.: Proxemic interaction: designing for a proximity and orientation-aware environment. In: ACM International Conference on Interactive Tabletops and Surfaces, pp. 121–130. ACM (2010)
12. Greenberg, S., Boyle, M., LaBerge, J.: Pdas and shared public displays: Making personal information public, and public information personal. Personal Technologies 3(1-2), 54–64 (1999)

13. Paul, S.A., Morris, M.R.: Cosense: enhancing sensemaking for collaborative web search. In: Proceedings of the SIGCHI Conference on Human Factors in Computing Systems, pp. 1771–1780. ACM (2009)
14. Widjaja, W., Yoshii, K., Haga, K., Takahashi, M.: Discusys: Multiple user real-time digital sticky-note affinity-diagram brainstorming system. Procedia Computer Science 22, 113–122 (2013)
15. Delbecq, A.L., Van de Ven, A.H.: A group process model for problem identification and program planning. The Journal of Applied Behavioral Science 7(4), 466–492 (1971)

# Integration of Product Conceptual Design Synthesis into a Computer-Aided Design System

Alexis Álvarez Cabrales[1], Enrique E. Zayas[2], Roberto Pérez[3], Rolando E. Simeón[3], Carles Riba[2], and Salvador Cardona[2]

[1] Technical Science Department, Granma University, Granma, Cuba
aalvarezc@udg.co.cu
[2] Mechanical Engineering Department, Polytechnic University of Catalonia, Barcelona, Spain
{enrique.zayas,carles.riba,salvador.cardona}@upc.edu
[3] CAD/CAM Study Center, Engineering Faculty, Holguin University, Holguin, Cuba
roberto.perez@facing.uho.edu.cu, simeon@cadcam.uho.edu.cu

**Abstract.** Commercial Computer-Aided Design systems have been mainly focused in give support to the process of capturing and representing geometric shapes and incorporating technological information. Conversely, few utilities in these systems are present to facilitate decision making in the early stages of the design process, such as the capture, modeling and conceptual design synthesis of solutions. Typical tasks of the conceptual design process in mechanical design are intended for applications stand-alone or are based on the heuristic knowledge of the designer. Such approaches are non-interoperable with the commercial computer-aided design systems which results in non-continuous information in the design process. This study addresses this subject and proposes a method to improve the integration of product conceptual design synthesis into a Computer Aided Design system. To validate the feasibility of the approach implemented, a prototype application based on a Computer Aided Design system was developed and a study case is presented.

**Keywords:** Conceptual design, design synthesis, CAD, collaborative.

## 1 Introduction

Nowadays, the traditional linear engineering design and manufacturing processes are being replaced by a new paradigmatic concurrent approach that aims to facilitate an integrated product development process. To remain competitive in this continuously evolving design and manufacturing scenario, SMEs are now focusing more and more on collaborative engineering tools in the design and manufacturing phases of the product lifecycle. In order to develop this collaborative-concurrent vision, there is a need for the formulation and application of collaborative engineering tools with the intention of supporting a virtual product design process in the new concurrent engineering approach [1].

The purpose of the conceptual design phase is to generate conceptual solutions that will meet the functional requirements of the problem (specifications), and subsequently form the basis for developing the basic and detailed system [2, 3].

Y. Luo (Ed.): CDVE 2014, LNCS 8683, pp. 214–221, 2014.
© Springer International Publishing Switzerland 2014

In the conceptual design solution, concepts are derived from the functional requirements of the design problem. This is characterized by managing information that is often inaccurate, inadequate and informal. Although the identification and generation of functional requirements and generating solutions are closely related at the conceptual stage, there is little understanding of how this process occurs [4].

The challenge then is how to support designers to increase the chance of producing the best concepts? The key to answering this question lies in the fact that it is usual to find multiple alternative solutions to a given problem. Therefore, if you can facilitate and encourage to the designer in the process of generation and exploration of concepts, the potential for better concepts would increase [4].

Authors in the field have worked in developing generic and specialized models to represent the conceptual design process. An increasing number of researchers are using computer aided design tools for their conceptual product development. These tools are characterized by 3D computer graphics visualization, but with little support to generate and evaluate conceptual solutions. A significant amount of literature is related to conceptual design of the product development. Below, advances which are considered closest to the present research are described.

Inoue et al. [5] propose a method that was applied to a real industrial multi-objective design problem (i.e. an automotive front-side frame design). This study discusses the suitability of proposed approach for obtaining the multi-objective satisfactory solu-tions that reflect the different design preferences of different designers in their design solutions for collaborative engineering. The authors do not address the conceptual modeling of solutions.

Ma et al. [6] propose an adapted Gero's Function–Behavior–State model to aid creative design activities during conceptual design stage by introducing an integrated cross-domain knowledge representation methodology, to increase robustness by reusing existing cases knowledge through retrieval algorithm, and to realize effectiveness by putting forward a design synthesis methodology. His approach is not oriented CAD systems. Torres et al. [7] define a continuous product design information flow from the conceptual design up to the detailed design phase and to implement it into a prototype application within a commercial CAD system. Research does not address the conceptual synthesis of solutions.

Song et al. [8] propose a framework of collaborative product innovation network at the project level based on the review of innovation network. Technology solutions for collaborative product innovation network (modular product innovation network development and ontology-based knowledge integration) have also been proposed. An application in electric water heater development to demonstrate the implementation and potentials of the framework proposed is also given. The authors do not address the conceptual synthesis of solutions.

Tseng et al.[9] describe the development of an intelligent system based on concurrent engineering for generating design alternatives at the conceptual design stage. The proposed system encompasses a design analysis module, a design evaluation module, a knowledge acquisition and storing module, a user interface and databases. Research is not aimed at the inclusion of the synthesis of solutions in the CAD systems. Kurtoglu et al. [10] introduces a tool called the designer preference modeler (DPM) that analyzes the designer's decision making during concept evaluation, and constructs a designer preference model to be used for evaluation of automatically generated design alternatives. Researchers do not address the synthesis of conceptual solutions.

The present research aims to understand the process of converting the functional requirements of a product to schematic descriptions, and develop a computational tool that supports the synthesis of solutions. Through a case study of a biomass stove, is exposed the development of a computational tool based on a CAD system to evaluate the design criteria's taking into account the possible combinations of product's components.

## 2    Model for Conceptual Synthesis of Solutions

In classical systematic design methodologies, especially in the conceptual design stage, it is observed as weakness the existence of ambiguity and uncertainty, both in the information to be transmitted and specifying, as in the transmission of the information between each one the sub-stages that make up the conceptual design phase. Even, can be added the lack of formalization that facilitates the evaluation of concepts from the intensive reasoning of the functional requirements.

As one of the essential characteristics of this stage, it may be mentioned that in the early stages of the design process, the information is inaccurate and therefore it is difficult to use the computer aided tools. Computer-assisted methods, such as solid modeling, optimization, the simulation and analysis of mechanisms, etc. are not suitable for this stage, thus requiring an accurate representation of the object.

In order to respond to the problematic described above, a reference model for conceptual synthesis of solutions oriented CAD systems is presented below (Figure 1). The model builds on the description of the various stages that make up the conceptual design phase of a product. Different relationships between the various sub-stages are shown. At the same time, describes how the functional requirements flow from initial specification to obtain the different concepts.

In the process of refinement of functional requirements are observed two complementary approaches. The first approach is derived from the classical paradigm of concurrent engineering, where each functional requirement is stratified according to the type of guidance that represents (DFM, DFE, etc.). Although this process helps to characterize the functional requirements, it does not provide for later use in the evaluation process. Then, a second approach that allows expressing qualitatively the functional requirements, in order to serve as a criterion for further evaluation, is proposed. Requirements with qualitative orientation can be classified according to various techniques, in the case of this research, the Kano method was used as a classification criterion.

This transformation of functional requirements expressed by the client, in qualitative requirements, allows the definition of a model for the synthesis of solutions oriented to CAD systems. Figure 1 shows the conceptual model here proposed.

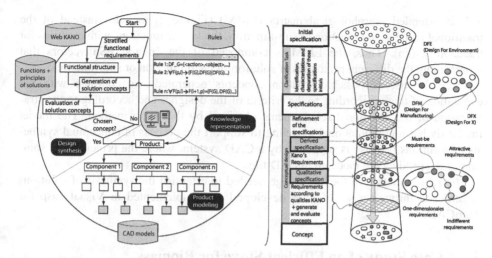

**Fig. 1.** Conceptual model for the synthesis of solutions in CAD systems

The model consists of three main stages. A stage corresponding to the synthesis of design, it is just the algorithmic representation of the conceptual design. From this process, was implemented in Visual Lisp programming an AutoCAD-oriented tool that facilitates dialogue with the user in each of the steps that the algorithm provides.

The computational tool developed has a link to a software application developed in Java that enables a collaborative environment in determining a set of surveys according to the Kano method, get group responses and make the corresponding analysis. Through a data file transfer (which in turn is stored in a database) the Java application in encrypted manner exports functional requirements to AutoCAD.

With this information, the application in AutoCAD facilitates the generation of functional structures using database functions, flows and coded signals. This structure allows the generation of concepts through the implementation of the extended morphological matrix represented as a matrix X with n and m number of functions associated with each function (Figure 2).

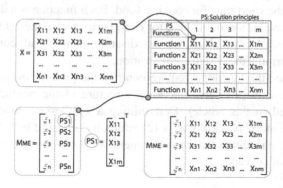

**Fig. 2.** Extended morphological matrix

The extended morphological matrix (EMM) (Figure 2) includes instead of the traditional name of the function or sub-function, the vector functions with qualities for traceability ($\xi n$). Thus, the EMM is composed of the $\xi n$ and PSn vectors that representing the different principles of solution of each function or sub-function.

Once the list of possible solution concepts generated, we continue with the evaluation of them, according to the criteria of the designer and according to the stratification of the functional requirements obtained by the Kano method. The model implicitly has a computational modeling to support the process of conceptual synthesis of solutions because is supported by a CAD system, where the principles of solution of the product are modeled in CAD files.

The representation of the knowledge needed to establish the synthesis of solutions is achieved through a set of rules developed and implemented in Visual Lisp for AutoCAD.

## 3     Case Study of an Efficient Stove for Biomass

In a metal mechanics company located in the eastern region of Cuba, the manufacture of a cooking stove is requested. Fuel is the waste of forest health treatment. A summary of the key stages of the design process used is exposed below, in the order established by the method of conceptual synthesis solutions oriented to CAD systems, here developed.

Through surveys and expert analysis on a collaborative web environment by using the Kano method, criteria and user requirements are established. The C$\Phi$A vector, defined in expression (1.1) contains the set of qualities of stove from this analysis (A: Attractive, I: Indifferent, U: One-dimensional).

$$C\Phi A = [A\ I\ A\ I\ A\ AA\ I\ U\ UU\ A\ AAAAA\ U\ U]^T \qquad (1.1)$$

The augmented matrix of functional requirements for efficient biomass stove is obtained from the vector Kn associated with each function. After this analysis, it is determined that the performance indicators will be given by the low cost, low power consumption and the short time for cooking food. Each function is a decision variable and the system provides a certain value for each performance indicator in each of the different solutions. All variables are of discrete nature and constitute general decisions that determine the design configuration.

Having identified the functional requirements of the product and having expressed through the expression (1.1), the functional structure of the product is determined (step not evaluated in this article). Determining a synthesized functional structure allows to generate morphological matrix [2] which is expressed in Table 1. This table also notes, genetic encoding used for the numerical calculation of the different possible combinations of concepts.

**Table 1.** Morphological matrix (not extended) developed for efficient biomass stove

The analysis of the relationship between functions and their solutions (Table 1) allows us to determine the size of the field theoretical solutions (TCS) (1.2 and 1.3).

$$TCS = \prod_{p=1}^{q} PS_p = 3 * 3 * 2 * 2 * 2 * 2 = 144 \qquad (1.2)$$

Each component of the design itself can group all functions, each with a solution and each feature in each solution has values that distinguish his influence on the set of efficiency indicators. Multiple Criterion value Z (1.3), taking into account the increased distance of Tchebysheff, is used as objective function [11].

$$Z = \max_{1 \le v \le n} W_i \frac{|Y_v - Y_{id}|}{|Y_{id}|} + \sum_{v=1}^{n} 0.001 \frac{|Y_v - Y_{id}|}{|Y_{id}|} \qquad (1.3)$$

where: Z - value of the objective function for the variant analyzed, $W_i$ - coefficient reflecting the importance attached by the user to efficiency indicator $Y_i$; $Y_{id}$ - Ideal value of the efficiency criterion $Y_i$, $Y_v$ - efficiency criterion value obtained according variant solution is analyzed.

In the case study there are three indicators of cost: efficiency (Co), fuelwood (Le) and cooking time (Ti), as each function n with m solutions provides Conm, Lenm and Tinm values. The value of each $Y_{id}$ is determined by equation (1.4) for indicators of fuelwood consumption and cooking time, if the amount of the cost function is assumed as n = 1, this allows to get the Coid, Leid and Tiid values.

$$Y_{id} = \frac{\sum_{i=1}^{n} \min_{1 \le j \le m} Y_{ij}}{n} \qquad (1.4)$$

where: i - Function, j - Solution, n - Number of functions; $Y_{ij}$ - Performance indicator function for the solution i with j.

Meanwhile, Yv also takes the average value of the sum of the Yi values variant analyzed according to equation (1.5).

$$Y_{id} = \frac{\sum_{i=1}^{n} \min_{1 \le j \le m} Y_{ij}}{n}$$  (1.5)

where: Yi - value of indicator i, efficiency function variant analyzed.

Each solution of variant of design will tend to value Z = 0 as the solution is more efficient, and depend on the values of weights Wi assigned by the user. The sum of the weights Wi is always 1. For this analysis a software application on a CAD system has been developed. From the weights assigned, an evaluation is performed (the results are shown in Figure 3).

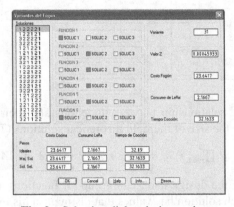

**Fig. 3.** Selection dialog design variants

The solutions generated from the morphological matrix are numerically encoded for better study and analysis. In Figure 3, the solutions and description on the selected version are identified. Once selected the solution, the combination of the principles of solution (Figure 4) is shown.

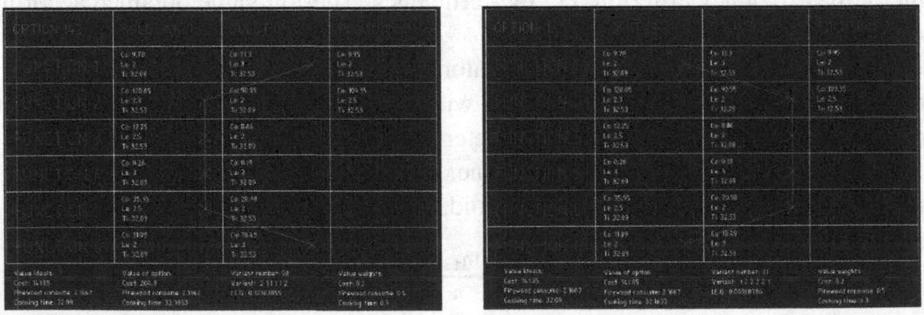

**Fig. 4.** Left - Worst design choice and Right - Better design option based on the values of weights assigned

The developed tool facilitates CAD environment, as demonstrated by its use in the case study analyzed. Also facilitates the decision-making process for the designer in the conceptual design process. The procedure developed promotes the generation of solutions and the utilization of system theory engineering enables obtaining optimized solutions.

# 4    Conclusions

The implementation of the proposed methodology in the case study discussed, indicates that the systematic formalization of the integration of the different sub-steps in the conceptual design process, permits the generation of strength concepts in a form sufficiently structured and facilitates decision-making in concept evaluation.

The development of similar systems to applied in the assessment of the case of study support the use of CAD systems in processing aspects of subjective information and in the evaluation of concepts, step linking the conceptual design with the preliminary design of a product and facilitates decision making designer.

# References

1. Pérez, R., Riba, C., Molina, A., Romero, D., Hernández, L.W., Quesada, A.M.: Concurrent Conceptual Evaluation of Tolerances' Synthesis in Mechanical Design. Concurrent Engineering: Research and Applications 19, 175–186 (2011)
2. Pahl, G., Beitz, W., Feldhusen, J., Grote, K.H.: Engineering Design. A Systematic Approach. Springer-Verlag, Londres (2007)
3. Hubka, V., Eder, E.W.: Engineering Design: General Procedural Model of Engineering Design, Zürich, Switzerland (1992)
4. Chakrabarti, A., Bligh, T.P.: An Approach to Functional Synthesis of Mechanical Design Concepts: Theory, Applications and Emerging Research Issues. Artificial Intelligence for Engineering Design, Analysis and Manufacturing 10, 313–331 (1996)
5. Inoue, M., Nahm, Y.E., Tanaka, K., Ishikawa, H.: Collaborative engineering among designers with different preferences: Application of the preference set–based design to the design problem of an automotive front-side frame. Concurrent Engineering: Research and Applications 21, 252–267 (2013)
6. Ma, J., Hu, J., Zheng, K., Peng, Y.H.: Knowledge-based functional conceptual design: Model, representation, and implementation. Concurrent Engineering: Research and Applications 21, 103–120 (2013)
7. Torres, V.H., Ríos, J., Vizán, A., Pérez, J.M.: Approach to integrate product conceptual design information into a computer-aided design system. Concurrent Engineering: Research and Applications 21, 27–38 (2013)
8. Song, W., Ming, X., Wang, P.: Collaborative product innovation network: Status review, framework, and technology solutions. Concurrent Engineering: Research and Applications 21, 55–64 (2013)
9. Tseng, K.C., El-Ganzoury, W.: An intelligent system based on concurrent engineering for innovative product design at the conceptual design stage. International Journal of Advanced Manufacturing Technology 63, 421–447 (2012)
10. Kurtoglu, T., Campbell, M.I.: An evaluation scheme for assessing the worth of automatically generated design alternatives. Research in Engineering Design 20, 59–76 (2009)
11. Arzola, J.: Sistemas Ingenieriles. Félix Varela, La Habana (2000)

# Implementation Challenges of Annotated 3D Models in Collaborative Design Environments

Jorge Camba[1], Manuel Contero[2], and Gustavo Salvador-Herranz[3]

[1] Engineering Design Graphics, Texas A&M University, College Station, TX, USA
camba@tamu.edu
[2] I3BH, Universitat Politècnica de València, València, Spain
mcontero@upv.es
[3] Dpto. Exp. Gráfica, Proyectos y Urbanismo, Univ. CEU Cardenal Herrera, València, Spain
gsalva@uch.ceu.es

**Abstract.** Recent studies in the area of collaborative design have proposed the use of 3D annotations as a tool to make design information explicitly available within the 3D model, so that different stakeholders can share information throughout the product lifecycle. Annotation practices defined by the latest digital definition standards have formalized the presentation of information and facilitated the implementation of annotation tools in CAD systems. In this paper, we review the latest studies in annotation methods and technologies and explore their expected benefits in the context of collaborative design. Next, we analyze the implementation challenges of different annotation approaches, focusing specifically on design intent annotations. An analysis of the literature suggests that the use of annotations has a positive effect on collaborative design communication as long as proper implementation practices, tools, and user interaction mechanisms are in place.

**Keywords:** annotated 3D models, collaborative design, design communication.

## 1 Introduction

Globalization and advances in manufacturing and information technologies are driving engineering organizations towards concurrent distributed design processes, which allow for reduced development times and costs. In this context, communication and coordination are two of the most critical activities for effective teamwork and overall organizational performance [1, 2]. Modern engineering teams, often comprised of specialists from various backgrounds must frequently work together in environments coordinated through technologies such as Product Lifecycle Management (PLM) systems [3]. Communication is critical, as a significant portion of engineers' time is spent exchanging information [4].

In the context of collaborative methodologies, the role of CAD models has been progressively transformed from mere representations of 3D geometry to elements that carry design information and can be shared among designers throughout the different stages of the product lifecycle [5-7]. Some reasons for this change include the

Y. Luo (Ed.): CDVE 2014, LNCS 8683, pp. 222–229, 2014.

popularization of the Model-Based Engineering (MBE) paradigm [8] and related technologies. In recent years, an interest in 3D annotation techniques as built-in knowledge repositories has been increasing. The development of standards for Digital Product Definition Data Practices [9, 10] and the implementation of these standards in major CAD packages have encouraged researchers to explore annotations as mechanisms to explicitly communicate design information. The significance of annotations and their role to mediate interactions were described by many authors [11-13]. A number of prototypes have also been developed [12, 14, 15]. Nonetheless, it is agreed that these roles are poorly addressed by current industrial tools.

In this paper, we review recent advances in annotation technologies and explore its expected benefits in the context of collaborative design. Next, we analyze the challenges of putting different annotation methods into practice, focusing specifically on annotations that communicate design information. Finally, we conclude our paper with a summary and a discussion of future research directions.

## 2    Annotations in Computer Aided Design

In Computer-Aided Design, the term annotation refers to a piece of information (usually text) that points to a specific aspect of the 3D model and provides additional explanations about the part [16]. Because annotations are linked to the geometry of the model, they are also called model-based annotations or 3D annotations. Annotations have been used to complement engineering drawings by providing information that is difficult or impossible to convey otherwise, such as manufacturing instructions and tolerances. Despite support from CAD packages for many years, most tools were proprietary and software-dependent, which made information exchange difficult. The lack of common rules created inconsistencies, which has had negative impacts in the adoption of annotations in industrial environments.

With the high demands of industry, researchers began to study the suitability of 3D annotations to carry design information [12, 15, 17]. The knowledge captured in CAD models is not merely helpful for design; it represents a major source of value for an organization. This knowledge includes the modeling process and its design intent. Many researchers noted that the efficient communication of design intent has a direct impact on reusability, which is a key issue to leverage current parametric CAD systems [6, 18, 19]. The importance of an explicit representation of design intent was summarized by [18] and yields the following benefits:

- In complex projects, the ability to store, process, and retrieve information about design changes can significantly improve productivity.
- When design intent information is represented explicitly and is easily available for review, the overall quality of the product increases.
- Explicit representation leads to a better use of resources and knowledge.
- Efficient communication of design intent is essential for integrating solutions and transferring design knowledge.

Companies have reported savings by capitalizing on reusable design elements [6] and identified obstacles involved in implementing reusability practices as well as the procedures to mitigate them. One obstacle was stated as "only original designer can change models successfully" and the procedure as "detail design information in model." Although standards have formalized how some of this information is presented, to ensure reusability design intent must be added so users understand how and why models were created in a specific manner. Because of its heterogeneous nature, managing design information is a difficult task, and the use of annotations has proven to be promising but challenging. In the next section, we discuss the challenges involved in implementing annotation mechanisms with the purpose of communicating design intent information.

## 3     Implementation Challenges

While specific challenges in using annotated models as carriers of design knowledge have been identified [16, 20], it is useful to review the scientific literature and assess the practical application of the proposed solutions to try to determine the direction of future developments. In addition to the review, we have elaborated on the subject, identified new challenges, and suggested our own approaches. We describe five major challenges related to the practical implementation of annotations: storage, representation, interface, visualization, and user motivation.

### 3.1     Annotation Storage

Annotations require efficient data structures to represent information. These structures demand tools to store, visualize, and interact with the content as well as instruments to manage the anchoring mechanism of the annotation [16]. It is also necessary that representations are unified to make annotations platform-independent and avoid compatibility and portability issues [20].

Based on how data is stored, annotations are classified as in-line (internal), stand-off (external), and hybrid. [15, 21]. In-line annotations store the information internally within the model, whereas stand-off annotations save the information in an external repository. The pros and cons of these methods are shown in Table 1. Hybrid approaches combine the strengths of both methods.

Stand-off annotations are generally more appropriate for use with CAD models [20, 22], particularly if the data needs to be shared. Since the information is kept separately, they allow flexible updates of the data without affecting the geometry of the model. Additionally, multiple annotation files can be linked to the same model to provide different annotated views to different users [22]. In terms of implementation, eXtensible Markup Language (XML) and SQL databases (particularly, in collaborative environments with PLM systems) have been recognized as common data description standards [13, 23]. Nevertheless, stand-off annotations are difficult to implement in distributed environments, mainly because of the problem of persistent references [24], which describes the inconsistencies generated in the annotation structures when the geometry of the model being annotated changes or when there is a simultaneous writing access to the model from multiple users. Hybrid representation approaches have been proposed, where annotation information is stored both externally and internally [15, 24].

**Table 1.** Annotation representation strategies (adapted and extended from [21])

| Strategy | Pros | Cons |
|---|---|---|
| In-line | Easy implementation | Original document changes |
| | Wide applications | Difficult to have multiple |
| | Full integration with the model (low maintenance) | independent sets of markup |
| | Efficiency in terms of processing and | Difficult to share information |
| | manipulation | in collaborative |
| | Already supported by most CAD systems | environments |
| Stand-off | Non-change of representation for the original | Difficult to implement |
| | object | Persistent references |
| | Support of multiple independent sets of markup | Lack of robust maintenance |
| | Support of progressively information update | method of references |
| | Reorganization of information for different | File maintenance |
| | purposes and applications | |
| | Easy distribution of information. | |
| | Information can be processed separately. | |

## 3.2 Annotation Representation

An additional challenge regarding the implementation of annotated models involves the annotation content structure, i.e. what information needs to be included and in what form, so information is communicated effectively. Naturally, decisions need to be made as to how design intent can be captured and communicated using annotations. Although some semi-automated capturing tools have been implemented [11, 25, 26] (many of them based on IBIS [27]), capturing design intent is a task that cannot be completely automated [28], requiring designers to be properly trained.

To provide computational support, design intent information must be represented in a structured manner [28]. With a formal syntax, it is relatively simple for a computer to process this information. However, fixed structures can also limit expressiveness and become intrusive to the user, which has in fact hindered the adoption of these tools in industry. For a designer, it is more intuitive to use natural language, particularly because of the difficulty of representing heterogeneous information (such as design intent) with fixed structures. A recent approach proposed by [29] suggests logging the actions performed by a designer in a CAD session and interpreting patterns found in these actions, which minimizes user intervention in the process. Regardless of the technology, when users are allowed to use natural language, new challenges appear, such as minimizing the effects of writing style and language on communication effectiveness, determining the optimum annotation length so annotations are not ignored, and implementing natural language processing mechanisms so computational support can still be provided.

## 3.3 Annotation Interface

Methods to support interaction with annotations must allow users to enter and retrieve data easily and intuitively [16], as designers are often reluctant to spend additional time adding information to their models [30]. The lack of adequate tools for knowledge-acquisition is in fact the major cause for the knowledge-acquisition bottleneck [30]. Interface simplicity and integration with existing tools are crucial factors for the successful implementation of design annotations.

Although a number of prototypes have been developed [12, 14, 15], integration of the annotation tools with the CAD application provides users with an already familiar interface, which minimizes the learning curve and the need to constantly switch between applications. In this context, Product and Manufacturing Information (PMI) modules available in modern CAD systems are already popular among engineers and designers so they are natural vehicles to interact with annotations [15].

### 3.4     Annotation Visualization

From an interaction standpoint, an ever increasing number of annotations can quickly result in a cluttered model, which often creates confusion and a feeling of information overload in the user. When too much data (or when data is not well organized) is displayed on a too small area, the value of information diminishes [31].

Previous studies on visual clutter have focused on algorithms for annotation styles [32], layouts to prevent occlusion [33], and the automatic arrangement of information [34]. However, none of the current model-based standards provides guidelines to reduce visual clutter (although they do recommend the use of groups to simplify interaction), and thus, no implementations are available in current PMI modules. Advanced filtering and interactive navigation based on the model's features have been proposed [15] as alternatives. These methods are generally faster as they do not rely on the user to create the groups and distribute the annotations within these groups.

### 3.5     User Motivation

Most annotation and knowledge representation techniques have proven to be valuable, but the majority do not find acceptance in industry, as designers are reluctant to spend time annotating their designs [35]. One reason is that the designer that has to implement the annotations has no further use of them. Why should the designer do something that is only beneficial for people that come after her? In many cases, incentives are missing.

Convincing users to use annotations can be a challenge, especially if the argument focuses exclusively on the collaborative aspect of helping other users. Even if the designer is forced to annotate her work, it is unclear that she will create quality annotations. On the other hand, just as computer programmers comment their source code to document algorithms, designers also need proper documentation to remember all model changes. Therefore, automatic tools that kept a historical record of annotation information could motivate and incentivize designers. After all, historical annotation information may not just be valuable for future users of a model, but also for the original creators.

### 3.6     Summary of Approaches

A summary of the most representative 3D annotation approaches and how they implement the challenges presented are shown in Table 2.

**Table 2.** Summary of 3D annotation approaches

| Approach | storage | representation | interface | visualization |
|---|---|---|---|---|
| Multiple Viewpoint [17] | Stand-off | Structured | Add-on | Not specified |
| LIMMA [23] | Stand-off | Freestyle and Structured | Add-on | Not specified |
| MATRICS [36] | Not specified | Freestyle | Knowledge-Based | Not specified |
| Space Pen [37] | Inline | Freestyle | Pen | Not specified |
| 3DAF [38] | Stand-off | Structured | Knowledge-Based | Not specified |
| Web-standards [39] | Inline and Stand-off | Structured | Knowledge-Based | Not specified |
| ModelCraft [40] | Stand-off | Freestyle | Pen | Not specified |

## 4    Discussion

The use of annotations as tools to incorporate product information within CAD models has proven to be a viable option for collaborative product development activities, partly because of the standardization of practices and the popularization of the Model-Based Enterprise paradigm. However, important challenges appear if the role of annotations is extended to communicate design information. Although some studies suggest that annotations may serve this purpose effectively, proper mechanisms must be put in place. Specifically, the problems of visual clutter, effective interfaces, and the automatic processing of freestyle text are challenges that will likely be addressed by upcoming versions of standards and PMI modules. User motivation challenges require integrated approaches that simplify annotation processes and incentivize users to document their designs.

In this review paper, we have examined the background, approaches, and issues in model annotation technology, as well as the impact of these mechanisms on design communication. This review is a crucial step to identify the aspects that are relevant to collaborative design activities. Selected technical literature has been analyzed to determine the aspects that must be considered in practical implementations.

The existing gap between engineering design and communication technologies is gradually being reduced as access to information becomes easier and new frameworks for product development become more distributed and collaborative. The use of model annotations to represent, capture and reuse design information is a promising subject, but mechanisms for indexing, searching, processing, and retrieving this information are needed. Additionally, commercial CAD manufacturers must provide tools that facilitate knowledge capture, reuse, and integration. It can be expected that collaborative design processes will be substantially affected by new advancements in annotation technologies.

## References

1. Katzenbach, J.R., Smith, D.K.: The Discipline of Teams. Harvard Business Review 71(2), 111–120 (2005)
2. Campion, M.A., Medsker, G.J., Higgs, A.C.: Relations between Work Group Characteristics and Effectiveness: Implications for Designing Effective Work Groups. Personnel Psychology 46, 823–850 (1993)

3. Chudoba, K.M., Wynn, E., Lu, M., Watson-Manheim, M.B.: How Virtual Are We? Measuring Virtuality and Understanding its Impact in a Global Organization. Information Systems Journal 15, 279–306 (2005)
4. Lahti, H., Seitamaa-Hakkarainen, P., Hakkarainen, K.: Collaboration Patterns in Computer Supported Collaborative Designing. Design Studies 25, 351–371 (2004)
5. Chang, K.H., Silva, J., Bryant, I.: Concurrent Design and Manufacturing for Mechanical Systems. Concurrent Engineering 7, 290–308 (1999)
6. Jackson, C., Buxton, M.: The Design Reuse Benchmark Report: Seizing the Opportunity to Shorten Product Development. Aberdeen Group, Boston (2007)
7. Lang, S., Dickinson, J., Buchal, R.O.: Cognitive Factors in Distributed Design. Computers in Industry 48, 89–98 (2002)
8. Alemanni, M., Destefanis, F., Vezzetti, E.: Model-Based Definition Design in the Product Lifecycle Management Scenario. International Journal of Advanced Manufacturing Technology 52(1-4), 1–14 (2011)
9. ASME: ASME Y14.41-2012 Digital Product Definition Data Practices. The American Society of Mechanical Engineers, New York (2012)
10. ISO: ISO 16792:2006 Technical Product Documentation – Digital Product Definition Data Practices. Organisation Internationale de Normalisation, Genève, Suisse (2006)
11. Bracewell, R.H., Wallace, K.M.: A Tool for Capturing Design Rationale. In:14th International Conference on Engineering Design, Design Society, Stockholm, Sweden (2003)
12. Boujut, J.F., Dugdale, J.: Design of a 3D Annotation Tool for Supporting Evaluation Activities in Engineering Design. Cooperative Systems Design, COOP 6, 1–8 (2006)
13. Alducin-Quintero, G., Rojo, A., Plata, F., Hernández, A., Contero, M.: 3D Model Annotation as a Tool for Improving Design Intent Communication: A Case Study on its Impact in the Engineering Change Process. In: ASME International Design Engineering Technical Conferences & Computers and Information in Engineering Conference, Chicago, Illinois (2012)
14. Sandberg, S., Näsström, M.: A Proposed Method to Preserve Knowledge and Information by Use of Knowledge Enabled Engineering. In: ASME International Design Engineering Technical Conferences & Computers and Information in Engineering Conference, Las Vegas, Nevada (2007)
15. Dorribo-Camba, J., Alducin-Quintero, G., Perona, P., Contero, M.: Enhancing Model Reuse through 3D Annotations: A Theoretical Proposal for an Annotation-Centered Design Intent and Design Rationale Communication. In: ASME International Mechanical Engineering Congress & Exposition, San Diego, California (2013)
16. Ding, L., Ball, A., Patel, M., Matthews, J., Mullineux, G.: Strategies for the Collaborative Use of CAD Product Models. In: 17th International Conference on Engineering Design, vol. 8, pp. 123–134 (2009)
17. Davies, D., McMahon, C.A.: Multiple Viewpoint Design Modelling through Semantic Markup. In: ASME International Design Engineering Technical Conferences and Computers and Information in Engineering Conference, Philadelphia, PA, vol. 3, pp. 561–571 (2006)
18. Pena-Mora, F., Sriram, D., Logcher, R.: SHARED-DRIMS: SHARED Design Recommendation-Intent Management System. Enabling Technologies: Infrastructure for Collaborative Enterprises, 213–221 (1993)
19. Iyer, N., Jayanti, S., Lou, K., Kalyanaraman, Y., Ramani, K.: Shape-based Searching for Product Lifecycle Applications. Computer-Aided Design 37(13), 1435–1446 (2005)
20. Li, C., McMahon, C., Newnes, L.: Annotation in Product Lifecycle Management: A Review of Approaches. In: ASME International Design Engineering Technical Conferences and Computers and Information in Engineering Conference, vol. 2, pp. 797–806 (2009)

21. Ding, L., Liu, S.: Markup in Engineering Design: A Discourse. Future Internet 2, 74–95 (2010)
22. Patel, M., Ball, A., Ding, L.: Curation and Preservation of CAD Engineering Models in Product Lifecycle Management. In: Conference on Virtual Systems and Multimedia Dedicated to Digital Heritage, University of Bath, pp. 59–66 (2008)
23. Ding, L., Davies, D., McMahon, C.A.: The Integration of Lightweight Representation and Annotation for Collaborative Design Representation. Research in Engineering Design 20(3), 185–200 (2009)
24. Patel, M., Ball, A., Ding, L.: Strategies for the Curation of CAD Engineering Models. International Journal of Digital Curation 4(1), 84–97 (2009)
25. Ganeshan, R., Garrett, J., Finger, S.: A Framework for Representing Design Intent. Design Studies 15(1), 59–84 (1994)
26. Myers, K., Zumel, N., Garcia, P.: Acquiring Design Rationale Automatically. Artificial Intelligence for Engineering Design, Analysis and Manufacturing 14(2), 115–135 (2000)
27. Kunz, W., Rittel, H.: Issues as Elements of Information Systems. Working paper 131. Center for Planning and Development Research, Berkeley (1970)
28. Shum, S.J.B., Selvin, A.M., Sierhuis, M., Conklin, J., Haley, C.B., Nuseibeh, B.: Hypermedia Support for Argumentation-Based Rationale: 15 Years on from Gibis and Qoc. Rationale Management in Software Engineering, 111–132 (2006)
29. Sung, R., Ritchie, J.M., Rea, H.J., Corney, J.: Automated Design Knowledge Capture and Representation in Single-User CAD Environments. J. of Eng. Design 22(7), 487–503 (2011)
30. Chandrasegaran, S.K., Ramani, K., Sriram, R.D., Horváth, I., Bernard, A., Harik, R.F., Gao, W.: The Evolution, Challenges, and Future of Knowledge Representation in Product Design Systems. Computer-Aided Design 45(2), 204–228 (2013)
31. Ellis, G., Dix, A.: A Taxonomy of Clutter Reduction for Information Visualisation. IEEE Transactions on Visualization and Computer Graphics 13(6), 1216–1223 (2007)
32. Cipriano, G., Gleicher, M.: Text Scaffolds for Effective Surface Labeling. IEEE Transactions on Visualization and Computer Graphics 14(6), 1675–1682 (2008)
33. Stein, T., Décoret, X.: Dynamic Label Placement for Improved Interactive Exploration. In: 6th International Symposium on Non-Photorealistic Animation and Rendering, pp. 15–21 (2008)
34. Götzelmann, T., Hartmann, K., Strothotte, T.: Agent-Based Annotation of Interactive 3D Visualizations. In: Butz, A., Fisher, B., Krüger, A., Olivier, P. (eds.) SG 2006. LNCS, vol. 4073, pp. 24–35. Springer, Heidelberg (2006)
35. Szykman, S., Sriram, R., Regli, W.: The Role of Knowledge in Next-Generation Product Development Systems. J. of Computing and Inf. Science in Engineering 1(1), 3–11 (2001)
36. Aubry, S., Thouvenin, I., Lenne, D., Olive, J.: A Knowledge Model to Read 3D Annotations on a Virtual Mock-up for Collaborative Design. In: 11th International Conference on Computer Supported Cooperative Work in Design, pp. 669–674 (2007)
37. Jung, T., Gross, M.D., Do, E.Y.L.: Sketching Annotations in a 3D Web Environment. In: CHI 2002, Extended Abstracts on Human Factors in Computing Systems, pp. 618–619 (2002)
38. Bilasco, I.M., Gensel, J., Villanova-Oliver, M., Martin, H.: An MPEG-7 Framework Enhancing the Reuse of 3D Models. In: 11th International Conference on 3D Web Technology, Columbia, Maryland (2006)
39. Pittarello, F., De Faveri, A.: Semantic Description of 3D Environments: A Proposal Based on Web Standards. In: 11th International Conference on 3D Web Technology, Columbia, Maryland (2006)
40. Song, H., Guimbretière, F., Hu, C., Lipson, H.: ModelCraft: Capturing Freehand Annotations and Edits on Physical 3D Models. In: 19th Annual ACM Symposium on User Interface Software and Technology, pp. 13–22 (2006)

# Metamorphic Controller for Collaborative Design of an Optimal Structure of the Control System

Tomasz Klopot, Dariusz Choiński, Piotr Skupin, and Daniel Szczypka

Faculty of Automatic, Electronics and Computer Science Control,
Silesian University of Technology,
ul.Akademicka 16, 44-100 Gliwice, Poland
{tomasz.klopot,dariusz.choinski,piotr.skupin}@polsl.pl,
krequs@o2.pl

**Abstract.** When designing a control system, the customer specifies some control requirements and the expert provides the parameterized optimal controller. A change of the control algorithm to a more advanced one may lead to a better performance of the closed loop system. On the other hand, implementation and parameterization of the advanced controllers require more extensive knowledge. A possible solution is a group of cooperating experts that are able to determine the most suitable control algorithm, depending on the customer's requirements. However, in practice, hiring more experts is an expensive approach. Hence, the performance of majority of industrial systems is not optimal. The paper presents the metamorphic controller with extended functionality for selection of an optimal control algorithm (including advanced controllers). As a result, only one expert, cooperating with the customer, is sufficient to ensure the optimal system performance. The proposed solution has been implemented and tested on the industrial controller.

**Keywords:** Metamorphic controller, collaborative design, programmable logic controller (PLC).

## 1 Introduction

Synthesis of the control system requires cooperation between customer and control engineers (experts), because the experts (being more experienced) posses sufficient knowledge to determine the controller structure and to tune its parameters according to the customer's requirements. In practice, the choice of the controller structure (control algorithm) depends on the simplicity of its implementation and the required knowledge of its operation. For these reasons, the most common industrial controller is the PID (proportional-integral-derivative) controller or its simplified form (the PI controller without derivative action) [1], [2]. Of course, there are other more advanced control algorithms such as B-BAC (Balance-Based Adaptive Control) [3] or a class of predictive controllers (e.g. DMC – Dynamic Matrix Control or PFC – Predictive Functional Control), [3], [4]. The application of these algorithms may result in a much better quality of control than by using the classical PID controller [4].

Y. Luo (Ed.): CDVE 2014, LNCS 8683, pp. 230–237, 2014.
© Springer International Publishing Switzerland 2014

However, the implementation of the advanced controllers is more difficult and requires more extensive knowledge (Fig.1a). In majority of cases, the control engineers (experts) specialize only in one type of the controller. Hence, to implement various control algorithms, it would be necessary to employ several experts. Depending on the customer's requirements, the experts would have to cooperate with each other to determine which type of the control algorithm to choose and how to tune its parameters (Fig.1b). On the other hand, such solution is unacceptable in industrial practice, because hiring more experts increases the overall costs. In effect, the performance of the majority of industrial control systems is not optimal.

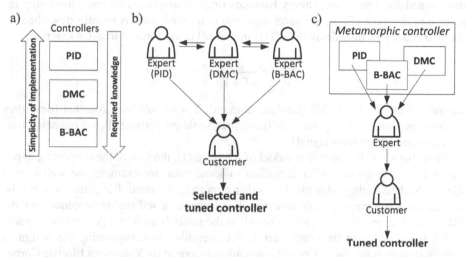

**Fig. 1.** Selection of the controller structure and its parameterization: a) comparison of the available controllers; b) selection of the controller by cooperation; c) metamorphic controller for selection of the optimal controller structure

Currently, many manufacturers of the control equipment offer a number of useful tools that support control engineers (experts) in the designing process of control systems. However, the functionalities of these tools are limited to the parameterization of one type of controller (usually the PID control algorithm) with no possibilities of changing its structure, which could lead to a better system performance.

Based on our previous research in this field for biotechnological plants [5], [6], it is proposed the metamorphic controller that allows for selection of an optimal control algorithm according to the customer's requirements (Fig.1c). In effect, only one expert, cooperating with the customer, is enough to tune the selected controller. Moreover, the expert (e.g. control engineer or process operator) does not have to possess knowledge on how to implement and how to select the optimal control algorithm for a desired operating point of the process. The proposed solution has been implemented and tested on a real industrial programmable logic controller (PLC). The implementation details and the effectiveness of the application are presented in the paper.

## 2    Related Work

One of the basic tasks of each control system is minimization (or elimination) of the control error, which is a difference between set point (SP) and process variable (PV). As mentioned in the introduction, controller selection and its parameterization are fundamental problems in the designing of control systems. Hence, the manufacturers of control equipment offer additional tools and supporting applications (intended mainly for the PID controllers) to facilitate the designing process.

Most of these tools use a mathematical model of the controlled plant, which can be determined from mass and energy balances or, in a simplified manner, from step response of the plant [7]. In the latter case, the controlled plant is usually described by the first order plus time delay (FOPTD) model [8] in the form of transfer function:

$$K(s) = \frac{k}{sT+1} e^{-sT_0} \tag{1}$$

where: s – complex variable (Laplace domain), T – overall time constant (describes dynamic properties), k – plant gain (describes static properties), $T_o$ – time delay (delay in response to control signal).

Then, based on the simplified model of the plant (1), the task of the supporting application is to tune the controller according to some rules, for example, the well-known Ziegler-Nichols tuning rules [9]. In another approach, the controller parameters can be chosen so as to optimize some criterion. For instance, a self-tuning procedure for the PID controller, presented in [10], is based on the minimization of a performance index, which is a function of the control error. An interesting tool, supporting the design of control system, is the Super Control application proposed by Yokogawa Electric Corporation [11]. The Super Control is based on the fuzzy logic and allows tuning the controller for one of the three available modes [12]: I – overshot suppression, II – large stability margin, III – fast response of the control system. Yet another interesting example is a self-tuning procedure for the PID controller that uses neural networks and step response data of the plant [13]. More examples and details on the tools supporting the designer of control system can be found in the review paper by Li et al. [12].

However, it should be emphasized that some of the supporting applications require additional and expensive hardware modules. Moreover, practically all the supporting applications do not allow to change the controller structure during normal operation of the control system. Because, the stiff controller structure may limit the performance of the whole control system, therefore, the possibility of switching between various control algorithms for the same process, and for the same criterion, may result in a better quality of control and lower costs.

In the literature, the problem of switching between several controllers is generally known. For example, metamorphic controllers for the manufacturing systems have been described in [14], [15]. In this case, the adaptation of the controller structure (its metamorphosis) results from constant changes in the manufacturing environment. The selection of a proper control algorithm can also be realized with the help of fuzzy logic rules. Such an approach was proposed in [16] for autonomous vehicle control. In turn, the selection of the most suitable control algorithm presented in [10], [17] was realized by minimizing a criterion function. However, most of the proposed solutions use the advanced control algorithms, which require more extensive knowledge and experience.

Given the above considerations, the presented paper describes a metamorphic controller with extended functionality that allows for selection of the most suitable control algorithm (including advanced controllers) depending on the customer's requirements and operating point of the controlled process. The implementation details on the industrial PLC are presented in the next section.

# 3    The Structure of Metamorphic Control System

As shown in Figure 2, selection of the optimal structure of controller and its initial parameterization is realized by additional function units. The function units are responsible for: identification of parameters of the FOPTD model, controller parameterization, simulations of the closed loop (CL) system with each individual controller and calculation of the performance indices. In the presented case, the metamorphic controller uses three various control algorithms: PI controller (the most common in practice), DMC controller (effective for plants with variable time delay) and B-BAC controller (effective in attenuation of disturbances).

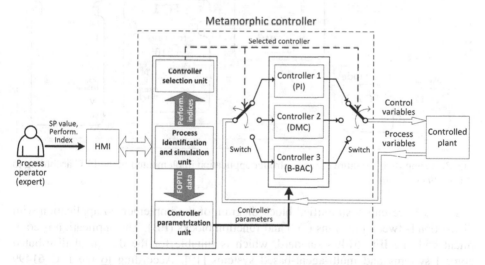

**Fig. 2.** The general scheme of the metamorphic controller

In this case, based on the customer requirements, the user of system (e.g. process operator) is responsible for determination of the process operating point (SP value), the amplitude of CV signal (for model identification purposes) and for selection of one of the three performance indices: IAE (Integral of the Absolute Error), ITAE (Integral of Time multiplied by the Absolute Error), ISE (Integral Square Error), which are defined as follows [18]:

$$IAE = \int_0^{T_f} |e(t)|dt, \ ITAE = \int_0^{T_f} t \cdot |e(t)|dt, \ ISE = \int_0^{T_f} e^2(t)dt \qquad (2)$$

where: e – control error at instant t, $T_f$ – final instant (dependent on the overall time constant). The overall performance of the CL system is strictly dependent on the form of minimized performance index. The ITAE weights error with time and ensures fast transients, IAE – ensures small overshoots, ISE – is a compromise between sufficiently fast transients and small overshoots [18]. The metamorphic controller selects the control algorithm associated with the smallest value of the chosen performance index. The application was implemented and tested in the industrial PLC S7-300 series (Siemens). An interaction with the metamorphic controller is realized by means of a human machine interface (HMI) created in ProTool software.

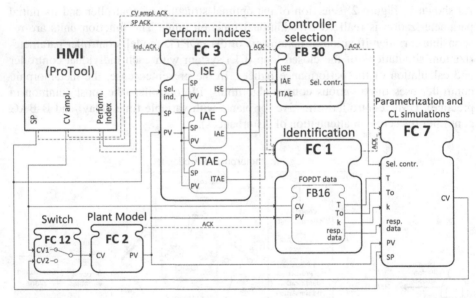

**Fig. 3.** A simplified structure of the controller application implemented in the PLC according to IEC 61499 standard

Figure 3 presents a simplified block diagram of the implemented application with distinction between functions (FC) and function blocks (FB). The application is compliant with the IEC 61499 standard, which is suitable for the design of distributed control systems and multi-agent-based systems [19]. According to the IEC 61499 standard, there is a distinction between data inputs (continuous arrows) and event inputs (dashed arrows) in each function block (Fig.3). An example of an event is the acknowledgement signal (ACK) sent to another function block once the calculations are finished. The procedure for controller selection and its parameterization is followed by the determination of operating point of the process, the CV amplitude and one of the performance indices. In the first phase, the system uses a mathematical model of the plant (implemented in block FC2) to calculate its step response for a desired operating point of the process. In this way, there is no need to excite the real plant that, in some cases, is undesirable or impossible [12]. Based on the step response data, the block FC1 calculates parameter values of the FOPTD model (1). These parameters (i.e., k, T and $T_o$) and the step response data are necessary for initial tuning of each controller, which is realized by the function FC7. The initial tuning procedures are based on the methods presented in [20], [21]. Then, for each candidate controller and model of the plant, the CL system simulations are performed. The results of these simulations are used by the function FC3 to calculate the performance indices. Once the calculations are finished, the function block FB30 selects the optimal structure of the metamorphic controller.

## 4 Results

In order to asses the effectiveness of the metamorphic controller, a nonlinear model of the hydraulic system (irregular shaped tank) [22] has been chosen:

$$A_1 \dot{h} = F_{in} - c_1 \sqrt{h} \quad \text{for} \quad h \leq h_o \quad (3)$$

$$A_2(h)\dot{h} = F_{in} - c_2 \sqrt{h + h_o} \quad \text{for} \quad h > h_o \quad (4)$$

where: h – liquid level in the tank ($\dot{h}$ – time derivative of h), $F_{in}$ – input flow rate (CV), $c_1$, $c_2$, $A_1$, $A_2(h)$, $h_o$ – model parameters. The nonlinear model of the controlled plant is implemented in the block FC2 and numerically integrated with a time step $\Delta t=100[ms]$, which is achieved by the cyclic interrupts in the controller. The cycle time of 100[ms] was sufficient to perform the necessary calculations.

Depending on the operating point of the system (3)-(4), parameters of the simplified model (1) of the plant can significantly vary. Table 1 shows the obtained results for each performance index, and for each candidate control algorithm.

Table 1. Performance index values for two different operating points of the plant

| Contr. | The first operating point | | | The second operating point | | |
|---|---|---|---|---|---|---|
|  | IAE | ITAE | ISE | IAE | ITAE | ISE |
| PI | 108.8 | 342.1 | 1907.1 | **117.8** | 391.1 | 1915.1 |
| DMC | **104.7** | **300.0** | 3378.7 | 119.7 | **344.3** | 3471.6 |
| B-BAC | 256.4 | 2209.6 | **90.0** | 266.4 | 2311.2 | **97.0** |

The optimal controller structures, determined by the metamorphic controller, were marked by bold numbers. For a given criterion, one can achieve a better performance of the CL system by changing the controller structure. This justifies a modification of the controller during normal operation of the system, which is not proposed in the existing solutions (limited to a single control algorithm). The information about the selected controller is displayed in the panel in ProTool environment for the final decision to be made by the user (e.g. process operator or control engineer). After approval of the new controller structure, the system switches to the new controller in a bump-less manner.

The proposed solution has also been tested for several other models of plants and in each case, depending on the plant's dynamics and the scan cycle of the controller, the time needed to perform the entire procedure was on the order of a few minutes or less. In comparison to the response times of real industrial plants, this is an acceptable solution.

# 5     Concluding Remarks

The metamorphic controller allows using more advanced control algorithms without the need of employing several cooperating experts. In this case, the role of the user is limited to the selection of operating point and the criterion (performance index) that determines the behavior of the CL control system. As a result, less experienced engi-neer or process operator is able to use more advanced controllers. As shown by the experimental results with the use of industrial PLC, modification of the controller structure may lead to a better performance of the CL system. Compliance with the IEC 61499 standard simplifies implementation of the metamorphic controller in the distributed control system using various hardware platforms, but the versatility of the system makes it applicable in any time-determined networking environment [23]. Moreover, to increase the effectiveness of the proposed solution (e.g. to reduce the computational time), it is possible to exploit the advantages offered by the cloud ser-vices. In this case, a part of time-consuming calculations can be carried out in the cloud that is shared between several metamorphic controllers in the distributed control system. Then, the obtained results will allow to select the optimal controller structure.

**Acknowledgments.** This work was supported by the National Science Centre under grant No. 2012/05/B/ST7/00096 and by the Ministry of Science and Higher Education under grants BK-UiUA and BKM-UiUA.

# References

1. Yu, C.C.: Autotuning of PID Controllers: Relay Feedback Approach. Springer, New York (1999)
2. Li, Y., Ang, K., Chong, G.: PID control system analysis and design. IEEE Control Syst. Mag. 26, 32–41 (2006)
3. Czeczot, J.: Balance-Based Adaptive Control of a Neutralization Process. Int. J. Con-trol. 79, 1581–1600 (2006)
4. Nocon, W., Metzger, M.: Predictive Control of Decantation in Batch Sedimentation Process. AICHE J. 56, 3279–3283 (2010)
5. Choinski, D., Metzger, M., Nocon, W.: MAS-Based Cooperative Control for Biotechno-logical Process-A Case Study. In: Mařík, V., Strasser, T., Zoitl, A. (eds.) HoloMAS 2009. LNCS, vol. 5696, pp. 175–182. Springer, Heidelberg (2009)

6. Choinski, D., Metzger, M., Nocon, W.: Cooperative operating control based on virtual resources and user-suited HCI. In: Luo, Y. (ed.) CDVE 2009. LNCS, vol. 5738,
   pp. 216–223. Springer, Heidelberg (2009)
7. Gyoongy, I.J., Clarke, D.W.: On the automatic tuning and adaptation of PID controllers.
   Control Eng. Pract. 14, 149–163 (2006)
8. Metzger, M.: Comparison of the RK4M4 RK4LIN and RK4M1 methods for systems with
   time-delays. Simul. 52, 189–193 (1989)
9. Ziegler, J.G., Nichols, N.B.: Optimum settings for automatic controllers. Trans.
   ASME. 64, 759–768 (1942)
10. Paul, A., Akar, M., Safonov, M.G., Mitra, U.: Adaptive power control for wireless net-
    works using multiple controllers and switching. IEEE Trans. Neural. Netw. 16, 1212–1218
    (2005)
11. Wilson, C., Callen, C.: Close process control translates to quality heat treated parts. Ind.
    Heating - Pittsburg then Troy. 71, 25–28 (2004)
12. Li, Y., Ang, K., Chong, G.: Patents, software, and hardware for PID control. IEEE Control
    Syst. Mag. 26, 42–54 (2006)
13. Weinzierl, K.: Method for Generating Conrol Parameters From a Response Signal of a
    Ccontrolled System and System for Adaptive Setting af a PID Controller. U.S. Patent
    6,353,766 B1 (2002)
14. Balasubramanian, S., Brennan, R.W., Norrie, D.H.: An architecture for metamorphic con-
    trol of holonic manufacturing systems. Comp. Ind. 46, 13–31 (2001)
15. Brennan, R.W., Zhang, X., Xu, Y., Norrie, D.H.: A Reconfigurable Concurrent Function
    Block Model and its implementation in Real-Time Java. Integr. Comput.-Aided Eng. 9,
    263–279 (2002)
16. Abdullah, R., Hussain, A., Warwick, K., Zayed, A.: Autonomous Intelligent Cruise Con-
    trol Using a Novel Multiple-Controller Framework Incorporating Fuzzy-Logic Based
    Switching and Tuning. Neurocomputing 71, 2727–2741 (2008)
17. Wang, R., Paul, A., Stefanovic, M., Safonov, M.G.: Cost-detectability and stability of
    adaptive control systems. In: 44th IEEE Conference on Decision and Control and Euro-
    pean Control Conference, Seville, pp. 3584–3589 (2005)
18. Davendra, D., Zelinka, I., Senkerik, R.: Chaos driven evolutionary algorithms for the task
    of PID control. Comput. Math. Appl. 60, 1088–1104 (2010)
19. Vyatkin, V.: IEC 61499 Function blocks for embedded and distributed control systems de-
    sign. ISA, Research Triangle Park (2007)
20. Stebel, K., Czeczot, J., Laszczyk, P.: General tuning procedure for the nonlinear balance-
    based adaptive controller. Int. J. Control. 87, 76–89 (2014)
21. Skupin, P., Klopot, W., Klopot, T.: Dynamic Matrix Control with partial decoupling. In:
    11th WSEAS International Conference on Automation & Information, Iasi, pp. 61–66
    (2010)
22. Klopot, W., Klopot, T., Laszczyk, P., Czeczot, J., Metzger, M.: Practical Implementation
    of the Nonlinear Control of the Liquid Level in the Tank of Irregular Shape. In: Lee, J.,
    Lee, M.C., Liu, H., Ryu, J.-H. (eds.) ICIRA 2013, Part II. LNCS, vol. 8103, pp. 178–188.
    Springer, Heidelberg (2013)
23. Polakow, G., Metzger, M.: Performance evaluation of the parallel processing producer-
    distributor-consumer network architecture. Comp. Stand. Inter. 35, 596–604 (2013)

# BIM-Enabled Design Collaboration
# for Complex Building[*]

Jun Wang[1], Heap-Yih Chong[1], Wenchi Shou[1], Xiangyu Wang[1,**] and Jun Guo[2]

[1] Australasian Joint Research Centre for Building Information Modelling,
Curtin University, Australia
[2] CCDI Group, China
{jun.wang1,heapyih.chong,wenchi.
shou,xiangyu.wang}@curtin.edu.au,
guo.jun@ccdi.com.cn

**Abstract.** Fragmented practices are common in construction industry due to the traditional procurement system and poor adoption of advanced technologies and approaches for construction projects. Building Information Modelling is an emerging technology and able to transform the conventional practice. It can create a collaborative working platform for a project, particularly during the design stage. Therefore, the research aims to improve the conventional design practices by incorporating the BIM technology in addressing the design collaboration for a complex building. A case study was adopted from a complex building in Beijing, China. The data were collected and observed during the design process. A framework was developed to explain the design collaboration process. The findings show the duration of the design has significantly shortened and also improved the design performance in the project. The research renders an important insight into promoting BIM-based design collaboration in the construction industry.

**Keywords:** Fragmentation, Collaboration, BIM, Design.

## 1 Introduction

Traditional procurement system or project delivery method always relies on inputs provided by construction professionals individually in numerous stages of the project life cycle. All the project stakeholders would have different objectives and goals in the project. It is caused by the contractual relationship and agreement on the job scopes. This fragmented practice will lead to poor coordination and productivity issues in the construction industry [1, 2].

Many innovative procurement systems or joint venture approaches were proposed [3.4]. Yet, the 'reluctant to change' attitude has remained in the construction industry,

---

[*] The 11th International Consference on Cooperative Design, Visualization and Engineering, p. 238, 2014.
[**] Corresponding author.

Y. Luo (Ed.): CDVE 2014, LNCS 8683, pp. 238–244, 2014.

where the traditional procurement system or project delivery method is still the preferred option. This procurement system is still the most popular method in construction industry and conflicts or disagreements are bound to be happened [5,6]. Building Information Modelling recognizes as an advanced technology in architectural, engineering, construction and operation (AECO) sectors, where all the geometric information will be shared as a platform for collaborative service using a three-dimensional model. The research aims to improve the conventional fragmented practices by incorporating BIM technology in addressing the design collaboration for a complex building. An approach of case study was adopted, where a complicated art building in Beijing, China. The details of each process were demonstrated and explained in a framework. The distinguished savings in terms of duration and design performance would be analysed and highlighted based on the design collaboration of the project. The research contributes in addressing and overcoming the highly fragmented design process in the construction industry.

## 2    Collaborative Working Practices and Technologies

An effective collaboration is not a new agenda in the construction industry. However, the recent and fast development in computing technologies has triggered and brought the need of collaboration into many areas of a construction project [7,8,9,10]. Notably, BIM is an emerging information technology and receives tremendous responses and supports from both academia and industry [11]. However, one of the obvious barriers of using this technology is many perceptions and concepts towards BIM's actual agenda and philosophy [12,13]. This has caused the slow adoption of BIM around the world [14].

Yet, the need of adding more data into the conventional two dimensional drawings is obvious. Numerous data could be added into a basic design, such as like costs, quantities, time, energy or environment data[15]. Therefore, an effective collaboration is a must as other data as mentioned above require inputs from different professionals. BIM is could be the best solution on the collaborative working environment. A wide range of software applications can contribute to the creation, analysis, enhancement and communication towards the BIM project. As a result, the interoperability among the software or designs is the important aspect for its effective implementation and collaboration for the BIM project [16,17,18].

The problems of incompatible among the software and designs have been encountering for some time. It is about the inability to use and exchange the data with one another. This situation was originally addressed in 1994, where an initiative to exchange with industry competitors or vendors in forming a *"A neutral, international and unique non for profit organisation supporting open BIM through the life cycle"* in order to *"Develop and maintain international standards for openBIM"* [19].

Thus, The Industry Foundation Classes (IFC) specification has been developed. It is a neutral data format to describe, exchange and share information in relation to construction industry [20]. Apart from that, International Framework for Dictionaries (IFD) and Information Delivery Manual (IDM) were also developed. They provide flexibility and better coordination for data and process required in IFC-based BIM projects.

Apart from that, BIM is moving to a cloud based platform, which is able to expand the collaboration and facilitate the all the processes involved in the project life cycle [21,22,23,24]. It will improve coordination processes and networks among the project stakeholders. Besides, cloud computing makes business processes easier for companies to scale their services, whether up or down, as the resources can be deployed very fast from the cloud [25].

## 3    Research Approach

An approach of case study was adopted in the research, where most of the primary data were obtained from a complex building in Beijing, China. The total built-up area is approximately 16524 square meters. The project mainly adopted following software during the design stage, such as Autodesk Revit Architecture, Autodesk Revit Structure, Autodesk Revit MEP, Autodesk 3DS MAX, Navisworks, Rhinoceros, CATIA and Auto CAD.

Observational methods are varied in terms of its disturbance on the subject matter being studies [26]. Two types of observations were conducted in the case study namely, personal observations and mechanical/technical observations. The former method was to detect any coordination issues and problems among the project participants, while the latter means was to synchronize and assist into developing the BIM-enabled design collaboration via a more interfering approach. Subsequently, the related processes were recorded. Moreover, a framework was developed to explain the philosophy behind the design collaboration as illustrated in the following section.

## 4    BIM-Based Design Collaboration System

### 4.1    BIM-Based Collaborative Design

In a conventional two dimensional (2D) coordination practice, the processes will be carried out in a step by step manner, where the designated precedent process must be completed before the others. The design duration would be longer as poor coordination from the different disciplines of professionals. On the other hand, the BIM-based design collaboration system transforms the conventional practice. It is able to shorten the design process as illustrated in Figure 1.

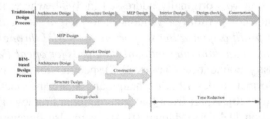

**Fig. 1.** Comparison between traditional design process and BIM-based design process

   The BIM-based design collaboration was organised according to project directory control using three dimensional (3D) models. All the files were allocated into designated folders and standards. The project participants were working on a similar 'Integrated Central Model' as illustrated in Figure 2. Certain authorities and rights were assigned for the project participants in terms of reading and editing. Design reviewer and coordinator would check and synchronize the designs produced by each designer. This process would improve the productivity and avoid any potential conflicts and clashes in the design. Meanwhile, the 3D models also promote direct visualization and communication on the design process. Eventually, it would improve the quality of the model.

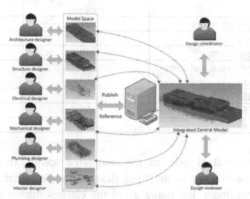

**Fig. 2.** BIM-based collaborative design

## 4.2   Case Study

Two similar buildings were selected for investigation in the project as initiated by the client. The comparative data below was recorded based on reports generated from the project. The first comparative result was the duration required to develop the completed design model. The traditional design method required to spend an additional four weeks compared to the BIM-based design collaboration as shown in Table 1. This result was contributed significantly due to less rework and effective communication in the BIM approach.

**Table 1.** Comparative analysis on duration

| Week (W) | W1 | W 2 | W 3 | W 4 | W 5 | W 6 | W 7 | W 8 | W 9 | W 10 | W 11 | W 12 |
|---|---|---|---|---|---|---|---|---|---|---|---|---|
| Traditional design method | | | | | | | | | | | | |
| BIM-based collaborative design | | | | | | | | | | | | |

Apart from that, after the design completed, the performance analysis was carried out to determine number of errors from both designs. Table 2 shows a total of 392 errors were reported in the traditional design method; whereas only 143 errors were identified from the BIM approach. The clashes were the main source of errors for both designs, especially, the clashes between MEP and structure. The results also revealed that personal errors were obvious especially in MEP design. Nevertheless, the BIM approach performed effectively to reduce the clashes involved.

**Table 2.** Comparative analysis

|  | Traditional design method | BIM-based collaborative design |
|---|---|---|
| Architecture design errors | 23 | 15 |
| Structure design errors | 34 | 29 |
| MEP design errors | 40 | 34 |
| clashes between architecture and structure | 16 | 4 |
| clashes between MEP and structure | 224 | 45 |
| clashes between MEP and architecture | 55 | 16 |
| Total | 392 | 143 |

Traditional design method relies on the completed designs from various parties to identify and solve the clashes in the final design. On the other hand, the BIM approach is able to coordinate and make good the clashes during the design development process. Figure 3 illustrates the details of the clashes that were identified along the process development. The analysis also revealed that most of the clashes were identified and solved in Week 5.

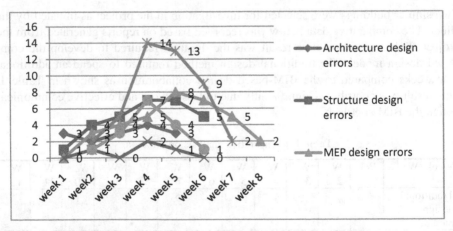

**Fig. 3.** Number of clashes during the BIM design development

# 5    Conclusion

The case study was analysed and explained the improvements in terms of duration and design performance by incorporating the BIM technology in addressing the design collaboration for a complex building. The BIM has significantly shortened the duration for the whole design development over 30% compared to the traditional design approach. It is also able to resolve the clashes during the design process. There were some clashes identified in the BIM approach due to coordination problems. This limitation should be addressed by having a more optimized and collaborative platform using a real-time BIM model in the future.

# References

1. Cheng, J.C., Law, K.H., Bjornsson, H., Jones, A., et al.: A service oriented framework for construction supply chain integration. Automation in Construction 19(2), 245–260 (2010)
2. Kagioglou, M., Cooper, R., Aouad, G., Sexton, M.: Rethinking construction: the generic design and construction process protocol. Engineering Construction and Architectural Management 7(2), 141–153 (2000)
3. Adnan, H., Chong, H.-Y., Morledge, R.: Success criteria for international joint ventures: The experience of Malaysian contractors in the Middle East. African Journal of Business Management 5(13), 5254–5260 (2011)
4. Nippa, M., Beechler, S.: What do we know about the success and failure of international joint ventures? in search of relevance and holism. Advances in International Management 26, 363–396 (2013)
5. Chong, H.-Y., Zin, R.M.: The behaviour of dispute resolution methods in Malaysian construction industry. In: IEEE International Conference on Industrial Engineering and Engineering Management, IEEM 2009. IEEE (2009)
6. Chong, H.-Y., Zin, R.M.: Selection of dispute resolution methods: factor analysis approach. Engineering, Construction and Architectural Management 19(4), 428–443 (2012)
7. Chong, H.Y., Balamuralithara, B., Chong, S.C.: Construction contract administration in Malaysia using DFD: a conceptual model. Industrial Management & Data Systems 111(9), 1449–1464 (2011)
8. Chong, H.Y., Zin, R.M., Chong, S.C.: Employing Data Warehousing for Contract Administration: e-Dispute Resolution Prototype. Journal of Construction Engineering and Management 139(6), 611–619 (2012)
9. Lin, Y.-C.: Construction 3D BIM-based knowledge management system: A case study. Journal of Civil Engineering and Management 20(2), 186–200 (2014)
10. Miettinen, R., Paavola, S.: Beyond the BIM utopia: Approaches to the development and implementation of building information modelling. Automation in Construction 43, 84–91 (2014)
11. Singh, V., Gu, N., Wang, X.: A theoretical framework of a BIM-based multi-disciplinary collaboration platform. Automation in Construction 20(2), 134–144 (2011)
12. Gu, N., London, K.: Understanding and facilitating BIM adoption in the AEC industry. Automation in Construction 19(8), 988–999 (2010)
13. Barlish, K., Sullivan, K.: How to measure the benefits of BIM—A case study approach. Automation in Construction 24, 149–159 (2012)

14. Sattineni, A., Bradford, R.: Estimating with bim: a survey of US construction companies. In: Proceedings of the 28th International Symposium on Automation and Robotics in Construction, Seoul, Korea (2011)
15. Nejat, A., Darwish, M.M., Ghebrab, T.B.: Teaching Strategy for construction engineering students (2012),
http://www.asee.org/public/conferences/8/papers/5582/download
16. Wang, X., Dunston, P.S.: Design, Strategies, and Issues towards an Augmented Reality-based Construction training Platform. Journal of Information Technology in Construction (ITcon) 12, 363–380 (2007)
17. Wang, X., Gu, N., Marchant, D.: An Empirical Case Study on Designer's Perceptions of Augmented Reality within an Architectural Firm. Journal of Information Technology in Construction (ITcon) 13, 536–552 (2008)
18. Cerovsek, T.: A review and outlook for a 'Building Information Model'(BIM): A multi-standpoint framework for technological development. Advanced Engineering Informatics 25(2), 224–244 (2011)
19. buildingSMART. About us, http://buildingsmart.org/
20. buildingSMART. IFC Wiki,
http://www.ifcwiki.org/index.php/Main_Page
21. Tao, J., Marten, H., Kramer, D., Karl, W.: An intuitive framework for accessing computing clouds. Procedia Computer Science 4, 2049–2057 (2011)
22. Fathi, M.S., Abedi, M., Rawai, N.: The potential of cloud computing technology for construction collaboration. Applied Mechanics and Materials 174, 1931–1934 (2012)
23. Sawhney, A., Maheswari, J.U.: Design Coordination Using Cloud-based Smart Building Element Models. International Journal of Computer Information Systems and Industrial Management Applications 5, 445–453 (2012)
24. Marston, S., Li, Z., Bandyopadhyay, S., Zhang, J., et al.: Cloud computing—The business perspective. Decision Support Systems 51(1), 176–189 (2011)
25. Chong, H.Y., Wong, J.S., Wang, X.: An explanatory case study on cloud computing applications in the built environment. Automation in Construction 44, 152–162 (2014)
26. McBurney, D., White, T.: Research methods. Cengage Learning (2009)

# The Impact of Expertise on the Capture of Sketched Intentions: Perspectives for Remote Cooperative Design

Jennifer Sutera[1], Maria C. Yang[2], and Catherine Elsen[1]

[1] LUCID-ULg, University of Liège, Belgium
jsutera@alumni.ulg.ac.be, catherine.elsen@ulg.ac.be
[2] Department of Mechanical Engineering and Engineering Systems Division,
MIT, Cambridge, USA
mcyang@mit.edu

**Abstract.** The paper describes the way expertise and field-knowledge can impact the transfer of graphical intentions during architectural cooperative design. The analysis of 28 controlled experiments reveals what matters in transmitting architectural intents and more specifically underlines how novices' intuitive, deductive processes based on previous and embodied experiences interestingly complement experts' knowledge of the architectural field and its semantics. The results directly inform how we, as researchers, designers and engineers, should take advantage of both novices' and experts' strategies to develop tools, methods or interfaces to support next generation cooperative design.

**Keywords:** Cooperative design in architecture, transfer of design intents, expertise.

## 1 Introduction

Cooperative situations are nowadays the norm in almost any design field and architecture is no exception. At any design stage of an architectural project, stakeholders from different backgrounds and levels of expertise are frequently seen working together in dynamic environments, and remotely from each other. Among the numerous issues stakeholders face in such working environments, preserving efficient and effective communication certainly remains a decisive goal: anyone involved in transmitting an intention wants to be correctly understood.

The chosen medium for communication to support this transmission depends on the field, the type of collaboration, the stakeholders involved and the type of project. In the field of architecture, this communication traditionally occurs through graphical exchanges, naturally augmented with conversations and gestures. More specifically during the early stages of a design project, free hand sketching remains one of the preferred tools for architects because of its intuitive, natural and efficient characteristics [1; 2]. The use of digital tools to support remote collaborative design is also spreading, from emailing CAD representations to immersive environments that re-create a virtual sense of co-presence [3]. In the field of Sketch-Based Interfaces,

Y. Luo (Ed.): CDVE 2014, LNCS 8683, pp. 245–252, 2014.

researchers also look into free-hand sketching's natural and intuitive qualities to develop tools to support graphical remote cooperation [4].

Through our research, we want to help those researchers better understand how designers share information and intentions, in order to make these next generation tools, interfaces and methodologies more efficient and more reflective of real working habits.

## 2    State of the Art

In vernacular societies, where human-made objects were conceived, made, and used by the same person [5], the design process could be theoretically estimated as the result of a single actor. The industrial revolution, however, confirmed the necessity of tasks' repartition between several stakeholders, among them the *designer* (or engineer - the person who conceives an object), the *maker* (the person who produces it), the *consumer* (the person who orders it) and the *user* (the person who experiences it). Today, putting aside the fact that design projects constantly and dynamically grow in size and in complexity, one also has to deal with the geographical distance separating (for instance) teams of architects or engineers from building or production sites.

These distant situations require adapted, augmented solutions for efficient remote cooperative design. In order to gain desirability and quick adoption, those next-generation interfaces, tools and methods should be innovative while respectful of stakeholders' practices and needs. As Norman and Verganti adequately summarize: "radical innovation driven by meaning change can be design driven through better understanding of potential patterns of meanings" [6]. In the case of cooperative design, one should consequently take a leap forward and project new ways to work and design together distantly, while always preserving the essential, qualitative aspects of cooperation.

In that regard, Baker, Détienne and Burkhardt researched the key indicators to assess the quality of collaboration (seen as a process rather than simply an outcome). Among the seven highlighted keys, two are of particular interest for this paper: to sustain first some *mutual understanding* and, second, the *information exchanges during problem solving* [7]. We summarize here those two keys under the overall goal of *efficiently transferring intentions*.

Several aspects could endanger this transmission of intentions: the erosion of psycho-social relations, due to the absence of physical co-presence; the incompleteness and inadequacy of shared information, weakened by less straightforward knowledge-sharing models; the illegibility of the shared information, impacted by badly designed IT environments or by lacking common ground between stakeholders of various backgrounds. In the field of distant architectural design, and more specifically during early stages of the design process, efficiency of remotely shared external representations is another key aspect underlying this intricate process of transferring intentions [8].

The role graphical representations play in supporting remote collaborative architectural design has already been extensively studied [9]. Some of our previous work in product design has specifically investigated how designers deal with foreign external representations, underlying the graphic strokes essential to the faithful transmission of an intention [10]. This current research rather focuses on architectural design, and more specifically on 2D plan representations, supposedly more straightforward in transferring and understanding intentions given the limited set of (quasi) universal architectural symbols and codes used in this field [11]. This paper questions whether this limited set of symbols and codified representations could constitute an interesting safe-pass to efficient transmission of intentions, and how the wide diversity of stakeholders taking part to a building project (from the architectural creative process to the building site) and the discrepancy of their respective expertise might impact this transmission.

## 3    Approach

To investigate how the level of expertise might impact the capture of architectural intentions, a series of controlled experiments (20 to 45' in duration) was set up. Participants with diverse architectural backgrounds were asked to copy a reference sketch (provided in hardcopy, see Figure 1) representing a two-dimensional house plan, intentionally blurry and incomplete but presenting a layout familiar to a wide range of participants and composed by a limited set of traditional architectural symbols. Free hand sketching was favored here because of its popularity among trained architects and its ease-of-use given the low expertise of some participants in dealing with other design tools.

Participants were trained to the think aloud method [12] (through a simple Hanoi tower exercise) and then asked to verbally comment their re-copying process, with no additional requirements in terms of exactness, style or time-efficiency. Strokes and verbalizations were recorded through the Smartpen™ technology that allowed a sequential replay of the data.

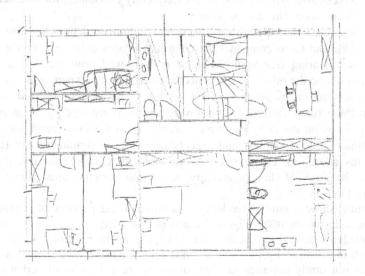

**Fig. 1.** The reference sketch of a two-dimensional, first-floor house plan

To investigate the impact of expertise on capturing the sketched architectural intention, 28 participants (mainly graduate students) were selected based on their level of architectural knowledge and were classified following three categories:

• 10 participants with no specific knowledge in architecture (i.e., not following any class in architecture) were selected as "novices";
• 8 participants with a limited background in architecture (e.g. did not major in architecture but did take lessons or had significant contacts within this field) were considered as "familiar";
• 10 participants specifically studying architecture and close to finishing their degree were selected as "experts".

Once all experiments completed, graphical elements of each copied sketch were coded in regard to the reference elements in the reference sketch. Graphic and verbal recorded data was analyzed quantitatively and qualitatively from different perspectives, such as the expertise of each participant, its interpretation and perception of the reference elements and the nature of the reference components.

## 4    Results

The first important result concerns the overall capture of the reference sketch. Interestingly, and in spite of its blurry and incomplete aspects, it appears that the reference sketch is globally accurately copied by all participants, regardless of the expertise level. Indeed, 43% of the reference elements (graphic units of the reference sketch, e.g. a door, a bed, a wall…) were copied by 100% of the participants, and 76% of those elements were even captured by 93% of the participants. This confirms the (quasi) universal quality of 2D architectural plan representations: surpassing the blurry aspect of the reference sketch, even participants with no architectural expertise were able to recognize symbols that we all frequently encounter, for instance in real estate advertisements or fire-escape plans.

In previous research focusing on concurrent cognitive actions involved during design, Kavakli and Gero compared the cognitive processes of one novice and one expert architect during free-hand sketching and showed how the design thinking differed from one to the other. Their results revealed that the expert architect required three times less actions to reach the final version of his sketch; realized the design experiment three times faster than the novice and demonstrated an organized mind with strong focus on the task. The novice architect, on the other hand, did generate and investigate several options and aspects of the task simultaneously (therefore scattering his attention), but was also more inclined to more creative, innovative discoveries because of his potentiality to create much more unconventional associations [13].

Our results show a similar tendency this time in the process of capturing and interpreting a drawn intention. Figure 2 illustrates how experts extensively used their field-knowledge when recopying the sketch (44,7 % of their actions being supported by a reflection nurtured by this architectural knowledge), while another 44,7 % of actions was not orally commented (demonstrating the difficulty to verbalize highly usual, implicit actions). The remaining 10,6 % was performed using an indirect reflection, defined by Hattenauer as parallel strategies (association, intuition and similarity) people use when facing unknown situations [14]. Novices, on the other hand, used references to architectural knowledge in only 34 % of the occurrences, relying more on indirect reflections (38,1 % of actions), nurtured by their personal way of experiencing space and previous experiences as an "inhabitant" of a house (for instance in terms of what furniture to expect inside a bedroom).

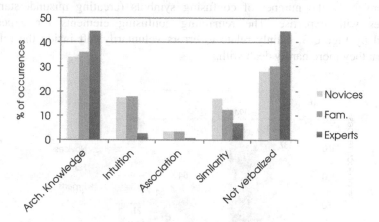

**Fig. 2.** Strategies used by different levels of expertise in the process of capturing a sketched intention

Interestingly, our results additionally show how the three groups of participants differently dealt with the blurry and erroneous parts of the reference sketch. Figure 3 for instance shows how a 'door' element, originally badly drawn in the reference sketch (with a triangular shape instead of its standard "quarter-circle" representation, see picture extract on the right) is differently appropriated. It appears that while novices and familiar participants all recopy the item and correctly verbalize it as 'a door', most experts do not perceive it as such, some erroneously understanding it, others deciding not to copy it at all (perhaps considering it as a design mistake).

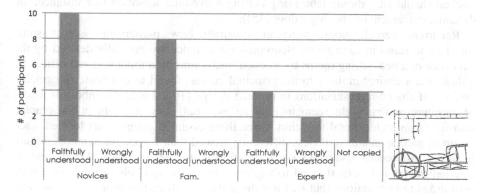

**Fig. 3.** Various understandings of a 'door' element

We suggest that experts mainly base their recopying process on concepts and symbols that they have previously learned. They automatically react to the reference sketch by using their knowledge of architectural semantics, favoring efficiency and preferring not to spend too much time on what could not be immediately understood. Novices, on the other hand, are less trained to read these symbols and therefore approach them differently. Figure 4 illustrates two learning curves, showing how the number of key symbols (triggering the recognition process) increases with expertise, while conversely the number of confusing symbols (creating misunderstandings) diminishes with expertise. The remaining confusing elements for experts, as suggested by Figure 3, mainly relate to errors voluntarily left inside the reference sketch that they more hardly dealt with.

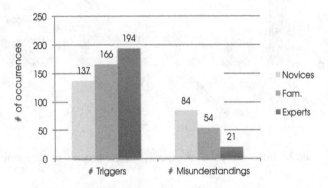

**Fig. 4.** Impact of expertise on perception of elements

Besides being more disposed to discovery during design [13], the results of our study moreover suggest that the novice participants, with their flexibility, logical thinking and open-mindedness, better understand the most vague, unclear and erroneous parts of a sketch. They make more frequent reference to previous experiences, identifying parts of the blurry sketch thanks to what they encounter during everyday-life. They thus more easily identify symbols representing a real piece of furniture (for instance a toilet seat), clearly figuring a function (not too far from a kitchen should sit a dining table) or picturing a dynamic sensation (for instance, the dynamic movement of opening a door [15]).

Recurrent verbalizations moreover illustrate how participants expect some furniture to stand in each room. Bedrooms for instance are basically defined by the existence of a bed, sitting rooms by a couch, bathrooms by a toilet seat and offices by a desk and a chair. Similarly to the principal curves, found to constitute the graphic essence of shared representations in product design [10], standard symbols of pieces of furniture at first sight seem to play an essential, semantic role in the graphic transfer of an architectural intention. Once these essential components located, each group of participants nevertheless differently treated their respective symbols. Figure 5 shows differences related to strict faithfulness to the reference sketch (and its original intentions) : experts tend to slightly modify the symbols to implement their own drawing conventions (but still matching the overall codification), while novices are more respectful of the original drawing.

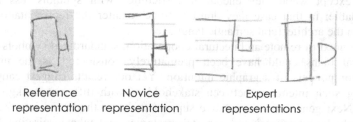

Reference              Novice                    Expert
representation    representation        representations

**Fig. 5.** Different representations of a desk, in regard of the level of expertise

All drawn symbols of pieces of furniture cannot yet be considered as essential to a robust transfer of intent, as illustrated by Figure 6. Three representations of a closet (traditionally represented by a rectangle crossed by two diagonals) are displayed, respectively the reference, novice and expert representations. If the experts have no problem recognizing and copying the closet, novices experience more difficulties in apprehending the object since it is less intuitively assimilable to any lived experience. Most of the time not understanding its meaning, novices sketched something completely different from the reference sketch, therefore totally ignoring the standard semantic architectural codes. Interestingly, novices indeed faithfully copied elements especially when they were positive about their functions, and otherwise would not pay attention to any particular convention, the "mysterious objects" making no sense, requiring no particular attention and consequently being altered.

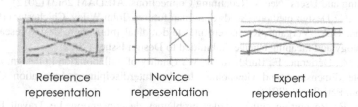

Reference              Novice                    Expert
representation    representation        representation

**Fig. 6.** Different representations of a closet, in regard of the level of expertise

## 5    Conclusion

The results of this preliminary study suggest that architectural intentions carried out by free-hand sketches are globally well captured by all but that there are differences in understanding and appropriating those graphic intentions according to the level of architectural expertise.

Experts, given their high knowledge in architectural semantics, easily and quickly capture most of the intentions without investing a lot of time or attention. While misunderstanding fewer elements, they also grant less interest to more blurry and erroneous parts of the reference sketch and tend to more systematically apply their own drawing conventions.

Novices, on the other hand, more extensively rely on previous living and bodily experiences to understand the sketch and therefore more easily deal with the blurriest parts of the freehand sketch. They tend to more faithfully represent the initial intention, except when they encounter difficulties with symbols less intuitively understandable: in that case they don't hesitate to alter the representations and to depart from the architectural semantic language.

In the context of remote architectural cooperation, standardized symbols inside 2D architectural plans could have been prematurely considered as the unique and essential components of a graphic intention. Yet our results suggest caution when transferring such intentions between stakeholders with different backgrounds and expertise. Next generation cooperative support tools, methods and interfaces should keep at sight both novices' and experts' strategies and take inspiration from both intuitive, deductive novices' embodied experiences and field-knowledge experts' efficiency in order to insure optimal cooperation between stakeholders experiencing some geographical and background distance.

# References

1. Schön, D.A., Wiggins, G.: Kinds of Seeing and their Functions in Designing. Design Studies 13(2), 135–156 (1992)
2. Dogan, F., Nersessian, N.J.: Generic abstraction in design creativity: the case of Staatsgalerie by James Stirling. Design Studies 31, 207–236 (2010)
3. Dorta, T., Kalay, Y., Pérez, E., Lesage, A.-M.: Comparing immersion in remote and local collaborative ideation through sketches: a case study. In: CAAD Futures, Proceedings (2011)
4. Elsen, C., Demaret, J.-N., Yang, M.-C., Leclercq, P.: Sketch-Based Interfaces for Modeling and Users' Needs: Redefining Connections. AIEDAM 26(3) (2012)
5. Jones, J.C.: Design methods: Seeds of human futures. John Wiley, Chichester (1970)
6. Norman, D.A., Verganti, R.: Incremental and radical innovation: design research versus technology and meaning change. Submitted to Design Issues (2012)
7. Baker, M., Détienne, F., Burkhardt, J.-M.: Quality of collaboration in design: articulating multiple dimensions and viewpoints. In: 1st Interdisciplinary Innovation Conference, Telecom ParisTech. (2013)
8. Darses, F.: Résolution collective des problèmes de conception. Le Travail Humain 72, 43–59 (2009)
9. Safin, S., Juchmes, R., Leclercq, P.: Use of graphical modality in a collaborative design distant setting. Work: A Journal of Prevention, Assessment and Rehabilitation (suppl.1) (2012)
10. Elsen, C., Darses, F., Leclercq, P.: What Do Strokes Teach Us about Collaborative Design? In: Luo, Y. (ed.) CDVE 2012. LNCS, vol. 7467, pp. 114–125. Springer, Heidelberg (2012)
11. Dessy, J.: De l'emploi des symboles dans les esquisses architecturales. Thesis, Université de Liège (2002)
12. Van Someren, M., Barnard, Y., Sandberg, J.: The Think Aloud Method: A Practical Guide to Modelling Cognitive Processes. Academic Press, London (1994)
13. Kavakli, M., Gero, J.S.: The Structure of Concurrent Cognitive Actions: a Case Study on Novice and Expert Designers. Design Studies 23(1), 25–40 (2001)
14. Hattenhauer, D.: The Rhetoric of Architecture: a Semiotic Approach. Communication Quarterly 32, 71–77 (1984)
15. Eco, U.: Function and Sign: the Semiotics of Architecture. In: Signs, Symbols and Architecture, pp. 11–69 (1980)

# Use of Tangible Marks with Optical Frame Interactive Surfaces in Collaborative Design Scenarios Based on Blended Spaces

Gustavo Salvador-Herranz[1], Manuel Contero[2], and Jorge Camba[3]

[1] Dpto. de Expresión Gráfica, Proyectos y Urbanismo,
Universidad CEU Cardenal Herrera, Valencia, Spain
gsalva@uch.ceu.es
[2] I3BH, Universitat Politécnica de Valencia, Valencia, Spain
mcontero@upv.es
[3] Engineering Design Graphics, Texas A&M University, College Station, TX, USA
camba@tamu.edu

**Abstract.** In this paper, we present new methods of interaction with multi-touch surfaces implemented with optical frames by using tangible elements. Since interactive surfaces typically allow simultaneous detection of a large number of touch points, we propose the use of physical objects (which can be 3D printed) to reproduce different touch patterns, similar to using finger gestures on the table. These patterns are identified and recognized by our system and used to calculate the position and orientation of the mark on the surface. We propose the use of these tangible elements as a method to manage information locally in an interactive surface and also to exchange information between different surfaces to support collaborative design work.

**Keywords:** human-computer interaction, natural interfaces, blended spaces, interactive surfaces, tabletops.

## 1 Introduction

Teamwork is an essential element in engineering and industrial design activities, particularly during the early stages of the design process, where creativity plays a major role. In fact, many creativity techniques only make sense within multidisciplinary work groups. In these early stages, effective communication and exchange of ideas are critical. A major concern during the initial working sessions is to avoid introducing barriers that may hinder the communication process.

Although technology certainly improves the exchange of information among team members, it can also become a barrier during the early creative stages where communication must be direct and personal. Face-to-face meetings where designers sit around a table to discuss or generate new ideas (typically using some creativity technique such as brainstorming) are common. In this context, systems based on Natural Interfaces can make technology transparent to users so it does not interfere with the

Y. Luo (Ed.): CDVE 2014, LNCS 8683, pp. 253–260, 2014.

creative process. Similarly, Blended Spaces simplify the synthesis between analog and digital worlds, allowing users to move and manage information from one space to another in a natural and intuitive way.

Large multi-touch interactive surfaces are suitable systems for collaborative work. Such devices offer a large interactive surface that simulates a traditional work table. This environment facilitates face-to-face communication and promotes discussion and exchange of ideas. To be effective, these interactive surfaces must be multi-touch and multi-user, allowing multiple users to interact with the system simultaneously.

Interactive surfaces are particularly attractive when used as part of Blended Interactive Spaces, which are ubiquitous computing environments for computer-supported collaboration that builds on and enhances the pre-existing motor, spatial, social, and cognitive skills of groups of users [1-4]. Such spaces hide the complexity of technology and enhance Human Computer Interaction (HCI), making it more natural. Tangible User Interfaces play an important role in Blended Spaces, as they allow a type of human-machine interaction that is similar to natural processes.

Interactive surfaces have been implemented with different types of technology [5]. In this paper, we focus on the use of multi-touch systems constructed from optical marks. Such frameworks can transform any type of display device (projective or not) into an interactive multi-touch surface. In particular, flat-panel TVs with optical frames have been widely used as they can be turned into powerful systems with excellent image quality at a reasonable cost.

We present new forms of interaction with interactive multi-touch surfaces implemented with optical frames by using tangible elements, which are elements not originally designed for these devices. Since interactive surfaces typically allow simultaneous detection of 32+ touch points, we propose the use of physical objects (which can 3D printed) to reproduce different touch patterns, similar to using finger gestures in certain positions on the table. These patterns can be identified and recognized by the system, providing its position and orientation on the interactive table.

## 2    3D Tangible Marks

Tangible user interfaces have been widely used as mechanisms to interact with digital information in a physical manner and a number of authors have demonstrated their benefits [6, 7]. A variety of items can be used depending on the implementation of the interactive surface.

In general, for every tangible item in the system, it is necessary to maintain a unique identifier (ID) and track its position and orientation on the interactive table. For example, in rear projection based interactive surfaces (tabletops) a camera located below the surface recognizes predefined marks printed on the bottom faces of the tangible elements [8,9], and calculates its position and orientation. Other implementations use radio frequency (RF) tracking methods. In this case, each tracked object contains an LC tag that resonates at a unique frequency. The position of the tag on the table is determined by measuring the resonance of the tag with different antenna elements on the tabletop. The problem with these systems is that only the XY position of the object on the surface (and in some cases an ID) is returned, but not the element orientation. Also, additional hardware is required, which increases the overall cost.

We propose the use of tangible elements in combination with interactive surfaces based on optical frames capable of detecting multiple touches (typically 30+) simultaneously. Touch gestures in such systems are recognized when users' fingers interrupt the optical barrier created by the framework. However, there is no need to use fingers, as any object can be used to interrupt the optical beam. The main contribution of this study is the use of flat elements with pins located at the bottom that can interrupt the light beam generated by the optical frame. Digital information can be linked to and manipulated by these elements.

At least three pins are necessary (the vertices of a triangle) to always define a plane (see Fig. 1). The triangle defined by the three pins is isosceles so its position and orientation on the tabletop can be determined easily. As explained in the next section, the two long sides of the triangle are used to get the position and orientation of the mark on the tabletop. Additional pins placed between those that define the shortest side of the triangle are used to encode a unique ID of the mark in binary form. The higher the resolution of the optical frame, the more pins can be placed on the element and thus the more physical elements can be used. In the example shown in Fig. 2, three pins are used to encode eight different ID's. Fig. 3 shows another example in which 4 distinct marks are encoded, this time using just two pins. With this method, a total of $2^n$ unique IDs can be encoded, where $n$ is the maximum number of pins that can be placed in the shortest side of the triangle.

 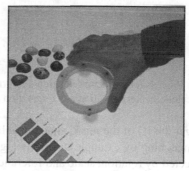

**Fig. 1.** Examples of Tangible Marks. Digital model (left) and real mark on tabletop (right).

## 3     Information Retrieval from Tangible Marks

To detect the location of the tangible marks on the interactive surface we use simple clustering techniques. The API of the optical frame provides a method to return the number and XY coordinates of each user action, which can be understood as a point cloud. To determine the clusters we use the Quality Threshold (QT) clustering algorithm. This is a simple method that does not provide the desired number of clusters (like in K-Means), but the maximum distance allowed for the cloud to be considered a cluster. In this case, the maximum distance is known (the diameter of the tangible mark). Although this algorithm is computationally intensive, the number of elements to classify is relatively small (about 32, depending of the capabilities of the optical frame), so real-time classification is still possible.

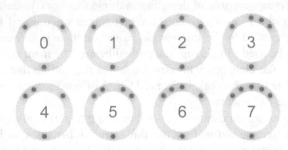

**Fig. 2.** Eight possible Tangible Marks using three encoding pins

Once the clusters are found, a convex hull for each of them is generated (see Fig. 3). Next, vectors $\overrightarrow{v1v2}$ and $\overrightarrow{v1v4}$ are defined using the two longest sides of the polygon, and added together to determine the direction vector of the mark. Additionally, the center $C$ of the mark can be found by transforming the direction vector into its unit vector and multiplying it by the radius of the mark.

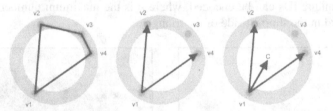

**Fig. 3.** Process for extracting position and orientation of a Tangible Mark: Convex hull (left). Main vectors (center). Position and orientation vector (right).

To get the ID of the mark, shape matching techniques can be applied [10]. We use shape matching by example using the algorithm described in [11]. This algorithm is not affected by rotation, scale and reference point, and also has a reasonable computational cost. The polygons that can be generated with two encoding pins are illustrated in Fig. 4.

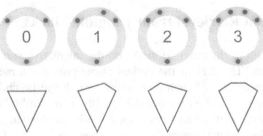

**Fig. 4.** Polygons associated with Tangible Marks

# 4     Distribute Collaborative Design Scenarios Using Tangibles

The combination of tangible marks with optical frame-based interactive surfaces represents a cost effective yet powerful mechanism to implement collaborative design scenarios based on Blended Spaces. In previous studies, [12] we proposed the use of interactive surfaces and designed a system based on natural interfaces that hides the complexity of technology and promotes face-to-face communication. Our system allows managing, organizing, and structuring digital two-dimensional graphical information and text in a natural way by simulating a physical workbench where designers traditionally work with paper, handwritten notes, sketches, pictures, and charts. This interactive surface can also be used to add information to the system in a variety of ways, such as by using shared folders in the cloud, via social networks like Twitter, or by sending messages with text and pictures.

A major feature of our system involves its distributed architecture, which allows teamwork in a co-localized manner. This means that different designers, or groups of designers (who may be geographically dispersed), can work collaboratively in real time using a common virtual board. The objective is to simulate a large common working plane (see Fig. 5) that can be shared by all users. An application server provides Internet support to the working plane and each device attached to the system acts as an interactive window to a section of this plane. These windows can be dragged and moved using simple finger gestures.

**Fig. 5.** Representation of the virtual work plane

In this paper, we propose the use of tangibles as a method to manage information locally in an interactive surface and also to exchange information in a simple way between different interactive surfaces, thus extending the idea of blended spaces in distributed environments.

## 4.1     Using Tangibles to Manage Information

Our system can associate a tangible mark (using its identifier) to a data storage operation. When the mark is placed on the interactive surface, it is automatically recognized (as previously discussed) and data elements arranged on the tabletop can be linked to it simply by dragging them to touch the mark (the link is displayed graphically). If an object is already bound to the mark, repeating the same operation the object is unlinked. If the physical mark is removed from the table, all linked items disappear but remain stored in the application server (still associated with the identifier of the mark). Therefore, when the mark is placed again on the table, all elements reappear. If the mark is moved or rotated, all linked elements follow it hierarchically.

Similarly, it is possible to associate a mark with a deletion operation. In this functioning mode, when the mark is placed on the table objects can still be linked to it, but when removed, linked objects are removed from the application server. Therefore, if the mark is placed back over the table, elements will not reappear.

### 4.2     Using Tangibles to Exchange Information between Different Interactive Surfaces

Tangible marks can also be used to exchange information in a simple and natural way between different interactive surfaces connected to the same application server. In addition, we can associate a mark with a "clipboard" so it can be used to perform copy-and paste operations, similar to the managing operations explained in the previous section, but without removing the information items from the interactive surface of origin.

## 5     System Architecture

Using the API functionalities provided by the optical frame manufacturer, we implemented a daemon process that continually samples touch gestures on the interactive surface and returns them as XY coordinates. With this information, the number of marks placed on the table as well as their respective IDs, position and orientation can be obtained, as described in section 3. At this point, using TUIO protocol [13], multiple TUIO "object" frames that correspond to those marks on the table and contain all their information (ID, position and orientation) are generated and sent to the system via UDP. All points that are not classified into any cluster (and thus do not belong to any mark) are sent as single points in single TUIO "point" frames. This feature allows compatible interaction with the multi-touch table using both tangible marks and hand gestures.

The application for collaborative work described in section 4 has been implemented using the Unity3D engine, which provides extensive support for developing graphical and networking applications (originally designed for the development of online games). Building on this engine, our system architecture is designed as a client-server application (see Fig. 6), where a server component supports the system, and multiple clients connect to it via TCP/IP.

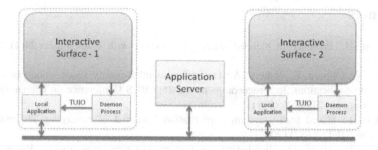

**Fig. 6.** Distributed System Architecture

The entire virtual workspace is managed by the server and each client has a view of it. Any action performed by a client is transmitted to the server, which immediately updates the scene and, in return, sends the changes back to the clients. The operation is similar to a network video game, where a common virtual world is stored on a server, and each player connects to it as a client. With this feature each interactive table has a view of a different area of a common space. For example, when a tangible mark is removed from a table, the associated items still exist in the application server (except in the case of delete operations) and are simply marked as hidden. When the mark placed again on the same or on another table, linked objects are moved to the new location and orientation, and re-marked as visible.

## 6    Conclusions and Future Work

In this work, we have presented a new interaction mechanism based on tangible elements and interactive surfaces built with optical frames. The availability and gradually lower costs of large format flat screen TVs in conjunction with optical frames are providing affordable yet powerful tools to develop large interactive multi-touch systems with excellent image quality at reasonable prices.

With the incorporation of tangible items, interactive surfaces can be effectively integrated in environments based on Blended Spaces and Ubiquitous Computing. Although different methods to include tangible elements within these devices have been developed (such as those based on radio frequency or fiducial marks and overhead cameras), they all require additional hardware and occlusion problems may occur. The solution we propose uses existing hardware with no additional elements, which simplifies the system substantially. Additionally, our marks are passive and can be easily 3D printed. We have also integrated the TUIO protocol, which makes the system multiplatform and compatible with other development systems, thus simplifying the creation of new applications.

We are currently developing new tools and interaction mechanisms that use tangibles marks. Our goal is to facilitate teamwork and increase productivity by improving the ubiquitous aspects of the system. We are also interested in conducting a formal usability study of our tool to compare user performance and satisfaction when tangible marks are used.

# References

1. Benyon, D.: Presence in blended spaces. Interacting with Compututers 24(4), 219–226 (2012)
2. Hoshi, K., Öhberg, F., Nyberg, A.: Designing blended reality space: conceptual foundations and applications. In: Proceedings of the 25th BCS Conference on Human-Computer Interaction, pp. 217–226 (2011)
3. Müller, D.: Mixed reality systems. International Journal of Emerging Technologies in Learning (iJET) 5 (S2) (2009)
4. Benyon, D., Mival, O.: Blended spaces for collaborative creativity. In: Proceedings of Workshop on Designing Collaborative Interactive Spaces, AVI 2012 (2012)
5. Müller-Tomfelde, C. (ed.): Tabletops - Horizontal Interactive Displays. Springer, London (2010) ISBN 978-1-84996-113-4
6. Ishii, H., Ullmer, B.: Tangible bits: towards seamless interfaces between people, bits and atoms. In: Proceedings of the SIGCHI Conference on Human Factors in Computing Systems (CHI 1997), pp. 234–241 (1997), doi: 10.1145/258549 .258715
7. Ishii, H.: Tangible user interfaces. In: Sears, A., Jacko, J.A. (eds.) The Human-Computer Interaction Handbook. Fundamentals, Evolving Technologies, and Emerging Applications, pp. 469–487 (2007)
8. Patten, J., Recht, B., Ishii, H.: Interaction Techniques for Musical Performance with Tabletop Tangible Interfaces. In: Advances in Computer Entertainment (2006)
9. Jordà, S., Geiger, G., Alonso, M., Kaltenbrunner, M.: The Reactable: exploring the synergy between live music performance and tabletop tangible interfaces. In: Proceedings of the 1st International Conference on Tangible and Embedded Interaction, pp. 139–146 (2007)
10. Veltkamp, R.C.: Shape matching: Similarity measures and algorithms. In: International Conference on Shape Modeling and Applications, SMI 2001, pp. 188–197 (2001)
11. Arkin, E.M., Paul, L., Keden, K., Mitchell, J.: An Efficiently Computable Metric for Comparing Poygonal Shapes. Technical Report 89-1007. Department of Computer Science. Cornell University (1989)
12. Salvador, G., Bañó, M., Pérez, D., Contero, M.: A distributed collaborative learning tool based on a conceptual map paradigm and natural interfaces applied to the case of product design studies. In: Proceedings of the Research in Engineering Education Symposium (2003)
13. Kaltenbrunner, M., Bovermann, T., Bencina, R., Costanza, E.: TUIO - A protocol for table-top tangible user interfaces. In: Proceedings of the 6th International Workshop on Gesture in Human-Computer Interaction and Simulation (2005)

# A Creative Approach to Conflict Detection in Web-Based 3D Cooperative Design

Xiaoming Ma[1], Hongming Cai[2], and Lihong Jiang[3]

Shanghai Jiaotong University, Shanghai, China
xinj2012sjtu@sjtu.edu.cn, {cai-hm,jiang-lh}@cs.sjtu.edu.cn

**Abstract.** In the process of web-based 3D cooperative design, it is difficult to avoid concurrent design conflicts among designers. B/S structure requires that most computational work must be done in service side, so conventional solution to desktop-based cooperative system is not well applicable to web-based one. Therefore, during the conflict detection process, when to make conflict detection, conflict resolution and broadcast result operations to all cooperative sites become a key problem. In this article we propose a novel web-based 3D cooperative design framework and a concrete implementation to conflict detection.

By this framework we can achieve automatic operation submission, real-time conflict detection based on dynamically adjustable time, and automatic conflict resolution with designers' customization, which is much different from conventional solutions that require frequent participation of designers to submit changes and resolve conflicts. And through tests and analysis our solution shows good performance, scalability and design interactivity.

**Keywords:** Co-design; design interactivity; cooperative; conflict detection; web-based 3D.

## 1    Introduction

It is very difficult to avoid cooperative conflicts when more than one designer edit the same 3D scene. However, the core problems of cooperative design platform are conflict detection (CD) and conflict resolution (CR) [1, 2, 3, 4], so how to define, detect and resolute conflicts are the key issues we must solve. In this paper we mainly aim at solving conflicts of editing operations to atomic 3D models or sub-scenarios, whereas the multi-level operations will be considered in our future work. While resolving those problems, we also have to ensure the design platform's interactivity and real-time performance.

Taking these into consideration, we propose a novel web-based 3D cooperative design framework with automatic operation submissions, real-time CD based on dynamically adjustable time, which is much different from conventional solutions that require frequent participation of designers. Then we show its performance, scalability and design interactivity by experiments and analysis.

Y. Luo (Ed.): CDVE 2014, LNCS 8683, pp. 261–268, 2014.

## 2     Related Work

The current solutions to collaboration design problems can be mainly divided into three types: authority mechanism, operation transformation (OT), and other synchronous or asynchronous ones. Authority type takes the way of avoiding conflicts, while the other two allow conflicts to arise and then resolve them.

By authority mechanism [5, 6, 7], designers must apply for system's permissions before modifying shared data, so operations will execute sequentially thus ensuring data consistency among all workstations. But these methods also decrease designer experience, and dead lock may arise if some workstation is down. OT transforms conflict operations to enable them executed sequentially, and is commonly used in cooperative word editing system (CWES) [8, 9, 10]. However, it requires complex calculations to   transform operations of 3D models, and in 3D cooperative design only one of conflict operations of the same type can be reserved, which is different from CWES. Also a novel OT solution [11] is proposed to solve the dependency conflicts among 3D models, but dependency conflicts are just similar to the position conflicts in CWES, so it cannot resolve the cooperative editing conflicts of 3D models. Additionally, other solutions are primarily designers-motivated synchronous ones. Both operation submissions and conflict resolution require designers' frequent participation, which would disturb the design work pace.

On the basis of those problems, we propose the solution of the dynamic time related real-time CD.

The remainder of this paper is as follows: In section three we describe our cooperative model and some basic concepts; then we present our CR strategy in section four; at last we evaluate out framework and cooperative solution by experiments and analysis.

## 3     Background

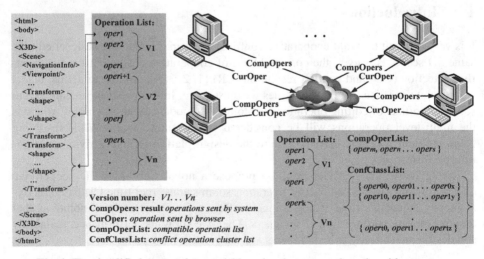

**Fig. 1.** The simplified system data model based on browser and service-side structure

## 3.1    Cooperative Model

We use X3D format models as design material for their XML schema (Fig 1). Based on the characteristic, all X3D files in a HTML file can be abstracted into an X3D tree with many nodes; and any updates on X3D models can be reflected to X3D document object model (DOM) tree. Since X3D DOM tree has a hierarchical structure, designers can modify the same node, the different node, or the parent and the child nodes cooperatively; however, in this paper we mainly make CD for operations of atomic models and sub-scenarios and we will handle the last situation in our future work.

We use browser and service-side architecture to design our framework (Fig 1). With storage-type and data processing-type cloud platforms, the service-side can be divided into several modules that are responsible for designer management, real-time CD, version controlling and sending result operations to sites; while browsers are responsible for performing compatible operations, undoing conflict operations and updating local version number.

To minimize the data transfer volume between browsers and service-side, and to satisfy the need to undo conflicting operations we adopt the operation-based scene state change [4]. Besides, we use fully replica design structure in which every browser end maintains the same history operation lists and version number as service-side, thus designers can edit models without constraints.

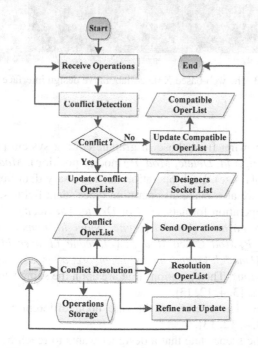

**Fig. 2.** Primary function flow chart in the service-side

The specific processes of our solution is as follows (Fig 2): Firstly, a designer edits a scene model in local browser (Fig 3); the operation is sent to CD service module automatically; then it makes conflict comparison and puts it into different operation lists according to the result. Meanwhile, the CR service module decides whether to start conflict resolution based on dynamic adjustable time. If does, it automatically resolves conflicts, refines the dynamic time and updates version number; then the designer management service module sends the results to all sites, and the storage-type service module saves result operations.

After receiving the result operations and message tips sent by system, every site undoes local conflict operations, performs compatible operations and updates local version number automatically. However, even though the conflict operations are undone, he or she can still decide whether to submit them for the new version (Fig 3).

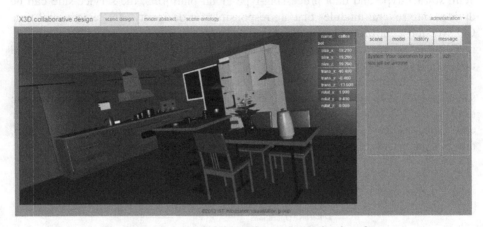

**Fig. 3.** The web-based X3D collaborative design interface

## 3.2    Basic Concepts

*Operation Type*: Borrowing from those in graphic editing system [12], we consider five types of operation: *Add*, *Delete*, *Mod_P* (modify position), *Mod_C* (modify color) and *Mod_S* (modify size). Each operation has necessary data fields as the operation format. Besides, we also make all operation types' data fields scalable for future needs. Here are the operation formats: *Add* or *Delete*: {*id, scene_id, user_id, operation_type, version_no, params*: [{*model*:{*scene_model_id, name, style, trans, color, size* ... } ... }]}. *Mod_P*, *Mod_C* and *Mod_S*: {*id, scene_id, user_id, operation_type, version_no, params*: [{*model*: {*scene_model_id, before, after* ...} ...}]}.

*Concurrent Operations*: The operations that are upon the same version are called *Concurrent Operations* [3, 4, 12, 13].

*Causal Operations*: The operations that are upon different versions are called *Causal Operations* [3, 4, 12, 13].

*Operation Will*: The scene state that a designer wants to reach by operating. In order to protect designers' *operation will* fairly we suppose all concurrent operations are timeless, and only one of the conflict operations of the same type can be reserved.

*Conflict Operations*: When more than one designer modifies the same model's same attribute to the same or different values, we say their operations are conflicting

[3, 4, 12, 13]. However, although they are conflicting, we still need to handle several special cases: when designer A and B delete the same model, or modify the same model' same attribute to same value, keeping either of these two operations has the same effect, but we have to reserve them and regard them as conflicting; this is because the corresponding designers may have different authority values that can be used as basis when making automatic CR. However, when the same designer modifies the same model' same attribute repeatedly, we just keep the last one.

## 4     Conflict Detection

In this section, we describe the core process of CD, give our time strategy and then refine this process by leak filling.

### 4.1     Conflict Detection

Apparently, all conflict operations can only happen among concurrent operations, so we simply need to conduct CD for concurrent operations. However, when to start and how to make CD are the key issues we should figure out in this section.

***Question 1***: *When and how to make CD?*
As mentioned above, we intend to realize real-time CD to balance the calculation loads, so the specific CD process is as follows: when the system receives the first operation, just puts it into the compatible operation list (ComOL); but after receiving the second operation the system compares it with the first since they are concurrent, then makes different processing depending on the comparison result. For subsequent operations, the system first compares them with operations in ComOL, then the operations in ConOL one by one.

### 4.2     Time Strategy

The results we get from CD are ComOL and ConOL; and if we do not make CR, the sizes of ComOL and ConOL will become larger and larger, which will make CD more time-consuming. So the system needs to select an appropriate time to make automatic CR, so as to limit the sizes of ComOL and ConOL to a small range.
   Before presenting our time strategy, we propose a rule first.

***RULE 1:*** If the time is too long, the real-time performance will get poorer. Since designer A cannot know in time whether his or her operations already sent to service-side have conflicts with those of others, and if yes, since the conflicts cannot be resolved immediately, A may perform more conflict operations next. On the contrary, if the time is too short, more concurrent operations may be treated as causal operations, so some conflict operations may be missed and designers' *operation will* may not be well protected.   Here we present our time strategy by answering three questions.

***Question 2***: *If   the selected time is too long or too short?*

RULE 1 has described the different situations caused by time selection, so we can judge the time by identifying these two situations. We use two indexes calculated at the end of each version period to indicate them roughly.

*avoidableConflictNo*: This refers to the number of conflict operations that could have been avoided if we select an appropriate time. We use this index to indicate that the selected time is too long. Because when it is too long, conflict operations will accumulate constantly and some unnecessary conflict operations may appear due to the time delay to make automatic CR.

*lateOperNo*: This refers to the number of operations that had been received late by system and is used to indicate that the time selected is too short. Because if the time is too short, the server starts CR untimely, and may miss a lot of concurrent operations; and when CR is finished, the version number will be updated, then the system may receive operations whose version number is smaller than the current one.

***Question 3***: *How to initialize the time?*
Because of the uncertainties of designers number, operation features and network conditions and so on before design work begins, we decide to start CR when the first avoidable conflict operation is detected or the total operation number is equal to the number of designers, then we use this time interval in the next version period.

***Question 4***: *How to update the time before entering the next version period?*
By the two indexes we can estimate whether the time is long or short, and we should increase or decrease it in the next version period to keep them in a range as small as possible. We cope with this problem based on our experimental data. Experiments show that the average processing time for one operation is about two milliseconds, so when one hundred designers operate the same scene and each sends one operation concurrently, the total time would be two hundred milliseconds. But in fact, it is nearly impossible for all the designers to operate concurrently, so the time may be more than two hundred milliseconds. Hence, to better ensure all designers' operation will, we make the time no less than the product of number of designers and two milliseconds.

### 4.3    Leak Filling

Because of the uncertainties mentioned above, even though the time is dynamically adjustable, a problem may still exist: the system can still receive operations on former versions after the version has been updated. So we have to remedy this problem:

After the version number is updated, the system will reserve the CR result for one or more version periods; and when receiving the late operations, the system will compare them with the reserved operations individually, there comes two results: First, if they have conflicts, ignore them and let them handled by browser ends, because browser end has already performed this operation before it was sent to service-side; then the browser end would undo this operation, so we don't have to handle them. Second, if they have no conflict, the system changes the operation's version number to the present one, treats it as current operation and continues processing.

By this solution, this problem is well solved and designers' *operation will* is well protected too.

## 5    Analysis and Evaluation

**Extensibility:** Firstly, authorized designers can define new data fields of operation to perform more elaborate design work. Secondly, they can set up new time strategy themselves, or use our time solution to enhance collaboration interactivity and timeliness. Thirdly, we use web socket technology to implement designers' management, and this supports designer's dynamic joining and leaving. Fourthly, authorized designers can also choose to reserve more versions of operations to protect the operations that are upon old versions.

**Interactivity:** By selecting an appropriate CR time every designer can know other's operations as soon as possible, so as to provide them with better interactivity; we also try to prevent potential and avoidable conflicting operations from arising, so we can save designers much work time taken by making and resolving those conflicting operations; besides, automatic CR also makes the design work more efficient.

**Evaluation:** We implement the system framework and run an instance in cooperative home design. We use *avoidableConflictNo* and *lateOperNo* to measure the protection degree for designers' operation will, and use operation processing time to show system response performance. We use threads to simulate designers, and use the suspended time of threads to simulate the operating time interval of designers or network delay. We simulate fifty and eighty designers respectively and produce operations by combining the five operation types according to the requirements of different scenarios. According to experiment results, the avoidable conflict operations are well prevented and the total time cost is well accepted based on designers' operating habits; but the number of late operations is relatively high, this is because we make the time interval between which the operations are sent so tight as to increase the system's request load. In fact, designers won't operate so frequently, the number of conflicting operations won't be so great and the running hardware environment will be faster too. Besides, most of the late operations can be well handled by the leak filling.

## 6    Conclusion

This paper proposes a novel, web-based, scalable and efficient framework with high interactivity for X3D cooperative design. By dynamic adjustable time we have realized real-time CD. Besides, the solution can well protect designers' operation will, improve the design work efficiency and provide designers with better interactivity. Moreover, we have made our framework more scalable in operation fields, time strategy, and parameter strategy, etc. However, in this paper only the editing operations of X3D atomic models or sub-scenario are considered and the time strategy is not so perfect, these are the issues we will consider in our future work.

**Acknowledgement.** This research is supported by the National Natural Science Foundation of China under No. 61373030, 71171132. We would like to thank 3D CAD browser for providing us with many X3D format models.

# References

1. Ahmed-Nacer, M., Urso, P., Balegas, V., Preguiça, N.: Concurrency control and awareness support for multi-synchronous collaborative editing. In: 2013 9th International Conference on Collaborative Computing: Networking, Applications and Worksharing (Collaborate-com), pp. 148–157. IEEE (October 2013)
2. Dewan, P., Hegde, R.: Semi-synchronous conflict detection and resolution in asynchronous software development. In: Dewan, P., Hegde, R. (eds.) ECSCW 2007, pp. 159–178. Springer, London (2007)
3. Koegel, M., Helming, J., Seyboth, S.: Operation-based conflict detection and resolution. In: Proceedings of the 2009 ICSE Workshop on Comparison and Versioning of Software Models, pp. 43–48. IEEE Computer Society (May 2009)
4. Koegel, M., Herrmannsdoerfer, M., von Wesendonk, O., Helming, J.: Operation-based conflict detection. In: Proceedings of the 1st International Workshop on Model Comparison in Practice, pp. 21–30. ACM (July 2010)
5. Agrawal, A.K., Ramani, K., Hoffmann, C.M.: CADDAC: multi-client collaborative shape design system with server-based geometry kernel. ASME (2002)
6. Bidarra, R., van den Berg, E., Bronsvoort, W.F.: Web-based collaborative feature modeling. In: Proceedings of the sixth ACM Symposium on Solid Modeling and Applications, pp. 319–320. ACM (May 2001)
7. Jing, S.X., He, F.Z., Han, S.H., Cai, X.T., Liu, H.J.: A method for topological entity correspondence in a replicated collaborative CAD system. Computers in Industry 60(7), 467–475 (2009)
8. Li, D., Li, R.: An admissibility-based operational transformation framework for collaborative editing systems. Computer Supported Cooperative Work (CSCW) 19(1), 1–43 (2010)
9. Shao, B., Li, D., Gu, N.: A sequence transformation algorithm for supporting cooperative work on mobile devices. In: Proceedings of the 2010 ACM Conference on Computer Supported Cooperative Work, pp. 159–168. ACM (February 2010)
10. Shao, B., Li, D., Lu, T., Gu, N.: An operational transformation based synchronization protocol for web 2.0 applications. In: Proceedings of the ACM 2011 Conference on Computer Supported Cooperative Work, pp. 563–572. ACM (March 2011)
11. Sun, C., Xu, D.: Operational transformation for dependency conflict resolution in real-time collaborative 3D design systems. In: Proceedings of the ACM 2012 Conference on Computer Supported Cooperative Work, pp. 1401–1410. ACM (February 2012)
12. Sun, C., Chen, D.: Consistency maintenance in real-time collaborative graphics editing systems. ACM Transactions on Computer-Human Interaction (TOCHI) 9(1), 1–41 (2002)
13. Sun, D., Xia, S., Sun, C., Chen, D.: Operational transformation for collaborative word processing. In: Proceedings of the 2004 ACM Conference on Computer Supported Cooperative Work, pp. 437–446. ACM (November 2004)

# Matching Workflow Contexts for Collaborative New Product Development Task Knowledge Provisioning

Tingyu Liu and Huifen Wang

School of Mechanical Engineering, Nanjing University of Science and Technology,
Nanjing 210094, P.R. China
tyliu@njust.edu.cn

**Abstract.** The variety of product types and spesifications make new product development (NPD) tasks tough work in discrete manufacturing enterprises, which makes it a common strategy to refer to similar outcomes (e.g. the product drawings, work instructions, etc.) of former tasks during NPD processes. To improve the efficiency of discovering similar historical outcomes, this paper presents a novel approach to measure the similarity between task execution contexts in process-aware information systems, and exploit it for runtime task knowledge recommendation. In our framework, the measurement of similarity is preceded by 1) modeling the task context with ontology theory, 2) using the ontology matching algorithms to evaluate the similarities between the corresponding context ontology entities of different tasks instances. The TD-IDF is then utilized to compute the context cohesion between the user's current task and historical tasks, and the tasks with the highest similarity will be recommended to the task executors, along with their outcomes. Comparative evaluation is performed using TF-IDF, Levenshtein and Affine Gaps, and results demonstrate that the proposed approach achieves good precision and recall, and is efficient in task knowledge recommendation.

**Keywords:** context-aware workflow; collaborative knowledge management; ontology matching; TF-IDF.

## 1    Introduction

Collaborative new product development (NPD) is a complex, geographically distributed, and highly intellectual process that provides automation challenges in the areas of process and knowledge management [1]. As a significant basic technology in EIS, workflow technology is widely utilized to track process-related information and status of NPD processes as it moves through an organization[2]. For the knowledge-intensive nature of NPD processes, there is a virtual explosion in the amount of raw data available to the designers[3-5].The following information overload issue makes some of the engineers heavily burdened, which is a drag on productivity and the adoption of new technology [6].

Therefore, to promote knowledge sharing among workers in collaborative NPD lifecycles, many distributed knowledge sharing approaches have been presented in enterprise information systems (EIS) [7-9]. Early studies in this area are the process oriented knowledge management based on document analysis/recommendation[10,

Y. Luo (Ed.): CDVE 2014, LNCS 8683, pp. 269–276, 2014.

11], which uses the text analyzing technology for document recommendation; Another famous approach is knowledge flow approach [12-14] proposed by Hai Zhuge, it utilizes the knowledge flow model along with the workflow models and the related management mechanism for realizing an ordered knowledge sharing and cognitive cooperation in distributed team software development processes; The most recent research with respect to process-centric knowledge management falls in information collaborative filtering[15], recommender system in workflow space[16], document recommendation based on the knowledge flow technology[17], etc. However, current works usually do not take into consideration the the dynamically changing contexts of product developing processes [18, 19]. Therefore, the effective and timely knowledge support and its concrete utilization in the product development process remains problematic.

It is our goal in this paper to explore ways of recommending similar historical contributions to current task executers. This paper proposes a novel approach based on workflow contextual information to facilitate runtime NPD task knowledge supply.

Our approach has two major advantages. Firstly, it solves the runtime NPD knowledge recommending issue in the workflow perspective, which avoids unperfect similarity calculations between complex CAD models. Secondly, the ontology theory is utilized to organize the NPD workflow context knowledge, and we can easily use the ontology matching technology to obtain the cohesion between different NPD tasks, both efficiently and effectively.

This remainder of this paper is organized as follows: In Section 2, we design a context-aware workflow task knowledge recommending framework and a hierarchical workflow context model named HOWCN. In Section 3, a novel context matching approach based on TF-IDF is presented. Later on in Section 4, we empirically compare two edit-distance-based ontology matching algorithms (Affine Gaps, and Levenshtein) with TF-IDF in the approach. Finally in Section 5, a conclusion is drawn.

## 2     HOWCN: A Hierarchical Ontology-Based Workflow Context Model for NPD

In the runtime of NPD workflow processes, all the historical contextual information of the tasks, and outcome data are organized and stored in an ontology-based workflow context repository $HC = \{c_1, c_2, ..., c_x, ..., c_n\}$. When a new process instance is activated, the current task context ontology $c_0$ can be automatically built, and so is the similarity between $c_0$ and $c_x \in HC$. The historical context ontology of the high similarity with $c_0$ will be in the recommended list, ranked by similarity values. In this way, the executor of current NPD task can reach to historical task outcomes much easier.

Ontology has been commonly recognized as the most promising context modelling method in literature [20-22], and there have already been a lot of context models for pervasive computing, mobile computing, etc. However, to the best of our knowledge, research on ontology-based context model in workflow space for product development remains blank and is still worth exploring.

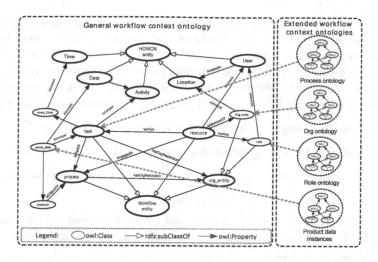

**Fig. 1.** The graph of HOWCN

In this paper, we study the main influence factors (location, user, time, data and activity, etc.) for NPD task execution in workflow space, and construct an ontology-based NPD workflow context model named HOWCN, and its main structure is shown in Fig. 1.

As depicted in Fig. 1, HOWCN is a hierarchical context model, which consists of two layers. The upper layer is the general workflow context ontology (GWCO), which indicates the key entities in the model and their main relations; the lower layer is the extended workflow context ontologies (EWCO), where the domain ontology knowledge and structured data (e.g. the organization tree data and workflow role structure, etc.) are stored. In HOWCN ontology, GWCO is usually stable, whereas EWCO is structured (in tree or net graph) and thus is extensible and easy to maintain.

# 3  A Workflow Context Ontology Matching Based on TF-IDF

The goal of this work is to output the best guess from the historic task outcomes based on the contextual information of NPD tasks. Here in this paper we use a famous natural language processing (NLP) technology named TF-IDF to measure the cohesions between current task and historical ones. Firstly, we use a naive VSM named stem-based VSM[23] to retrieve term vectors from the textual descriptions, which can be extracted from the RDFS tags such as *rdfs:label*, *rdfs:comment*, etc. With these term vectors, we then use TF-IDF to compute the similarities between current task context instance and the historical ones in HOWCN ontology. Finally, the outcomes of the tasks with the highest score are then recommended to the executor of current task for reference, ordered in similarities.

We use the operator $TEXT(c_j)$ to derive textual information from the *rdfs:label* and *rdfs:comment* tags of a context ontology $c_j$. To reduce inflectional and related forms of a word to a more basic form, we use one of the most popular stemmers, the Porter stemmer[24] to remove common derivational affixes. For example: *Stem(organize, organizes, organized, organizing, organization) = organiz*. Thus we can extract terms from all the textual documents, and these terms are listed as *index term set* of the documents. We use *it* to represent an index term, and the *index term set* is represented as $its = (it_1, it_2, ..., it_z)$. Using *its*, we transform the textual descriptions of a HOWCN instance $c_j$ into the *context vectors*: $TEXT(c_j) \rightarrow \vec{V}(c_j)$. These vectors are weighted for scoring different terms, where: $\vec{V}(c_j) = (w_{1j}, ..., w_{zj})^T$. Where $z = |its|$, and $w_{sj}$ is the *stem weight* of term $s$ in $\vec{V}(c_j)$. Likewise, we also get the term vector of current context $c_0$: $\vec{V}(c_0) = (w_{10}, ..., w_{z0})^T$.

We use the *term frequency, inverse document frequency (tf-idf)* weighting scheme[23, 25] $w_{sj}$ to represent the relative importance of the index stem $s$ in description document $j$, where

$$w_{sj} = tf - idf(s, j) = tf(s, j) \times \text{idf}(s) \tag{1}$$

Where $tf(s, j)$ is the *term frequency*, which is the number of times stem $s$ appears in description document $j$. The $idf(s)$ is the *inverse document frequency*.

$$idf(s) = \log\frac{N}{df(s)} + 1 \tag{2}$$

Where N is the total number of the document collections and $df(s)$ is the number of documents containing the stem $s$. As we can see from Equ (2) above, that the *idf* value of a rare term would be high, and the *idf* value of a term appearing in all the documents would near to zero, and would be added into the *stop list*. Therefore, the weight measure $w_{sj}$ is proportional to the term frequency of stem $s$ in document $j$, and is inversely proportional to the frequency of document containing stem $s$. For all the context vectors, we get the $z \times n$ *historical context matrix* $M_{HC}$:

$$M_{HC} = \begin{bmatrix} \vec{V}(c_1) & \vec{V}(c_2) & ... & \vec{V}(c_n) \end{bmatrix} = \begin{bmatrix} w_{11} & w_{12} & ... & w_{1n} \\ w_{21} & w_{22} & ... & w_{2n} \\ ... & ... & ... & ... \\ w_{z1} & w_{z2} & ... & w_{zn} \end{bmatrix} \tag{3}$$

Therefore, we use the cosine similarity of current task context $\vec{V}(c_0)$ and $\vec{V}(c_j)$ to quantify the cohesion between the current task $c_0$ and $c_j$:

$$Sim(c_0, c_j) = cosine(\vec{V}(c_0), \vec{V}(c_j)) = \frac{\vec{V}(c_0) \cdot \vec{V}(c_j)}{\|\vec{V}(c_0)\|\|\vec{V}(c_j)\|} = \frac{\sum_{m=1}^{z}(w'_{m0}w_{mj})}{\sqrt{\sum_{m=1}^{z}w'^2_{m0}}\sqrt{\sum_{m=1}^{z}w^2_{mj}}} \tag{4}$$

Where the denominator is the product of *Euclidean lengths* of the vectors $\vec{V}(c_0)$ and $\vec{V}(c_j)$, and the numerator represents their *dot product*. Furthermore, we use the VSM similarity between $\vec{V}(c_0)$ the matrix $M_{HC}$ to compute the cohesion measure between $c_0$ and all the historical task contexts:

$$Sim(c_0, C_H) = Sim_{VSM}(\vec{V}(c_0), M_{HC}) = M_{HC}^T \vec{V}(c_0) \tag{5}$$

# 4    Evaluation

To evaluate the presented approach, we use the testing document corpus and task data distracted from our former work[9, 26] to construct a HOWCN ontology with 232 task instances. The related NPD workflow process diagram is depicted in Fig. 2. This process is modeled in a Petri-net-like model referred to as WF-NET[27]. This process includes five tasks (A, B, C, D, and E), a parallel routing (the AND-Split and the AND-Join), and two selective routings (OR-Split $P_1$ and OR-Join $P_6$).

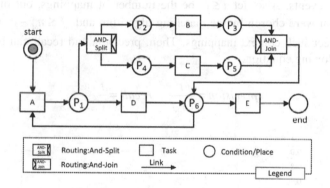

**Fig. 2.** A sample NPD workflow process modeled using WF-NET

Entities in this diagram are: process, task, and routing, etc. First, in Task A, the system automatically searches the database for similar cases. If there are cases meeting the requirements, the process would be submitted to Task D, and the designer will download the case documents and alert them. Otherwise, the work would be passed through a parallel routing to both Task B and Task C, and new design tasks will be assigned to corresponding designers for Task B and co-designer for Task C. When both the Task B and C are finished, the designed document will be archived in Task E and the whole design process ends.

As we can see from Fig. 3, 1633 stem items are derived from the entire document corpus, and the term frequency counts are also illustrated in the figure, the count of the most frequent term reaches as high as 763. Hence the weighted vector of the documents generate according to the stem set.

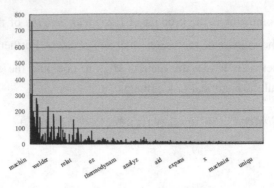

**Fig. 3.** The overall term frequency distribution of the test data

For the empirical evaluation of the performance, we use two famous metrics and their combinations in information retrieval, namely precision and recall, higher values of both precision and recall imply a better matching algorithm. Assume that out of the $n_M$ similarity computes, there are $c \leq n_M$ correct matching instances, with respect to the historical events. Also, let $t \leq c$ be the number of mappings, out of the correct mappings, that were chosen by the matching algorithm and $f \leq n_M - c$ be the number of incorrect such context mappings. Then, precision and recall can be computed using the following equation:

$$precision = \frac{t}{t+f} \ , \quad recall = \frac{t}{c} \tag{6}$$

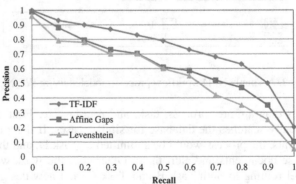

**Fig. 4.** The precision and recall curves showing the relative performance of TF-IDF, Affine Gaps, and Levenshtein

For comparison, we use another two edit-distance-based similarity computing methods named Levenshtein[28] and Affine Gaps[29] in the ontology matching phase, the experiment result is illustrated in Fig. 4. We find that different mapping methods perform differently in both precision and recall. We carefully analyze the testing data and to find that the reason why the TF-IDF method performs best is probably that in different dimensions of HOWCN, the user and data plays the most critical role, and their textual descriptions are relatively long and the word order is unimportant, which makes the token-based TF-IDF method the better choice.

Based on all the three curves in Fig.4, we conclude that the presented approach is efficient to achieve good recommending quality.

# 5    Conclusion

This paper proposes a novel approach based on NPD task context matching to make timely knowledge support for engineers. A comparative experiment is performed for demonstration and achieves a good prediction quality.

**Acknowledgements.** This work is funded in part by the NSFC under Grant 51275246 and National S&T Major Project of China under grant 2012ZX04010-011.

# References

1. Chandrasegaran, S.K., Ramani, K., Sriram, R.D., Horváth, I., Bernard, A., Harik, R.F., Gao, W.: The evolution, challenges, and future of knowledge representation in product design systems. Computer-Aided Design 45, 204–228 (2013)
2. Xu, L.: Enterprise systems: state-of-the-art and future trends. IEEE Transactions on Industrial Informatics 7, 630–640 (2011)
3. Vanderfeesten, I., Reijers, H.A., Van der Aalst, W.M.: Product-based workflow support. Information Systems 36, 517–535 (2011)
4. Harmon, P.: The scope and evolution of business process management. In: Handbook on Business Process Management, vol. 1, pp. 37–81. Springer (2010)
5. Alexopoulos, K., Makris, S., Xanthakis, V., Chryssolouris, G.: A web-services oriented workflow management system for integrated digital production engineering. CIRP Journal of Manufacturing Science and Technology 4, 290–295 (2011)
6. Farhoomand, A.F., Drury, D.H.: Managerial information overload. Commun. ACM 45, 127–131 (2002)
7. Zhen, L., Jiang, Z., Song, H.-T.: Distributed knowledge sharing for collaborative product development. International Journal of Production Research 49, 2959–2976 (2011)
8. Li, B.M., Xie, S.Q., Xu, X.: Recent development of knowledge-based systems, methods and tools for One-of-a-Kind Production. Knowledge-Based Systems 24, 1108–1119 (2011)
9. Liu, T., Cheng, Y., Ni, Z.: Mining Event Logs to Support Workflow Resource Allocation. Knowledge-Based Systems 35, 320–331 (2012)
10. Abecker, A., Bernardi, A., Maus, H., Sintek, M., Wenzel, C.: Information supply for business processes: coupling workflow with document analysis and information retrieval. Knowledge-Based Systems 13, 271–284 (2000)
11. Abecker, A.: Business-process oriented knowledge management: concepts, methods, and tools. Forschungszentrum Informatik, vol. Doctor. University of Karlsruhe (TH), Karlsruhe (2004)
12. Zhuge, H.: A process matching approach for flexible workflow process reuse. Information and Software Technology 44, 445–450 (2002)

13. Zhuge, H.: Knowledge flow management for distributed team software development. Knowledge-Based Systems 15, 465–471 (2002)
14. Zhuge, H.: A knowledge flow model for peer-to-peer team knowledge sharing and management. Expert Systems with Applications 23, 23–30 (2002)
15. Zhen, L., Huang, G.Q., Jiang, Z.: Collaborative filtering based on workflow space. Expert Systems with Applications 36, 7873–7881 (2009)
16. Zhen, L., Huang, G.Q., Jiang, Z.: Recommender system based on workflow. Decision Support Systems 48, 237–245 (2009)
17. Liu, D.-R., Lai, C.-H., Chen, Y.-T.: Document recommendations based on knowledge flows: A hybrid of personalized and group-based approaches. Journal of the American Society for Information Science and Technology 63, 2100–2117 (2012)
18. Harms, R., Fleschutz, T., Seliger, G.: Life cycle management of production facilities using semantic web technologies. CIRP Annals - Manufacturing Technology 59, 45–48 (2010)
19. Christophe, F., Bernard, A., Coatanéa, É.: RFBS: A model for knowledge representation of conceptual design. CIRP Annals - Manufacturing Technology 59, 155–158 (2010)
20. Strang, T., Linnhoff-Popien, C.: A Context Modeling Survey. In: Workshop on Advanced Context Modelling, Reasoning and Management, UbiComp 2004 - The Sixth International Conference on Ubiquitous Computing (2004)
21. Bettini, C., Brdiczka, O., Henricksen, K., Indulska, J., Nicklas, D., Ranganathan, A., Riboni, D.: A survey of context modelling and reasoning techniques. Pervasive and Mobile Computing 6, 161–180 (2010)
22. Bolchini, C., Curino, C.A., Quintarelli, E., Schreiber, F.A., Tanca, L.: A data-oriented survey of context models. ACM Sigmod Record 36, 19–26 (2007)
23. Salton, G., Wong, A., Yang, C.S.: A vector space model for automatic indexing. Commun. ACM 18, 613–620 (1975)
24. Porter, M.: An algorithm for suffix stripping. Program 14, 8 (1980)
25. Christopher, D., Manning, P.R.: Hinrich Schütze: Introduction to Information Retrieval. Cambridge University Press, Cambridge, England (2009)
26. Liu, T., Ni, Z., Jiao, L., Liu, X.: The stem-based vector space model for automatic resource allocation in workflow. In: 2010 2nd International Conference on Computer Engineering and Technology (ICCET), pp. V1-631–634 (2010)
27. van der Aalst, W., van Hee, K.: Workflow Management: Models, Methods, and Systems. The MIT Press (2004)
28. Ristad, E.S., Yianilos, P.N.: Learning string-edit distance. IEEE Transactions on Pattern Analysis and Machine Intelligence 20, 522–532 (1998)
29. Bilenko, M., Mooney, R.J.: Adaptive duplicate detection using learnable string similarity measures. In: ACM SIGKDD, pp. 39–48 (2003)

# A Collaborative Manufacturing Execution System Oriented to Discrete Manufacturing Enterprises

Huifen Wang, Linyan Liu, Yizheng Fei, and Tingting Liu

School of Mechanical Engineering, Nanjing University of Science and Technology,
Nanjing, Jiangsu 210094, China
nust8351121@126.com, {llylgy01,liuingtingwy}@163.com,
Yizheng.Fei@cn.bosch.com

**Abstract.** Collaborative manufacturing execution system (c-MES) is very important for manufacturing enterprises to realize informatization under the networked manufacturing environment. Production characteristics, typical production flow and collaborative management requirements of multi-workshop production in discrete manufacturing enterprise is analyzed. An architecture oriented to discrete manufacturing enterprises of c-MES is put forward. Main functions of c-MES and key technologies to realize c-MES are analyzed. Finally some system interfaces are introduced by a case study.

**Keywords:** Networked Manufacturing; c-MES; Architecture.

## 1 Introduction

Information and computer network technology has profoundly changed the world economy, but also the manufacturing industry into a new era of global competition. For many manufacturing enterprises, the location is no longer a hindrance, remote collaboration becomes possible, and products can be manufactured and sold through the Internet worldwide. [1-3]

Under the networked manufacturing environment, the enterprise integrated management model is different from traditional manufacturing enterprise. Modern manufacturing enterprises must use the computer network and database technology to effectively collaborate with partners and to achieve enterprise-wide integrated management of product design, process planning, manufacturing and production operation, so as to improve the flowing speed of information within the enterprise, shorten product development cycle and enhance the competitiveness of enterprises. As we have described in paper [3], the implementation of manufacturing enterprise integrated management requires the support of two platforms, one is networked manufacturing platform to support collaborative design and manufacture among cooperative enterprises, another one is manufacturing workshop integrated management platform to support enterprises realizing rapid product manufacturing.

Under the networked manufacturing environment, manufacturing workshop is a flexible integrated manufacturing system which can not only achieve the production

Y. Luo (Ed.): CDVE 2014, LNCS 8683, pp. 277–285, 2014.

management and control, but also to ensure the accuracy and reliability of the product. Workshop integrated management must ensure the data sharing and communication among functional departments under the supporting of network and database, so as to realize the whole process coordination and control, involving product design, process design, parts machining, resource allocation and management. As shown in figure 1, the entire manufacturing enterprise information management system can be logically divided into three layers involving design management, management control and process control. A workshop production management platform based on c-MES (Collaborative Manufacturing Execution System) is responsible for all aspects involved in the workshop execution process. It has played a role of a connecting link between enterprise plan and production control so as to achieve the transition from management to production.

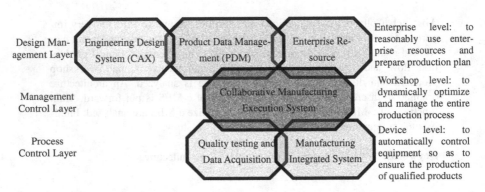

**Fig. 1.** Manufacturing enterprise information integration framework

Manufacturing Execution System (MES) is a shop floor-oriented management information system proposed by American Institute of Advanced Manufacturing Research in 1990. [4] But existing MES system lacks of effective coordination and rapid response capability, thereby weakening the effect of its application and even leads to the failure of its implementation, because its production management process is a serial management method from planning, execution, controlling to feedback. C-MES is a new concept combined with MES and collaboration, which breaks the information barriers in production management process, optimizes production processes of various operations, thereby enhances the capability of parallel collaboration, information integration and rapid response among different workshops, departments and information systems. With the flattening of enterprise management, c-MES is becoming one of important technical means for enterprises to improve their competitiveness, which can support enterprises to achieve effective integration of production activities and business activities, effective control and management of multi-workshop collaborative production process. So it is very important to establish a c-MES which can effectively realize manufacturing execution, information integration and collaboration, so as to promote the informationization process of discrete manufacturing enterprises, realize rapid response manufacturing and improve management level.

Based on the analysis of typical producing characteristics and needs of discrete manufacturing enterprises, discrete manufacturing business process model is established. According to the collaborative management requirements of multi-workshop production under the networked manufacturing environment, the universal c-MES architecture suitable for discrete manufacturing enterprises is put forward. Based on this, main functions are designed in detail and key technologies to realize c-MES are analyzed. Finally the system interface and case study are given.

## 2    Literature Review

### 2.1    MES and c-MES

An MES is the main software production management tool between production planning at the company management level and control/automation systems at the shop-floor level [5].

The C-MES model focused on how core operations activities interact with business operations in a model that represented issues such as increased competition, outsourcing, supply chain optimization, and asset optimization. Inside the c-MES box, the model depicts functions typically found in the integrated MES product offerings at that time. The c-MES world then interfaces to the other business operations areas around the edges.

MESA White Paper [6-9] outlines the objectives of this model: "What characterizes Collaborative Manufacturing Execution Systems (c-MES)? These systems combine earlier generation MES functionality to operate and improve plant operations and add better ability to integrate with other systems and people in the enterprise and value chain/stream. Although some of this data has been shared through traditional communications, the Internet and web-based technologies such as XML and web services provide a significant leap in accuracy and timeliness of communications."

### 2.2    Research Works on c-MES

With the promotion of digital manufacturing, MES research has made a lot of achievements. Compared to the MES, universities and research institutions began to research c-MES from the start of the 21st century and also obtained some research results. In china, 863 national CIMS hi-tech research and development program issued that MES is one of the key development projects in 2002, which promoted the domestic colleges and scientific research institution to study the MES system and its related technologies.

Research on Yang F, etc. [10] proposed an agent-based MES structure of press industries. Zhou H, etc. [11] established a kind of model-driven agent-based manufacturing execution system. Hao GK, etc. [12] researches the reconfigurability of service-oriented MES by making a reference to CIM-OSA and proposes three views, including function reconfigurability, data reconfigurability and process reconfigurability. Service-oriented MES is designed in a multi-tier architecture. Then researched how to control and implement three views of reconfigurability in MES based on

Service Component Architecture, Service Bus, Service Data Object and standards for business process. Service-oriented MES is well reconfigurable so that it can facilitate system fast practices and workshop business agility.

Song XY, etc. [13] set up a physical model and network structure of collaborative MES and applied it in a tobacco factory. We [14] built an architecture of c-MES for the collaboration manufacturing of discrete military manufacturing enterprises, gave the multi-plant planning and scheduling processes, designed a collaboration genetic algorithm for multi-plant planning and scheduling problem, proposed a multi-plant production data acquisition solution and developed the collaborative manufacturing execution system which has been proved effective, feasible and well meeting the actual demands of application enterprise. Peng GL, etc. [15] proposed a collaborative platform under network-based manufacturing environment for space products development and a kind of dynamic job shop scheduling algorithm which is used to realize rapid response and adjust manufacturing plan when production or process plan has changed. Zhang J, etc. [16] proposed a control model oriented to fit the MTO production, designed the data-collection scheme and the control system of material-flows according to the requirements on the information visualization and material synchronization, so as to realize a cooperative manufacturing system.

The above research work just focused on one specific manufacturing and lacked industrial applications. To tackle these problems, this paper tries to put forward universal c-MES architecture suitable for discrete manufacturing enterprises under the networked manufacturing environment and provide an industrial solution.

## 3    Architecture of c-MES

### 3.1    Requirements Analysis

Usually discrete manufacturing enterprise organizes its production in a discrete or non-continuous manner, which production methods, product structure and manufacturing processes are relatively complex, and so its production is characterized by complex resource management, complex and changeable product processes, highly dynamic production environment, parallel asynchronous production, a large redundancy of device functions and so on. With the continuous progress of modernization process, a variety of research and development tasks for complex high-tech products are also increased. Most of discrete manufacturing enterprises urgently need to resolve many problems existing in the workshop production process, such as production scheduling confusion, no timely feedback of production data, the lack of effective coordination in the production processes and so on. To solve these problems appear in the workshop production process, a typical production flow model of discrete manufacturing enterprise under the collaborative environment is established in this paper. As shown in figure 2, the production operations planning process is divided into two phase: one is planning and decomposition which is mainly do production planning, material requirements planning, job shop scheduling, program coordination and validation to ensure smooth and continuous production process; the other one is task execution and monitoring which is mainly do production dispatching, product machining, quality inspection and task submitting, production data feedback and re-scheduling.

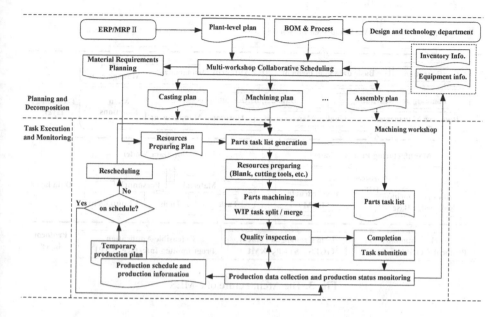

**Fig. 2.** Typical production flow of discrete manufacturing enterprise

To meet the requirements of the above collaborative production process, c-MES system should meet some functional requirements such as multi- workshop collaborative production, efficient planning and scheduling mechanism, real-time data acquisition and processing as well as effective control of the production process, in order to achieve stable product quality and improve the overall operating efficiency.

## 3.2    Architecture of c-MES

Based on the collaborative management requirements of multi-workshop production, this section outlines the architecture of c-MES. There are four layers in this architecture, which are called protocol layer, data layer, technology layer and application layer. Explanations of these four layers are as follows:

**(1) Protocol Layer:** This layer mainly specifies the protocol of the network protocol among the internal c-MES modules, as well as the platform and external information systems. In addition, data exchange protocol and API are both in this layer.

**(2) Data Layer:** This layer mainly stores and manages the information and data to maintain the consistency of data in the c-MES. The data is divided into the following:

**(3) Technology Layer:** This layer provides crucial functions of each c-MES module, including system management, planning and scheduling, data acquisition and processing, resource management, quality management, document management.

**(4) Application Layer:** The application layer provides user views to the clients and integrates the interfaces with DNC systems and others.

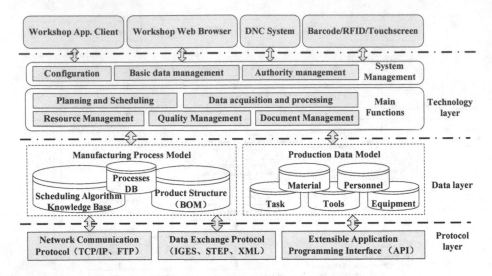

**Fig. 3.** The Architecture of c-MES

# 4    Main Functions and Its Implementation

## 4.1    Main Functions of c-MES

There are six functions in the c-MES, as showed in Figure 4, namely plan management, data collection & processing, document management, quality management, resources management and system management.

**(1) Plan Management:** Plan management module provides plant production plan according to the orders. It integrates advanced multi-workshop collaborative scheduling optimization algorithm for multi-workshop scheduling and provides the workshop production plan. This module includes plant production plan, workshop production plan and production status query.

**(2) Data Collection and Processing:** Data collection & processing is mainly responsible for the production data collection and processing in the shop floor. With computer terminals, handheld data collection devices and other devices, the production data can be collected timely. Thus the data of the task progress, material information, tooling status, and other production information can be stored in c-MES. The shop managers can query and monitor production status and timely adjust the production timely by production data analysis. This module mainly includes production data collection, task progress tracking, and material status query and production process analysis.

**(3) Document Management:** Document management provides a tool for the workshop managers and operators. They can query various documents in the production process. The documents include BOM, process documents, production flow sheets and quality check lists. Thus the production documents are well managed and shared.

**(4) Quality Management:** With quality management module, the quality control staffs can track and analyze the product quality in processing. It includes quality managements, quality analysis and quality control.

**(5) Resources Management:** Resource management includes equipment maintain and fixture management. This module manages the equipment information of the failure, maintenance and scrapping and the fixture information of storage, inventory, and other daily use.

**(6) System Management:** The module system management is constructed for system configuration, basic data management and system role management.

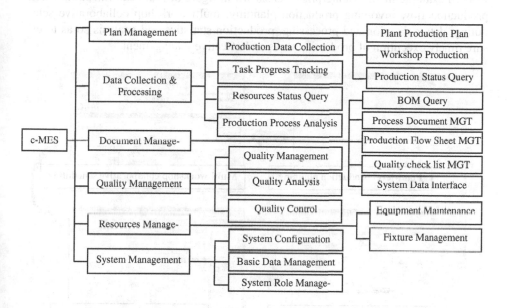

**Fig. 4.** Main Functions of c-MES

## 4.2    Key Technologies to Realize c-MES

To realize main functions of c-MES, we should resolve following key technologies:

**(1) Optimization Algorithm for Multi-Workshop Cooperative Scheduling:** to set up reasonable and efficient scheduling model and optimization algorithm so as to realize the reasonable allocation of manufacturing resources, scheduling and optimization of production operations.

**(2) Workshop Production Data Collection and Processing:** to collect, process and statistical analyze the workshop production data completely, efficiently and timely, in order to achieve effective monitoring and management of personnel, equipment, process, operations planning and production quality.

**(3) Information Security of c-MES:** to ensure production data security for manufacturing enterprises by authentication, access control, secure communications and other security measures.

Due to the limited length of this paper, key technologies mentioned above will be discussed in detail in subsequent papers.

### 4.3     System Interface and Case Study

Based on the proposed architecture of c-MES and its main functions, a prototype is developed. Feasibility of the proposed prototype is demonstrated by presenting a worked example in XXX enterprise. As shown in figure 5, users can finish the whole production flow involving production planning, multi-workshop collaborative scheduling, data collection and processing, production statistics and analysis so as to ensure timely execution of production tasks and effective management.

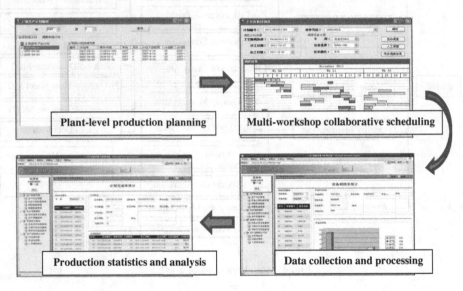

**Fig. 5.** System interface and case

## 5     Conclusion

Based on the production status and characteristics of discrete manufacturing enterprise under the collaborative environment, needs of c-MES system is analyzed. Then a typical production flow of discrete manufacturing enterprise under the collaborative environment is established and architecture of c-MES oriented to multi-workshop cooperation is put forward, functional structure of collaborative manufacturing execution system is designed, key technologies to realize c-MES is analyzed. Finally the system interface and case study are given. This system can provide great support for discrete manufacturing enterprises to improve production efficiency and market competitiveness.

**Acknowledgements.** This project is funded by the Priority Academic Program Development (PAPD) of Jiangsu Higher Education Institutions.

# References

[1] Cheng, T., Hu, C.H., Wu, B., Yang, S.Z.: On a Concept of Distributed Networked-Manufacturing System. China Mechanical Engineering 10(11), 1234–1238 (1999)

[2] Wang, Q.F.: Research on Manufacturing Execution System for Discrete Manufacturing Enterprise. Group Technology & Production Modernization 25(1), 9–11 (2008)

[3] Wang, H.F., Liu, T.T., Zhang, Y.L.: Design and Implementation of Integrated Management System of Digitized Manufacturing Shop. Defense Manufacturing Technology (2), 44–48 (2009)

[4] Huang, Y.B.: Optimization of Resource Reconfiguration and Job-shop Scheduling for c-MES. Nanjing University of Aeronautics and Astronautics, Nanjing (2006)

[5] Rolón, M., Martínez, E.: Agent Learning in Autonomic Manufacturing Execution Systems for Enterprise Networking. Computers & Industrial Engineering 63, 901–925 (2012)

[6] Swanton, B.: MES Five Years Later: Prelude to Phase III. American: AMR report 13725 (1995)

[7] MESA International, MES Explained: A High Level Vision. White Paper 6 Pittsburgh: Manufacturing Execution Systems Assoc. (1997)

[8] MESA International, Controls Definition & MES to Controls Data Flow Possibilities. White Paper3 Pittsburgh: Manufacturing Execution Systems Assoc. (1997)

[9] MESA International, MES Functionalities & MRP to MES Data Flow Possibilities. White Paper2 Pittsburgh: Manufacturing Execution Systems Assoc. (1997)

[10] Yang, F., Xiao, D.Y.: Research on Agent-based MES Structure of Press Industries. Computer Integrated Manufacturing System 9(2), 107–111 (2003)

[11] Zhou, H., Liu, M., Wu, C.: A Kind of Model-driven Agent-based Manufacturing Execution Systems. Control Engineering of China 12(1), 80–100 (2005)

[12] Hao, G.K., He, W.P., He, Y.L., Yan, H.: Research on Reconfigurability of Service-Oriented Manufacturing Execution System. In: Proceedings of the 2009 IEEE 10th International Conference on Computer-Aided Industrial Design & Conceptual Design (CAID&CD 2009), pp. 591–595 (2009)

[13] Song, X.Y., Zhuo, Z.B., Bai, X.B., Xue, J.S.: Construction the Collaborative Manufacturing Execution System Based on NetworK. Information and Control 34(4), 466–469 (2005)

[14] Fei, Y.Z.: Discrete Manufacturing-oriented Collaborative Manufacturing Execution System and Its Key Technology. Nanjing University of Science and Technology, Nanjing (2012)

[15] Peng, G.L., Jiang, Y., Xu, J., Li, X.: A Collaborative Manufacturing Execution Platform for Space Product Development. The International Journal of Advanced Manufacturing Technology 62(5-8), 443–455 (2012)

[16] Zhang, J., Yu, H.L., Liao, W.X.: Cooperative Manufacturing System Realization for MTO Production of Bearing [J]. Journal of Zhejiang Industry & Trade Vocational College 13(1), 35–39 (2013)

# A Steerable GA Method for Block Erection of Shipbuilding in Virtual Environment

Jinsong Bao, Qian Wang, and Aiming Xu

Shanghai Jiao Tong University, Shanghai, China, 20040
bao@sjtu.edu.cn, wangqian1992511@sjtu.edu.cn

**Abstract.** Solving the dispatch and optimization of block erection of shipbuilding is a complex problem, especially when the spatial constraints are considered. The block erection scheduling problem can be defined as an identical parallel machine scheduling problem with precedence constraints and machine eligibility (PCME) restrictions, as well as limited layout space. An enhanced genetic algorithm (GA) is proposed to find the near-optimal solution, and a few lower bounds. Also, the percentage of the reduced makespan is defined to evaluate the performance of the proposed algorithm. The proposed GA method of steering optimization produces quicker and lesser values of makespan than the RANDOM heuristic algorithm for the collected real instances. It not only allows users to steer a computing towards effective direction and leverages computing, but also is guided by the intelligence of human to get a global view when the users are in immersive environment. The dispatch of block erection to the crane is modeled into a parallel machine scheduling problem with spatial constraints. Meanwhile a 3D layout of block erection is modeled with real size, and an interactive GA optimization is developed to solve this problem with the objective of minimizing makespan.

**Keywords:** Steerable Genetic algorithm, Scheduling, Parallel machines, Shipbuilding, Virtual environment.

## 1 Introduction

The manufacturing process of shipbuilding includes pre-processing, fabrication, assembly, painting, pre-erection and block erection, according to the necessary operations to build a ship. The block erection process is the process of constructing ships by assembling blocks transported to docks by cranes. The block erection process is the last stage in shipbuilding, but it is the first stage and basis of the flow of manufacturing plans. In any shipyard, most bottlenecks form around the building dock area. To minimize the block occupancy at the dock, the cranes are equipped as much as possible. Two main studies are focused on these areas:

- **How to model sufficiently:** The block erection scheduling problem can be defined as a parallel machine scheduling problem with PCME restrictions, as well as limited layout space. Much attention has been paid to the optimization of fabrication

Y. Luo (Ed.): CDVE 2014, LNCS 8683, pp. 286–293, 2014.

(Okumoto and Iseki, 2005), block assembly (Park et al., 1996), and pre-erection (Varghese and Yoon, 2006; Yoon and Varghese, 2007). Lee et al. (1997) used the constraint directed graph search technique to generate block erection schedule. However, they not only did not consider the machine (crane) eligibility restrictions, but also did not consider the spatial constraints, without which the result will not reflect the real manufacturing. Aho and Mäkinen (2006) solved the parallel machine scheduling problem, consisting of $m$ parallel machines, $n$ tasks with precedence constraints, and unit processing time, but they only considered the precedence constraints, and did not address the machine eligibility.

- **How to resolve efficiently**: Lin et al. (2004) presented a polynomial algorithm for the parallel machine scheduling problem with unit-length jobs. Many people successfully developed the genetic algorithm for parallel machine scheduling problem with different constraints and objective, such as minimizing the completion on non-identical parallel machines with fuzzy logic (Alcan and Başlıgil, 2011), minimizing the weighted completion time with precedence (Ramachandra and Elmaghraby, 2005), minimizing the maximum lateness with dynamic job arrivals (Malve and Uzsoy, 2007), and multi-objective (Gasior and Seredynski, 2013). However, there is a noticeable gap between the theory and the practice of scheduling, because some real situations are ignored. Dispatch optimization of block erection will become a very complicated problem when the constraints, such as sequence, resources and spatial, are considered.

Most relative researches on optimization focused on producing algorithms that are more efficient than previous algorithms. An algorithm's efficiency is judged by the value of the solutions it produces, according to a given, well-defined objective function, as well as amount of computation required to produce these solutions. Klau et al. (2010) has given a human-guided search optimization. Interactive optimization which provides simple and general visual metaphors, related to local search operations that allow users to guide the exploration of the search space, is presented. This approach to evaluating optimization systems is, however, insufficient for many real-world contexts in which optimization problems arise. Caprace et al. (2013) posted a heuristic algorithm to tackle the 3D bin-packing. We present a steerable GA and it will be guided in a 3D virtual environment.

## 2    Problem Description and Modeling

### 2.1    Description of Erection Processes of Shipyard

Three constraints should be considered in the erection processes of shipyard: manufacturing processes constraints, resource constraints and time.

- **Manufacturing processes constraints:** They refer to the sequences of block assembly sequences which guarantee the assembly accuracy and smooth of erection of ship. For example, in Fig. 1, bottom blocks should be assembled ahead of top blocks. Meanwhile left and right side of the blocks should generally be lifted simultaneously, in order to reduce the welding deformation and to improve the construction accuracy. This erection constraints network includes ten blocks (or total blocks) and it shows the relationship between the erection sequence constraints. A large ship includes hundreds of blocks or the total blocks, so the erection network will also include dozens or even hundreds of nodes.

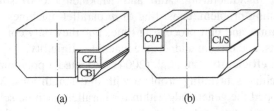

(a)                                        (b)

**Fig. 1.** (a) Up and down sequence (b) Left and right sequence

- **Resource constraints:** They include erection devices (such as cranes) and storages, as shown in Fig. 2 Erection devices include two types: gantry crane and portal crane. Storages include field of dock and platform near dock. For example, Fig. 2 describes resources of dock. The status of cranes may be busy or idle (gantry crane: M1; portal cranes: M1-M3); the status of storages may be occupied and empty (storages: A0~A3, B0~B3).

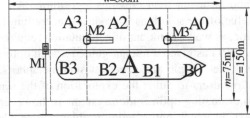

**Fig. 2.** Resources of a dock

- **Time constraints:** The time during erection process include transport time, assembly time and weld time. They should be limited as standard operation time.

### 2.2    The Formulation of the Model

$$\text{Mini:} \quad Z = \sum_{i=1}^{n} w_i C_i \tag{1}$$

Subject to:

$$\sum_{i=1}^{n} Q_{it} \leq M, 1 \leq t \leq S \tag{2}$$

$$t_j + p_j \leq t_i, \forall j \in D_i, 1 \leq i \leq n \tag{3}$$

$$S = \max\{t_i | i = 1, 2, \dots n\} \tag{4}$$

$$t_i, t_j \in Z^+, (1 \leq i, j \leq n) \tag{5}$$

The objective of scheduling is to minimize the weighted total completion time. Every block is assigned a weighting factor according to its importance. One machine can process only one task at any time instant. Some blocks need only one machine to complete, while some blocks require two machines simultaneously. The total number of occupied machines at particular time $t$ cannot exceed the total capacity of all machines $M$. The crane machine capacity constraints are represented by constraint (2). A task cannot be started until its direct preceding tasks are finished and a task requires a specific amount time for processing. The precedence constraints in this problem aim on the precedence of different blocks to be processed. Constraint (3) is the formulation of task precedence constraints. Here, $t_i$ is the decision variable; $S$, $C_i$ and $O_{it}$ are the dependent variables. Constraint (5) indicates that the start time of a task is a positive integer.

## 3 Steerable GA Algorithm

The known GA is a powerful and broadly applied stochastic search and optimization technique based on principles of evolution theory. In the recent years, GA has received considerable attention for solving difficult combinatorial optimization problems. The basic elements of a GA that must be specified for any given implementation are representation, population, evaluation, selection, operators and parameters. A drawback of genetic algorithm is that a solution is "better" only in comparison to other. This means that a genetic algorithm never knows for certain when to stop aside from the length of time, the number of iterations and candidate solutions that you wish to allow it to explore.

### 3.1 Chromosome Representation

Each chromosome string, representing a feasible solution, has a number of positions equal to the number of jobs to be scheduled. The number in one position represents a job. A set of these chromosomes is called a population. The precedence constraints among the jobs are considered appropriately, and the population can be generated by selecting the job for each position from the assignable job set randomly. For instance, consider an example problem with 25 jobs. One feasible solution satisfying the precedence constraints can be randomly generated as following: {1 2 4 5 13 7 6 8 3 11 9 14

18 15 12 22 17 20 10 16 21 19 23 24 25}. Because the chromosome representation does not directly provide the schedules for *m* machines, a decoder is necessary to transform the chromosome into the schedule for each machine. The decoder is defined as following: the latter job in the above list cannot be processed before the former job. Considering the machine eligibility restrictions, the completed assignment is thus:

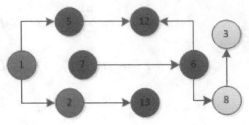

**Fig. 3.** Steerable mobility elements

— Machine 1: 1 2 5 13 8 6 9 14 18 12 17 20 16 21
— Machine 2: 4 7 6 9 14 18 22 10 16 21
— Machine 3: 3 11 15 10 19 23 24 25

### 3.2    Genetic Operators

Mobility of HuGS (Klau et al. 2002) provides a general mechanism that allows users to visually annotate elements of a solution, in order to guide a local search to improve this solution. However, the mobility only defines a character: priority. The mobility cannot meet the complex process where spatial constraints and process constraints are considered. The proposed method defines three elements for mobility: priority, direction and spatial constraints. Priority of mobility can be assigned as high, medium, low or disable with the corresponding color as red, yellow, green and grey. Direction is assigned as a vector matrix and spatial constraints are defined as a bound box of elements, which will be shown as Fig. 6 in the experimental results (Section 4). The search algorithm is only allowed to explore solutions that can be reached by applying a sequence of moves to the current solution such that each move operate on a high-mobility element and not alter any low-mobility elements, as shown in Fig. 3.

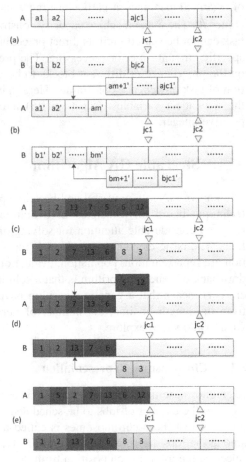

**Fig. 4.** Crossover operator of genetic algorithm ($jc1 = 7, jc2 = 12$)

The traditional GA crossover and mutation operators may violate the precedence constraints, thereby generating invalid lists. So, other genetic operators should be defined. Fig. 4 demonstrates an example. The crossover mechanism of a double-point order crossover operator is accomplished through the following steps:

1. Randomly select two chromosomes, named Parent A and Parent B and randomly select two cutoff points (the same for both parents as $jc1$ and $jc2$) in each of these two chromosomes.
2. Note the same jobs before $jc1$ in A as $a_1' a_2' \ldots a_m'$ and in B as $b_1' b_2' \ldots b_m'$. Note the distinct jobs before $jc1$ in A as $a_{m+1}' a_{m+2}' \ldots a_{jc1}'$ and in B as $b_{m+1}' b_{m+2}' \ldots b_{jc1}'$.
3. Insert $a_1' a_2' \ldots a_m'$ to the beginning of B and insert $b_1' b_2' \ldots b_m'$ to the beginning of A.
4. Search for all the precedence of $a_{m+1}'$ in $b_1' b_2' \ldots b_m'$ and place $a_{m+1}'$ right after its last precedence in $b_1' b_2' \ldots b_m'$. Process similarly with $a_{m+2}'$, $a_{m+3}'$, ..., $a_{jc1}'$.
5. Repeat step 4 for $b_{m+1}' b_{m+2}' \ldots b_{jc1}'$.
6. Repeat step 2 to step 5 for $a_{jc2+1}' a_{jc2+2}' \ldots a_n'$ and $b_{jc2+1}' b_{jc2+2}' \ldots b_n'$.

The mutation mechanism of a swapping operator is accomplished as following steps with a dynamic mutation rate.

1. Randomly choose one chromosome, named C.
2. Randomly select one jobs $c_j$ to swap in C.
3. The following condition is defined and used to generate the interchangeable jobs set: if job $c_j$ leads job $c_k$ when there is no successor of job $c_j$ or predecessor of job $c_k$ between them or if job $c_k$ leads job $c_j$ when there is no successor of job $c_k$ or predecessor of job $c_j$ between them, then job $c_j$ and $c_k$ can be swapped. For example, job 5 and 7 of A in Fig. 4 can be swapped, since there is only job 2 between them, and it is neither successor of job 5 nor predecessor of job 7 according to Fig. 4.
4. Notice that at least one of the two jobs should have a high mobility and none of the two jobs can have a low mobility.
5. Randomly select one job from the interchangeable job set, and swap them to produce a new chromosome.

# 4    Computing Steering and Experimental Results

The experiment to be conducted in this paper is the scheduling problem of block erection in a shipyard located in Shanghai, China. The hull block construction method is to divide hulls into many blocks and to build them up at dock. During the blocks division, the vessel type and the tonnage are mainly considered. The manual scheduling system of block erection, based on the random heuristic algorithm, is used in the shipyard, while the solution quality is poor and it cannot react quickly to the dynamic environment, which is the major incentive for us to develop a more efficient and effective GA method to improve the system performance. The prototype application of erection scheduling and planning is developed with MS C#. The steering GA has been coded in C ++ and is called as Dynamic link library. The 3D simulation scene of erection running in Dassualt's Delmia Quest can be driven by the prototype system, as Fig.5.

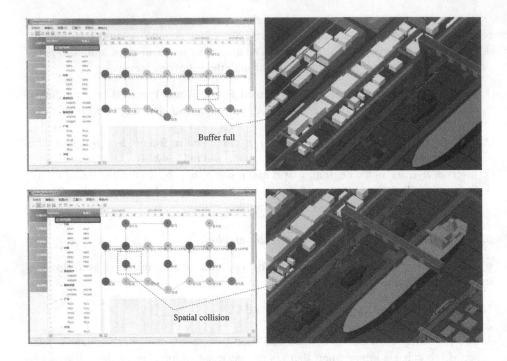

**Fig. 5.** The human-interactive for steer GA search and simulation

Table 1 presents the comparison among Heuristic A* search, classic GA and steerable GA. Those specifying constraints have significantly cut down the search space.

**Table 1.** Interaction experiment results

|                     | Minimal makespan | Time of get optimal result |
|---------------------|------------------|----------------------------|
| Heuristic A* search | 235 hr.          | 783 sec.                   |
| Un-steerable GA     | 183.3 hr.        | 956 sec.                   |
| Steerable GA        | 162.4 hr.        | 302 sec.                   |

## 5     Conclusions and Future Works

Solving the dispatch and optimization of block erection of shipbuilding is a complex problem, since PCME restrictions as well as limited layout space should be considered. Traditional solutions to the job scheduling problems can only be applied to 2D problems with the help of linear programming, heuristic algorithms or genetic algorithms. However, these approaches cannot fully solve the dispatch and optimization of block erection of shipbuilding. Moreover, these algorithms are encapsulated in a black-box and not visualized. Therefore, it is impossible to control the searching process. Since the searching space is not optimized, the process will be lengthened and the efficiency will be reduced.

This paper proposed a steerable GA method to solve this problem. By defining three mobilities, users are allowed to steer the crossover and mutation mechanism. Meanwhile, the process can be displayed through the 3D simulation scene so that human-computer interaction can be applied to change the GA search direction. This method reduces the search space, increases the search efficiency and obtains a satisfying result. In the future, other algorithms, such as heuristic algorithms, will be developed to be steerable in order to solve scheduling with large scale.

# References

1. Aho, I., Mäkinen, E.: On a parallel machine scheduling problem with precedence constraints. Journal of Scheduling 9(5), 493–495 (2006)
2. Alcan, P., Başlıgil, H.: An application with non-identical parallel machines using genetic algorithm with the help of fuzzy logic. Proceedings of the World Congress on Engineering 45(1), 272–280 (2011)
3. Caprace, J.D., Petcu, C., Velarde, M., Rigo, P.: Optimization of shipyard space allocation and scheduling using heuristic algorithm. Journals of Marine Science & Technology 18(3), 404–417 (2013)
4. Gasior, J., Seredynski, F.: Multi-objective Parallel Machines Scheduling for Fault-Tolerant Cloud Systems. In: ICA3PP(1), pp. 247–256 (2013)
5. Klau, G.W., Lesh, N., Marks, J., Mitzenmacher, M.: Human-guided search. Journal of Heuristics 16(3), 289–310 (2010)
6. Klau, G.W., Lesh, N., Marks, J., Mitzenmacher, M., Schafer, G.T.: The HuGS platform: A toolkit for interactive optimization. In: Proceedings of the Working Conference on Advanced Visual Interfaces, pp. 324–330. ACM (May 2002)
7. Lee, J.K., Lee, K.J., Park, H.K., Hong, J.S., Lee, J.S.: Developing scheduling systems for Daewoo shipbuilding: DAS project. European Journal of Operational Research 97(2), 380–395 (1997)
8. Lin, Y., Li, W.: Parallel machine scheduling of machine-dependent jobs with unit-length. European Journal of Operational Research 156(1), 261–266 (2004)
9. Malve, S., Uzsoy, R.: A genetic algorithm for minimizing maximum lateness on parallel identical batch processing machines with dynamic job arrivals and incompatible job families. Computers & Operations Research 34(10), 3016–3028 (2007)
10. Okumoto, Y., Iseki, R.: Optimization of steel plate cutting sequence using the tabu search method. Journal of ship production 21(2), 134–139 (2005)
11. Park, K., Lee, K., Park, S., Kim, S.: Modeling and solving the spatial block scheduling problem in a shipbuilding company. Computers & industrial engineering 30(3), 357–364 (1996)
12. Ramachandra, G., Elmaghraby, S.E.: Sequencing precedence-related jobs on two machines to minimize the weighted completion time. International Journal of Production Economics 100(1), 44–58 (2006)
13. Varghese, R., Yoon, D.Y.: Shipbuilding erection network optimization: a TSP method. Journal of ship production 22(3), 139–146 (2006)
14. Yoon, D.Y., Varghese, R.: Looking-forward scheduling approach applied in pre-erection area of a shipyard. Journal of Ship production 23(1), 30–35 (2007)

# Service Evaluation-Based Resource Selection in Cloud Manufacturing

Yan-Wei Zhao[1] and Li-Nan Zhu[1,2,3]

[1] Key Laboratory of Special Purpose Equipment and Advanced Processing Technology,
Ministry of Education, Zhejiang University of Technology, Hangzhou 310014, PRC
[2] College of Computer Science and Technology,
Zhejiang University of Technology, Hangzhou 310023, PRC
[3] College of Educational Science and Technology,
Zhejiang University of Technology, Hangzhou 310023, PRC
{zyw,zln}@zjut.edu.cn

**Abstract.** With the development of cloud computing, cloud manufacturing has been gained more and more attention. According to the peculiarity of cloud manufacturing, the resource designated as manufacturing service is always massive, complex and heterogeneous, and the high degree of user participation, and user diversity are also the main features. This paper presents a method of resource selection based on service evaluation, which consists of predictive evaluation and recommended evaluation. In detail, predictive evaluation is based on user's historical service evaluations which may have different influence according to the experience in different time. Recommended evaluation is given by the recommenders who are generated by 2-step selection and have different recommended weight according to their similarities and objectivities. Finally, experiment results show that the proposed algorithm has better performance.

**Keywords:** cloud manufacturing, resource selection, service evaluation.

## 1 Introduction

Attributed to cloud computing theory and application, cloud manufacturing and cloud service, as the extension and development of networked manufacturing, was put forward in the early 2000s and has gradually risen and become the main direction of manufacturing industry. Cloud manufacturing reflects the idea of "distributed resources are integrated to be used for one task" and "integrated resources are distributed to be used", and achieves the many-to-many service model, which provides multiple users with services at the same time by aggregating and centralized managing distributed resources and services. In cloud manufacturing, service efficiency is very important in resource selection. The paper proposed a method of service evaluation-based resource selection under cloud manufacturing environment, including predictive evaluation and recommended evaluation.

Y. Luo (Ed.): CDVE 2014, LNCS 8683, pp. 294–302, 2014.

## 2    Structure of Cloud Manufacturing

Cloud Manufacturing System (CMS) is composed of Cloud Manufacturing Platform (CMP) and Cloud End (CE), and CE contains Cloud Demander (CD) which is corresponding to resource demander and Cloud Provider (CP) which is corresponding to resource provider. Showed as Fig.1, CP publishes, updates, cancels and provides manufacturing resource and service through CMP; CD propose the requirement to CMP and get corresponding products or services through CMP; CMP just like a great resource pool consist of several sub-CMPs, which can interacts with each other and receives the requirement from CD and searches the most appropriate resource. Of course, in many cases, a CE is both a CD and a CP [1].

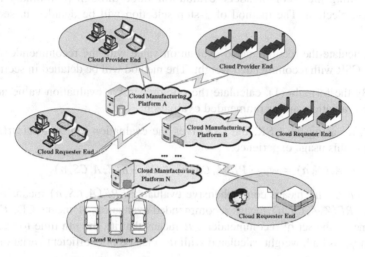

**Fig. 1.** Cloud Manufacturing System Structure

## 3    Evaluation Model

In this paper, we propose a service evaluation model of Cloud Service Resource (CSR). The model is composed of two parts: user's (DE's) own predictive evaluation and recommender's evaluation. In predictive evaluation, the predicted value results from user's historical service evaluations which may have different influence depending on user's own experience at that time, and the result should be modified according to the predictive bias, so the experience factor and modifying factor are introduced to the predictive evaluation model. In recommended evaluation, recommended value is just the predicted value of other users who are called as recommender, so recommender selection is very important. Well, we make the preliminary selection based on users' usage history, and make the further selection based on similarity and objective of users' evaluation.

So, the evaluation process is as follows:

**Step 1:** Calculate the predictive evaluation value according to CD's previous evaluation to the CSR which the CD may intend to use. The method of prediction will be detailed in section 4;

**Step 2:** Set the recommender selection condition. That is setting the time range $T$ and the minimum evaluation amount $N$. For example, the CE who should have used the CSR and given evaluation $3(N = 3)$ times in the past $5(T = 5)$ years;

**Step 3:** Getting the CD's historical evaluation value of the CSR, and calculate the predictive evaluation value, which will be detailed in section 4;

**Step 4:** Getting the recommenders' evaluation value through preliminary selection and further selection. The method of 2-step-selection will be detailed in section 5.1 and 5.2;

**Step 5:** Calculate the recommended evaluation value with the recommenders' evaluation to the CSR with recommended weight. The method will be detailed in section 5.3;

**Step 6:** By the formula (1), calculate the comprehensive evaluation value according predictive evaluation and recommended evaluation;

**Step 7:** After using the CSR, the CD gives the evaluation $DEvaluation(A, CS, n)$ according to this usage experience.

$$E(A, CS, n) = w_{PE} \cdot PE(A, CS, n) + w_{RE}RE(Z, A, CS, n) \qquad (1)$$

Here, $E(A, CS, n)$ means comprehensive evaluation, $PE(A, CS, n)$ means predictive evaluation, $RE(Z, A, CS, n)$ means recommended evaluation, $A$ means CD, $CS$ means CSR, $Z$ means the set of recommenders, $n$ means that it's the $n$th time to use the $CS$, $w_{PE}$ and $w_{RE}$ is both weight calculated with the method of coefficient variation.

## 4    Predictive Evaluation

### 4.1    The Method of Predictive Evaluation

Assume, a CD named $CUser$ tends to use the CSR named $CS$, the predictive evaluation calculation method is as follows.

**The 1st Time:** Because of no historical usage data, the predictive evaluation value is set to 0.5. That is $PE(CUser, CS, 1) = 0.5$, and we abbreviate as $PE_1 = 0.5$ for the sake of convenience. After using $CS$, $CUser$ gave direct evaluation $DE(CUser, CS, 1)$ according to this usage experience, and we also abbreviate as $DE_1$ for the sake of convenience.

**The 2nd Time:** The $CUser$ make predictive evaluation by the first direct evaluation with the formula (2). Here, $f(1)$ is experience factor, and $a_2$ is modifying factor. After using $CS$, $CUser$ gave direct evaluation $DE_2$ according to the second usage experience.

$$PE_2 = \frac{1}{f(1)} \cdot f(1)a_2 \cdot DE_1 = a_2 \cdot DE_1 \qquad (2)$$

**The 3rd Time:** The *CUser* make predictive evaluation by the first direct evaluation with the formula (3). Here, $f(1)$ and $f(2)$ are both experience factor, and $a_3$ is modifying factor. After using *CS*, *CUser* gave direct evaluation $DE_3$ according to the third usage experience.

$$PE_3 = \frac{a_3}{f(2)+f(1)} \cdot (f(2) \cdot DE_2 + f(1) \cdot DE_1) \tag{3}$$

**The *n*th Time:** The *CUser* make predictive evaluation by the direct evaluation before $t$ times with the formula (4). Here, $f(n-i)$ is experience factor, $a_n$ is modifying factor, and $t$ is the step length. After using *CS*, *CUser* gave direct evaluation $DE_n$ according to the *n*th usage experience.

$$PE_n = \frac{a_n}{\sum_{i=1}^{t} f(n-i)} \cdot \left( \begin{array}{c} f(n-1) \cdot DE_{n-1} \\ + \cdots + f(n-t) \cdot DE_{n-t} \end{array} \right) = \frac{a_n \sum_{i=1}^{t} f(n-i) \cdot DE_{n-i}}{\sum_{i=1}^{t} f(n-i)} \tag{4}$$

## 4.2    Experience Factor

The direct evaluation occurred in different time with different experience would has different influence on this predictive evaluation, the closer direct evaluation occurred to current, the bigger the influence is, otherwise the opposite. The formula of experience factor is very simple, just like formula (5). Here, $t_0$ is the time when the CSR established, $t_i$ is the time when the direct evaluation was given, and $t_n$ is the time at once.

$$f(i) = \frac{x \cdot e^{t_i - t_0}}{x \cdot e^{t_n - t_0}} = e^{t_i - t_n} \tag{5}$$

## 4.3    Modifying Factor

Because the *CS* has continuously changed, the experience factor can't reflect the service well. So, we adopt the modifying factor $a_i$ ($a_i \in (0,1)$) which can update by itself, and the update calculation method is as follows.

**Step 1:** When *CUser* uses *CS* the first time and the second time, the experience factor is 1 for default. That is $a_1 = 1$.

**Step 2:** When *CUser* uses *CS* the *n*th time ($n \geq 2$), he make the predictive evaluation (4). The formula can seen as a formula about the experience $a_n$, just like formula (6).

$$PE_n(a_n) = \frac{a_n \cdot \sum_{i=1}^{t} f(n-i) DE_{n-i}}{\sum_{i=1}^{t} f(n-i)} \tag{6}$$

**Step 3:** Because of the experience factor, the $PE_n$ and $DE_n$ must not be the same, so we get the formula (7). The new experience is $a_n'$, and that is $a_n' = a_n + \Delta a$.

$$\Delta E_n = DE_n - PE_n = DE_n - \frac{a_n \cdot \sum_{i=1}^{t} f(n-i) DE_{n-i}}{\sum_{i=1}^{t} f(n-i)} \tag{7}$$

**Step 4:** Calculate derivative of the formula (6), and get the formula (8).

$$\Delta PE_n(a_n) = \frac{\sum_{i=1}^{t} f(n-i) DE_{n-i}}{\sum_{i=1}^{t} f(n-i)} \cdot \Delta a \tag{8}$$

**Step 5:** The formula (7) and (8) should be equal, so get the formula (9) to calculate $\Delta a$.

$$\Delta E_n = \Delta PE_n(a_n)$$

$$DE_n - PE_n = \frac{\sum_{i=1}^t f(n-i)DE_{n-i}}{\sum_{i=1}^t f(n-i)} \cdot \Delta a \tag{9}$$

$$\Delta a = \frac{(DE_n - PE_n)\left(\sum_{i=1}^t f(n-i)\right)^2}{\sum_{i=1}^t f(n-i)DE_{n-i}}$$

**Step 6:** When $CUser$ uses $CS$ the $(n+1)$th time, the new experience factor $a'_n$ would be adopted as $a_{n+1}$, just like formula (10).

$$a_{n+1} = a'_n = a_n + \Delta a = a_n + \frac{(DE_n - PE_n)\left(\sum_{i=1}^t f(n-i)\right)^2}{\sum_{i=1}^t f(n-i)DE_{n-i}} \tag{10}$$

# 5    Recommended Evaluation

When the CD makes service evaluation to a certain CSR, he should refer to other users' evaluation. But in cloud manufacturing environment, there are massive evaluation data, some of which has no reference value and should be eliminated. The recommender selection need two steps: the first step is preliminary selection based on usage history, and the second step is further selection based on evaluation similarity and objectivity. After the two steps above, the CD can get the recommended evaluation value with the formula (11). Here, $m$ means the sum of elements in recommender set, $g(z_i)$ means recommended weight of recommender $z_i$, $n_i$ means the $n_i$th time the recommender $z_i$ would use $CS$ next time.

$$RE(Z, A, CS, n) = \frac{1}{\sum_{i=1}^m g(z_i)} \cdot \sum_{i=1}^m PE(z_i, CS, n_i)g(z_i) \tag{11}$$

## 5.1    Preliminary Selection of Recommender

Preliminary selection of recommender is based on usage history, which means that the CE who has used the same resources with the CD during a certain time will be selected into primary set. Assume, the CD $CUser$ tends to use the CSR $CS$, and the calculation method is as follows.

**Step 1:** Set the time range $T'$ and the number $K$ of resource they have both used. So, there must be $T' < T$.

**Step 2:** Traverse all CEs in set $Z$ who used to use $CSource$, and select the CEs who has used $CSource$ more than $N$ times during the past time $T'$ into set $CSU$, and that is $CSU = \{u_1, u_2, \cdots, u_n\}$.

**Step 3:** Get the CSRs that $CUser$ has used during the past time $T'$, and that is $CUse\_source = \{CUs_1, CUs_2, \cdots, CUs_k\}$.

**Step 4:** Compare the element in set $CUse\_source$ with the resources used by CEs in set $CSU$, and the CEs who have more than $K$ common resources would be selected into primary set $SU = \{su_1, su_2, \cdots, su_j\}$, and there must be $SU \subseteq CSU$.

## 5.2    Further Selection of Recommender

In order to eliminate the CEs who has given malicious evaluation or has low reference value, the further selection of recommender based on evaluation similarity and objective will be proposed. Assume that in the service resource pool, there are $k$ resources, every one of which has $m$ evaluation index, so there must be an evaluation matrix $Q$ like formula (12).

$$Q = \begin{pmatrix} q_1 \\ q_2 \\ \vdots \\ q_k \end{pmatrix} = \begin{pmatrix} q_{11}, & q_{12}, & \cdots & q_{1m} \\ q_{21}, & q_{22}, & \cdots & q_{2m} \\ \cdots & \cdots & \ddots & \cdots \\ q_{k1}, & q_{k2}, & \cdots & q_{km} \end{pmatrix} \tag{12}$$

During a certain time, the average of evaluation index is matrix $\overline{Q}$ like formula (13).

$$\overline{Q} = \begin{pmatrix} \overline{q_1} \\ \overline{q_2} \\ \vdots \\ \overline{q_k} \end{pmatrix} = \begin{pmatrix} \overline{q_{11}}, & \overline{q_{12}}, & \cdots & \overline{q_{1m}} \\ \overline{q_{21}}, & \overline{q_{22}}, & \cdots & \overline{q_{2m}} \\ \cdots & \cdots & \ddots & \cdots \\ \overline{q_{k1}}, & \overline{q_{k2}}, & \cdots & \overline{q_{km}} \end{pmatrix} \tag{13}$$

Some $sus$ selected by preliminary selection and $CUser$ has the common resource set $SimCR = \{s_1, s_2, \cdots, s_n\}$, so $CUser$'s predictive evaluation to every element in $SimCR$ is $Q^{CUser} = \{(s_1, q_1^{CUser}), (s_2, q_2^{CUser}), \cdots, (s_n, q_n^{CUser})\}$, $su$'s predictive evaluation to every element in $SimCR$ is $Q^{su} = \{(s_1, q_1^{su}), (s_2, q_2^{su}), \cdots, (s_n, q_n^{su})\}$, and the average value of predictive evaluation given by every $sus$ and $CUser$ is $\overline{Q} = \{\overline{q_1}, \overline{q_2}, \cdots \overline{q_n}\}$. In this paper, we adopt vector angle cosine to calculate the similarity and objectivity with formula (14) and (15). The $su$ whose similarity and objectivity both reach the threshold will be selected into set $SimU$ as the final recommender, and there must be $SimU \subseteq SU \subseteq CSU$.

$$Rsim(su) = cos(Q^{CUser}, Q^{su}) = \sum_{i=1}^{n} \frac{q_i^{CUser} \times q_i^{su}}{\sqrt{\sum_{i=1}^{n}(q_i^{CUser})^2} \times \sqrt{\sum_{i=1}^{n}(q_i^{su})^2}} \tag{14}$$

$$Rtrust(su) = cos(Q^{su}, \overline{Q}) = \sum_{i=1}^{n} \frac{q_i^{su} \times \overline{q_i}}{\sqrt{\sum_{i=1}^{n}(q_i^{su})^2} \times \sqrt{\sum_{i=1}^{n}(\overline{q_i})^2}} \tag{15}$$

## 5.3    Recommended Weight

In section 5.1 and 5.2, we have gotten the recommenders and their evaluation similarity and objectivity, so we can calculate the recommended weight with the formula (16). Here, $z_i$ is the recommender, and $\alpha \in [0,1]$.

$$g(z_i) = \alpha Rsim(z_i) + (1 - \alpha)Rtrust(z_i) \tag{16}$$

To $CUser$, the more $z_i$ has used $CSource$, the more important $z_i$'s objectivity. Based on this consideration, we set a using threshold $\theta_r$ ($\theta_r \geq N$), when $z_i$ has used $CSource$ more than $\theta_r$ times, the objectivity is more important than similarity, otherwise the opposite, calculated as formula (17).

$$\alpha = \begin{cases} \dfrac{\theta_r}{2x}, & x \geq \theta_r, \\ 1 - \dfrac{x}{2\theta_r}, & N \leq x < \theta_r. \end{cases} \tag{17}$$

## 6    Experiment and Analysis

In the first experiment, we assume that a CD uses a certain CSR 100 times and gives direct evaluation which is generated randomly and floats on both sides of the before direct evaluation with the range of $[-0.1, 0.1]$ every time, and the step length is 10. The CSR's establish time is 0, the time when the CD used it the first time is 50, and the interval time between two adjacent use is also a random value between 0 and 10. In experiment result showed in Fig.2, the solid line is direct evaluation, and the dashed line is predictive evaluation. The figure shows that the slop of the two line is almost similar, so it means that the predictive evaluation changes along with direct evaluation and has good sensitivity.

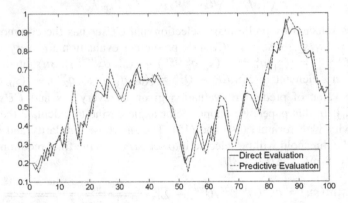

**Fig. 2.** Comparison Figure of Direct Evaluation and Predictive Evaluation

The second experiment is based on the first experiment, so the predictive evalua-tion is designed as the same as the first experiment. The preliminary selection of rec-ommend is simply based on usage history. Here we assume 6 recommenders selected under the rule have used 3-6 the same CSRs with the CD. In experiment result showed in Fig.3, the solid line is direct evaluation, the dashed line is predictive evalu-ation, and the dot-dashed line is comprehensive evaluation. The figure shows that: (1) The slop of the solid line and dot-dashed line is almost similar, it means comprehen-sive evaluation changes along with direct evaluation and has good sensitivity; (2) The dot-dashed line fluctuates smaller than dashed line even when the solid line generated randomly fluctuates large, it means the comprehensive evaluation has stability because of the influence of recommended evaluation.

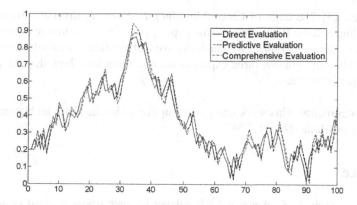

**Fig. 3.** Comparison Figure of Direct, Predictive and Comprehensive Evaluations

The third experiment is based on the first and second experiments. The *CUser*'s evaluation and recommenders' evaluations are established, and several interferers with evaluation values randomly generated are added. In the experiment result showed in Fig.4, the solid line is direct evaluation, the dashed line is predictive evaluation, the dot-dashed line is comprehensive evaluation with recommender selection, and the dotted line is comprehensive evaluation without recommender selection. The figure shows that the dotted line fluctuates larger than dot-dashed line, it means the recommender selection can eliminate interference well.

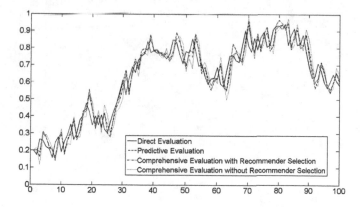

**Fig. 4.** Comparison Figure of evaluations with and without interference

## 7    Conclusion

It is now acknowledged that cloud manufacturing is one of the most important manufacturing models, and will become a main model in the future. From the recent achievement all over the world and preliminary work, this paper summarized the main features of cloud manufacturing: (1) The resources which appear as manufacturing services are massive, complex and heterogeneous; (2) The degree of user participation is very high; (3) The users of Cloud Manufacturing is very diversity. Based on this understanding and the Beth's theory, this paper gives a new method of resource selection based on service evaluation, which consists of predictive evaluation and recommended evaluation. Finally, three experiments are given and show that the algorithm has better performance.

**Acknowledgements.** This work was partly supported by the National Natural Science Foundation of China (No. 51275477).

# Reference

1. Zhu, L.N., Zhao, Y.W., Wang, W.L.: A bilayer resource model of cloud man-ufacturing services. Math. Probl. Eng., Article ID: 607582, 10 pages (2013), doi: 10.1155/2013/607582

# SaaS Approach to the Process Control Teaching and Engineering

Grzegorz Polaków and Witold Nocoń

Faculty of Automatic Control, Electronics and Computer Science,
Silesian University of Technology, Gliwice, Poland
{grzegorz.polakow,witold.nocon}@polsl.pl

**Abstract.** In light of the rapid development of network technology, the general concept of software requires redefinition. New opportunities provided by broadband networking, distributed processing, and available network resources i.e. what is widely called a cloud, makes the classic software architecture obsolete. In this paper it is proposed to apply the web service oriented approach and cloud-related techniques to the tasks of the control algorithms design, engineering and training. Basing on the literature, the necessary concepts are defined and the limitations specific to the considered domain are identified. Next, with the two specific applications as the examples, it is described how to apply the new approach to the classic tasks, in order to turn the classic software into the cloud-based software.

**Keywords:** SaaS, process control, control systems engineering, cloud computing, web services.

## 1 Introduction

Recent advances in computer networking, resulting in increase of available bandwidth and lowering prices of hardware, make the tasks of application developers quite different than even a decade ago. The particularly topical subject is processing and storing data in the cloud. The "cloud" term became so trendy and ubiquitous, that it is actually difficult to clearly define it properly. In this regard, for example, particularly famous became the speeches of Oracle's CEO Larry Ellison, who claims that most of what is referred to as a cloud computing was already there, before the term coined (see [1] for example). Anyway the term became popular, and is typically defined as follows: "cloud computing refers to both the applications delivered as services over the Internet and the hardware and system software in the data centers that provide those services" [1]. This means that the key functionality in the field of cloud computing is providing the software as a service, which is referred to as SaaS. Apart from SaaS, the terms of PaaS and IaaS are often used. Good and clear definition of them is present for example in [2]:

- "IaaS. Infrastructure-as-a-service products deliver a full computer infrastructure via the Internet.
- PaaS. Platform-as-a-service products offer a full or partial application development environment that users can access and utilize online, even in collaboration with others."

Y. Luo (Ed.): CDVE 2014, LNCS 8683, pp. 303–310, 2014.

In the case of the SaaS approach, the attention is often drawn to the possibilities provided by the further spread of monolithic applications into multiple separate services able to communicate with each other. This results in the architecture known as Service Oriented Computing (SOC), in which the individual services are building blocks of larger services and of applications [3]. This architecture, however, poses a number of challenges in terms of organizing the services, i.e. their discovery, delivery and composition. These issues are discussed, among others, by [3] and [4].

This paper presents an attempt to implement these modern software architectures in the domain of continuous control of industrial processes. Due to the very specific requirements in the field, such as real-time data processing, deterministic communication, guarantees of the reliability, and safety procedures, the straightforward implementation of the service-based approach is rarely possible. However, the paper attempts to identify the part of the field, where the cloud techniques are possible to implement and where it gives the potential benefits.

## 2    The Specifics of the Domain

In the process automation in production applications it is difficult to speak of any virtualization of infrastructure, platform, nor software, because the key part of the software i.e. the control algorithm is the part of the closed feedback loop. The loop works in the time-determined manner and is usually embedded in a low-level hardware at the factory floor. Such a mode of work results in the specific requirements for software and hardware, and all the tools must be developed to take the requirements into account (as in [5]). However, if only the supervisory control is under the consideration, the cloud-like approach is already well established. The specific architecture of software, hardware and network links is usually referred to as a SCADA (Supervisory Control And Data Acquisition), and is shown in the Fig. 1. The architecture actually meets the criteria of SaaS and so it can be seen from the operator's point of view. SCADA is, however, a technique well recognized, which does not leave much place for innovations and additional benefits.

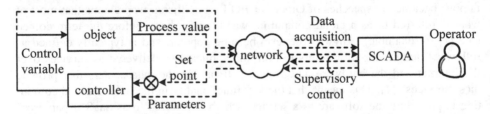

**Fig. 1.** Typical SCADA system can be treated by an operator as a SaaS

Applications for cloud technology can, however, be found in the process of design and engineering of control systems. However, an indication of the tasks, for which the cloud technology provides potential benefits, must be preceded by definition of the subtasks forming the whole cycle of a process control design and engineering. Good analysis of this subject is provided by Choinski et al. in [6], where the sequence of the tasks is additionally analyzed in order to optimize the whole process by the proper formalization of knowledge. In general, the engineering begins with the analysis of the features of the plants and given technological guidelines. Based on this, the developed system is decomposed into subsystems, which are easier to cope with (the choice of the number and the detail level of the subsystems is crucial). The connections between subsystems form the architecture of the whole system, which is then developed as a software. Often the formal analysis of the features and guidelines is skipped, when the system is developed by smaller numbers of closely cooperating engineers (as seen in the Fig. 2). Because the end result of the design and engineering process often requires continuous fine-tuning and/or maintaining (for example, because of changing guidelines), the process is cyclically repeated.

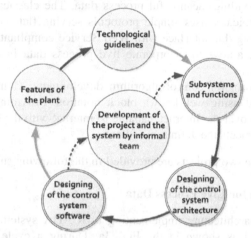

**Fig. 2.** The life cycle of process control engineering [6]

The software tools supporting the design and engineering according to the present cycle can be delivered as PaaS and support remote cooperation, which is particularly important, since experts in many areas of automated processes are uncommon and enabling them to work remotely cuts the costs of the process significantly. Of course, the algorithm itself, which is developed and tested with the PaaS platform must later be downloaded and, with the help of classical software tools, embedded as a part of the hardware control loop.

Moreover, cloud technology offers great opportunities in another field of teaching and training the control system operators, because it allows them to work simultaneously, including the work on simulated processes. Significance of cooperative training of process control engineers is presented in e.g. [7], where the problem of allowing the multiple operators share the same SCADA system was considered. In a summary, the cooperative work on virtual processes, allows the accelerate the education and provides measurable financial and time savings because, first, wrong decisions of trained operators in simulated process will carry no negative implication in the actual process, and second, the simulated process can train the operators for emergency situations, which cannot be arranged in operating production plant.

The opportunities for cloud computing in the process control engineering identified above are presented in the next sections using the examples of software solutions developed by the authors.

# 3    Examples

At the Control Systems & Control Instrumentation Group of the Silesian University of Technology the work on cooperative learning, design and engineering of process control is carried out for many years. Two of the developed applications are particularly adequate to serve as an examples to present the idea of cloud computing in process control. These are:

— Web Service providing meaningful process data. The classical data interface of control system typically uses simple protocols serving flat data without any description. Replacing this interface with Web Service compliant to the knowledge-related standards, allows to incorporate live process data in modern distributed network applications.
— cooperative platform for control algorithm development. Control algorithms are usually developed using well-known block notation. Providing the users with a software working over the Internet, capable to interact with the blocks stored in the main application meets the definition of PaaS.

More details on these two projects are provided in the following subsections.

## 3.1    Web Service for Live Process Data

A typical software architecture implementing a SCADA system with the structure shown in the Fig. 1 is shown in the Fig. 3a. During a cycle of control system engineering a specific tasks for the control system are defined and grouped into subsystems and corresponding functions. The knowledge about the subsystems and functions is then used to develop the software, which is deployed in the location where the control system's supervisors work. This results in a closed and static architecture, because the knowledge about the controlled system is embedded within the software, and non-codified. All further modifications to the software, as well as the development of another programs for related tasks, require another full cycle of design and engineering, in which the previously accumulated knowledge is reused. Because the application is monolithic and stored offline, all of its modified versions must undergo a process of deployment, which is not always simple.

The only data that is accessible dynamically during the runtime provides numerical values of the variables in the system. Typically, the data are provided without any description, which means that without the knowledge of the subsystems, their functions and architecture, the data are useless. In addition, the data are typically served by a service, which is optimized for performance and ease of communication, not a semantic standards compliance. Connecting to a service, without the knowledge of the specific platform, plant and control algorithms used to build the system would require tedious reverse engineering and, although theoretically feasible, impracticable.

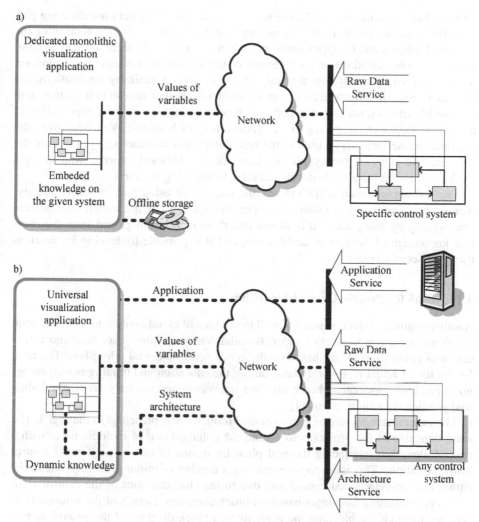

**Fig. 3.** Modification of the classical SCADA architecture to enable SOC support

According to the cloud computing and service oriented computing methodologies it is proposed to modify the architecture of the system according to the Fig. 3b. Thus, the knowledge on the system architecture has to be codified, and made available through an additional Web Service. The general idea has been researched by authors (see [8]) before the cloud computing notion emerged, but now the idea has to be reorganized according to the established terminology of cloud computing. To the service which provides the online raw data, it is proposed to add another Web Service, that provides the knowledge about the structure of the system using one of the well-recognized standards of knowledge sharing (a good overview of such standards with regard to their suitability for cloud computing is presented in [4]). The software application itself can be dynamic and available as a web application through a separate service. The combination of all three services results in the system not differing particularly from the previous monolithic application, however, the advantages of the proposed solution can be appreciated only when using the individual services as components of other solutions on the principle of service oriented computing. Therefore, the data served by the system are fully usable in other visualizing applications, the provided visualization application can be used for another automation system with compatible services, and most importantly it provides a possibility for applications of agent based software according to the methodology of Semantic Web. Moreover, the Architecture Service can be used in the next design and engineering cycles (from the Fig. 2). The steps of the cycles can incorporate additional experts, who can get the knowledge on the already developed subsystems using the service.

The test implementation ([8]) shows the benefits of using this approach. The dynamic architecture was a result of cooperative editions of the system architecture concurrently by many users. It is shown that there is a benefit gained from the codified knowledge of the system architecture, and it is possible to develop applications using the set of services.

## 3.2    PaaS for Process Control Algorithms

Another ongoing project, which fits well to the idea of cloud computing is the system, developed for a few years, that supports collaborative creation, execution and verification of control algorithms based on the actual semi-industrial pilot plant. The need for the use of actual real-world plants during the education and training is well recognized [9], [10], especially when it involves innovative and not fully verified in industrial practice algorithms, as in [11].

The general architecture of the developed framework is presented in the Fig. 4. The main objective of the project is to enable the collaboration of multiple users with a control algorithm interfacing the real plant by means of off-the-shelf retail control instrumentation. This issue requires solving a number of minor problems, due to the nature of time-determined control and due to the characteristics of the control algorithms programming languages based on block diagrams. Details of the solution concern the methods for blocking the portions of a block diagram of the control system edited by separate programmers, and developing the interface between the dynamic middleware and static control instrumentation, and are provided in [12].

Attention should be paid to the analogy between the developed solution and a well-known cloud computing PaaS model. Whether it is the teaching the students, training the process operators, or cooperative development of production control algorithms for a given class of processes, the presented framework is a standalone platform taking the interaction with the users. Using appropriate client software, an user can develop software running on the platform (in the form of blocks in the OOP convention) and as a result he can modify the control system and retrieve its specification from any network location.

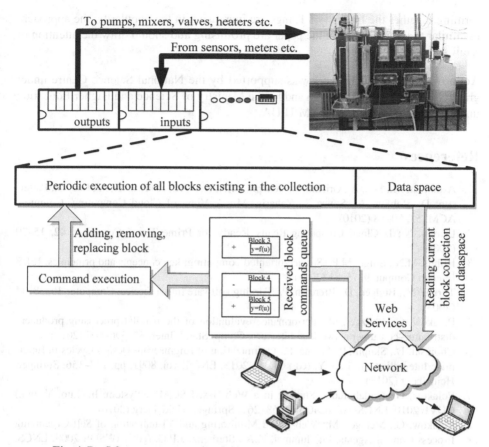

**Fig. 4.** PaaS for process control training and cooperative algorithm engineering

## 4    Concluding Remarks

Implementation of the presented ideas relies on the recent developments in the distributed computing domain i.e. web services and corresponding protocols. While codification of the knowledge may seem an abstract task, there are file formats and protocols for storing abstract knowledge (i.e. ontologies, taxonomies) for a relatively long time (see [4]). The only real obstacle to the new distributed approach is the well established thinking, preserved by classical software development tools used traditionally in automation. Some change in thinking is displayed by the growing use of event-based programming based on models of systems with open structure according to the IEC61499 standard,  holonic approach to automation systems, and agent-based approach to the development of control systems software.

The tests of the pilot implementations of the ideas presented above show that they provide significant benefits, in the form of shortening design and development cycle and they increase the flexibility and openness of the developed software. Since the ideas of distributed computing, automated reasoning and artificial intelligence, forming together the Internet of Things are increasing in the popularity, the approaches similar to the presented in the paper are promising and should draw the attention of retail software developers.

**Acknowledgments.** This work was supported by the National Science Centre under grant No. 2012/05/B/ST7/00096 and by the Ministry of Science and Higher Education under grants BK-UiUA and BKM-UiUA.

# References

1. Armbrust, M., Fox, A., Griffith, R., Joseph, A.D., Katz, R., Konwinski, A., Lee, G., Patterson, D., Rabkin, A., Stoica, I., Zaharia, M.: A View of Cloud Computing. Commun. ACM. 53, 50–58 (2010)
2. Leavitt, N.: Is Cloud Computing Really Ready for Prime Time? Computer. 42, 15–20 (2009)
3. Huhns, M.N., Singh, M.P.: Service-oriented computing: key concepts and principles. IEEE Internet Comput. 9, 75–81 (2005)
4. Turner, M., Budgen, D., Brereton, P.: Turning software into a service. Computer 36, 38–44 (2003)
5. Polaków, G., Metzger, M.: Performance evaluation of the parallel processing producer–distributor–consumer network architecture. Comp. Stand. Inter. 35, 596–604 (2013)
6. Choinski, D., Skupin, P., Szajna, E.: Optimization of Engineering Design Cycles in Enterprise Integration. In: Luo, Y. (ed.) CDVE 2013. LNCS, vol. 8091, pp. 153–156. Springer, Heidelberg (2013)
7. Polaków, G.: Collaboration Support in a Web-Based SCADA System. In: Luo, Y. (ed.) CDVE 2010. LNCS, vol. 6240, pp. 258–261. Springer, Heidelberg (2010)
8. Polaków, G., Metzger, M.: Web-Based Monitoring and Visualization of Self-Organizing Process Control Agents. In: Hummel, K.A., Sterbenz, J.P.G. (eds.) IWSOS 2008. LNCS, vol. 5343, pp. 325–331. Springer, Heidelberg (2008)
9. Metzger, M., Polaków, G.: Holonic Multiagent-Based System for Distributed Control of Semi-industrial Pilot Plants. In: Mařík, V., Vyatkin, V., Colombo, A.W. (eds.) HoloMAS 2007. LNCS (LNAI), vol. 4659, pp. 338–347. Springer, Heidelberg (2007)
10. Doelitzscher, F., Sulistio, A., Reich, C., Kuijs, H., Wolf, D.: Private cloud for collaboration and e-Learning services: from IaaS to SaaS. Computing 91, 23–42 (2011)
11. Metzger, M.: A comparative evaluation of DRE integration algorithms for real-time simulation of biologically activated sludge process. Simulat. Pract. Theory 7(7), 629–643 (2000)
12. Nocoń, W., Polaków, G.: Object-Oriented Framework for Cooperative Testing of Control Algorithms for Experimental Pilot-Plants. In: Luo, Y. (ed.) CDVE 2013. LNCS, vol. 8091, pp. 197–204. Springer, Heidelberg (2013)

# Author Index

Alves, Tatiana P.V.   151
Aragon, Cecilia R.   1, 64

Bao, Jinsong   286
Batrouni, Marwan   103
Bauer, Christine   88
Borges, Marcos R.S.   151
Borri, Dino   179
Boton, Conrad   159
Bredin, Hervé   163
Brooks, Michael   1
Bruneau, Pierrick   163
Budnik, Mateusz   163

Cabrales, Alexis Álvarez   214
Cai, Hongming   261
Camarda, Domenico   179
Camba, Jorge   222, 253
Cardona, Salvador   214
Castro, Omar   199
Charoy, François   191
Chi, Jing   68
Choiński, Dariusz   72, 80, 230
Chong, Heap-Yih   44, 143, 238
Conejero, José María   118
Contero, Manuel   222, 253
Cuenca, David   167

Didry, Yoann   175
Didry, Yoanne   60
Dossick, Carrie Sturts   134
Dyrgrav, Kjetil   9

Elsen, Catherine   245

Fei, Yizheng   277
Ferreira, Hugo Sereno   199

Goo, Boncheol   167
Grishin, Vladimir   19, 27
Guo, Ji-Dong   68
Guo, Jun   44, 143, 238

Halin, Gilles   159
Hong, Sungsoo (Ray)   1

Hou, Lei   143
Huang, Aihua   96
Huang, Weidong   111
Huang, Xiaodi   111

Ignat, Claudia-Lavinia   191
Ivanov, Alex   36

Jiang, Lihong   261

Kirschner, Ursula   183
Klopot, Tomasz   230
Kovalerchuk, Boris   19, 27
Kubicki, Sylvain   159

Lai, Wei   111
Lee, Jang Ho   171
Liu, Changan   96
Liu, Linyan   277
Liu, Tingting   277
Liu, Tingyu   269
Liu, Xin   143

Ma, Xiaoming   261
Melnikov, Jiri   167
Metzger, Mieczysław   80
Mileva, Emma   36
Mladenow, Andreas   88
Morales-Chaparro, Rober   51
Mory, Maik   126

Navratil, Jiri   167
Newman, Meagan   191
Nocoń, Witold   80, 303

Oster, Gérald   191
Otjacques, Benoît   163

Parisot, Olivier   60, 175
Pérez, Roberto   214
Pluchinotta, Irene   179
Poignant, Johann   163
Polaków, Grzegorz   80, 303
Preciado, Juan Carlos   51, 118

Riba, Carles   214
Rieder, Helmut   175
Robinson, John J.   1
Rodríguez-Echeverría, Roberto   118

Salvador-Herranz, Gustavo    222, 253
Sánchez-Figueroa, Fernando    51, 118
Sandnes, Frode Eika    9
Santana, Ivani    167
Shalin, Valerie    191
Shou, Wenchi    44, 238
Simeón, Rolando E.    214
Skupin, Piotr    72, 230
Sousa, Tiago Boldt    199
Starbird, Kate    64
Stefas, Mickaël    163
Strauss, Christine    88
Sutera, Jennifer    245
Szczypka, Daniel    230

Takahashi, Makoto    203
Tamisier, Thomas    60, 163, 175
Torkildson, Megan K.    1, 64

Ubik, Sven    167

Vajna, Sandor    126
Vierke, Gero    175
Vivacqua, Adriana S.    151

Wang, Huifen    269, 277
Wang, Jun    44, 143, 238
Wang, Qian    286
Wang, Xiangyu    44, 143, 238
Węgrzyn, Anna    80
Widjaja, William    203
Wiesner, Martin    126
Wodołażski, Artur    72
Wünsch, Andreas    126

Xu, Aiming    286

Yang, Chengwei    68
Yang, Maria C.    245
Yoshii, Keito    203
Yuan, Juntang    96

Zayas, Enrique E.    214
Zhao, Yan-Wei    294
Zhou, Lin    96
Zhu, Li-Nan    294